# Basic
# Industrial
# Resources
# of the

U · S · S · R

# Basic
# Industrial
# Resources
# of the

# U · S · S · R

*by Theodore Shabad*

Columbia University Press

*New York & London*    *1969*

Theodore Shabad, now Editor for Soviet Affairs, Foreign News Desk, *The New York Times,* was former correspondent for *The New York Times* in Moscow. He is also editor of *Soviet Geography* (a monthly translation journal of the American Geographical Society), and author of *Geography of the USSR,* published in 1951 by Columbia University Press.

To Leslie, Steven, and Peter

# PREFACE

Despite an increasing emphasis on the production of consumer goods, basic heavy industry continues to be the mainstay of the Soviet Union's economic growth. An expansion of heavy industry, in turn, must be supported by development of the nation's resource base, particularly fuel and energy resources, metals, and other minerals for the chemical industry. Soviet progress in opening up these resources, especially since the end of World War II and through the 1950s and the 1960s, is the subject of this book. It is thus designed to bring up to date some of the aspects covered in the author's *Geography of the USSR, a Regional Survey*, published in 1951.

Fuels, electric power, metals, and chemical raw materials have been singled out for discussion on two grounds. First, these primary industries, involving extraction and basic processing of raw materials for later fabricating and manufacturing, form a cohesive chain in which fuels provide the source of electric power, and the metal and basic chemical industries, in turn, are major consumers of electric power. Second, extractive and raw-material–oriented industries are among the elements of the Soviet economy that have played a leading role in remaking the map of the country through the growth of mining towns and industrial complexes, the construction of access railroads and other means of transport, the laying of oil and gas pipelines, and changes in the locational pattern of industry.

The economic sectors selected here are also the ones in which the most dramatic changes have taken place in the Soviet Union since the mid-1950s. In fuels, it has been a radical shift in emphasis from the previous reliance on coal production to priority development of more economical oil and natural-gas resources. In electric power, the trend has been from a multitude of small, local generating plants to the construction of large central electric stations, the interconnection of power grids, and the long-distance transmission of large blocks of electricity from sources of cheap power production to major consuming areas. In metals, the expansion of the basic iron and steel industry has been associated with increasing diversification and sophistication of the use of resources, including one-time "minor" metals like titanium, beryllium, germanium, zirconium, and, of course, uranium, that have found new uses in nuclear energy, electronics, high-speed flight, missiles, and space exploration. Finally, the chemical industry, long a lagging sector of the Soviet economy, has been the focus of a high-priority expansion program, based to a large extent on the use of petrochemicals from petroleum and natural gas.

Throughout the discussion, the actual development of resources is emphasized. The date that operation of specific mines, power plants, and primary processing industries began is given whenever possible, and information on capacity of production or actual output is given when such data are obtainable from Soviet sources. Potential resources are mentioned only if they are in the process of being developed or figure in early plans for development. Because of this emphasis on the actual economic use of resources for production, data on geological reserves and potential deposits have been sparsely used and attention has been concentrated on the exploitation of resources.

Mention must be made here of previous studies of Soviet mineral resources by Demitri B. Shimkin and Jordan A. Hodgkins. Shimkin's *Minerals: A Key to Soviet Power* (Harvard University Press, 1953) was an exhaustive survey of mineral resources, with a pronounced emphasis on geological considerations and potential availability of minerals. Hodgkins' *Soviet Power: Energy Resources, Production, and Potentials* (Prentice-Hall, 1961) brought the situation up to date for mineral fuels. A second study by Shimkin, *The Soviet*

*Mineral Fuels Industries, 1928–1958* (U.S. Bureau of the Census, 1962) was a historical statistical survey in mineral economics.

The present book in a sense complements the previous studies with specific and up-to-date material on Soviet resource development, including both minerals and electric power. The information presented has been culled over a period of fifteen years from a multitude of Soviet periodicals (mainly daily newspapers) and Soviet monographs. The principal sources are listed in the bibliography.

The book is arranged in two parts. Part I briefly discusses the general production trends and locational patterns of each resource sector, with emphasis on changes over the last two decades. Part II is a regional survey of specific mining centers and related resource complexes by major regions, with information on start of operations, output, and development problems. Because of the availability of statistics by republics, the Soviet Union has been broken down arbitrarily in the regional discussion into its fifteen constituent republics, with the Russian Soviet Federated Socialist Republic, the nation's largest, further divided into eight regions: four in European Russia—the North, the Center, the South (Northern Caucasus), and the Volga region; the Urals; and three in Siberia—West Siberia, East Siberia, and the Soviet Far East.

The focus on resource development does not properly reflect the relative importance of Soviet regions as integrated economic entities. Central European Russia, for example, a core area of the Soviet Union in terms of population settlement, agriculture, and the development of manufacturing, occupies relatively little space in the discussion because it is a region poor in resources that relies for its industrial potential on long-haul raw materials and long-distance power and fuel transmission from other resource-rich parts of the Soviet Union. The resulting imbalance in the presentation of data is further compounded by an uneven coverage of source materials. Because of the availability of detailed studies and separate daily newspapers for each constituent republic of the Soviet Union, data on resource development for, say, the Central Asian republics tend to be more complete than for a major economic region within the RSFSR, such as the Urals, for which fewer comprehensive sources are available.

The statistical tables in Part I are intended to provide data on the regional distribution of the production of those basic resources that could be documented from Soviet sources. Most of the tables have been compiled from a wide range of Soviet publications in an attempt to present consistent time series. Some statistical data appeared directly in Soviet sources; others were computed from indirect indications, such as percentages and other mathematical relationships, given in Soviet publications. The detailed source references, procedures, and computations have been omitted for reasons of space.

Much of the material is derived from the "News Notes," regularly prepared by the author for *Soviet Geography: Review and Translation,* the monthly translation journal published by the American Geographical Society of New York.

# CONTENTS

# MAPS

# I

## PART

## General
## Production
## Trends

# 1

# FUEL INDUSTRIES

The development of the modern Soviet fuel industries can be conveniently divided into two periods distinguished by different fuel policies and development priorities. The first, from the early stages of Soviet industrialization about 1930 until the early 1950s, was marked by emphasis on the development of coal and relative neglect of the use of petroleum and natural gas. The second period, which began in the 1950s and which is expected to continue in the foreseeable future, has been distinguished by rapid development of oil and gas resources and a slower growth of coal output.

Several reasons have been given in Soviet sources for the long persistence of an economic policy based on coal while other industrial nations, notably the United States, were already enjoying the advantages of lower-cost oil and gas. One major factor was the easy accessibility of coal deposits in the earlier period of economic development when coal resources were already relatively well known, but the prospecting and exploration of oil and gas deposits were lagging behind. Although geological exploration for oil and gas subsequently uncovered important deposits, the rigidity of Soviet planning machinery delayed the translation of the new discoveries into actual economic exploitation. A related factor was an official policy favoring the development of local fuel resources, partly as an element in a strategic program of decentralization of production, partly as an effort to reduce expensive long hauls of fuels, especially coal, that were overburdening a strained railroad network. The local-fuels policy led to the development of easily available fuels, even if they were of low grade, as in the case of brown coal, peat, and oil shale. Little concern was shown for the economics of fuel production, and development was based on strategic, political, and other noneconomic considerations. The preservation of a coal-dominated economy was also promoted by the existence of powerful national industrial ministries, including a coal ministry, intent on building up economic sectors under their jurisdiction regardless of economic effectiveness or the overall national interest.

As a result of the reliance on coal, heavy industry was concentrated largely in coal-producing areas such as the Donets Basin, the Urals, the Kuznetsk Basin, and the Karaganda area. This was true not only of the iron and steel industry, for which the availability of coking coal was often a decisive locational factor, but also of the chemical industry, then based largely on the use of coal-tar derivatives obtained from coke ovens. Despite the promotion of local fuel sources, the reliance on coal led to long coal hauls by railroad from sources of supply to often distant consuming areas. In 1950, coal shipments accounted for almost 30 percent of the Soviet Union's total railroad freight traffic (178.2 billion out of 602.3 billion ton-kilometers), burning up a large share of the shipment in transportation, which was then still 95 percent steam traction. The predominance of coal can also be illustrated by the coal-petroleum output ratio. In 1930, the Soviet Union produced 2.5 tons of coal for every ton of crude oil. By 1950, the ratio was 6.8 tons of coal for every ton of oil.

The reversal of the fuel policy in favor of oil and gas development, starting in the early 1950s, stemmed from a variety of factors. An intensive exploration program after World War II had demonstrated the existence of large reserves of both petroleum and natural gas. An increasingly diversified Soviet iron and steel industry had the capability of producing the pipeline needed for long-distance transmission of the newly developed fuels. Strategic considerations of industrial decentralization, based on older military concepts of ground warfare, were less applicable in an age of nuclear missile weapons. The emphasis on local-fuel development was also abandoned as an ever more complex Soviet economy called for greater attention to cost-accounting factors. On a strict cost basis, it was often found more advantageous to transport high-grade fuels over long distances instead of using higher-cost, low-grade local fuels.

At any rate, crude-oil production soared during the 1950s and 1960s, and natural-gas production also increased as rapidly as pipelines could be completed. New industrial complexes, based on petroleum refining and petrochemicals, arose both in the oil-producing areas (the Ishimbay–Salavat–Sterlitamak and Ufa complexes in Bashkiria, the Kuybyshev–Novokuybyshevsk complex on the Volga River, and the new Nizhnekamsk complex on the lower Kama River in the Tatar ASSR) and along the oil and gas pipelines. By 1965, the coal–oil ratio of 1930 had been restored, as 1 ton of crude oil was being produced for every 2.4 tons of coal. Although the production of coal in 1965 was more than double the 1950 level and still constituted the principal commodity on the railroads, its share in the total freight traffic had dropped from almost 30 percent in 1950 to 20 percent in 1965 (397 billion out of 1,950 billion ton-kilometers). Moreover, less coal was being consumed on the railroads as a result of conversion to diesel and electric traction. Steam traction accounted for 15.5 percent of all freight traffic in 1965 compared with 95 percent in 1950.

The rise of the oil and gas industries has been associated with a relative decline of some of the less efficient local fuels that were promoted under the earlier fuels policy. This applied particularly to peat and to costly underground brown coal. However, it was still found economical to use such fuels as brown coal and oil shale for power generation if they could be mined cheaply in open-pit operations and burned in minehead electric stations without additional transport costs.

The changing pattern of Soviet fuel production and consumption is illustrated in Table 1, which compares the relative importance of fuels by reducing them to standard fuel units of 7,000 kilogram calories (12,600 British thermal units). The table shows that petroleum increased substantially in importance relative to other fuels after a decline from 1940 to 1945 related to the drop of production at Baku. Subsequent growth stemmed mainly from the expansion of the Volga–Urals oil production. Natural gas became significant only after 1955, when the discovery of large fields began to be associated with the construction of pipelines.

The relative significance of coal production has been declining steadily since 1950 as underground brown-coal mines have been shut down and stress is placed on higher-ranking coals, particularly coking coals, and strip mining of brown coal and other coals for use in on-site power plants. Of the lower-ranking fuels, only oil shale has been holding its own in relative terms, mainly because of the expansion of the Estonian operations in conjunction with the construction of two large shale-burning power stations. Peat remains significant only in Central European Russia and the northwest of the USSR, and the significance of firewood, once an important industrial fuel in Russia, has been declining rapidly, especially since the greater availability of gas for residential use.

*Table 1*

Fuel Structure of the USSR, in Percent

|             | 1940 | 1945 | 1950 | 1955 | 1958 | 1960 | 1965 |
|-------------|------|------|------|------|------|------|------|
| Petroleum   | 18.7 | 15.0 | 17.4 | 21.1 | 26.3 | 30.5 | 35.9 |
| Natural Gas | 1.9  | 2.3  | 2.3  | 2.4  | 5.5  | 7.9  | 15.6 |
| Coal        | 59.1 | 62.2 | 66.1 | 64.8 | 58.8 | 53.9 | 42.9 |
| Peat        | 5.7  | 4.9  | 4.8  | 4.3  | 3.4  | 2.9  | 1.7  |
| Oil Shale   | 0.3  | 0.2  | 0.4  | 0.7  | 0.7  | 0.7  | 0.8  |
| Firewood    | 14.3 | 15.4 | 9.0  | 6.7  | 5.3  | 4.1  | 3.1  |

Note: The fuel structure is calculated by converting the production of various
types of fuels to standard fuel units of 7,000 kilogram calories (12,600
British thermal units).

## Coal

Soviet coal basins may be conveniently divided into two groups: basins that produce coals with high heating value or special qualities, as in coking coals, justifying long hauls to serve a large market area (Donets Basin, Kuznetsk Basin, Karaganda, Pechora), and basins that produce coals with low heating value that cannot be transported economically over long distances and are best used in the vicinity of the mines, preferably at minehead electric power plants. The higher-ranking coals are anthracite and bituminous coals; the lower-ranking coals are the brown coals, corresponding to the subbituminous and lignitic coals in United States classification (Fig. 1).

Soviet production of anthracite, which has been relatively steady over the last decade at about 80 million tons, is concentrated in the Donets Basin, mostly in its southern and southeast sections. Bituminous coal, mined in all four major basins producing higher-ranking coals, has been steadily increasing over the years from 216 million tons in 1955 to 297 million in 1960 and 347 million tons in 1965, including 139 million tons for coking. The production of brown coal, concentrated in the Moscow Basin, the Urals, Ekibastuz in northeast Kazakhstan, and in Siberia, has also remained relatively stable, rising from 143 million tons in 1958 to 150 million in 1965. Total Soviet coal output in 1965 was 578 million tons of all ranks (Table 2).

*Table 2*

Soviet Coal Output by Major Classes
　　(in million metric tons)

|  | *1940* | *1945* | *1950* | *1955* | *1958* | *1960* | *1965* |
|---|---|---|---|---|---|---|---|
| Anthracite | 36.4 | 17.6 | 41.8 | 60.8 | 78.1 | 78.0 | 80.5 |
| Bituminous (total) | 103.6 | 81.8 | 143.4 | 215.8 | 274.9 | 296.9 | 347.4 |
| Coking | 35.3 | 29.8 | 51.7 | 77.7 | 94.4 | 110.2 | 139.0 |
| Others | 68.3 | 52.0 | 91.7 | 138.1 | 180.5 | 186.7 | 208.4 |
| Brown Coals | 25.9 | 49.9 | 75.9 | 114.6 | 143.1 | 138.3 | 149.8 |
| Total | 165.9 | 149.3 | 261.1 | 391.3 | 496.1 | 513.2 | 577.7 |

By far the most important coal basin of the Soviet Union is the Donets Basin, situated favorably near the main population centers and manufacturing districts of the European part of the country. Because of its nearness to major markets, the output of the basin has been growing steadily during the Soviet period despite an unfavorable geology and deep, thin seams requiring increasingly deeper mines. Production rose from a pre-World War II peak of 94.4 million tons in 1940 to 206 million in 1965, including 174 million in the Ukrainian part of the Donbas and 32 million in the basin's eastern section extending into Rostov Oblast of the Russian Re-

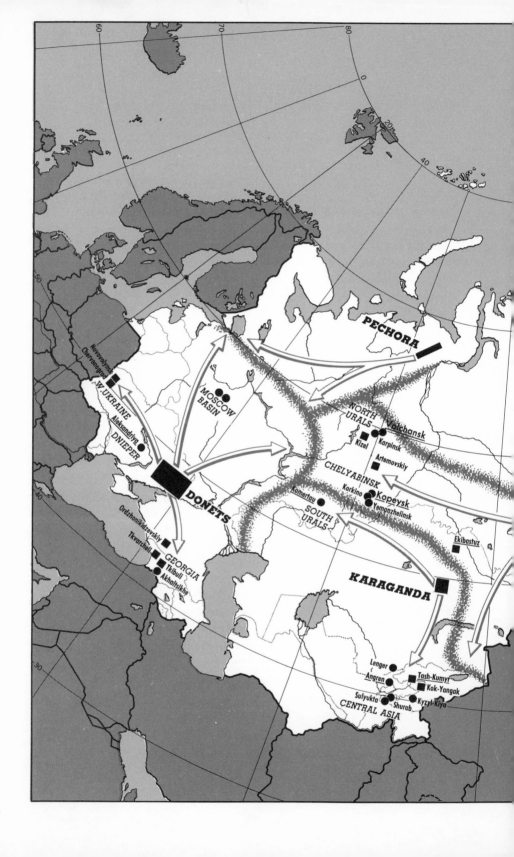

PECHORA

MOSCOW
BASIN

Novovolynsk
Chervonograd

W. UKRAINE

Aleksandriya

DNIEPER

NORTH
URALS    Volchansk

Kizel    Karpinsk

Artemovskiy

CHELYABINSK

Korkino    Kopeysk

Kumertau    Yemanzhelinsk

SOUTH
URALS

Ekibastuz

DONETS

Ordzhonikidsevskiy

Tkvarcheli

GEORGIA

Tkibuli

Akhaltsikhe

KARAGANDA

Lenger

Angren    Tash-Kumyr

Kok-Yangak

Sulyukta    Shurab    Kyzyl-Kiya

CENTRAL ASIA

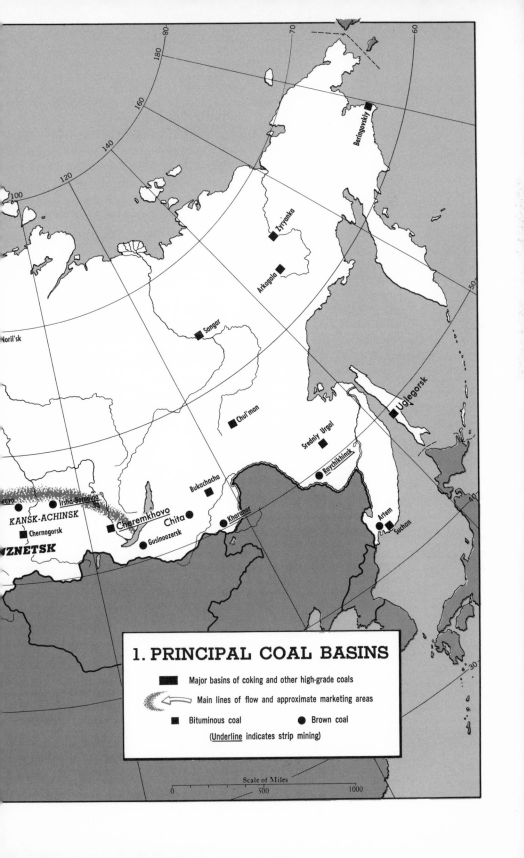

# 1. PRINCIPAL COAL BASINS

Major basins of coking and other high-grade coals

Main lines of flow and approximate marketing areas

■ Bituminous coal          ● Brown coal

(<u>Underline</u> indicates strip mining)

Beringovskiy

Zyryanka

Arkagala

Sangar

Noril'sk

Chul'man

Srednly Urgal

Raychikhinsk

Uglegorsk

Bukachacha

Irsha-Borodino

KANSK-ACHINSK

Cheremkhovo  Chita ●

Kharanor

Artem

Suchan

Chernogorsk

Gusinoozersk

ZNETSK

Scale of Miles

0          500          1000

public. In addition to supplying the important iron and steel industry of the Ukraine with coking coal (Table 3), the Donets Basin ships steam coals to almost all of the Soviet Union west of the Urals.

*Table 3*

Soviet Output of Coking Coal by Basins
  (in million metric tons)

|  | 1940 | 1945 | 1950 | 1955 | 1958 | 1960 | 1965 |
|---|---|---|---|---|---|---|---|
| European USSR | 27.4 | 11.4 | 28.6 | 47.2 | 59.4 | 70.9 | 87.4 |
| European Russia | 0.1 | 0.9 | 1.3 | 3.2 | 5.6 | 6.7 | 8.3 |
| Pechora | — | — | 0.2 | 0.9 | 2.5 | 3.8 | 4.7 |
| Rostov (Donbas) | 0.1 | 0.9 | 1.1 | 2.3 | 3.1 | 2.9 | 3.6 |
| Ukraine (Donbas) | 27.3 | 10.5 | 27.3 | 42.1 | 51.4 | 62.0 | 77.0 |
| (*Total Donbas* | *27.4* | *11.4* | *28.4* | *44.4* | *54.5* | *64.9* | *80.6*) |
| Georgia | — | — | — | 1.9 | 2.4 | 2.2 | 2.1 |
| Urals (Kizel) | 0.7 | 2.3 | 2.7 | 2.1 | 2.2 | 2.3 | 2.3 |
| Asian USSR | 7.2 | 16.0 | 20.4 | 28.4 | 32.7 | 37.1 | 49.3 |
| Kuznetsk Basin | 5.9 | 12.9 | 14.9 | 21.4 | 25.7 | 28.5 | 38.0 |
| Noril'sk | — | — | — | 0.3 | 0.4 | 0.3 | 0.3 |
| Karaganda | 1.3 | 3.1 | 5.5 | 6.7 | 6.6 | 8.3 | 11.0 |
| Total USSR | 35.3 | 29.8 | 51.7 | 77.7 | 94.4 | 110.2 | 139.0 |

Despite the production rise in the Donets Basin, its share in the total Soviet coal output has been steadily declining as other basins, mainly east of the Urals, have expanded. The eastern basins are distinguished by large reserves and a favorable geology, with thick seams near the surface, often suitable for strip mining. Foremost of the eastern basins is the Kuznetsk Basin of Siberia, where production rose from 22.6 million tons in 1940 to almost 100 million in the mid-1960s. The Kuzbas supplies coking coal to its own iron and steel industry and to the Urals, and ships steam coals to most of Siberia.

The third bituminous coal basin is at Karaganda in central Kazakhstan, which serves the coking coal needs of its own steel industry as well as that of the Urals, and the steam coal requirements of most of Soviet Central Asia. Output at Karaganda rose from 6.3 million tons in 1940 to about 30 million in the mid-1960s, including about 45 percent coking coal. The Pechora Basin, in northern European Russia, has been limited in production, despite large reserves, because of adverse climatic and working conditions of the sub-Arctic. Resulting high mining costs limit the basin's marketing area to the Far North of European Russia, including the

Table 4

Regional Distribution of Soviet Coal Production
(in million metric tons)

|  | 1940 | 1945 | 1950 | 1955 | 1958 | 1960 | 1965 |
|---|---|---|---|---|---|---|---|
| European USSR | 106 | 63 | 138 | 208 | 263 | 268 | 289 |
| European Russia | 22 | 32 | 58 | 79 | 95 | 90 | 92 |
| Pechora Basin | 0.3 | 3 | 9 | 14 | 18 | 18 | 18 |
| Moscow Basin | 10 | 20 | 31 | 39 | 47 | 43 | 41 |
| Rostov (Donbas) | 11 | 8 | 18 | 25 | 32 | 32 | 32 |
| Ukraine | 84 | 30 | 78 | 126 | 165 | 172 | 194 |
| Ukrainian Donbas | 83 | 29 | 76 | 116 | 150 | 156 | 174 |
| (Total Donbas | 94 | 37 | 95 | 141 | 182 | 188 | 206) |
| L'vov–Volhynia | — | — | 0.2 | 0.7 | 2 | 4 | 10 |
| Dnieper basins | 0.4 | 1 | 2 | 8 | 11 | 11 | 10 |
| Georgia | 0.6 | 0.6 | 2 | 3 | 3 | 3 | 3 |
| Urals | 12 | 25 | 33 | 47 | 61 | 62 | 62 |
| Kizel | 5 | 8 | 10 | 11 | 12 | 12 | 10 |
| Chelyabinsk | 6 | 11 | 12 | 18 | 22 | 23 | 24 |
| Serov | 1.4 | 6 | 9 | 15 | 22 | 23 | 21 |
| Bashkiria | — | — | — | 2 | 4 | 4 | 7 |
| Asian USSR | 48 | 61 | 90 | 136 | 170 | 183 | 227 |
| Siberia | 39 | 47 | 69 | 103 | 131 | 143 | 172 |
| Kuznetsk Basin | 22 | 29 | 38 | 58 | 75 | 84 | 96 |
| Eastern Siberia | 9 | 8 | 18 | 27 | 36 | 37 | 47 |
| Far East | 7 | 7 | 13 | 17 | 20 | 22 | 29 |
| Kazakhstan | 7 | 11 | 17 | 28 | 31 | 32 | 46 |
| Karaganda | 6 | 11 | 16 | 25 | 24 | 25 | 30 |
| Ekibastuz | — | — | — | 2 | 6 | 7 | 14 |
| Central Asia | 1.7 | 1.4 | 4 | 6 | 8 | 8 | 9 |
| Angren (Uzbekistan) | — | 0.1 | 1.5 | 2.6 | 3.5 | 3.2 | 4.4 |
| Fergana Valley | 1.7 | 1.3 | 2.3 | 3.3 | 4.2 | 4.4 | 4.6 |
| Kirghizia | 1.5 | 1.1 | 1.9 | 2.7 | 3.4 | 3.5 | 3.7 |
| Tadzhikistan | 0.2 | 0.2 | 0.5 | 0.6 | 0.8 | 0.9 | 0.9 |
| Total USSR | 166 | 149 | 261 | 301 | 496 | 513 | 578 |

Note: Some subtotals do not add up because of rounding or the omission of minor producing areas.

coking coal needs of the Cherepovets iron and steel plant. The Pechora Basin, centered on Vorkuta, produced 17 to 18 million tons of coal in the mid-1960s. The regional distribution of Soviet coal output appears in Table 4.

Since the advent of the oil and gas era in the mid-1950s, the trend in the coal industry has been toward low-cost strip mining, a reduction of long hauls of low-value coals, the increasing use of strip-mined brown coal at minehead power stations, and the construction of large-capacity mines to reduce costs in underground operations. Strip mining, which yielded only 27 million tons of coal in 1950, rose to 140 million tons by 1965, mostly because of the exploitation of surface brown-coal deposits in the Urals and Siberia for generating power. One effect of the availability of natural gas was to put a virtual end to Soviet experiments at underground gasification of coals in the Donets, Moscow, and Kuznetsk basins. These experiments, designed to gasify coal in place, with air or oxygen, to produce a gas suitable for power generation and other industrial uses begin in the 1930s, but were found to be uneconomical even before the development of natural gas provided a far more economical fuel.

## Petroleum

Before World War II, 80 percent of Soviet crude-oil production was concentrated in the Caucasus, where commercial output dated from the 1870s at Baku and from the 1890s at Groznyy. Out of a total Soviet production of 31.1 million tons in 1940, Baku yielded 22.2 million, a record level that would not be reached again until the late 1960s, and Groznyy contributed 2.2 million tons, having dropped from a peak of about 8 million tons in the early 1930s. The Groznyy field was not to recover and surpass that record level until 1965, after the discovery of large oil deposits in Mesozoic strata, below the previously productive Tertiary beds, had resulted in a revival of Groznyy production. Before World War II, however, there was relatively little exploration for oil, as the national fuel policy favored the development of the coal industry. During the war, the Baku and Groznyy fields, though threatened by the German invasion, were not seized, but output nevertheless declined as the previously low level of exploration was reflected in production. Output at Baku dropped to half of its prewar level.

Under the pressure of the wartime emergency, greater attention was given to a vast new potential oil-bearing province that had been identified in the 1930s between the Volga River and the Urals. Although commercial production had begun there before the war, it accounted for only 6 percent of total Soviet crude-oil output in 1940. The intensified exploration of the Volga–Urals province during World War II and especially after the war uncovered the potentialities of the region, whose most productive oil-bearing horizons were associated with Devonian and Carboniferous strata. By 1949 the expanding Volga–Urals production had compensated for the wartime decline of the old Caucasus fields, and during the late 1950s the new great Volga producing areas, the Tatar ASSR, the Bashkir ASSR, and Kuybyshev Oblast, one after another surpassed the production levels of Baku. Growing Volga output raised the Soviet Union to second place among the world's oil producers when it passed Venezuela in 1961. By the mid-1960s the Volga region contributed 70 percent of a total Soviet crude-oil output of 243 million tons. The regional distribution of Soviet oil production appears in Table 5.

The Volga province is expected to retain its preeminent position in the Soviet petroleum industry in the foreseeable future, although the outlines of other major producing regions began to emerge in the mid-1960s. They were the Mangyshlak Peninsula, on the northeast coast of the Caspian Sea, and the West Siberian deposits around Surgut on the Ob' River. Adverse physical–geographic conditions—desert in the Mangyshlak and, particularly, remote Siberian forest in the Surgut area—are expected to slow the pace of development, but reserves were said to indicate high future production levels. Pipelines, railroads, and other services were under construction in both regions in the late 1960s as production slowly gained momentum. As in the revived North Causacus fields around Groznyy, the promising reserves of Mangyshlak and West Siberia are associated with Mesozoic formations, which also account for most of the oil production of the Middle East.

The changing distribution of crude-oil production was reflected in the locational pattern of oil refineries. Before World War II,

Table 5

Regional Distribution of Soviet Crude-Oil Production
(in million metric tons)

| | 1940 | 1945 | 1950 | 1955 | 1958 | 1960 | 1965 |
|---|---|---|---|---|---|---|---|
| European USSR | 27.5 | 14.9 | 26.6 | 48.8 | 82.2 | 108.4 | 172.7 |
| *(incl. Urals)* | *29.1* | *16.7* | *32.8* | *64.1* | *104.7* | *137.3* | *225.7)* |
| European Russia | 4.9 | 3.1 | 11.4 | 33.0 | 64.5 | 88.4 | 143.6 |
| *(incl. Urals)* | *6.5* | *4.9* | *17.6* | *48.3* | *87.0* | *117.3* | *196.6)* |
| Ukhta | 0.1 | 0.3 | 0.5 | 0.6 | 0.7 | 0.7 | 2.2 |
| North Caucasus | 4.6 | 1.8 | 6.0 | 6.5 | 12 | 12.1 | 20.7 |
| Groznyy | 2.2 | 1.4 | 2.5 | 2.1 | 2.3 | 3.3 | 9.0 |
| Krasnodar | 2.2 | 0.3 | 3.0 | 3.9 | | 7 | 6.1 |
| Stavropol' | — | — | — | — | | 1.5 | 4.6 |
| Dagestan | 0.1 | 0.1 | 0.5 | 0.4 | 0.2 | 0.2 | 1.0 |
| Volga | 0.2 | 1.0 | 4.7 | 25.9 | 51.3 | 73 | 117.4 |
| Tataria | — | — | 0.9 | 14.5 | 31.8 | 45 | 76.5 |
| Kuybyshev | 0.2 | 1.0 | 3.5 | 7.3 | 16 | 22 | 33.4 |
| Saratov | — | — | 0.4 | 1.8 | | 2 | 1.3 |
| Volgograd | — | — | — | 2.3 | | 5 | 6.2 |
| Urals | 1.6 | 1.8 | 6.3 | 15.3 | 22.5 | 31 | 56.3 |
| Bashkiria | 1.4 | 1.3 | 5.7 | 14.2 | 20.0 | 25 | 43.9 |
| Orenburg | 0.2 | 0.4 | 0.3 | 0.5 | | 2 | 2.6 |
| Perm' | 0.16 | 0.2 | 0.5 | 0.6 | | 3 | 9.8 |
| *(Volga–Urals)* | *1.8* | *2.8* | *11.0* | *41.2* | *73.8* | *104* | *173.7)* |

| | | | | | | | |
|---|---|---|---|---|---|---|---|
| Azerbaydzhan (Baku) | 22.2 | 11.5 | 14.8 | 15.3 | 16.5 | 17.8 | 21.5 |
| Ukraine | 0.4 | 0.3 | 0.3 | 0.5 | 1.2 | 2.2 | 7.6 |
| Belorussia | — | — | — | — | — | — | 0.039 |
| Kazakhstan | 0.7 | 0.8 | 1.1 | 1.4 | 1.5 | 1.6 | 2.0 |
| Asia USSR | 2.0 | 2.7 | 5.1 | 6.6 | 8.5 | 10.6 | 17.2 |
| Siberia | 0.5 | 0.8 | 0.6 | 1.0 | 1 | 1.6 | 3.4 |
| Tyumen' | — | — | — | — | — | — | 1.0 |
| Sakhalin | 0.5 | 0.8 | 0.6 | 1.0 | 1 | 1.6 | 2.4 |
| Central Asia | 0.8 | 1.1 | 3.4 | 4.2 | 6.0 | 7.4 | 11.8 |
| Turkmenia | 0.6 | 0.6 | 2.0 | 3.1 | 4.2 | 5.3 | 9.6 |
| Uzbekistan | 0.1 | 0.5 | 1.3 | 1.0 | 1.3 | 1.6 | 1.8 |
| Kirghizia | 0.024 | 0.019 | 0.047 | 0.1 | 0.5 | 0.5 | 0.3 |
| Tadzhikistan | 0.030 | 0.020 | 0.020 | 0.017 | 0.018 | 0.017 | 0.047 |
| Total USSR | 31.1 | 19.4 | 37.9 | 70.8 | 113.2 | 147.9 | 242.9 |

Note: Some subtotals do not add up because of rounding.

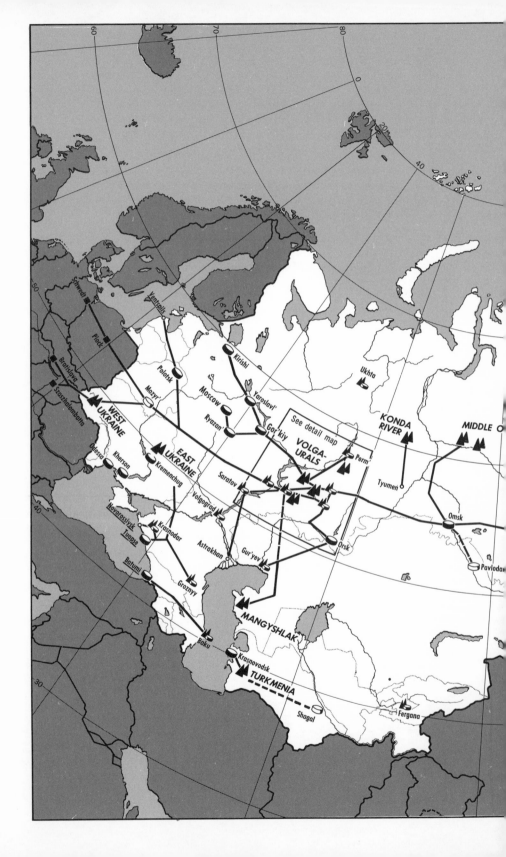

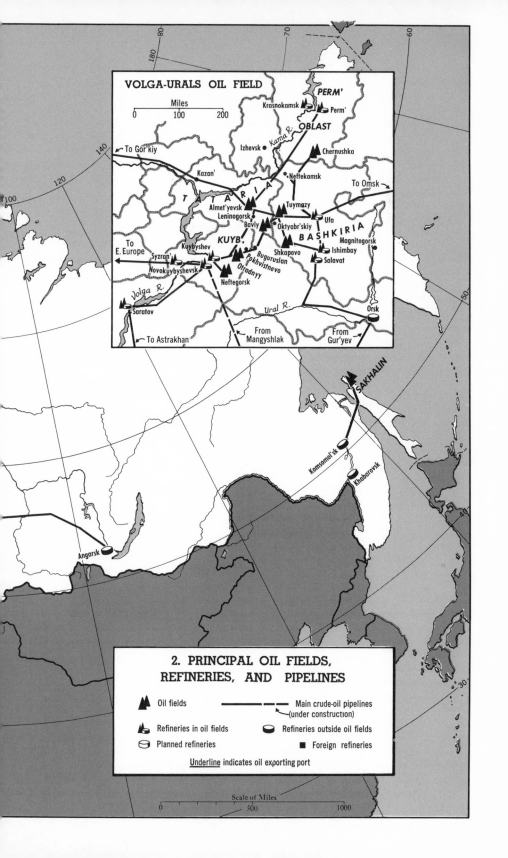

**VOLGA-URALS OIL FIELD**

Miles
0    100    200

To Gor'kiy

Krasnokamsk    *Perm'*    **PERM'**

Izhevsk    **OBLAST**

Kazan'    Kama R.    Chernushka

Neftekamsk    To Omsk

T A T A R I A

Almet'yevsk    Tuymazy
Leninogorsk    Ufa    **BASHKIRIA**
Bavly    Oktyabr'skiy    Magnitogorsk
**KUYB.**    Shkapovo    Ishimbay
Kuybyshev    Bugurusian    Salavat
To    Pokhvistnevo
E. Europe    Syzran'    Otradnyy
Novokuybyshevsk    Neftegorsk

Volga R.    Ural R.    Orsk
Saratov

To Astrakhan    From    From
Mangyshlak    Gur'yev

**SAKHALIN**

Komsomol'sk
Khabarovsk

Angarsk

**2. PRINCIPAL OIL FIELDS,
REFINERIES, AND PIPELINES**

▲ Oil fields ————— Main crude-oil pipelines
(under construction)

⛏ Refineries in oil fields    ⬭ Refineries outside oil fields

⬯ Planned refineries    ■ Foreign refineries

<u>Underline</u> indicates oil exporting port

Scale of Miles
0    500    1000

more than 80 percent of refining capacity was concentrated in the
Baku and Groznyy fields, supplying refined products to the major
consuming areas of European Russia by railroad tank cars. What
trunk pipelines there were—4,100 kilometers in 1940—were found
mainly in the Caucasus, linking oil fields with refineries and water
terminals on the Caspian Sea and the Black Sea.

The shift to the Volga–Urals region upset the prewar refining
and distribution system. Although refineries were completed in the
Volga region in the early postwar period, crude-oil production in
the expanding fields rose more rapidly than refining capacity, and
several million tons of oil a year were shipped by pipeline and
tanker from the Volga fields for refining at Baku and Groznyy,
where the wartime decline of crude-oil production had idled part
of the refining capacity. Starting in the mid-1950s, a new program
of establishing refineries began. Instead of concentrating refining
operations in the producing fields and then distributing refined
products to consuming centers, it was found more economical to
deliver crude oil by pipeline to new refineries to be located in consuming areas.

The new policy affected not only domestic oil distribution, but
also Soviet exports to Eastern Europe as the Friendship trunk pipeline, completed in 1964, carried Volga oil to new refineries in Plock
(Poland), Schwedt (East Germany), Bratislava (Czechoslovakia),
and Szaszhalombatta (Hungary). Within the Soviet Union, the
Trans-Siberian oil pipeline, completed in 1962, served new refineries
at Omsk and Angarsk (near Irkutsk) for products distribution
within Siberia. In European Russia, other pipelines delivered Volga
oil to new refineries in Perm' (opened in 1958), Gor'kiy (1958),
Ryazan' (1960), Yaroslavl' (1964), Kirishi (near Leningrad, 1966),
and Polotsk (1963). Pipeline construction involved in this new
program raised the total length of trunk pipelines in the Soviet Union
to 28,200 kilometers by 1965 (Fig. 2).

Despite an intensive program of refinery construction, the expansion of refining capacity failed to keep pace with crude-oil production. In 1958, when the Soviet Union produced 113 million tons of
crude oil, it had a net export balance of 8 million tons, suggesting a
refining throughput of about 105 million tons. By 1965, crude-oil
output rose to 243 million tons and throughput to almost 200 million

tons, resulting in an export balance of 43 million tons. The lag of expansion of refining capacity in general is associated with a shortage of cracking capacity in particular.

Aside from the advantage of increasing the total yield of gasoline, diesel oil, and other distillate products by cracking the low-value residual fuel oil left over from straight-run distillation, there were two reasons for increasing the deeper processing of crude oil under Soviet conditions. One was the growing petrochemical industry, some of whose basic materials, called aromatics, are obtained most efficiently by an advanced process called catalytic reforming. By altering the molecules of straight-run naphthas, this method converts some nonaromatic constituents into products containing aromatic compounds, such as benzene, used for manufacturing styrene (a constituent of synthetic rubber) and other synthetics. The second reason for the development of more reforming capacity lay in the high-sulfur character of the Volga crude oil. Catalytic reforming yields a large amount of by-product hydrogen needed to desulfurize the corrosive Volga diesel and other distillate fuel oils by a process known as hydrogenation.

## Natural Gas

Natural gas is an even more recent latecomer to the Soviet economy than mass production of petroleum. Before World War II, there were virtually not any nonassociated gas fields (producing gas and no oil) in the Soviet Union. Out of 3.2 billion cubic meters recovered in 1940, 80 percent consisted of gas associated with crude-oil production at Baku. The only separate gas field of any consequence was in the Dashava area of the Carpathians, which was annexed by the Soviet Union from Poland in 1939 and which supplied gas by pipeline to L'vov.

During World War II, in conjunction with the exploration of the oil resources of the Volga–Urals province, nonassociated natural-gas deposits with substantial reserves justifying long-distance transmission were found near Saratov, and in 1946 the Soviet Union's first major transmission gas main, a 12-inch, 500-mile-long pipeline, began to deliver Saratov gas to Moscow. (During World War II, a 90-mile-long pipeline was completed in 1943 from a gas

19

field near Buguruslan to Kuybyshev.) In this early program to supply natural gas to Moscow, a second long-distance transmission
main, this one 800 miles long and 20 inches in diameter, was completed from the Carpathian field of Dashava to Moscow in 1951.
(The Dashava–Kiev section opened in 1948.)

By 1955, total natural-gas production had risen to 9 billion cubic
meters, of which two-thirds was from gas fields and one-third from
oil fields. Natural gas was used primarily by residential consumers,
with virtually no industrial applications. One of the few exceptions
was the manufacture of carbon black in the Ukhta gas fields of
northern European Russia.

The discovery of large nonassociated natural-gas reserves in the
late 1950s inaugurated the era of gas utilization in earnest. Three
principal provinces were found to have reserves adequate to justify
the construction of major transmission systems to the fuel-poor
manufacturing centers in the Urals and the European part of the
Soviet Union. The new sources of natural gas were the Stavropol'
and Krasnodar areas of the Northern Caucasus, the Shebelinka field
southeast of Khar'kov in the eastern Ukraine, and the Bukhara fields
of the Uzbek SSR in Central Asia (Fig. 3).

A transmission system of three pipelines, first with a diameter of
30 inches, later 40 inches, was built within a few years (1956–60)
between the Northern Caucasus fields and Moscow, with an extension to Leningrad. It transmitted 30 billion cubic meters a year in
the mid-1960s. The Northern Caucasus fields were also connected
with Transcaucasia to supplement natural gas already being transmitted from Karadag in the Baku area. The Shebelinka field became
the source for a system of pipelines serving the Ukraine and central
European Russia. In the Bukhara area, the Gazli field fed natural
gas to the Urals via two transmission mains completed in 1963
and 1965, and other fields, Dzharkak and later Mubarek, southeast
of Bukhara, supplied the industrial centers of Central Asia. At the
same time, an expansion of reserves through exploration in the
older gas-producing areas of Dashava and Saratov led to the construction of additional pipelines; Dashava supplied Belorussia,
Lithuania, and Latvia, and the new Saratov field (at Stepnoye)
served the Upper Volga industrial centers of Gor'kiy, Yaroslavl',
and Cherepovets.

As the transmission systems expanded—the total length of transmission mains reached 41,800 kilometers by 1965—gas production soared. In 1965 the Soviet Union produced 128 billion cubic meters, including 111 billion from gas fields and 17 billion from oil fields. The use of gas pervaded all sectors of the economy. In the mid-1960s, 60 percent was used in industry, either as a fuel in iron and steel production, cement kilns, and metal fabrication, or as a raw material in the chemical industry; 25 percent was burned in central power stations, and domestic consumers absorbed only 10 percent.

Substantial savings for the economy as a whole resulted from the substitution of natural gas, a clean, flexible, relatively low-cost fuel, for the traditional long-haul coal. By supplementing petrochemicals derived from petroleum and its products, natural gas and its derivatives also promoted an expansion of the chemical industry, notably by providing low-cost hydrogen for ammonia synthesis and the nitrogen fertilizer industry.

The natural-gas industry expanded further during the late 1960s as new transmission systems were under construction from newly explored fields in northeast European Russia and the Kara Kum Desert of Central Asia. The first main of 40-inch pipe of the Central Asian system reached the Moscow area at the end of 1967. A second line of 48-inch pipe, under construction in the late 1960s, was planned to raise annual transmission along this system to 25 billion cubic meters, or as much as the entire country produced in 1957 as massive development of the natural-gas industry was just getting under way. The North European pipeline, also of 48-inch diameter, has its origins in the Vuktyl gas field, explored in the mid-1960s east of Ukhta. This transmission main reached Rybinsk in late 1968 and connected early the following year with the existing Moscow–Leningrad gas transmission system at Torzhok.

The North European pipeline is the first of a major transmission system that will carry gas from the newly discovered West Siberian fields to European Russia, the Baltic republics, Belorussia, the Ukraine, and countries of Eastern Europe. The transmission system is to be equipped first with 48-inch and 56-inch pipelines, later possibly with 80-inch and 100-inch transmission mains to handle the flow of large amounts of West Siberian gas in the late 1970s. In addition to the North European pipeline system, which

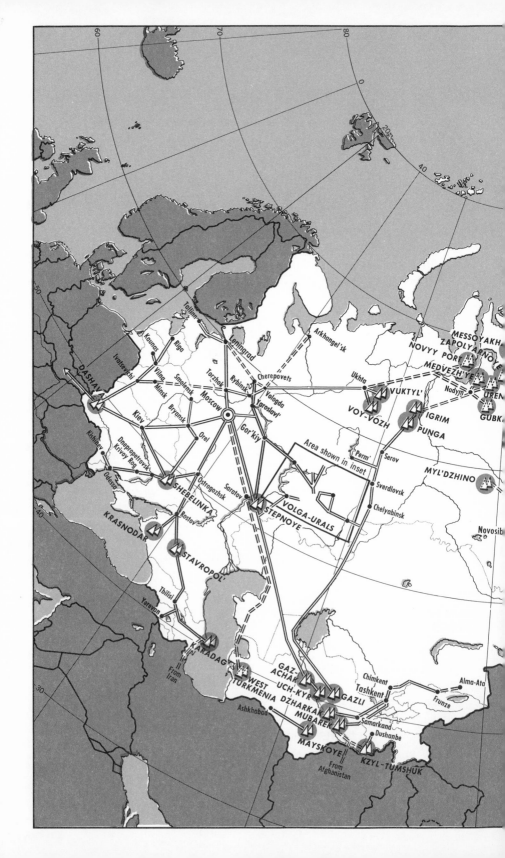

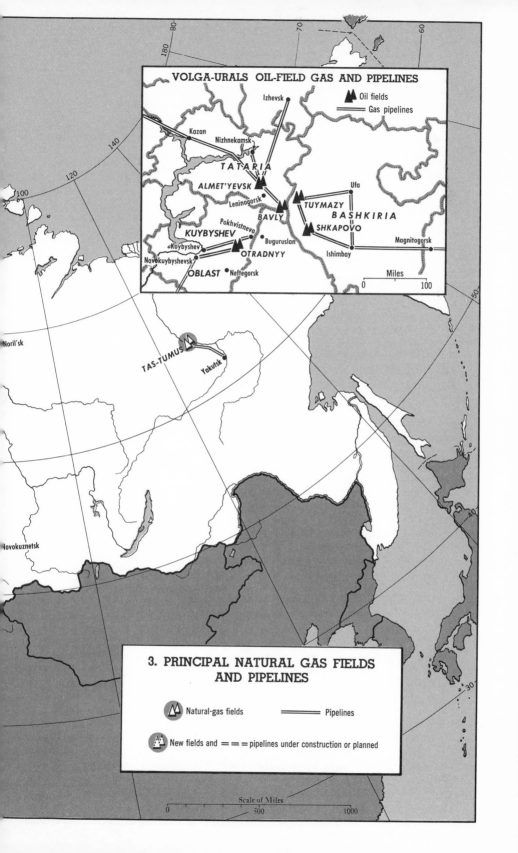

## VOLGA-URALS OIL-FIELD GAS AND PIPELINES

▲▲ Oil fields
— Gas pipelines

Izhevsk

Kazan
Nizhnekamsk

*TATARIA*

*ALMET'YEVSK*

Leninogorsk

Ufa

*BAVLY*        *TUYMAZY*

*BASHKIRIA*

Pokhvistnevo        *SHKAPOVO*

*KUYBYSHEV*        Buguruslan

Magnitogorsk

Kuybyshev

Novokuybyshevsk    *OTRADNYY*

Ishimbay

*OBLAST* • Neftegorsk

Miles
0        100

Noril'sk

TAS-TUMUS    • Yakutsk

Novokuznetsk

## 3. PRINCIPAL NATURAL GAS FIELDS AND PIPELINES

🛆 Natural-gas fields        ═══ Pipelines

🛆 New fields and ≡≡≡ pipelines under construction or planned

Scale of Miles
0        500        1000

will have its origin at the West Siberian collecting center of Nadym, the West Siberian gas fields are also expected to be connected with the Urals.

The regional distribution of Soviet natural-gas production, broken down into gas associated with oil production and nonassociated gas, appears in Table 6.

## Oil Shale & Peat

Although oil-shale deposits are widespread in the Soviet Union, this fuel has been of only local significance because of low heating value and high ash content. The largest mining operations are found in Estonia, where the extraction of shale, begun in World War I, was promoted during independence and especially under the Soviet regime in the absence of other fuel resources. Under the former policy of promoting the use of local fuels, even if of low grade, shale deposits were also developed in the 1930s in the Slantsy area of Leningrad Oblast, an extension of the Estonian basin, and in the middle Volga valley. At least two small mines in the Saratov area that supplied oil shale to a Saratov power station discontinued operations in the mid-1950s because of the competition of lower-priced petroleum products and natural gas. A second Volga oil-shale mine, at Kashpirovka, southern suburb of Syzran', continues to produce about 1.5 million tons a year for an adjacent power plant and for conversion into chemicals. Only in the Estonian–Leningrad area does the oil-shale industry continue to flourish as a source of fuel for local power stations. Estonia's production, in particular, has risen continuously, from 3.5 million tons in 1950 to 16 million tons in the mid-1960s (Table 7), providing fuel for a 1.6-million kilowatt central electric station, the world's largest shale-based power plant. Further expansion of shale production was planned in connection with inauguration of a second major power station in 1969. In addition to fueling power stations, the Estonian shale was also used in the 1950s and 1960s for the manufacture of gas that was transmitted to Leningrad and Tallinn. However, shale gas could not compete with the increasing availability of natural gas, which reached Estonia in 1969.

Like oil shale, peat was developed in the Soviet Union for power generation in areas where other fuels were not available and even

*Table 6*

Regional Distribution of Soviet Natural-Gas Production
(in billion cubic meters)

| | | 1940 | 1955 | 1960 | 1965 |
|---|---|---|---|---|---|
| European USSR | T | 3.18 | 8.6 | 44.2 | 109.2 |
| (incl. Urals) | G | 0.41 | 5.8 | 37.1 | 94.2 |
| | O | 2.77 | 2.8 | 7.1 | 15.0 |
| European Russia | T | 1.43 | 4.1 | 24.0 | 63.7 |
| (incl. Urals) | G | 0.05 | 2.4 | 18.7 | 53.4 |
| | O | 1.38 | 1.7 | 5.3 | 10.3 |
| Ukhta | T | — | 1.1 | 1.0 | 0.6 |
| | G | | 1.0 | 1.0 | 0.6 |
| Northern Caucasus | T | 0.195 | 0.6 | 14 | 39 |
| | G | 0.053 | 0.4 | 12.6 | 37.5 |
| | O | 0.142 | 0.2 | 1.4 | 1.5 |
| Krasnodar | G | — | 0.3 | 4.4 | 22.3 |
| Stavropol' | G | — | — | 8.2 | 15.1 |
| Volga–Urals | T | 0.015 | 2.4 | 9.4 | 24 |
| | G | — | 1.4 | 5.3 | 15.3 |
| | O | 0.015 | 1.0 | 4.1 | 9 |
| Volgograd | G | — | — | 2.3 | 6.6 |
| Saratov | G | — | 0.8 | 2.3 | 6.2 |
| Ukraine | T | 0.495 | 2.9 | 14.3 | 39.4 |
| | G | 0.408 | 2.8 | 13.8 | 37.8 |
| | O | 0.087 | 0.1 | 0.5 | 1.6 |
| Dashava | G | 0.4 | 2.8 | 4.9 | 9.5 |
| Shebelinka | G | — | — | 8.9 | 26.2 |
| Azerbaydzhan (Baku) | T | 2.5 | 1.5 | 5.8 | 6.2 |
| | G | — | 0.5 | 4.5 | 3.0 |
| | O | 2.5 | 1.0 | 1.3 | 3.2 |
| Asian USSR | T | 0.02 | 0.4 | 1.1 | 18.5 |
| | G | — | 0.1 | 0.5 | 17.0 |
| | O | 0.02 | 0.3 | 0.6 | 1.5 |
| Bukhara (Uzbek) | G | — | — | 0.4 | 16.4 |
| Total USSR | T | 3.2 | 9.0 | 45.3 | 127.7 |
| | G | 0.4 | 5.9 | 37.6 | 111.2 |
| | O | 2.8 | 3.1 | 7.7 | 16.5 |

Abbreviations: T = Total natural-gas output
G = Gas output not associated with oil
O = Oil-associated gas output

*Table 7*

Regional Distribution of Soviet Oil-Shale Production
(in million metric tons)

|  | 1940 | 1945 | 1950 | 1955 | 1958 | 1960 | 1965 |
|---|---|---|---|---|---|---|---|
| Estonia | 1.9 | 0.9 | 3.5 | 7.0 | 9.0 | 9.3 | 15.8 |
| Slantsy (Leningrad Oblast) | 0.4 | — | 0.4 | 2.1 | 3.0 | 3.5 | 4.2 |
| Total Northwest | 2.3 | 0.9 | 3.9 | 9.1 | 12.0 | 12.8 | 20.0 |
| Kashpirovka | 0.2 | 0.3 | 0.4 | 1.2 | 1.2 | 1.4 | 1.3 |
| Saratov Oblast | 0.1 | 0.3 | 0.4 | 0.6 | — | — | — |
| Total Volga | 0.3 | 0.5 | 0.8 | 1.7 | 1.2 | 1.4 | 1.3 |
| Total USSR | 2.6 | 1.4 | 4.7 | 10.8 | 13.2 | 14.2 | 21.3 |

a low-value fuel such as peat was able to compete with long-haul steam coal. Such conditions existed in central European Russia, Belorussia, the Baltic republics, and the Leningrad area. At least in the early phase of the oil and gas era, the use of peat for power generation continued, and during the late 1950s and 1960s total production remained at 50 to 70 million tons.

# 2

# ELECTRIC POWER

As in the case of fuels, the mid-1950s marked a turning point in the Soviet Union's electric power industry. Previously central electric stations were developed with relatively small- and medium-size capacities in a more or less even distribution throughout the industrial areas of the country. This was in keeping with a policy of industrial decentralization and the use of local fuel resources. Central stations served relatively small areas, and the transmission of electric power was limited to a radius of 50 to 100 miles at relatively low voltages (100 kilovolts).

Small stations, though suited to the early stages of Soviet industrialization, proved inadequate as the economy expanded and became more complex. A more diversified Soviet industrial system required a more rapid expansion of power generation than could be assured by the construction of stations of 100,000- and 200,000- kilowatt capacity. It also required the interconnection of electric grids via high-voltage lines to enable transfers of electric power according to shifting demands of industry. About 1955 the Soviet Union therefore adopted a new development program for the electric power industry, calling for the construction of large central electric stations of 1 million kilowatts or more and the construction of major power transmission lines.

Before World War II and in the early postwar period small electric power complexes developed on the basis of local fuels in

European Russia, which accounted for more than three-fourths of the total electric power output of the Soviet Union in 1940. Peat furnished the fuel for a system of power plants around Moscow, Leningrad, and in Belorussia. Other power complexes arose on the basis of the brown coal of the Moscow Basin, south of the Soviet capital, and of culm (anthracite fines) of the Donets Basin. These local fuels were supplemented by long-haul Donets steam coals, which were often shipped over great distances. Hydroelectric power was at first also developed mainly in European Russia, notably the first Dnieper station at Zaporozh'ye, which opened in 1932 and, with a capacity of 560,000 kilowatts, long remained the nation's largest hydroelectric plant. It was in conjunction with the need for transmission of the larger capacities of the early stations that the first higher-voltage lines of up to 220 kilovolts were constructed in the 1930s. The small stations yielded relatively small annual increases in electrical capacity as the total installed capacity in the Soviet Union rose slowly from 11 million kilowatts in 1940 to 20 million in 1950 and 37 million in 1955.

The advent of the oil and gas era combined with the new policy of low-cost strip mining of brown coal in Siberia introduced new elements into the distributional pattern of thermal power stations. On the one hand the long-distance transmission of crude oil and natural gas made it possible to base large central stations burning gas and fuel oil at points along the pipelines. On the other hand, advances in the long-distance transmission of electric power made it economical to transport large blocks of power from generating stations at Siberian brown-coal strip mines to distant consumers. Beginning in the mid-1950s, central stations with capacities of 600,000 to 1.2 million kilowatts went into construction. In the period of the seven-year plan (1959–65), a number of stations with ultimate capacities of 2.4 million kilowatts were begun, using generating units of 200,000 and 300,000 kilowatts. The trend toward ever larger units continued in the late 1960s as 500,000-kilowatt generators were installed at Nazarovo, a major brown-coal based station in Siberia, and 800,000-kilowatt units were used at the Slavyansk thermal power station in the Donets Basin (Fig. 4).

The shift to large stations had a marked effect on the growth of installed power capacity and on production. From 37 million kilowatts in 1955, total generating capacity increased to 67 million in 1960 and 115 million in 1965. During the mid-1960s about 10 million kilowatts a year were being added, or roughly the equivalent of the country's total electrical generating capacity of 1940. The rapid rise of capacity was reflected in total electric power output, which rose from 170 billion kilowatt-hours in 1955 to 292 billion in 1960 and 507 billion in 1965 (Table 8).

Thermal stations, because they cost less and take less time to construct than do hydroelectric stations, were given priority. However, construction of hydroelectric projects continued in areas where abundant stream flow, mountainous terrain, and other physical factors favored such development. Hydroelectric stations had a total installed capacity of 22 million kilowatts compared with 93 million in thermal power, and contributed about 17 percent of the total electric output in 1965. This ratio is expected to be maintained in the foreseeable future.

The most spectacular projects to be completed or under construction are on the great Siberian streams, particularly the Yenisey River and its tributary, the Angara. On the Angara, the 660,000-kilowatt Irkutsk station, using Lake Baykal as a natural storage reservoir, was opened in 1956 after six years of construction. It was followed by the Bratsk station in 1961. Originally planned for a total capacity of 4.5 million kilowatts, the Bratsk station had 18 of the planned 20 generators installed by the end of 1966, for a total capacity of 4.05 million kilowatts, making it then the world's largest hydroelectric power producer. A third Angara station, the Ust'-Ilimsk plant, was under construction in the late 1960s. It was also scheduled to have a capacity of about 4.5 million kilowatts when completed. On the Yenisey River, the first 500,000-kilowatt generators of a planned 6-million-kilowatt station went into operation in 1967 at Divnogorsk, near Krasnoyarsk, and the station reached 5 million kilowatts in early 1970. The 6.5-million-kilowatt Sayan plant was under construction in the late 1960s farther upstream.

One problem associated with the construction of these large capacities in relatively remote and underdeveloped parts of Siberia is the need for parallel construction of power-oriented industrial enterprises, such as aluminum reduction plants, to make use of the newly available amounts of electric power. In the case of the Bratsk

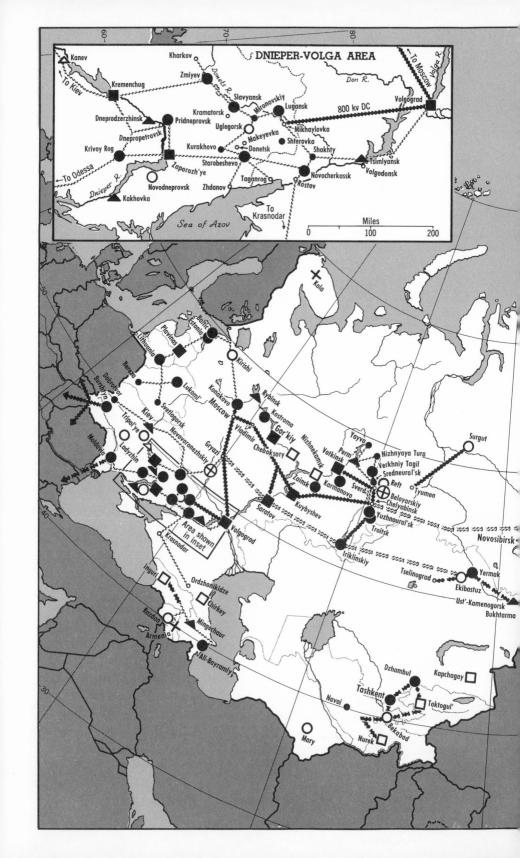

## DNIEPER-VOLGA AREA

Kanev

Kharkov

Zmiyev

Kremenchug

Slavyansk

Mironovskiy

Lugansk

To Moscow

Volga R.

Don R.

800 kv DC

Volgograd

Kramatorsk

Dneprodzerzhinsk

Pridneprovsk

Uglegorsk

Mikhaylovka

Dnepropetrovsk

Krivoy Rog

Kurakhovo

Makeyevka

Shterovka

Shakhty

To Odessa

Starobeshevo

Donetsk

Zaporozh'ye

Taganrog

Zhdanov

Novocherkassk

Volgodonsk

Tsimlyansk

Novodneprovsk

Rostov

Kakhovka

To Krasnodar

Sea of Azov

Miles

0    100    200

Kola

Baltic

Estonia

Dolitf

Plavinas

Lithuania

Kirishi

Reseva

Dobrotvor

Burshlyn

Lukoml'

Konakovo

Rybinsk

Moscow

Kostroma

Surgut

Tripol'ye

Kiev

Svetlogorsk

Vladimir

Gor'kiy

Yayva

Ladyzhin

Novovoronezhskiy

Cheboksary

Nizhnekamsk

Votkinsk

Perm

Nizhnyaya Tura

Verkhniy Tagil

Moldavia

Gryazi

Zainsk

Karmanovo

Sverd

Reft

Tyumen

Sredneural'sk

Beloyarskiy

Chelyabinsk

Saratov

Kuybyshev

Area shown in inset

Volgograd

Yuzhnoural'sk

Troitsk

Novosibirsk

Krasnodar

Iriklinskiy

Yermak

Inguri

Ordzhonikidze

Tselinograd

Ekibastuz

Chirkey

Ust'-Kamenogorsk

Bukhtarma

Razdan

Mingechaur

Armenia

Ali-Bayramly

Dzhambul

Kapchagay

Tashkent

Navoi

Toktogul'

Mary

Bekabad

Nurek

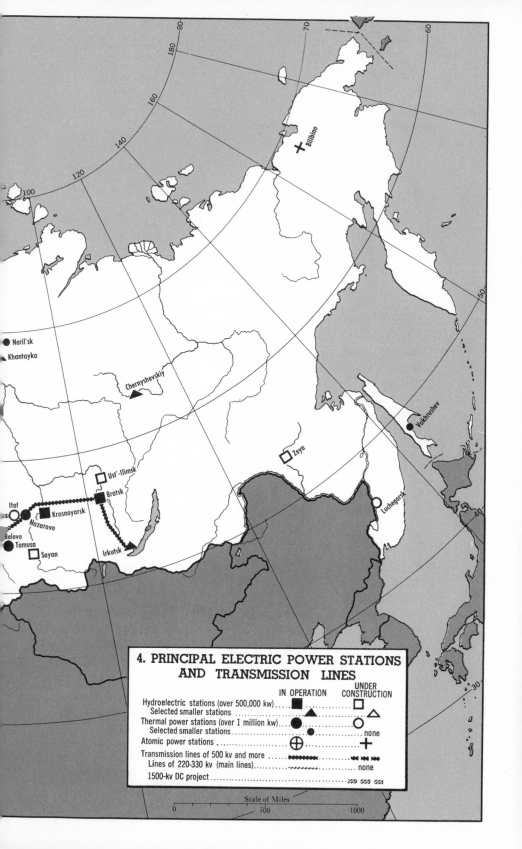

Noril'sk
Khantayka

Bilibino

Chernyshevskiy

Zeya

Yakhrushev

Ust'-Ilimsk
Bratsk

Itat
Krasnoyarsk
Nazarovo
Belovo
Tomusa
Sayan

Irkutsk

Luchegorsk

## 4. PRINCIPAL ELECTRIC POWER STATIONS AND TRANSMISSION LINES

|  | IN OPERATION | UNDER CONSTRUCTION |
|---|---|---|
| Hydroelectric stations (over 500,000 kw) | ■ | □ |
| Selected smaller stations | ▲ | △ |
| Thermal power stations (over 1 million kw) | ● | ○ |
| Selected smaller stations | ● | none |
| Atomic power stations | ⊕ | + |
| Transmission lines of 500 kv and more | ►►►► | ►► ►►►► |
| Lines of 220-330 kv (main lines) | | none |
| 1500-kv DC project | | 〰〰 〰〰 〰〰 |

Scale of Miles

0          500          1000

*Table 8*

Regional Distribution of Soviet Electric Power Output
(in billion kilowatt-hours)

| | 1940 | 1950 | 1955 | 1960 | 1965 |
|---|---|---|---|---|---|
| European USSR | 37.6 | 56 | 105 | 180 | 308 |
| European Russia | 22 | 35 | 62 | 104 | 169 |
| North | 5 | 7 | 13 | 17 | 25 |
| Central | 13 | 20 | 33 | 44 | 70 |
| Volga | 2 | 4 | 9 | 33 | 56 |
| North Caucasus | 2 | 4 | 7 | 10 | 18 |
| Ukraine | 12 | 15 | 30 | 54 | 95 |
| Moldavia | 0.02 | 0.1 | 0.3 | 0.7 | 3 |
| Belorussia | 0.5 | 0.8 | 1.9 | 4 | 8 |
| Baltic | 0.27 | 1.1 | 2.4 | 5 | 13 |
| Lithuania | 0.04 | 0.2 | 0.6 | 1 | 4 |
| Latvia | 0.13 | 0.5 | 0.9 | 1.7 | 1.5 |
| Estonia | 0.10 | 0.4 | 0.9 | 2 | 7 |
| Transcaucasia | 2.9 | 5 | 9 | 14 | 19 |
| Azerbaydzhan | 1.8 | 3 | 5 | 7 | 10 |
| Georgia | 0.7 | 1.4 | 2 | 4 | 6 |
| Armenia | 0.4 | 0.9 | 2 | 3 | 3 |
| Urals | 6 | 18 | 33 | 49 | 76 |
| Asian USSR | 4.5 | 17 | 31 | 63 | 123 |
| Siberia | 3.1 | 10 | 20 | 44 | 87 |
| Western Siberia | 1.8 | 6 | 12 | 23 | 35 |
| Eastern Siberia | 0.7 | 2 | 5 | 16 | 43 |
| Far East | 0.7 | 2 | 3 | 5 | 9 |
| Kazakhstan | 0.6 | 3 | 6 | 10 | 19 |
| Central Asia | 0.7 | 4 | 5 | 9 | 17 |
| Uzbekistan | 0.5 | 3 | 4 | 6 | 11.5 |
| Kirghizia | 0.05 | 0.2 | 0.5 | 0.9 | 2.3 |
| Turkmenia | 0.08 | 0.2 | 0.4 | 0.8 | 1.4 |
| Tadzhikistan | 0.06 | 0.2 | 0.3 | 1.3 | 1.6 |
| Total USSR | 48 | 91 | 170 | 292 | 507 |

Note: Some totals and subtotals do not add up because of rounding.

station, the construction of an associated aluminum plant lagged
behind the installation of generating capacity at the power station
so that much of the installed capacity was not fully used for some
years. The situation was alleviated only by the construction of a
500-kilovolt power transmission line from Bratsk westward to the

Krasnoyarsk industrial district, and ultimately by the inauguration of aluminum production at Bratsk itself. The big Siberian plants helped raise Siberia's share in the total power output to 18 percent in 1965, compared with 7 percent in 1940.

In European Russia, where the nation's manufacturing capacity is concentrated, only the construction of high-voltage transmission lines was needed to take advantage of the power generated by new systems of hydroelectric stations along the Volga River and the Dnieper River. The 2.3-million-kilowatt Kuybyshev station was linked by a 400-kilovolt line (later raised to 500 kilovolts) with Moscow and by a 500-kilovolt system with the Urals. A 500-kilovolt line also connected the 2.5-million-kilowatt Volgograd station with Moscow. These power transmission lines played a key role in forming an interconnected electric grid in European Russia in the late 1950s, linking the central regions with the Volga basin and the Urals. In connection with the prospective need for efficient power transmission systems from low-cost power sources in Siberia to consumers in European Russia, the Soviet Union has been experimenting with direct-current transmission, a system that is more economical than the conventional alternating-current transmission over distances of more than 750 miles. An experimental 800-kilovolt DC line has been in operation since 1962 between the Volga hydroelectric plant at Volgograd and the Mikhaylovka substation in the Donets Basin.

Atomic power does not play a significant role in the Soviet electric power industry although the Russians were the first to complete an experimental nuclear power station for public use. This was the pressurized, water-cooled, graphite-moderated 5,000-kilowatt station put in operation in 1954 at Obninsk, a reactor-testing center 70 miles southwest of Moscow. The first large Soviet power plant went into operation in 1958 somewhere in Siberia. The location of this installation, with a capacity of more than 600,000 kilowatts, is secret because it was built primarily for the production of plutonium for use in nuclear weapons.

The first major civilian nuclear power plant went into operation in 1964 at Beloyarskiy, east of Sverdlovsk, in the Urals. This station is of the boiling-water, graphite-moderated type, superheating steam in the reactor. The first unit of 100,000 kilowatts electrical capacity was supplemented in 1968 by a second unit of 200,000 kilowatts.

The second civilian power plant, opened later in 1964, is situated at Novovoronezhskiy, on the Don River south of Voronezh, in Central European Russia. It is of the pressurized water-cooled, water-moderated type. Its first unit, with an electrical capacity of 210,000 kilowatts, was supplemented in 1969 by a second unit of 375,000 kilowatts.

A 50,000-kilowatt power station of the boiling-water, water-moderated type is in operation at Melekess, in the middle Volga Valley, where a new reactor-development center has arisen.

In the late 1960s the Soviet Union announced that it would put pressurized-water reactors with an electrical capacity of 440,000 kilowatts, based on the principle of the Novovoronezhskiy station, into serial production for installation in several regional nuclear power plants. The standard regional station of this type will consist of two 440,000-kilowatt units for a combined capacity of 880,-000 kilowatts. Construction began on two such stations, one in the Kola Peninsula, south of Murmansk, the other in Armenia, near Yerevan. Both are in regions deficient in conventional fuels. Two standard 440,000-kilowatt units are also to be added to the Novovoronezhskiy station itself, bringing its total electrical capacity to 1.5 million kilowatts in the 1970s.

Two other nuclear power projects were under construction in the late 1960s. One was a 48,000-kilowatt boiling-water graphite-moderated reactor at Bilibino, major gold-mining center of northeast Siberia, in an area far from conventional power sources. The other was a sodium-cooled fast-breeder reactor with an electrical capacity of 350,000 kilowatts at Shevchenko, center of the Mangyshlak oil-producing district on the northeast desert shore of the Caspian Sea. The Shevchenko project will be a dual-purpose plant producing both commercial power and heat for a desalting installation that will supply fresh water to the arid oil district.

The Soviet Union has also been experimenting with tidal power. A small 800-kilowatt test installation was inaugurated late in 1968 at Kislaya Guba, an inlet of the Barents Sea on the Kola Peninsula. There are plans for larger commercial tidal power plants at the mouth of the Lumbovka River, on the northeast coast of the Kola Peninsula, and nearby at the mouth of the Mezen' River.

# 3

# METAL INDUSTRIES

## *Iron & Steel*

In the iron and steel industry, too, the 1950s marked a change in development policies. In this case the new orientation resulted from the approaching exhaustion of high-grade ore deposits, particularly in the more easily accessible upper horizons, and the need for the development of new iron ore sources for the expanding steel industry. This was achieved by reorienting a substantial part of the industry to the use of low-grade ores through concentration for blast-furnace smelting. In this development, paralleling the mining of low-grade magnetic taconite deposits in the Lake Superior district of the United States, the Soviet Union began exploiting low-grade ores mainly in open-pit mines, both in the Krivoy Rog basin, long the principal Soviet source of ores, and in new eastern deposits that supplied ore to a growing iron and steel industry in the Urals, Karaganda, and the Kuznetsk Basin (Table 9).

This latest emphasis on low-grade ores marks the newest phase in an industry that has been marked by substantial shifts in locational patterns since its inception. High-grade ore was produced in the seventeenth century in central European Russia and smelted in local charcoal reduction plants to satisfy the modest metal needs of the period. The eighteenth century marked the rise of metallurgy

*Table 9*

Regional Distribution of Soviet Iron Ore Production
(in million metric tons of usable ore)

| | 1940 | 1945 | 1950 | 1955 | 1958 | 1960 | 1965 |
|---|---|---|---|---|---|---|---|
| European USSR | 21.3 | 4.3 | 22.0 | 43.0 | 54.5 | 66.9 | 103.3 |
| European Russia | 1.1 | 0.5 | 0.9 | 2.2 | 3.4 | 6.6 | 18.1 |
| Kola Peninsula | — | — | — | 0.4 | 1.7 | 2.2 | 5.5 |
| Central Russia | 1.1 | 0.5 | 0.9 | 1.8 | 1.7 | 4.4 | 12.6 |
| Tula-Lipetsk | 1.1 | 0.5 | 0.9 | 1.5 | 1.4 | 1.7 | 0.6 |
| Kursk Magnetic Anomaly | — | — | — | 0.3 | 0.3 | 2.7 | 12.0 |
| Ukraine | 20.2 | 3.8 | 21.0 | 40.0 | 49.8 | 59.1 | 83.8 |
| Krivoy Rog | 18.9 | 3.8 | 21.0 | 37.4 | 46.8 | 54.8 | 79.2 |
| Crimea | 1.3 | — | — | 2.6 | 3.0 | 4.3 | 4.6 |
| Azerbaydzhan | — | — | — | 0.8 | 1.2 | 1.3 | 1.5 |
| Urals | 8.1 | 10.8 | 15.5 | 25.1 | 27.3 | 27.3 | 27.8 |
| Asian USSR | 0.5 | 0.8 | 2.2 | 3.8 | 7.0 | 11.7 | 22.3 |
| Siberia | 0.5 | 0.8 | 2.2 | 3.6 | 5.0 | 6.0 | 8.3 |
| Kuzbas area | 0.5 | 0.8 | 2.2 | 3.6 | 5.0 | 6.0 | 7.5 |
| Zheleznogorsk | — | — | — | — | — | — | 0.8 |
| Kazakhstan | — | — | — | 0.2 | 2.0 | 5.8 | 14.1 |
| Rudnyy | — | — | — | — | 1.1 | 4.5 | 11.4 |
| Karazhal | — | — | — | — | 0.8 | 1.2 | 2.6 |
| Total USSR | 29.9 | 15.9 | 39.7 | 71.9 | 88.8 | 105.9 | 153.4 |

Note: Some subtotals do not add up because of rounding.

in the Urals, where a combination of rich iron ore deposits and forest resources offered favorable conditions for development of the industry. In the mid-eighteenth century the Urals was the world's leading producer of iron, but soon lost this position as other nations, beginning with Britain, modernized their iron and steel industries by shifting from charcoal to coal furnaces. Russia was late to adopt the coke-smelting method, and by 1870 still produced virtually all its iron by charcoal. The era of railroad construction, which had also come relatively late to Russia, increased the demand for rails and other steel products beyond levels that could be met by the old charcoal-based industry of the Urals, and promoted a rapid shift from charcoal to coke smelting in larger, more productive blast furnaces. In the last two decades of the nineteenth century and the first decade of the twentieth, Russia's iron and steel industry shifted to a new resource base in southern European Russia, where the proximity of Krivoy Rog iron ore and Donets Basin coking coal furnished favorable conditions for the modern iron and steel industry. On the eve of World War I, the southern region accounted for 74 percent of the nation's total pig iron production of 4.2 million tons and the old charcoal furnaces of the Urals for 22 percent.

Under the Soviet regime, the Krivoy Rog basin has continued to supply most of the country's iron ore although its share in the national output has declined slightly as other ore sources have been developed. At the same time the ratio of crude to usable ore has increased as mining shifted increasingly after 1955 to low-grade ores requiring concentration. In 1940, the Krivoy Rog basin yielded 18.9 million tons, all of it direct-shipping ore, or 63 percent of the national total. In 1965, the output of the basin, about 80 million tons of usable ore, represented 52 percent of the entire Soviet ore output, but Krivoy Rog production now consisted of 60 percent direct-shipping ore and 40 percent concentrate derived from the low-grade ore. In addition to supplying ore to the entire Ukrainian iron and steel district, which accounts for 50 percent of Soviet pig iron production (Table 10), the Krivoy Rog also provides for exports to iron and steel centers in Poland, East Germany, Czechoslovakia, Hungary, and Rumania. These shipments amounted to 24 million tons in 1965.

The expansion of the iron and steel industry outside the dominant Ukrainian district began in the early 1930s with the operation of the so-called Urals–Kuzbas combine. This project involved the construction of two major iron and steel centers, one at Magnitogorsk, in the Urals, the other at Novokuznetsk (then called Stalinsk), in the Kuznetsk Basin. The two centers were to be supplied by iron ore from Magnitogorsk and by coking coal from the Kuznetsk Basin, with a 1,400-mile-long railroad shuttle carrying coking coal to the Urals and iron ore to the Kuznetsk Basin. The project, motivated largely by defense considerations and the desire to develop the eastern regions of the country, paid off despite the high transport costs involved when German armies overran the Ukrainian iron and steel industry in World War II and the war effort had to rely for

*Table 10*

Regional Distribution of Soviet Pig Iron Production
(in million metric tons)

|  | 1940 | 1945 | 1950 | 1955 | 1958 | 1960 | 1965 |
|---|---|---|---|---|---|---|---|
| European USSR | 10.6 | 2.1 | 10.1 | 19.0 | 23.7 | 28.1 | 40.9 |
| European Russia | 1.0 | 0.5 | 0.9 | 1.9 | 2.9 | 3.1 | 7.5 |
| Cherepovets | — | — | — | — | 1.1 | 1.3 | 3.1 |
| Tula–Lipetsk | 1.0 | 0.5 | 0.9 | 1.9 | 1.8 | 1.8 | 4.4 |
| Ukraine | 9.6 | 1.6 | 9.2 | 16.6 | 20.1 | 24.2 | 32.6 |
| Donets Basin | 5.2 |  | 5.7 |  | 10.7 | 13.1 | 15 |
| Dnieper area | 3.9 |  | 3.5 |  | 9.4 | 11.1 | 17 |
| Kerch' | 0.5 | — | — | — | — | — | — |
| Georgia (Rustavi) | — | — | — | 0.4 | 0.7 | 0.7 | 0.8 |
| Urals | 2.7 | 5.1 | 7.2 | 11.9 | 13.1 | 15.1 | 18.9 |
| Asian USSR | 1.5 | 1.6 | 1.9 | 2.4 | 2.8 | 3.6 | 6.4 |
| Siberia (Kuznetsk) | 1.5 | 1.6 | 1.9 | 2.4 | 2.8 | 3.3 | 4.8 |
| Karaganda | — | — | — | — | — | 0.3 | 1.6 |
| Total USSR | 14.9 | 8.8 | 19.2 | 33.3 | 39.6 | 46.8 | 66.2 |

a time entirely on the iron and steel production of the eastern regions. In 1940, the Urals accounted for 2.7 million tons of pig iron, or 18 percent of the national total, and the Kuznetsk plant for 1.5 million tons, or 10 percent of the total. From the late 1930s, when a crisis in transportation spurred a policy of developing local resources to achieve regional self-sufficiency, to the early 1950s, the ore and coal ties between the Urals and the Kuznetsk Basin were gradually loosened as Urals coking coal needs were met in part by the nearer Karaganda coal basin and the Kuznetsk plant relied increasingly on local iron ore resources (Fig. 5).

In the 1950s, when high-grade ores in the Urals seemed inadequate in the long run to support an expanding iron and steel industry in the region, steps were taken to develop two major low-grade ore sites. One, the Sokolovka-Sarbay deposit at the new iron-mining city of Rudnyy, in northwest Kazakhstan, was developed in the late 1950s as a source of ore for three major Urals plants: Magnitogorsk, the Soviet Union's largest; Chelyabinsk, dating from World War II; and Novotroitsk, opened in 1955. By 1965, Rudnyy was shipping 11 million tons of usable ore to these three plants. The other new source of ore for the Urals was a vanadium-bearing titaniferous magnetite deposit at Kachkanar, which yields a high-vanadium pig iron at an iron and steel plant that opened in 1940 at Nizhniy Tagil. The Kachkanar mining complex began operations in 1963. In 1965, the Urals iron and steel industry consumed about 39 million tons of usable ore to produce about 19 million tons of pig iron, or 28 percent of the Soviet Union's total pig iron output. Of the total Urals ore consumption, 28 million tons of usable ore came from the old ore mines of the Urals proper (including the newly opened Kachkanar site, which was then producing little more than 1 million tons), and 11 million tons originated in the nearby Rudnyy complex of Kazakhstan. The share of both the Kachkanar ore and the Rudnyy ore in total Urals consumption increased during the late 1960s.

Outside of the Ukrainian and Urals iron and steel districts, five less important areas have developed since the 1950s. In the Kuznetsk Basin, the old iron and steel plant of the 1930s has been supplemented since 1964 by a second major installation, the so-called West Siberian plant, also situated at Novokuznetsk. In addition to ore mines in the vicinity of the two plants, in the Gornaya Shoriya area' south of the Kuznetsk Basin, and in the Khakass Autonomous Oblast to the east, a more distant source of ore has been developed at the Korshunovo deposit at the new mining town of Zheleznogorsk, east of Bratsk in Irkutsk Oblast. In 1965, the iron and steel industry of the Kuznetsk Basin was consuming 8.3 million tons of usable ore to produce 4.8 million tons of pig iron. A second iron and steel center has been in operation since 1960 in the Karaganda area, based on local coking coal and on ore from the nearby Karazhal mines. These produced about 2.6 million tons of usable ore in 1965, yielding 1.6 million tons of pig iron.

The three lesser iron and steel complexes in European Russia are at Cherepovets, in the north; at Tula and Lipetsk, in the central area, and at Rustavi, in the Transcaucasian republic of Georgia. The Cherepovets plant, which opened in 1955, is based on distant sources of iron ore in the Kola Peninsula and of coking coal in the Pechora basin at Vorkuta. In 1965 the Cherepovets blast furnaces consumed about 5 million tons of iron ore concentrate to produce 3.1 million tons of pig iron. The two plants of central European Russia use direct-shipping ore and concentrate from Zheleznogorsk

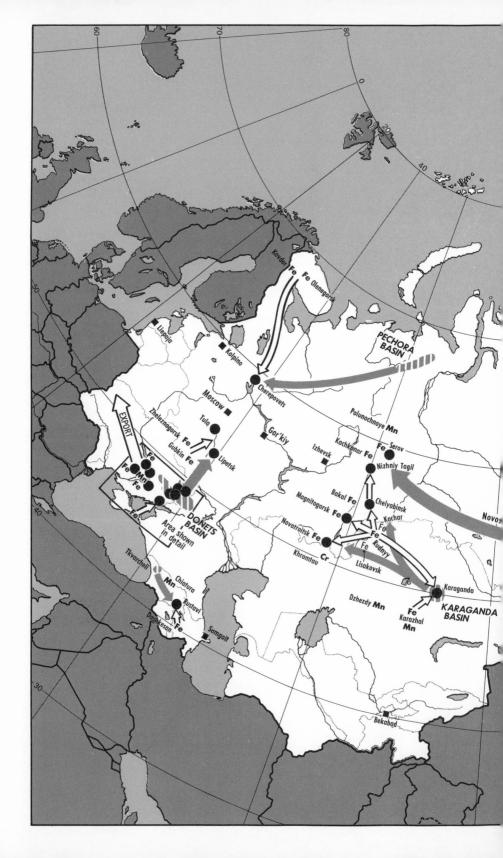

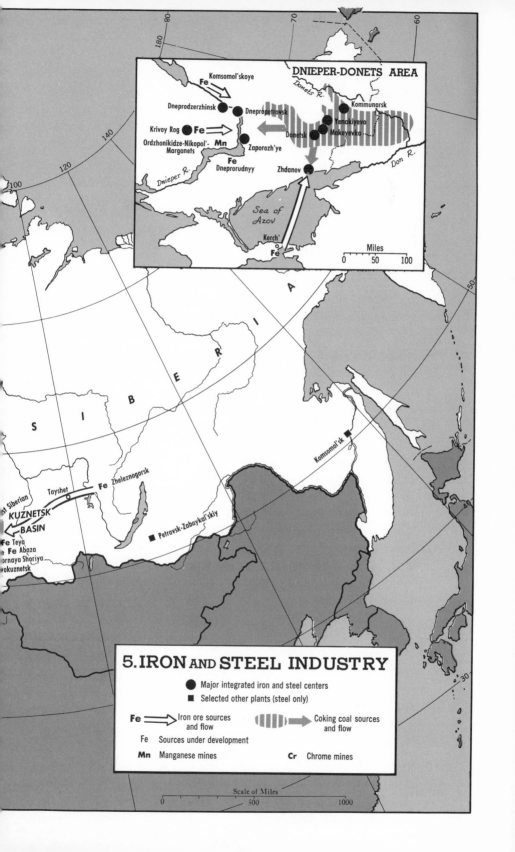

# DNIEPER-DONETS AREA

Komsomol'skoye

Fe

Donets R.

Dneprodzerzhinsk
Dnepropetrovsk

Kommunarsk

Yenakiyeva
Makeyevka

Krivoy Rog  Fe

Donetsk

Ordzhonikidze-Nikopol'-
Marganets

Mn

Zaporozh'ye

Don R.

Fe
Dneprodzerzhinsk

Dnieper R.

Fe
Dneprorudnyy

Zhdanov

Sea of
Azov

Miles

0    50    100

Kerch'
Fe

S        I        B        E        R        I        A

50

100

120

140

180

80

70

60

100

120

Komsomol'sk

West Siberian
Tayshet
Fe Zheleznogorsk

KUZNETSK
BASIN

Fe Teya
Fe Abaza
ornaya Shoriya
okuznetsk

Petrovsk-Zabaykal'skiy

30

# 5. IRON AND STEEL INDUSTRY

● Major integrated iron and steel centers

■ Selected other plants (steel only)

Fe ⟹ Iron ore sources
and flow

⬛⬛⬛⟹ Coking coal sources
and flow

Fe    Sources under development

Mn   Manganese mines          Cr   Chrome mines

Scale of Miles

0              500              1000

and Gubkin, two mining centers of the so-called Kursk Magnetic Anomaly, a vast iron-bearing zone whose development has been hampered by difficult geological conditions, particularly water-logged strata. In operation since 1959–60, the mines of Zhelezno-gorsk and Gubkin supplied about 12 million tons of usable ore to plants at Tula and Lipetsk, yielding about 4.4 million tons of pig iron. Finally, in the Transcaucasian complex, the Rustavi iron and steel plant, which began to smelt pig iron in 1954, uses 1.5 million tons of ore from the Dashkesan deposit of adjoining Azerbaydzhan to produce about 800,000 tons of pig iron.

The production of ingot steel, which uses scrap metal in addition to pig iron, is less closely tied to ore and coal resources than pig iron production and is therefore somewhat more decentralized. The Ukrainian district is the leading producer of ingot steel, with 37 million tons in 1965, followed by 30 million tons for the Urals, about 6 million tons for the Kuznetsk Basin, and a number of scattered lesser centers, including 13.5 million tons in steel plants of European Russia (Table 11). Total production of ingot steel in 1965 was 91 million tons, and it was increasing at a rate of 5 to 6 million tons a year in the late 1960s.

Technological progress has played an important role in the expansion of iron and steel production. As noted earlier, the ap-proaching exhaustion of high-grade ores, both in the Krivoy Rog basin and at Magnitogorsk, forced a major shift to the use of low-grade iron deposits and the beneficiation of this ore to usable con-centrate. In 1940, 90 percent of the total Soviet production of iron ore was direct-shipping ore and 10 percent was concentrate. In 1965, 47 percent was direct-shipping ore and 53 percent was con-centrate. Almost all the high-grade ore, or 72 million tons, stemmed from underground operations, while the low-grade ore was mined in open pits. In 1965 the total production of low-grade ore from open-pit mines was 171 million tons, which was converted into 81 million tons of usable concentrate.

Since the mid-1950s an increasing share of iron ore, particularly fine-grained ore and dust, has been agglomerated into self-fluxing sinter for more efficient blast-furnace operation. In the process, the ore is burned on open, moving belts to form a hard, lumpy agglom-erate or sinter. If crushed limestone (flux) is added during the

*Table 11*

Regional Distribution of Soviet Production of Ingot Steel
(in million metric tons)

| | 1940 | 1945 | 1950 | 1955 | 1958 | 1960 | 1965 |
|---|---|---|---|---|---|---|---|
| European USSR | 12.4 | 3.2 | 13.0 | 24.0 | 30.2 | 37.3 | 53.1 |
| European Russia | 3.4 | 1.7 | 4.4 | 5.9 | 7.0 | 9.2 | 13.6 |
| North | 0.6 | 0.2 | 0.6 | 0.9 | | | |
| Central | 1.5 | 1.1 | 1.9 | 2.6 | | | |
| Volga (Volgograd) | 0.9 | 0.3 | 1.2 | 1.5 | | | |
| North Caucasus | 0.5 | 0.2 | 0.7 | 0.9 | | | |
| Ukraine | 8.9 | 1.4 | 8.4 | 16.9 | 21.7 | 26.2 | 37.0 |
| Latvia (Liepaja) | — | — | — | 0.08 | 0.1 | 0.1 | 0.1 |
| Azerbaydzhan (Sumgait) | — | — | 0.04 | 0.4 | 0.4 | 0.6 | 0.8 |
| Georgia (Rustavi) | — | — | 0.1 | 0.6 | 1.0 | 1.1 | 1.4 |
| Urals | 4.0 | 6.5 | 10.7 | 16.4 | 19.0 | 21.9 | 29.8 |
| Asian USSR | 1.9 | 2.6 | 3.6 | 4.9 | 5.6 | 6.1 | 8.1 |
| Siberia | 1.9 | 2.6 | 3.4 | 4.5 | 5.0 | 5.5 | 6.7 |
| Uzbekistan (Bekabad) | — | — | 0.1 | 0.2 | 0.3 | 0.3 | 0.4 |
| Kazakhstan (Karaganda) | — | — | 0.1 | 0.2 | 0.3 | 0.3 | 1.1 |
| Total USSR | 18.3 | 12.3 | 27.3 | 45.3 | 54.9 | 65.3 | 91.0 |

sintering process, there is no need for limestone during the blast furnace operation, and the sinter becomes "self-fluxing." The proportion of self-fluxing sinter in the total usable ore production rose from about 35 percent in 1955 to about 70 percent in 1965. Following United States practice, the Russians have also begun the agglomeration of the self-fluxing sinter in the form of marblelike pellets for more efficient blast-furnace operation. The first Soviet pelletizing machines went into operation at the Rudnyy mining complex in 1965.

In pig iron production, the trend has been toward increasingly larger blast furnaces since the late 1950s. Throughout the postwar period, from 1945 to 1957, the maximum working volume of Soviet blast furnaces was 47,000 to 49,000 cubic feet. Then began a rapid increase as ever larger blast furnaces were erected. By 1960 the Soviet Union was installing furnaces with working volumes of 70,000 cubic feet and by 1967 the first 95,000-cubic-feet furnace, with an annual capacity of 1.7 million tons of pig iron, was inaugurated at Krivoy Rog. Others were placed into operation in 1969 at the Nizhniy Tagil and Cherepovets steel mills. The Soviet Union was reported to have fifteen of the world's twenty-seven blast furnaces with working volumes of 70,000 cubic feet or more. Most of the pig iron is being produced in modern furnaces that use natural gas as an additional fuel to save coke and use a higher oxygen content in the air blast to speed the smelting process.

Most ingot steel is still being produced in the traditional open-hearth furnaces (88 percent of all steel in 1965), but new construction of steelmaking capacity is entirely in the form of more efficient oxygen converters. Under the current five-year plan (1966–70), the share of oxygen-converter steel is to rise from 4 percent in 1965 to 20 percent in 1970. Another innovation being promoted is the continuous casting process, which has been found to reduce steel-mill operating costs by eliminating the need for the traditional ingot molds, soaking pits, and primary blooming mills by providing a short cut from the steel furnace to the rolling mill. Many of these innovations in pig iron and steel production were being installed in ten large Soviet mills that were receiving priority for expansion during the late 1960s. They are the Krivoy Rog mill and the two mills (Azovstal' and Il'yich) in Zhdanov, in the Ukraine; the new Lipetsk mill, in central European Russia; the Cherepovets mill, in northern European Russia; three Urals mills, at Magnitogorsk, Nizhniy Tagil, and Chelyabinsk; the West Siberian plant, in Novokuznetsk; and the Karaganda mill.

## Ferroalloys

A number of metals are used as alloying elements in the iron and steel industry to add special properties such as high strength or resistance to high temperature in an ever widening field of applications in the nuclear and space age (Fig. 6).

*Manganese.* The Soviet Union has long been the world's leading producer of manganese, an essential element in any iron and steel industry, used to counteract the harmful effects of sulfur in the production of steel and to impart toughness and hardness to certain steels. Virtually all the Soviet steel originates in two areas: the Chiatura area of Georgia, in Transcaucasia, and the Nikopol' area of the Ukraine. The Chiatura area has the higher-grade manganese ore and led in Soviet production before World War II, when it produced 1.45 million tons of usable ore compared with 0.9 million in the Nikopol' area. In the 1950s, Nikopol' undertook a major expansion program, involving the development of lower-grade surface deposits and the construction of beneficiation plants. Since the early 1960s, production at Nikopol' exceeds the Georgian output. Out of a 1965 Soviet manganese production of 7.6 million tons of usable ore and concentrate, Nikopol' contributed 4.7 million tons and Chiatura 2.9 million tons (Table 12). The increasing use of lower-grade ores is evident from the ratio of crude to usable ore. In 1950, 4.7 million tons of crude manganese ore yielded 3.4 million tons of concentrate. In 1965, 16.3 million tons of crude ore were mined to produce 7.6 million tons of concentrate.

*Table 12*

Regional Distribution of Soviet Production of Manganese
   (in million metric tons)

|  | 1940 | 1945 | 1950 | 1955 | 1958 | 1960 | 1965 |
|---|---|---|---|---|---|---|---|
| Ukraine (Nikopol') | 0.90 | 0.33 | 0.90 | 1.62 | 2.09 | 2.73 | 4.65 |
| Georgia (Chiatura) | 1.45 | 0.85 | 1.84 | 2.9 | 3.1 | 3.05 | 2.87 |
| Others | 0.2 | 0.3 | 0.6 | 0.2 | 0.2 | 0.1 | 0.06 |
| Total USSR | 2.56 | 1.47 | 3.38 | 4.74 | 5.37 | 5.87 | 7.58 |
| Total exports | 0.26 | 0.28* | 0.28 | 0.85 | 0.83 | 0.97 | 1.02 |

* 1946 data.

Small manganese deposits in the eastern regions of the USSR, including Polunochnoye in the northern Urals and Dzhezdy in Kazakhstan, are now of negligible importance, although they played a key role in supplying the eastern iron and steel industry in World War II when the Ukrainian manganese mines were put out of action by German occupation.

The Soviet Union exports about 1 million tons of manganese ore a year, mainly to the steel mills of Poland, East Germany, Czechoslovakia, Britain, and France. Because of Chiatura's favorable location with respect to the Black Sea port of Poti and its greater distance from the main iron and steel districts, the country exports about 20 percent of Chiatura's output compared with 10 percent of

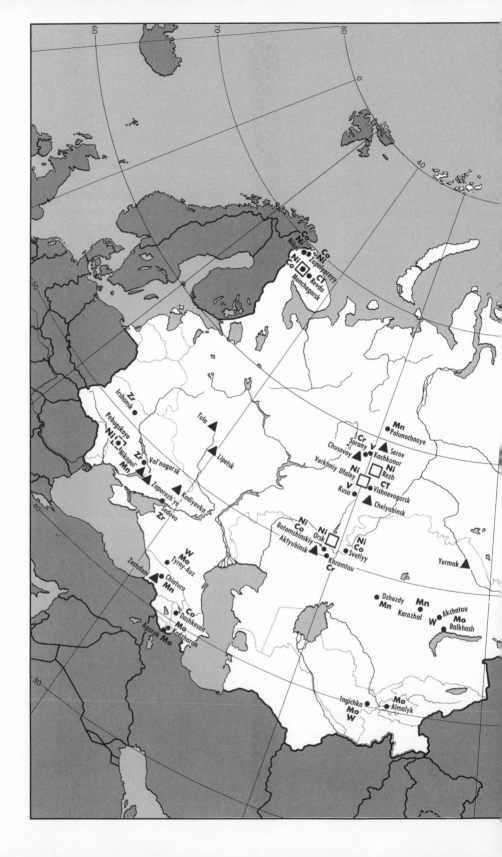

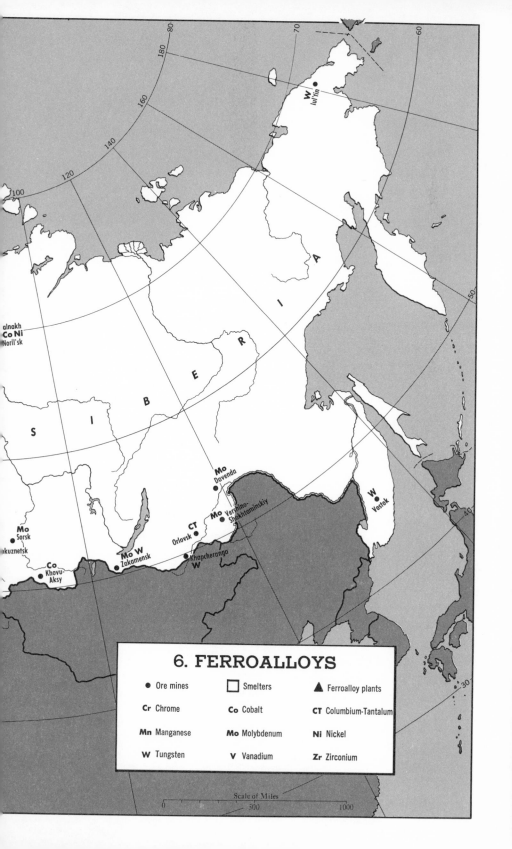

alnakh
**Co Ni**
Noril'sk

**W**
Iul'tin

**Mo**
Davenda

**Mo**
Sorsk

kuznetsk

**Mo W**
Zakamensk

**Co**
Khovu-
Aksy

Orlovsk

**CT**

**Mo** Vershino-
Shakhtaminskiy

**W**
Khapcheranga

**W**
Vostok

S  I  B  E  R  I  A

### 6. FERROALLOYS

● Ore mines        ▢ Smelters        ▲ Ferroalloy plants

**Cr** Chrome          **Co** Cobalt          **CT** Columbium-Tantalum

**Mn** Manganese       **Mo** Molybdenum      **Ni** Nickel

**W** Tungsten         **V** Vanadium         **Zr** Zirconium

Scale of Miles

0               500              1000

Nikopol's, which is mined in the immediate vicinity of the Ukrainian iron and steel industry.

*Chromium.* Like manganese, chromium resources are highly concentrated, with the two principal producing areas found in the Urals. The Soviet Union was long dependent on Sarany, the older of these two producers, whose low-grade chromite ores were suitable mainly for refractory and chemical uses. It was only after the discovery of high-grade chromite in the Khromtau (chrome mountain) deposit, at the southern end of the Urals in northwest Kazakhstan, that the Soviet Union disposed of metallurgical chromite, required in the manufacture of stainless and other alloy steels. This use accounts for 60 percent of the total chromite consumption, the rest going into refractories and chemicals. Much of the chromite of the Khromtau mine, in operation since World War II, is converted into ferrochromium and other ferroalloys at nearby Aktyubinsk for use in the steel industry. The USSR is the world's leading producer of chromite and the only major industrial nation that does not depend on imports of this ore. In the mid-1960s, output was believed to be about 1.4 million tons, or one-third of world production, with about one-half of the ore going for export. The principal customers for Soviet chromite were Western steel producers, such as the United States, Japan, West Germany, France, and Sweden.

*Nickel.* This important metal, used as an alloying element, both in steels and in nonferrous metallurgy, is produced in two widely separated general areas with different geological conditions. The nickel industry had its beginnings in the Urals, where reserves are in the form of soft, claylike serpentine surface deposits that are excavated in open-pit operations. The first smelter opened in 1933 at Verkhniy Ufaley, followed by another one at Rezh. These early deposits had small reserves that were soon exhausted and, in the late 1930s, the center of the Urals nickel industry moved southward to Orsk, where a smelter went into operation in 1939, processing first local nickel ores and, during World War II, increasingly the ore of a larger deposit at Batamshinskiy to the south in adjoining Kazakhstan. The latest Urals nickel development is the Svetlyy mine and smelter, about 100 miles east of Orsk, which went into operation in the mid-1960s. Cobalt and copper are co-products of these nickel deposits.

The second general nickel-producing region is the sub-Arctic of European Russia and Siberia, where nickel–copper sulfides similar to the Canadian deposits are associated with magmatic intrusions. Nickel mining and smelting began at Monchegorsk in the Kola Peninsula in 1938, but when World War II broke out the smelter was dismantled and transferred to Norilsk, in northern Siberia, where a similar deposit was under development. Norilsk, further expanded as a result of the development of the nearby Talnakh deposit in the mid-1960s, became one of the Soviet Union's principal nickel-producing centers. In the Kola Peninsula, the Monchegorsk complex, restored after the war, was supplemented by the former Petsamo (Pechenga) mines acquired from Finland and the newly developed deposit opened in the 1960s at Zapolyarnyy nearby. Unlike the Urals ores, which are smelted mostly with coke in shaft furnaces, the Arctic ore is refined electrolytically, yielding so-called cathode nickel and by-products. In addition to copper and cobalt, the Arctic ores also contain selenium and tellurium, two rare metals with increasing applications in electronics, and metals of the platinum group (platinum, palladium, iridium, osmium). In view of the virtual exhaustion of the old Urals platinum placers, the Arctic nickel deposits are now the Soviet Union's principal source of platinum-group metals. Total nickel output is believed to be about 80,000 to 90,000 tons, less than half of Canada's production, with two-thirds or more coming from the Arctic.

*Cobalt.* Virtually all the cobalt of the Soviet Union is associated with nickel production, both in the Arctic and in the southern Urals, with a ratio of about 1 ton of cobalt for every 70 tons of nickel. A small deposit at Dashkesan in Azerbaydzhan, in operation since before the Soviet regime, yields cobalt alone. A more important source of cobalt outside the nickel-producing areas is a rich cobalt–arsenic deposit in the process of being opened up in the late 1960s at Khovu-Aksy, in the Tuva Autonomous Republic, on the southern margins of Siberia.

*Molybdenum.* This important steel alloy is found in the Soviet Union mainly in association with copper ores or with tungsten ores. Before World War II, the molybdenum–tungsten mine at Tyrnyauz, on the northern slopes of the Caucasus, which first yielded molybdenum concentrate in 1938, accounted for 75 percent of the nation's molybdenum production. During World War II, when the Caucasus producer was lost to German occupation, molybdenum was produced mainly as a by-product of copper mining at Balkhash in Kazakhstan. The copper–molybdenum association became increasingly important after the war with the development of mines in Armenia (Kadzharan, Dastakert, and Agarak) and in Uzbekistan (at Almalyk).

A number of smaller deposits in Eastern Siberia yield molybdenum as the principal mineral component. The most important of these mining centers is the Sorsk complex in Khakass Autonomous Oblast, which began production in the early 1950s. Others are at Vershino-Shakhtaminskiy and Davenda, in Chita Oblast. A valuable product of molybdenum derived from the copper association is the rare metal rhenium, used increasingly in molybdenum and tungsten alloys. Soviet molybdenum production is estimated at 5,000 to 6,000 metric tons, or about one-sixth of the output of the United States, the world's leading producer, with its unique deposit at Climax, Colorado.

*Tungsten.* Like molybdenum, tungsten is used in the manufacture of high-speed tool steels and other alloys to impart hardness at high temperatures. Soviet tungsten output is associated mainly with tin or with molybdenum production. In the 1930s, the Russians derived tungsten mainly from the early tin-producing districts of Chita Oblast (Sherlovaya Gora and Khapcheranga), which have since been overshadowed by larger, if more remote, tin–tungsten deposits of the Soviet Far East, particularly at Iul'tin, in the Chukchi Peninsula, in operation since 1959. In addition to the major Tyrnyauz mine in the Caucasus, tungsten is associated with molybdenum in several Central Asian deposits, including Chorukh-Dayron (Tadzhik SSR) and Koytash, Lyangar, and Ingichka (Uzbekistan). The Soviet Union was long a net importer of tungsten, obtaining 60 percent $WO_3$ concentrate from China (6,000 metric tons in 1964 and in 1965) and exporting 3,000 to 4,000 tons to Western Europe. But in the late 1960s both imports and exports ceased. World production was about 40,000 tons, of which China was believed to produce almost half.

*Vanadium.* The principal sources of vanadium are deposits of vanadium-bearing titaniferous magnetites in the Urals. The relatively small deposits of Kusa, west of Chelyabinsk, and Pervoural'sk, west of Sverdlovsk, have been used since 1936 to produce ferro-vanadium at Chusovoy. Since the opening of the great titaniferous magnetite deposit at Kachkanar in 1963, the supply of vanadium-bearing material has been substantially increased. Kachkanar concentrate smelted at the Nizhniy Tagil iron and steel plant yields vanadium pig iron, which, when processed in oxygen converters, produces steel and a 15 percent vanadium slag. The slag is reduced in electric furnaces at Chusovoy to form ferrovanadium.

*Columbium (niobium) and tantalum.* These two alloying materials have gained in significance since the 1950s in heat- and corrosion-resistant applications in nuclear and space industries. The principal source of these two allied minerals in the Soviet Union is the Lovozero area of the Kola Peninsula, with a mining center at Revda. Columbium and tantalum are also mined on the eastern slopes of the Ural Mountains, mainly in Chelyabinsk Oblast, where the mining centers are believed to be Vishnevogorsk, near Kasli, dating from World War II, and Yuzhnyy, east of Magnitogorsk. The Ilmen Mountains in the Miass area are also associated with columbium–tantalum mineralization. In the 1960s Chita Oblast in Siberia became a major producing area.

*Zirconium.* This alloy and its co-product, hafnium, both in demand since the early 1960s for use in nuclear reactors, are re-covered commercially from heavy-mineral river gravels mined for titanium minerals. The principal heavy-mineral dredging operations have been under way since the 1950s in the Ukraine, in the Irsha River valley west of Kiev, and in the Samotkan' River valley at Vol'nogorsk, west of Dneprodzerzhinsk. In addition to these stream deposits, a beach deposit on the Sea of Azov is also believed to yield heavy minerals near Zhdanov, at Sedovo, since World War II.

## Base Metals

*Copper.* The Soviet Union is the world's second largest copper producer, with an estimated smelter production of about 700,000 to 800,000 metric tons, behind the United States and ahead of Zambia and Chile. Copper production dates back to the times of Peter the Great and continued to be concentrated in the Urals until the Soviet period, when developments in Kazakhstan and, more recently, in Uzbekistan came to the forefront. In the late 1960s these two Central Asian republics accounted for more than half of the Soviet Union's total copper smelter output.

In the Urals, pre-Soviet mining and smelting centers at Kirovgrad, Karabash, and Baymak and an electrolytic refinery at Kyshtym were supplemented during the 1930s by new mining and smelting centers at Krasnoural'sk, Revda, and Mednogorsk and by a second electrolytic refinery at Verkhnyaya Pyshma. As old copper deposits in the Urals were depleted, additional mines were opened up after World War II at Sibay and Uchaly (Bashkir ASSR) and Gay (Orenburg Oblast) (Fig. 7).

Production in Kazakhstan, begun on a small scale before the Soviet period, boomed after the start of operations in 1938 of the Balkhash smelter, which processed ore from the local Kounrad deposit and was expanding its raw-material base in the late 1960s to the Sayak copper deposit farther east. Dzhezkazgan, another major copper deposit of Kazakhstan, long shipped its ores and, after 1954, its concentrate to smelters in the Urals and at Balkhash. A long-delayed smelter at Dzhezkazgan was under construction in the late 1960s. An old smelter at Karsakpay, near Dzhezkazgan, has been dwarfed by subsequent developments. In a third copper-producing zone, in East Kazakhstan, copper is associated with zinc. There, too, an old copper smelter at Glubokoye is to be supplemented in the early 1970s by a new large smelter and refinery that will be processing copper–zinc ores from the Nikolayevka and Orlovka deposits, in process of development.

The newest development is the copper complex of Almalyk in Uzbekistan, in operation since the early 1960s. Armenia's copper mines at Kafan and Alaverdi, dating from before the Soviet period, have been supplemented by new developments at Kadzharan, Dastakert, and Agarak, significant mainly because of their association with molybdenum.

As noted earlier, copper is also a co-product of nickel in the Arctic mining centers of Norilsk and the Kola Peninsula. Significant future copper production is expected from the Urup deposits of the Northern Caucasus, under development in the late 1960s, and from the Udokan deposit in northern Chita Oblast of Eastern Siberia.

Until the development of the Almalyk copper complex, the Soviet Union was a net importer of copper metal and semimanufactures in the late 1950s and early 1960s, importing 80,000 to 100,000 tons, mainly from Zambia, Britain, West Germany, and exporting 60,000 to 70,000 tons to Eastern Europe. Imports virtually ceased in 1964, the year in which an electrolytic refinery went into operation in Almalyk. Exports rose to 120,000 tons in 1966.

*Lead and Zinc.* These two metals are usually found together in complex ore deposits, but the distribution of smelters and refineries differs. By far the greatest concentration of lead–zinc ores is in two areas of Kazakhstan, in East Kazakhstan and Chimkent oblasts, followed by the Altyn-Topkan mining complex at Almalyk, in Uzbekistan. There are scattered small mines elsewhere in Central Asia as well as at Tetyukhe, in the Soviet Far East, in the North Ossetian Republic of the North Caucasus, and at Salair, in the Kuznetsk Basin.

Although most mines have their own concentrators to process both zinc and lead, the concentrates then travel separately to their respective smelters or refineries. Lead concentrates from southern Kazakhstan and the smaller deposits of Central Asia are smelted at the Chimkent lead plant, opened in 1934. East Kazakhstan has an older installation at Leninogorsk, dating from 1926, and a new plant at Ust'-Kamenogorsk, opened in 1952. Other lead smelters, with substantially smaller capacity, operate at Ordzhonikidze, for the nearby North Ossetian mines, and at Tetyukhe in the Far East. With a smelter production of about 350,000 metric tons, the USSR rivals the United States for first position in the output of lead. For many years the Soviet Union has also been a net lead exporter. In 1967 it imported 30,000 tons, from North Korea, Bulgaria, and Yugoslavia, and exported 90,000 tons, mostly to East Germany and Czechoslovakia.

In contrast to lead smelters, zinc refineries are widely scattered throughout the Soviet Union because their large energy requirements make location near coal sources or low-cost electric power an economical necessity. Although Kazakhstan accounted for more than 40 percent of all zinc-concentrate production even before World War II, the absence of an electric power base in the republic required that the concentrate be shipped thousands of miles to

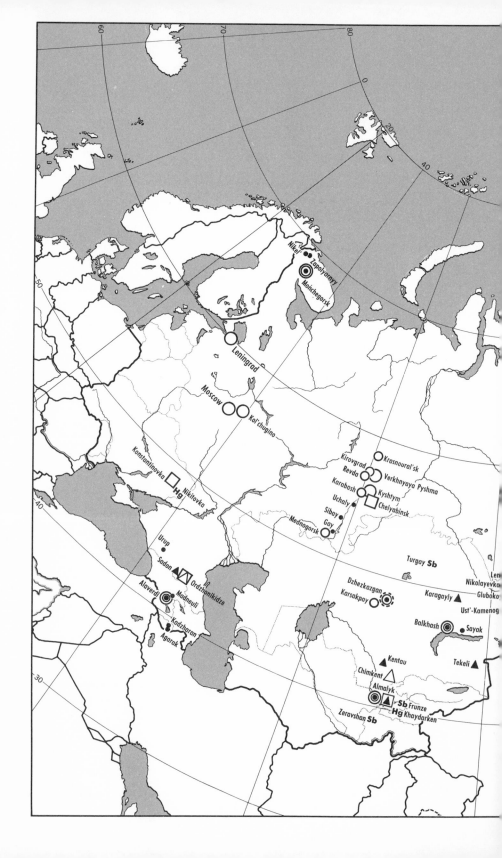

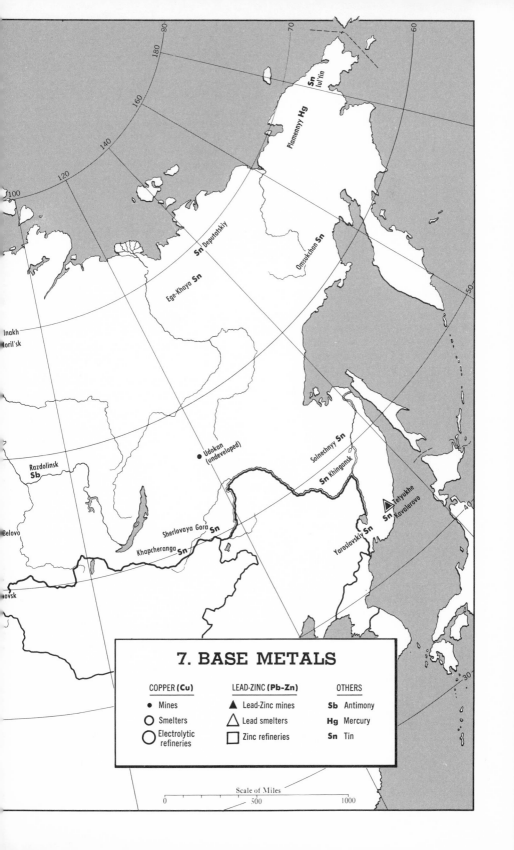

Sn Iul'tin

Plamennyy Hg

Sn Deputatskiy

Omsukchan Sn

Ege-Khaya Sn

Inakh

Noril'sk

Razdolinsk
Sb

Udokan
(undeveloped)

Solnechnyy Sn

Sn Khingansk

Tetyukhe
Sn Kavalerovo

Belovo

Sherlovaya Gora Sn

Khapcheranga Sn

Yaroslavskiy Sn

novsk

# 7. BASE METALS

### COPPER (Cu)

● Mines

○ Smelters

◯ Electrolytic refineries

### LEAD-ZINC (Pb-Zn)

▲ Lead-Zinc mines

△ Lead smelters

□ Zinc refineries

### OTHERS

Sb Antimony

Hg Mercury

Sn Tin

Scale of Miles

0      500      1000

refineries elsewhere in the country. The early refineries were distillation retort plants using coal or coke as a reducing agent and were therefore located in coal basins. Both the Konstantinovka plant, in the Donets Basin, and the Belovo plant, in the Kuznetsk Basin, began operations in 1930. Subsequent refineries used the electrolytic method. The first, at Ordzhonikidze in the Northern Caucasus, opened in 1934, followed the next year by a refinery at Chelyabinsk in the Urals. It was only after the construction of low-cost hydroelectric plants in East Kazakhstan that this center of lead–zinc mining also acquired its own zinc refineries. One at Ust'-Kamenogorsk opened in 1947, and a second at Leninogorsk in 1966. In the meantime the old distillation plant at Konstantinovka, destroyed in World War II, was converted in 1951 to the electrolytic method. In view of the growing importance of zinc production in Uzbekistan's Almalyk complex, an electrolytic refinery was under construction there in the late 1960s. Its completion will eliminate the need for shipping concentrates to Konstantinovka in the Ukraine.

On a world level, the zinc industry, with a smelter output of about 500,000 metric tons, is second after the United States, with more than 800,000 tons. The USSR is also a net exporter, shipping about 80,000 tons a year, mainly to East Germany and Czechoslovakia, and importing about 30,000 tons from Poland and North Korea.

*Tin.* The tin-mining industry of the Soviet Union is one of the extractive industries that has developed under the most adverse natural conditions in the sub-Arctic part of Siberia. Virtually nonexistent in prerevolutionary Russia, tin mining first developed in the early 1930s in Chita Oblast (Sherlovaya Gora and Khapcheranga) in small deposits that became soon exhausted. Larger deposits were developed in the 1940s in Yakutia, at Ege-Khaya, and in the Primorskiy Kray, in the Kavalerovo district near Tetyukhe, where production expanded further in the 1950s. Additional tin production began in 1958 near Ussuriysk and in 1963 in the area of Komsomol'sk. The Kolyma gold-mining district of northeast Siberia was a significant producer of tin during the period of forced labor, which ended in the mid-1950s. Thereafter the Kolyma tin mines, except one at Omsukchan, were found uneconomical and were closed. However, this northeastern corner of Siberia, with its eight-month sub-Arctic winter, continued to play a key role in tin production with the opening of the Iul'tin mining complex in 1959. Equally harsh conditions prevail at Deputatskiy, a tin center of northern Yakutia, where production began from tin placers in 1953 and was planned to expand through lode mining in the late 1960s.

The first tin smelter, opened in 1934, was situated at Podol'sk, south of Moscow. Since the 1940s most of the Siberian tin concentrate is smelted at a new plant in Novosibirsk. Tin production is estimated at 20,000 metric tons, and the country is a net importer. During the late 1950s and early 1960s, the Soviet Union imported as much as 20,000 tons of tin from China, an estimated three-quarters of total Chinese output, and reexported most of it. As the Soviet–Chinese rift deepened, Chinese tin shipments to the Soviet Union—and Soviet exports—ceased. Later the USSR imported some tin from Indonesia and Malaysia.

*Mercury and Antimony.* Among the lesser base metals, the Soviet Union has a significant production of mercury and antimony, both concentrated in the Kirghiz Republic of Central Asia. Before World War II, all of the Soviet Union's mercury supply came from a mercury mine at Nikitovka in the Ukraine's Donets Basin, which also yielded antimony as a by-product. During World War II, when the Donets Basin was occupied by the Germans, the Soviet Union developed a major mercury deposit at Khaydarken, in Kirghizia, not far from Kadamdzhay (later renamed Frunze), where antimony production had started a few years earlier. These two centers have remained the principal producers. Mercury is also mined at Aktash, in the Altay Mountain section of Western Siberia, and a new deposit was being developed in the late 1960s at Plamennyy, in the Chukchi Peninsula of northeastern Siberia. Lesser antimony deposits have been mined since the 1930s at Razdolinsk, in Krasnoyarsk Kray, and at Turgay, in northern Kazakhstan. Total Soviet output of mercury is believed to be about 1,200 metric tons (35,000 flasks), making it the third or fourth world producer after Italy, Spain, and perhaps China. In the late 1950s and early 1960s, the USSR imported almost the entire Chinese output (as much as 1,500 tons in 1960) and reexported as much as 600 tons. This trade virtually ceased in the mid-1960s.

*Cadmium.* As a leading zinc producer, the Soviet Union also has an important output of cadmium, which is almost entirely a by-product of zinc-bearing ores at zinc smelters, mainly in eastern Kazakhstan. Of an estimated production of 2,000 metric tons of cadmium, the Soviet Union exported about one-half (to Eastern Europe and the Netherlands), but it also imported about 200 tons from Poland. Of other minor base metals, bismuth is mostly a by-product of lead smelters, and arsenic is also recovered at lead and copper smelters.

## Light Metals

A common feature of all three major light metals—aluminum, magnesium, and titanium—is the large electric power requirements for metal reduction and the consequent location of reduction plants near cheap power sources. Magnesium and titanium, moreover, tend to be processed in single complexes because their technology is related (Fig. 8).

*Aluminum.* From the time its aluminum industry began in 1933, the Soviet Union has become the world's second largest producer with an annual output of about 1.5 million metric tons, or roughly half of the output of the United States. The USSR has won this position despite a generally unfavorable resource base. It is poor in the high-grade bauxite that provides the raw material for most of the world's aluminum production and has been forced to use low-grade bauxite and to pioneer in the use of other alumina-bearing materials such as nephelite, alunite, and kaolin. The first two aluminum plants, opened in 1933 at Volkhov, east of Leningrad, and at Zaporozhye, on the Dnieper River, used low-grade bauxite from the Boksitogorsk deposit, near Volkhov. Alumina, the intermediate product, was at first derived from bauxite at the two alumina plants themselves and, as requirements expanded, from an additional alumina plant opened in 1938 at Boksitogorsk.

The discovery of additional bauxite resources in the Urals in the mid-1930s led to the growth of an aluminum industry in that region, which was accelerated by the loss of aluminum capacity during World War II under German occupation. The first combined alumina and aluminum plant in the Urals opened in 1939 at Kamensk. During the war, equipment evacuated from the threatened plants at Zaporozh'ye and Volkhov was used in an aluminum plant built at Novokuznetsk in the Kuznetsk Basin, opened in 1943, and an alumina (1943) and aluminum (1945) installation at Krasnoturinsk, near the Urals' principal bauxite-mining center of Severoural'sk. As a result of these projects, aluminum production rose during World War II from 60,000 metric tons in 1940 to about 85,000 tons in 1945, despite the loss of the 36,000-ton Zaporozhye plant.

Since World War II, two major trends have been evident in the aluminum industry. One has been increasing reliance on the newly constructed hydroelectric capacity of Eastern Siberia for provision of the low-cost power needed for aluminum reduction. The other has been a gradual shift to the use of alumina-bearing raw materials other than bauxite. New aluminum plants opened production in Siberia at Shelekhov (near Irkutsk) in 1962, at Krasnoyarsk in 1964, and at Bratsk in 1966. Together with the older Novokuznetsk plant, Siberia accounted for 35 percent of the Soviet Union's total aluminum production in 1965, or about 350,000 tons out of 1 million. By 1970, according to the current five-year plan, Siberia is expected to account for 65 percent of the nation's aluminum, or 1.3 million of a planned total output of 2 million tons.

Until 1964 all the alumina consumed by the Siberian reduction mills had to be shipped eastward from the Urals, which continued to be the nation's principal alumina source. Since then an additional supply has opened up in northern Kazakhstan with bauxite mines at Arkalyk and alumina production at Pavlodar. The Pavlodar plant accounted for 8.7 percent of the Soviet Union's alumina in 1965, or about 170,000 tons out of 2 million. By 1970, Pavlodar and a long-delayed nephelite-based alumina plant at Achinsk are expected to supply 37 percent of the Soviet Union's alumina needs, or about 1.5 million tons. Since Siberia's alumina requirements then (based on a ratio of 2 tons of alumina to every ton of aluminum produced) are likely to be 2.6 million tons, more than 1 million tons of alumina will continue to be shipped from the Urals. In European Russia the only major aluminum reduction plant opened in the postwar period was the Volgograd mill, which began production in 1959 after the completion of the 2.5-million kilowatt hydroelectric plant on the Volga River.

The first non-bauxite material to be used commercially for alumina production in the Soviet Union was nephelite concentrate

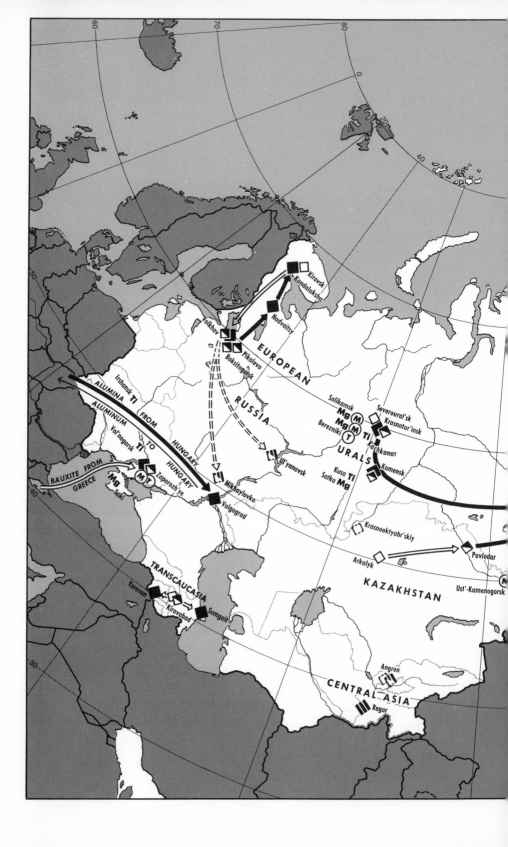

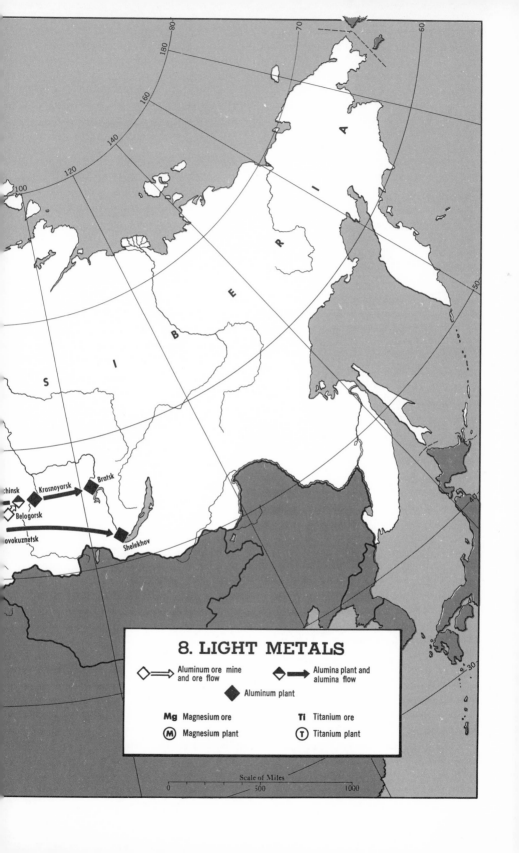

Krasnoyarsk  Bratsk

chinsk

Belogorsk

ovokuznetsk  Shelekhov

A

R

E

B

I

S

S

## 8. LIGHT METALS

◇⇨ Aluminum ore mine
and ore flow

◆➡ Alumina plant and
alumina flow

◆ Aluminum plant

**Mg** Magnesium ore

Ⓜ Magnesium plant

**Ti** Titanium ore

Ⓣ Titanium plant

Scale of Miles

0          500          1000

obtained as a by-product of apatite production in the Kola Peninsula of northern European Russia. The nephelite process, inaugurated in 1949 at the reconstructed Volkhov plant, requires large amounts of limestone (2 to 4 tons per ton of nephelite concentrate) and yields 9 to 10 tons of by-product cement for every ton of nephelite as well as one ton of soda and potash. The nephelite–alumina conversion is therefore economical only near abundant limestone and cement consumers.

The first specialized alumina plant using this process opened in 1959 at Pikalevo, on a rich limestone deposit near Boksitogorsk. The nephelite-based aluminum production is thus far confined to northwest European Russia. In addition to the Volkhov reduction plant, Pikalevo supplies nephelite-based alumina to aluminum mills at Kandalaksha, opened in 1951, and Nadvoitsy, inaugurated about 1954. Two more nephelite-based alumina complexes are under development in Siberia and Transcaucasia. One, at Achinsk, under construction since the late 1950s has been long delayed by technological problems and indecision over the choice of a resource base because the original nephelite source, at Goryachegorsk, was superseded by the discovery of a higher-grade deposit at Belogorsk. The second new nephelite complex is under development in Armenia at Razdan, as a new alumina supply source for the reduction plant at Yerevan, opened in 1950 and supplied in the past by Urals alumina.

Another pioneering development in the production of alumina has been the use of alunite in Azerbaydzhan. An alunite–alumina conversion plant began operations in 1966 at Kirovabad, processing ore from the nearby Alunitdag deposit for use in an aluminum reduction plant in operation since 1955 at Sumgait. Like Yerevan, Sumgait had been using Urals alumina pending completion of the local alumina source. The alunite process yields sulfuric acid as a by-product.

Finally there are plans for the use of kaolin near Angren, in Uzbekistan, where the construction of an alumina and cement plant is to be started in the late 1960s. A potential consumer of alumina from this plant is a reduction mill already under construction at Regar in Tadzhikistan. The Regar reduction plant, which will use low-cost power from the Nurek hydroelectric project, will also consume long-haul alumina from the Urals or from Transcaucasia, pending development of the kaolin-based process.

Virtually the entire aluminum industry is thus based on domestic raw materials. The only exception is the old Zaporozh'ye plant on the Dnieper River, which because of its location near water terminals finds it economical to use imported bauxite. Since the alumina department at Zaporozh'ye reopened in 1955, it has been using about 450,000 tons of Greek bauxite a year. In the early 1950s as much as 500,000 tons of Hungarian bauxite used to be shipped to Urals alumina plants, but these uneconomical transcontinental rail hauls ceased in 1955. Under an exchange that began in 1966, Hungary sends some of its surplus alumina to the reduction plant at Volgograd, which then returns the finished aluminum metal to Hungary. A future program affecting the raw-material base of the Volgograd plant involves the shipment of nephelite concentrate to limestone locations in the Volga valley (at Mikhaylovka or near Ul'yanovsk) for conversion to alumina and cement.

Regular aluminum exports suggest that the Soviet Union produces the metal in excess of needs. In 1966–67, exports were an average of 250,000 metric tons, or about one-fifth of the total production, going mainly to East Germany, Czechoslovakia, and other East European countries as well as to Britain and Japan.

*Magnesium.* In contrast to the United States, which derives almost all its primary magnesium from magnesium chloride obtained from sea water, the Soviet Union has relied mainly on magnesium-bearing minerals such as magnesite, found at Satka in Chelyabinsk Oblast, and carnallite, associated with the potash deposits of Solikamsk. Bischofite,.a hydrous magnesium chloride contained in salt-lake brine, has also been used, especially from the Saki complex in the Crimea. The first two Soviet magnesium plants were situated at Zaporozh'ye (inaugurated in 1935) and at Solikamsk (opened in 1936). During World War II, when half the magnesium capacity was lost through the German occupation of the Ukraine, a second magnesium plant was opened in 1943 in the Urals, at Berezniki, just south of Solikamsk. This plant, like the fourth and newest magnesium plant, opened in 1965 at Ust'-Kamenogorsk in East Kazakhstan, was associated technologically with titanium production, which requires magnesium metal as a reducing agent. With an estimated production of 35,000 metric tons of primary magnesium, the Soviet Union is the world's second producer, with an output of about one-half that of the United States.

*Titanium.* The technologically related titanium, once used almost entirely for the manufacture of pigments, has greatly gained in significance since the 1950s as a structural material in airplanes, especially supersonic aircraft, missiles, and spacecraft. The Soviet Union derives titanium from two sources: titanomagnetite lode deposits of the Urals (notably at Kusa and Kachkanar), which yield a 42 percent $TiO_2$ concentrate used for making titanium slag, and heavy-mineral river gravels, mainly in the Ukraine. The Urals titanomagnetites were the main sources until the late 1950s when stream deposits began to be dredged for heavy minerals. In addition to their titanium components (ilmenite and rutile), these operations also yielded zirconium concentrate and monazite concentrate containing rare earths and thorium. The principal Ukrainian dredging centers are on the Irsha River, west of Kiev, and at Vol'nogorsk, west of Dneprodzerzhinsk, on the Samotkan', a right tributary of the Dnieper.

Titanium metallurgy involves the chlorination of a titanium-bearing material to produce the tetrachloride, and then the reduction of the tetrachloride by magnesium metal. It is because of this technological association, in which the magnesium chloride formed in the reduction reaction is processed to recover magnesium metal, that the reduction of titanium is linked with magnesium production.

The first commercial titanium in the Soviet Union was produced in 1954 at the chemical–metallurgical plant of Podol'sk, south of Moscow, using ilmenite concentrate from the Urals. It was followed in 1956 by the start of titanium production at Zaporozh'ye, where the old magnesium plant, destroyed during World War II, was converted to titanium technology. The Zaporozh'ye plant also used Urals ilmenite until the first Ukrainian ilmenite concentrate from stream deposits became available in 1960. Two more titanium plants, both combined with magnesium production, opened in the 1960s. Titanium production was added to the Berezniki magnesium plant in 1962, and the Ust'-Kamenogorsk plant in East Kazakhstan began operations in 1965.

Two other light metals, lithium and beryllium, have been gaining in importance because of applications in nuclear energy and aerospace vehicles. Both are found in granite pegmatites in conjunction with feldspar, quartz, mica, and columbium–tantalum. Chita Oblast in Eastern Siberia is the principal Soviet source of lithium ores. In addition to being associated with lithium, beryllium is also found in mica-bearing pegmatites, as in the Mama area of Eastern Siberia and in northern Karelia, and in conjunction with emerald deposits, as in the Izumrud mines adjoining the Urals asbestos center of Asbest.

## Precious & Rare Metals

Gold. The USSR is believed to be the world's third-ranking producer of gold, after South Africa and Canada and ahead of the United States, using part of its production to settle its international trade balances. The mining of gold in the Soviet Union has undergone substantial changes both in geographical distribution and in technology in the last ten years. The precious metal was mined in the past almost entirely in the Urals and Siberia, with production shifting slowly eastward as old deposits were exhausted and new resources were explored. In the Urals, present production is centered in two lode-mining centers: Berezovskiy, dating from the eighteenth century, and Plast, where mining began in the nineteenth century. In Siberia, gold mining began in the Altay Mountains in the eighteenth century and in Lena Basin, around Bodaybo on the Vitim River in the nineteenth. In the Soviet period, production shifted farther eastward to Chita Oblast, where the gold-mining center is Baley, and in the 1920s to the Aldan district of Yakutia. In the mid-1930s, when much new resource development and construction were handled by political prisoners, the center of gold production shifted to the newly developed Kolyma district of northeastern Siberia (Fig. 9).

Although some of the western gold-mining areas began to employ mechanical equipment, such as dragline excavators and floating dredges, many easily accessible surface placers continued to be mined by small-scale hand methods, particularly in the Kolyma district, where the availability of forced labor delayed the introduction of machinery. It is only since the end of the forced-labor period

65

in the mid-1950s that there has been an increasing trend toward mechanization. In addition to exploiting low-grade placers previously thought uneconomical, the floating dredges and other mechanical equipment have also made possible the mining of shallow buried placers from which the overburden could be stripped. The gradual exhaustion of placer deposits and the availability of concentrating equipment have also enhanced the importance of lode mining, either in former placer districts or in entirely new areas.

In the 1960s gold mining spread from the Kolyma district still farther northeast into the Chukchi district, where operations began to center around Bilibino in large newly discovered placer deposits. At the same time lode deposits were being developed outside Siberia in areas not previously noted for gold production. They are the Zod deposit of Armenia; the Auezov deposit of East Kazakhstan; the Muruntau deposit at the new desert town of Zarafshan, in the Kyzyl Kum; and the Chadak deposit at the new town of Altynkan, in the Fergana Valley, the last two in the Uzbek Republic of Central Asia.

*Uranium.* This key metal of the nuclear age has been the subject of intensive development in the Soviet Union. The principal mining centers are believed to be in Central Asia in the Kirghiz SSR (the Tyuya-Muyun area and Min-Kush), in the Uzbek SSR (Yangiabad), and in the Tadzhik SSR (Taboshar). Outside of Central Asia, uranium mining is associated with the iron deposits of the Ukrainian Krivoy Rog basin (Zheltyye Vody) and with the Estonian oil shale (Sillimäe).

Most of the other rare metals are derived as by-products. Selenium and tellurium are derived during the electrolytic refining of copper; germanium, gallium, thallium, and indium are obtained commercially as by-products of zinc production; rubidium and cesium are obtained from the carnallite component of potash deposits.

## Selected Nonmetallics

*Asbestos.* Soviet production of asbestos, long second to Canada's, moved ahead in the mid-1960s when the Soviet Union began to exceed 1.5 million metric tons a year, or half of world production. Previously the USSR relied for its asbestos supply and exports almost entirely on a single mining complex in the Urals, the Bazhenovo deposit, in operation since the 1880s at the city of Asbest. The expansion of Soviet asbestos production during the middle 1960s stemmed from the development of three additional deposits. One, at Ak-Dovurak, in Tuva, which began production in 1964, is valuable for its higher content of spinning-grade fibers that can be woven into cloths. The two others are in the southern Urals. Dzhetygara, territorially within northwestern Kazakhstan, began production in 1965, and nearby Yasnyy, at the Kiyembay deposit in neighboring Orenburg Oblast, started shipments of asbestos-bearing rock the following year. About 250,000 tons of asbestos, or one-sixth of the national output, was being exported in the mid-1960s, mainly to Eastern and Western Europe.

*Diamonds.* Until the discovery of kimberlite pipes in Yakutia in the mid-1950s, the Soviet Union had no significant resources of industrial diamonds. Placer deposits in the Urals yielded a small amount and the country was largely dependent on imports. The Yakutian discovery placed the USSR among the world's leading producers of industrial diamonds. Output is concentrated in two areas: the Mirnyy district, where the first concentrating mill opened in 1957, and the Alakit-Daldyn district, astride the Arctic Circle, where the diamond centers of Aykhal and Udachnyy (Novyy) were developed in the late 1960s. According to Soviet sources, 20 percent of the total output consists of gem-quality diamonds and 80 percent of industrial diamonds.

*Fluorspar.* This material is used as a flux in steelmaking and in the electric reduction of aluminum, as a source of hydrofluoric acid and fluorine chemicals, and as a ceramic material. Early production was from Chita Oblast, where Kalanguy continues to be a major producer. Since World War II, two areas were opened up in Central Asia, at Takob, in the Tadzhik SSR, and at Toytepa, near Tashkent, in the Uzbek SSR. A third began operations in 1964 in the Soviet Far East at Voznesenka, north of Ussuriysk.

*Mica.* The most important commercial varieties are muscovite and phlogopite. Muscovite sheet mica is generally superior in many electrical properties, but phlogopite is important as an electrical insulator able to withstand high temperatures. Muscovite is

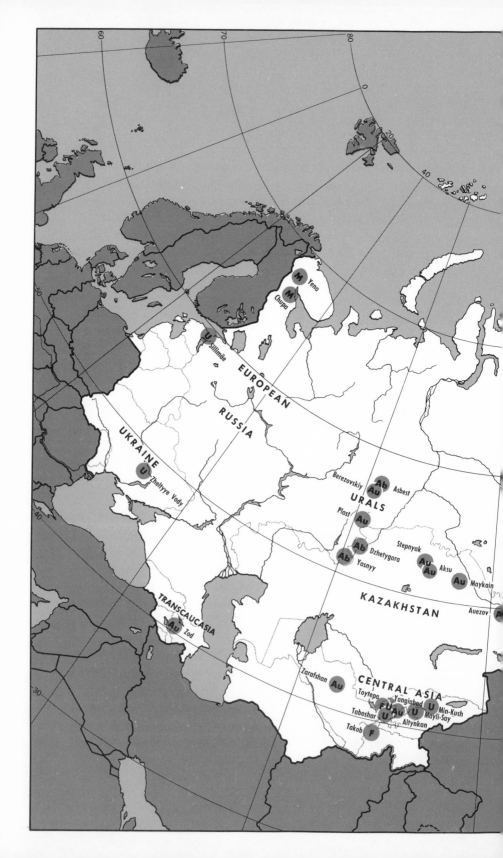

M Yena
M Chupa

U Sillimäe

EUROPEAN

RUSSIA

UKRAINE
U Zheltyye Vody

Berezovskiy    Ab Asbest
Au
URALS

Plast    Au

Ab Dzhetygara    Stepnyak
Ab Yasnyy    Au Aksu
Au
Au Maykain

TRANSCAUCASIA
Au Zod
KAZAKHSTAN

Auezov

Zarafshan    Au    CENTRAL ASIA
Toytepa    Yangiabad
F U Au U    U Min-Kush
Taboshar    U    Mayli-Say
Takob    F    Altynkan

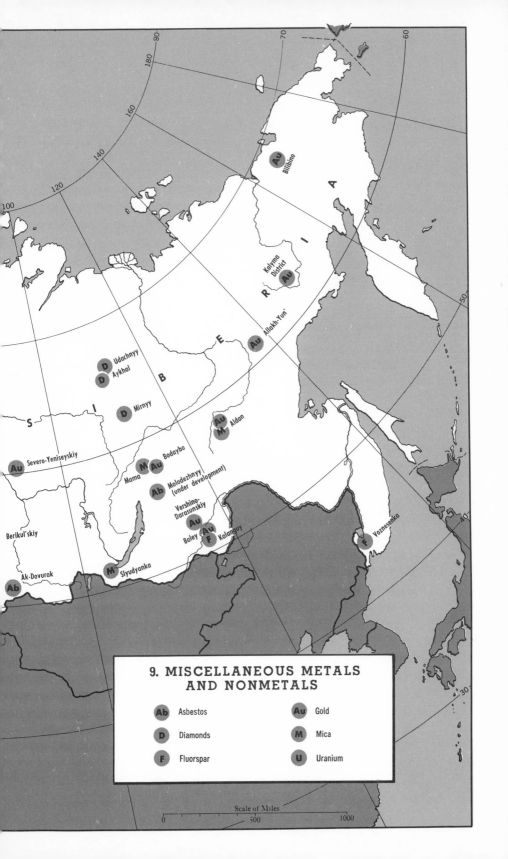

# 9. MISCELLANEOUS METALS AND NONMETALS

**Ab** Asbestos

**D** Diamonds

**F** Fluorspar

**Au** Gold

**M** Mica

**U** Uranium

Bilibino

Kolyma District

Allakh-Yun'

Udachnyy

Aykhal

Mirnyy

Severo-Yeniseyskiy

Mama Bodaybo

Aldan

Molodezhnyy
(under development)

Vershino-
Darasunskiy

Baley Kalanguy

Berikul'skiy

Ak-Dovurak

Slyudyanka

Voznesenka

Scale of Miles

0        500        1000

obtained from the Mama River district of Irkutsk Oblast, in Eastern Siberia, and from mines in northwest European Russia, at Chupa, in Karelia, and at Yena, in the Kola Peninsula. Phlogopite mica was originally produced at Slyudyanka (from *slyuda* = mica), at the southwestern tip of Lake Baykal. These mines, now exhausted, have been superseded since the 1940s by the development of the Aldan mica deposits.

*Graphite.* The Soviet Union now produces natural graphite from two major deposits: Zaval'ye, on the Southern Bug River, in the central Ukraine, and the Tayginka deposit at Kyshtym, in the Urals. Both deposits yield flake graphite with an average content of 7 percent, which is upgraded by flotation to about 90 percent carbon. The deposit at Tayginka yielded 389,000 tons of crude ore in 1964, and the Zaval'ye deposit 336,000 tons. A small deposit of low-grade amorphous graphite worked at Boyevka, 45 miles northeast of Kyshtym, became depleted and ceased operations in 1959.

# 4

# CHEMICAL INDUSTRIES

Chemical industries are considered here mainly as sources of raw materials and as basic processes affected by changing locational patterns and technology. The upper stages of chemical processing, with their intricate inter-industry relationships, are outside the scope of this book.

## Fertilizers

The Soviet Union is a major producer of the three principal categories of fertilizer: phosphates, nitrogenous fertilizers, and potash. Soviet fertilizer statistics are given in standard units, each corresponding to a fixed percentage of plant nutrient contained in the fertilizer. The standard unit of phosphate fertilizer is 18.7 percent $P_2O_5$; nitrogenous fertilizer, 20.5 percent nitrogen, and potash, 46.1 percent $K_2O$. A fourth basic fertilizer category is ground phosphate rock, for which the standard unit is 19 percent $P_2O_5$. Soviet production of mineral fertilizers by major types appears in Table 13. The regional distribution of fertilizer output, available only for all fertilizers combined, is shown in Table 14.

*Phosphates.* Before the Revolution of 1917, Russia's superphosphate industry relied to a large extent on imported phosphates from North Africa and even the United States. Because of these overseas connections, early superphosphate plants were situated in

*Table 13*

Soviet Production of Mineral Fertilizers by Types
(in million metric tons of standard units)

|  | 1940 | 1945 | 1950 | 1955 | 1958 | 1960 | 1965 |
|---|---|---|---|---|---|---|---|
| Nitrogenous | 0.97 | 0.75 | 1.91 | 3.01 | 4.12 | 4.89 | 13.22 |
| Phosphatic | 1.35 | 0.23 | 2.35 | 3.83 | 4.65 | 4.88 | 8.55 |
| Potash | 0.53 | 0.13 | 0.75 | 1.90 | 2.41 | 2.61 | 5.69 |
| Ground phosphate rock | 0.38 | 0.01 | 0.48 | 0.92 | 1.23 | 1.47 | 3.69 |
| Others (boron, magnesium) | — | — | — | 0.003 | 0.004 | 0.02 | 0.10 |
| Total | 3.24 | 1.12 | 5.50 | 9.67 | 12.42 | 13.87 | 31.25 |

Note: Some totals do not add up because of rounding.

ports (e.g., Leningrad, Riga, Odessa). Some of the old inland plants supplemented imported phosphates with lower-grade phosphate rock from nearby deposits (e.g., Vinnitsa, Perm', Dzerzhinsk). The discovery in the late 1920s of the rich apatite deposits of the Kola Peninsula provided a domestic phosphate source, supplanting all imports. Apatite concentrate containing 40 percent $P_2O_5$ became the principal raw material used at all Soviet superphosphate plants. Despite the long hauls involved in shipping Kola apatite to superphosphate plants all over the Soviet Union, this use of apatite concentrate was found economical because of its high content of plant nutrient and because most of the fertilizer output consisted of ordinary superphosphate with only about half the nutrient content of the concentrate. The ordinary superphosphate thus could not be transported economically and had to be manufactured close to markets.

Prerevolutionary superphosphate plants were supplemented in the 1930s by new installations at Voskresensk, at a newly developed low-grade phosphate-rock deposit near Moscow, and at Konstantinovka, in the Donets Basin. The Konstantinovka plant used sulfur gases from an adjoining zinc refinery to produce the sulfuric acid needed in the manufacture of superphosphate. Although some superphosphate plants were situated at or near phosphate rock deposits, this phosphate was suitable only for use as simple ground

*Table 14*

Regional Distribution of Soviet Production of Mineral Fertilizers
(in million metric tons of standard units)

|  | 1940 | 1950 | 1955 | 1960 | 1965 |
|---|---|---|---|---|---|
| European USSR | 2.2 | 3.2 | 5.6 | 8.3 | 20.8 |
| European Russia | 1.1 | 1.4 | 2.2 | 3.1 | 8.9 |
| North | 0.2 | 0.3 | 0.5 | | |
| Central | 0.9 | 1.0 | 1.7 | | |
| Ukraine | 1.0 | 1.5 | 2.7 | 3.9 | 7.3 |
| Belorussia | — | — | — | — | 1.9 |
| Baltic | 0.1 | 0.3 | 0.5 | 0.8 | 1.7 |
| Lithuania | — | — | — | — | 0.6 |
| Latvia | 0.1 | 0.2 | 0.3 | 0.3 | 0.3 |
| Estonia | — | 0.1 | 0.1 | 0.5 | 0.8 |
| Transcaucasia | — | 0.06 | 0.2 | 0.5 | 1.0 |
| Georgia | — | — | — | 0.3 | 0.4 |
| Azerbaydzhan | — | — | — | — | 0.4 |
| Armenia | — | 0.06 | 0.2 | 0.2 | 0.1 |
| Urals | 0.8 | 1.4 | 2.6 | 3.4 | 5.4 |
| Asian USSR | 0.2 | 0.9 | 1.4 | 2.2 | 5.1 |
| Siberia | 0.2 | 0.4 | 0.4 | 0.6 | 2.0 |
| Kazakhstan | — | — | 0.4 | 0.5 | 0.8 |
| Uzbekistan | — | 0.5 | 0.6 | 1.1 | 2.1 |
| Turkmenia | — | — | — | — | 0.2 |
| Total USSR | 3.2 | 5.5 | 9.7 | 13.9 | 31.3 |

Note: Some totals and subtotals do not add up because of rounding.

rock or, at best, as an added constituent in superphosphate manufacture in combination with the higher-grade long-haul apatite.

After World War II, the development of a second major phosphate deposit in the Kara-Tau mountains of southern Kazakhstan
spurred the construction of four superphosphate plants (Kokand,
Dzhambul, Samarkand, and Chardzhou) in Central Asia to fill the
superphosphate requirements of cotton growing. However, because
of the relatively low grade of the Kara-Tau phosphate, it, too, had
to be supplemented by apatite in superphosphate manufacture. By
1965, apatite thus still accounted for about 80 percent of the raw

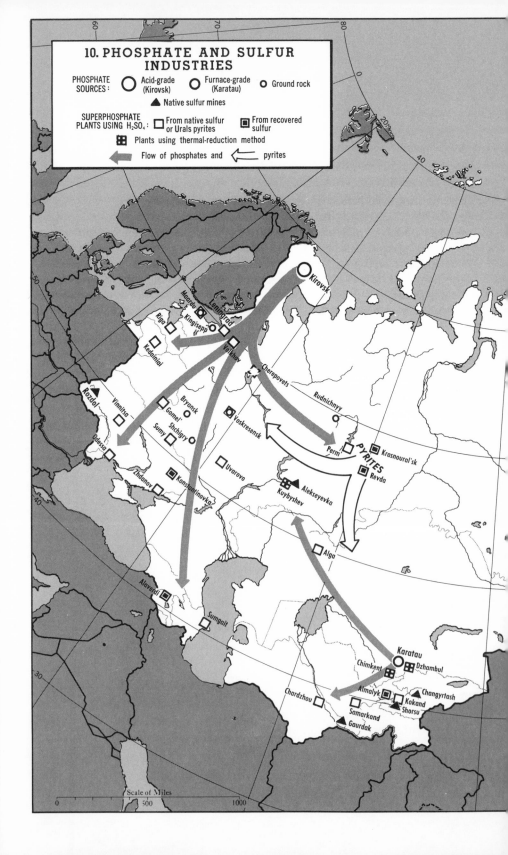

# 10. PHOSPHATE AND SULFUR INDUSTRIES

PHOSPHATE SOURCES:
○ Acid-grade (Kirovsk)  ○ Furnace-grade (Karatau)  ○ Ground rock
▲ Native sulfur mines

SUPERPHOSPHATE PLANTS USING H₂SO₄:
□ From native sulfur or Urals pyrites  ▣ From recovered sulfur
▦ Plants using thermal-reduction method

→ Flow of phosphates and  ⇦ pyrites

Scale of Miles
0        500        1000

material used in superphosphate manufacture; Kara-Tau phosphate about 15 percent, and the lower-grade phosphate rock, mainly in European Russia, about 5 percent. In the late 1960s, two technological trends became evident in the superphosphate industry. One was greater emphasis on double superphosphate and other higher-analysis fertilizers that carried a greater proportion of plant food and would be more transportable. As a result some of the older plants, situated in European Russia, were converted from simple to double superphosphate manufacture and new plants (Gomel, Kedainiai) also produced the more concentrated fertilizer. The second innovation is the use of the thermal reduction method (instead of the traditional sulfuric acid treatment) for decomposing phosphate rock. The thermal reduction method is to be applied to Kara-Tau phosphate rock, which is not economically processed by acid treatment because of its low $P_2O_5$ content and other technical reasons. The new method, requiring much electric power, is being used at Chimkent and Dzhambul, where natural gas piped from the Bukhara field provides the fuel for large power-generating complexes. Low-grade phosphate-rock deposits not suitable for superphosphate production will continue to be worked in European Russia for use as untreated ground phosphate rock, which can be effectively applied to combat excess acidity of the forest soils of central and northern European Russia (Fig. 10).

Superphosphate production consumes about 40 percent of all sulfuric acid (Table 15). Since the acid is not easily transportable and must be manufactured near large consumers, its production is usually linked with superphosphate plants. Until the 1950s, most of the sulfuric acid production (70 to 80 percent) was derived from iron pyrites mined in the Urals and shipped to sulfuric acid plants all over the Soviet Union. Native sulfur deposits at Alekseyevka, in the Volga valley near Kuybyshev, and in the Kara Kum Desert of Central Asia, constituted 5 to 10 percent of the sulfur-bearing raw materials. About 12 percent was derived from the smelting of sulfide ores of copper, lead, and zinc. In this case, metal-smelting centers, such as Krasnoural'sk, in the Urals, and Alaverdi, in Armenia, tended also to become producers of superphosphate because of the availability of sulfuric acid. However, since these smelters were usually in remote mountain areas, far from farm consumers, large

*Table 15*

Regional Distribution of Soviet Output of Sulfuric Acid
(in million metric tons)

|  | 1940 | 1945 | 1950 | 1955 | 1958 | 1960 | 1965 |
|---|---|---|---|---|---|---|---|
| European USSR | 1.3 | 0.7 | 1.4 | 2.4 | 2.9 | 3.3 | 5.2 |
| European Russia | 0.9 | 0.6 | 0.9 | 1.4 | 1.5 | 1.6 | 2.5 |
| Ukraine | 0.4 | 0.07 | 0.4 | 0.9 | 1.2 | 1.3 | 1.9 |
| Baltic | — | — | 0.06 | 0.1 | 0.2 | 0.3 | 0.6 |
| Estonia | — | — | — | — | 0.1 | 0.1 | 0.2 |
| Lithuania | — | — | — | — | — | — | 0.3 |
| Latvia | — | — | 0.06 | 0.1 | 0.1 | 0.1 | 0.1 |
| Transcaucasia | 0.03 | 0.02 | 0.05 | 0.09 | 0.09 | 0.09 | 0.15 |
| Azerbaydzhan | 0.03 | 0.01 | 0.02 | 0.03 | 0.03 | 0.03 | 0.13 |
| Armenia | — | 0.005 | 0.02 | 0.05 | 0.06 | 0.06 | 0.02 |
| Urals | 0.23 | 0.24 | 0.5 | 0.8 | 1.0 | 1.1 | 1.6 |
| Asian USSR | 0.07 | 0.06 | 0.2 | 0.6 | 0.9 | 1.0 | 1.7 |
| Siberia | 0.02 | 0.04 | 0.08 | 0.1 | 0.2 | 0.2 | 0.4 |
| Kazakhstan | 0.05 | 0.02 | 0.06 | 0.3 | 0.5 | 0.6 | 0.9 |
| Uzbekistan | — | — | 0.07 | 0.2 | 0.2 | 0.2 | 0.4 |
| Turkmenia | — | — | — | — | — | 0.02 | 0.1 |
| Total USSR | 1.6 | 0.8 | 2.1 | 3.8 | 4.8 | 5.4 | 8.5 |

development of superphósphate production based on smelter gases
was not always found economical. The sulfur supply underwent a
major shift in the mid-1950s with the discovery of rich native sulfur
deposits in the Carpathian foothills of the Ukraine. Deposits,
evidently representing an extension of the Polish deposits at Tar-
nobrzeg, were found at Rozdol, Yavorov, and Nemirov, south and
southwest of L'vov. Open-pit mining began in 1959 at Rozdol, and
plans were formulated for tapping deeper reserves by the hot-water
injection method known in the United States as the Frasch process.
The newly available native sulfur accounted for 26 percent of sulfuric acid output in 1965 and reduced the share of pyrite as a sulfur-
bearing raw material to 43 percent. Smelter gases accounted for 24
percent, and hydrogen sulfide, a by-product of the oil and gas
industry, for 7 percent.

*Nitrogenous fertilizers.* The most common method of making nitrogenous fertilizers is the synthetic ammonia process, which combines the nitrogen of the air with hydrogen to produce ammonia. A major factor in the location of ammonia-synthesis installations is the source of hydrogen. During the coal-dominated era (until the late 1950s), virtually all hydrogen was obtained from coal by water-gas reaction and from coke-oven gases so that the production of virtually all nitrogenous fertilizers tended to be concentrated in coal basins or coke–chemical centers. Plants at Gorlovka, in the Donets Basin; Dneprodzerzhinsk, a steel center on the Dnieper; Magnitogorsk, in the Urals; and Kemerovo, in the Kuznetsk Basin derived hydrogen from coke-oven gases. Fertilizer plants at Novomoskovsk in the Moscow coal basin and at Berezniki in the Kizel basin of the Urals used the water-gas reaction. The only ammonia-synthesis plant that did not fall into this pattern was the Chirchik plant near Tashkent, which derived its hydrogen from water by electrolysis. As late as 1958, 80 percent of the Soviet Union's hydrogen for ammonia synthesis was derived from coal, coke or coke gases, and 20 percent from water electrolysis (Fig. 11).

The next decade saw the expansion of the natural-gas industry, and the conversion of a large sector of the ammonia industry to this more economical raw material. Instead of being attached to coal and steel centers, the nitrogenous fertilizer industry became widely distributed as natural-gas pipelines made the new raw material available in many parts of the country, more cheaply and nearer to consumers. Central Asian gas supplied new plants at Fergana and Navoi; gas from Karadag and the Northern Caucasus served nitrogenous fertilizer plants in Transcaucasia, at Rustavi and Kirovakan; gas from the Carpathian fields led to the construction of plants at Grodno, in Belorussia, and Jonava, in Lithuania; the Stavropol' gas field served Nevinnomyssk, and so forth. By 1965, 51 percent of all ammonia synthesis was based on natural gas, 39 percent on coal, and 10 percent on electrolysis of water. The continuing trend toward the use of natural gas was accompanied by greater emphasis on improved types of nitrogen fertilizers. The previously dominant ammonium nitrate (75 per cent) and ammonium sulfate (22 percent) gave way after 1958 increasingly to more concentrated forms such as urea and other more effective types of fertilizers, for example, aqua ammonia.

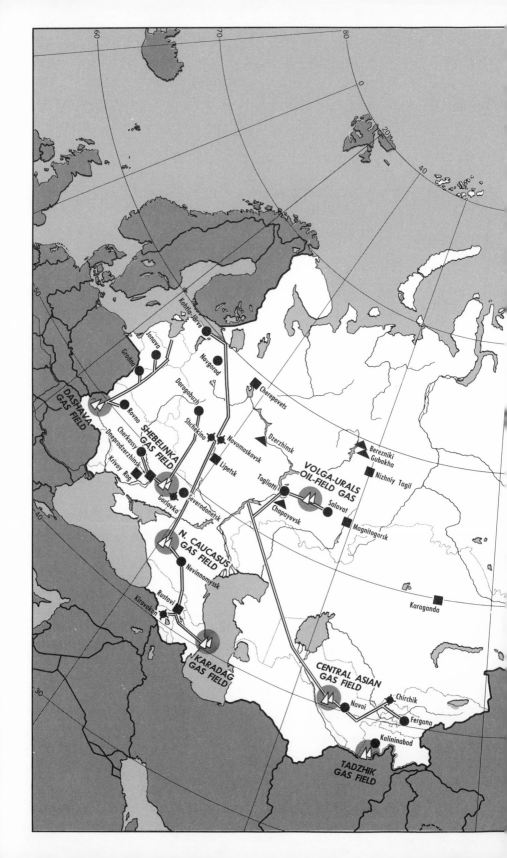

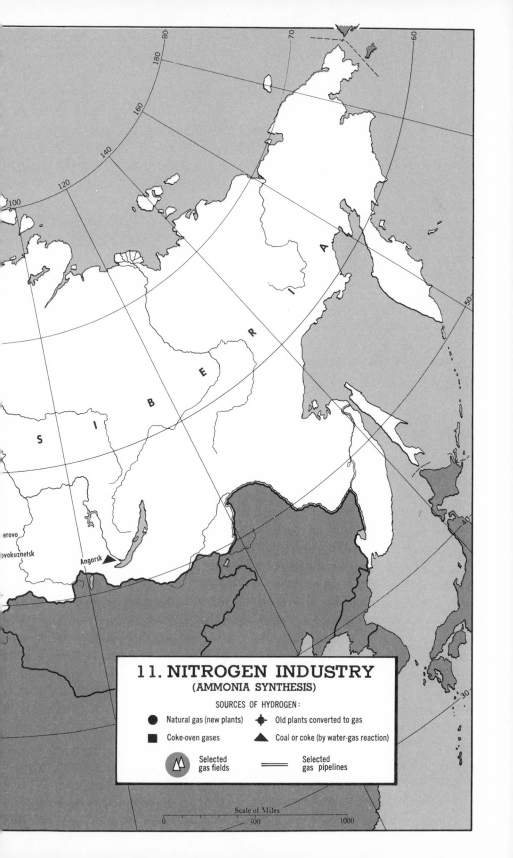

# 11. NITROGEN INDUSTRY
### (AMMONIA SYNTHESIS)

SOURCES OF HYDROGEN:

● Natural gas (new plants)　　◆ Old plants converted to gas

■ Coke-oven gases　　▲ Coal or coke (by water-gas reaction)

Selected gas fields

Selected gas pipelines

Scale of Miles

0　　　　500　　　　1000

Angarsk

erovo
ovokuznetsk

S　I　B　E　R　I　A

*Potash.* A major potash deposit developed in the 1920s in the Berezniki–Solikamsk district on the western slopes of the Urals has become the principal source of potassium fertilizers. The first potash plant went into operation in 1934 at Solikamsk, followed in 1954 by a second installation at Berezniki. Following the acquisition of the Western Ukraine in 1939, the Soviet Union gained two smaller Carpathian deposits at Kalush and Stebnik from Poland. The discovery of potash in Belorussia in the Soligorsk area and the start of operations on the new deposit in 1963 further expanded the resource base. Plans have also been announced for the development of potash reserves at Karlyuk in the southeast corner of the Central Asia republic of Turkmenia.

The Urals and Belorussian deposits yield mainly potassium chlorides (sylvite and carnallite), while the Carpathian deposits are made up mainly of sulfates (kainite and langbeinite). Although potassium chloride is the most widely used potassium compound in fertilizer, the sulfates are applied to some crops like grapes and tobacco, which cannot assimilate the chlorine-bearing fertilizer. Out of a total output of potassic fertilizers of 5.7 million metric tons in 1965, the Solikamsk–Berezniki district accounted for 3.4 million tons, Belorussia about 1.7 million tons, and the Carpathian deposits of the Ukraine about 600,000 tons (Table 16).

*Table 16*

Regional Distribution of Soviet Potash Production
(in million metric tons of standard units)

|  | 1940 | 1950 | 1955 | 1958 | 1960 | 1965 |
|---|---|---|---|---|---|---|
| Solikamsk–Berezniki | 0.46 | 0.64 | 1.61 | 2.09 | 2.26 | 3.44 |
| Belorussia (Soligorsk) | — | — | — | — | — | 1.7 |
| Ukraine | 0.07 | 0.11 | 0.28 | 0.32 | 0.35 | 0.6 |
| Stebnik | 0.02 | 0.04 | 0.12 |  |  |  |
| Kalush | 0.05 | 0.07 | 0.17 |  |  |  |

## Salts & Alkalies

While the production of sulfuric acid tends to be associated to a large extent with the manufacture of superphosphate, the largest consuming industry, the production of alkalies is based to a large extent on the availability of salt and limestone, as well as coal or cheap electric energy. Soviet production of soda ash, produced by the Solvay or ammonia-ash process, is concentrated in areas that combine salt, limestone, and coal resources (Table 17). Such combinations are found in the Donets Basin, at Slavyansk and Lisichansk, which account for about 30 percent of the output, and in the Urals–Volga region, at Berezniki and Sterlitamak, which produce 60 percent.

*Table 17*

Regional Distribution of Soviet Production of Soda Ash
(in million metric tons)

|  | *1940* | *1945* | *1950* | *1955* | *1958* | *1960* | *1965* |
|---|---|---|---|---|---|---|---|
| European USSR | 0.43 | 0.13 | 0.56 | 0.78 | 0.84 | 0.92 | 1.12 |
| European Russia | — | — | — | 0.03 | 0.05 | 0.11 | 0.23 |
| Ukraine | 0.43 | 0.13 | 0.56 | 0.75 | 0.79 | 0.81 | 0.85 |
| Urals | 0.09 | 0.08 | 0.13 | 0.60 | 0.9 | 0.91 | 1.72 |
| Siberia | 0.01 | 0.03 | 0.06 | 0.06 | 0.06 | 0.06 | 0.07 |
| Total USSR | 0.54 | 0.24 | 0.75 | 1.44 | 1.69 | 1.89 | 2.87 |

Caustic soda can be produced from soda ash, and about 30 percent of the Soviet Union's caustic soda originates in the Donets Basin and the Urals (Table 18). But since World War II an increasingly large share of caustic soda has been derived through

*Table 18*

Regional Distribution of Soviet Production of Caustic Soda
(in million metric tons)

|  | *1940* | *1945* | *1950* | *1958* | *1960* | *1965* |
|---|---|---|---|---|---|---|
| European USSR | 0.15 | 0.08 | 0.22 | 0.52 | 0.54 | 0.90 |
| European Russia | 0.06 | 0.07 | 0.16 | 0.39 | 0.36 | 0.66 |
| Ukraine | 0.08 | 0.008 | 0.05 | 0.09 | 0.11 | 0.15 |
| Transcaucasia | 0.003 | 0.006 | 0.02 | 0.04 | 0.07 | 0.1 |
| Urals | 0.04 | 0.04 |  |  | 0.15 | 0.24 |
| Siberia | — | 0.01 |  |  | 0.07 | 0.16 |
| Total USSR | 0.19 | 0.13 | 0.33 | 0.71 | 0.77 | 1.30 |

Note: Some totals and subtotals do not add up because of rounding.

electrolysis of salt, which also yields chlorine, a major chemical. Caustic-chlorine plants require large amounts of electric energy and have tended to be located near sources of low-cost hydroelectric power, such as the Volga valley around Kuybyshev and in Eastern Siberia around Irkutsk. Two additional caustic-chlorine complexes under development are situated at Pavlodar, where cheap electric power will be based on Ekibastuz brown coal, and at Yavan in the Tadzhik SSR, served by the Nurek hydroelectric station.

Outside these chemical complexes with their local salt resources, the principal salt producer is Lake Baskunchak, in the lower Volga valley, which accounts for about 30 percent of the national salt output. Baskunchak salt is hauled by rail and Volga shipping to chemical centers and other consumers.

## Synthetic Rubber

The geographical distribution of the synthetic-rubber industry has undergone substantial changes related to technological advances. When the Soviet Union emerged on the world scene in the 1930s as the first major producer of synthetic rubber, alcohol derived from grain, potatoes, and other farm products was the principal raw material and synthetic-rubber factories tended to be concentrated in the agricultural zone of central European Russia. The early plants, established in Yaroslavl' and Voronezh in 1932, in Yefremov in 1933, and in Kazan' in 1936, produced butadiene–sodium rubber, also known as Buna rubber, for the initial syllables of butadiene and natrium (sodium). The butadiene was derived from alcohol obtained from small farm distilleries in the region. These early rubber factories were situated close to the principal rubber consumers, the tire plants of Moscow, Voronezh, and Yaroslavl', which in turn served the automotive factories of Moscow, Yaroslavl', and Gor'kiy. The synthetic-rubber factories were also situated favorably with respect to another mass rubber consumer, the rubber footwear industry, concentrated in central European Russia and Leningrad (Fig. 12).

The only synthetic-rubber producer that did not fit into this pattern was the chloroprene rubber plant opened in 1940 in Yerevan (Armenia). Chloroprene, known in the United States as neoprene, was derived from acetylene, which in turn was produced in Armenia at that time by the calcium carbide process from limestone, using low-cost power from hydroelectric stations along the Razdan River.

This synthetic-rubber production pattern began to change about 1950. On the one hand, the primitive butadiene–sodium rubber gradually gave way to improved synthetic rubbers, such as the butadiene–styrene and the butadiene–methylstyrene polymers. On the other hand, farm-products alcohol was gradually replaced by synthetic alcohol derived from ethylene, an oil-refinery by-product gas. The first butadiene derived from synthetic alcohol was obtained in the USSR in 1953 at Sumgait, near the oil-refining center of Baku, and a synthetic-rubber plant opened at Sumgait in 1957. Other synthetic-alcohol plants attached to oil refineries at Orsk, Ufa, Saratov, and Novokuybyshevsk helped reduce the share of farm alcohol in synthetic-rubber production to 34 percent by 1958. Industrial alcohol was also derived during World War II and after the war through hydrolysis of wood cellulose from wood wastes, and this alcohol source furnished the basis for a synthetic-rubber plant opened in 1956 at Krasnoyarsk in Eastern Siberia.

Since 1958, with the expansion of the petroleum industry, the synthetic-rubber industry has shifted increasingly to oil-refining areas as new plants opened at Sterlitamak in 1960, Togliatti in 1962, Omsk in 1964, and Volzhskiy in 1966. At the same time, further technological changes eliminated reliance on alcohol-based butadiene. After 1958, butadiene was derived directly from butane and butylene, oil-refinery gases, bypassing the alcohol stage. While styrene–butadiene and methylstyrene–butadiene polymers replaced the old sodium–butadiene as the Soviet Union's principal general-purpose rubber in the early 1960s, still further diversification and technological improvement were under way. Polyisoprene rubber, the synthetic considered closest to natural rubber, went into commercial production at Sterlitamak, Togliatti, and Volzhskiy, and another advanced rubber, polybutadiene, was made at the converted Yefremov and Voronezh plants. Plans were made to introduce the ethylene–propylene terpolymer, another new rubber distinguished by great resilience and rebound. Chloroprene continued to be made in Armenia, but natural gas replaced calcium carbide as the source of acetylene in the middle 1960s. New synthetic-rubber plants were

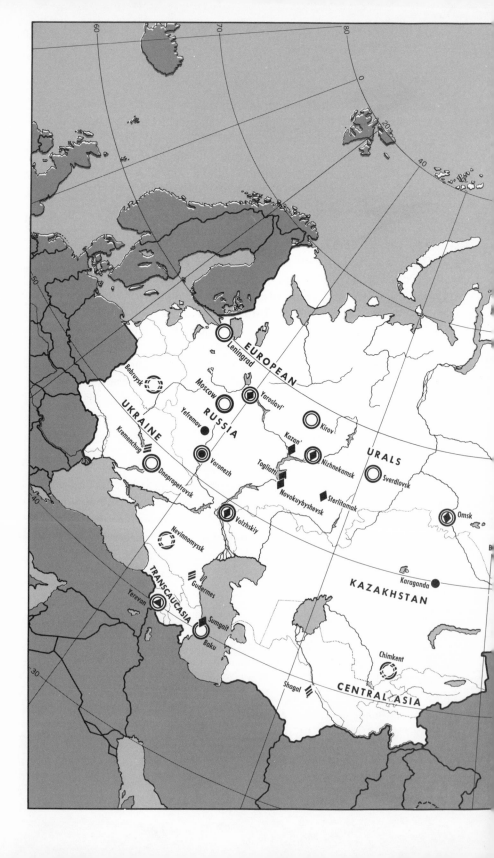

S I B E R I A

Krasnoyarsk

Usol'ye

## 12. SYNTHETIC-RUBBER INDUSTRY

TIRE PLANTS

SYNTHETIC-RUBBER PLANTS BASED ON:

◆ Oil-refinery gases          ● Synthetic alcohol

▲ Acetylene                   ■ Wood-hydrolysis alcohol

Scale of Miles

0          500          1000

entering production in the late 1960s at Nizhnekamsk in the Tatar oil fields, and at Gudermes, near Groznyy.

## Man-Made Fibers

Before World War II, the Soviet Union's modest man-made fiber industry was limited entirely to the production of rayon, the cellulosic fiber, mainly by the viscose process, with plants at Klin (Moscow Oblast), Mogilev (Belorussia), and Leningrad. The cuprammonium process of rayon manufacturing was used at two plants, in Kalinin near Moscow, and in Shuya near Ivanovo. During World War II, the Kalinin plant was evacuated to Kustanay in Kazakhstan, where the cuprammonium process is still being used. Other war-threatened installations were transferred to Aramil' in the Urals, and to Namangan in the Fergana Valley, where cotton linters supplied the raw material (Fig. 13).

World War II reduced output from 11,000 metric tons of fiber in 1940 to 1,100 tons in 1945. Although the prewar level was more than doubled by 1950, when 24,000 tons was produced, the real growth of man-made fiber industries began only in the 1950s. Expansion was at first mainly in the viscose field. The acetate rayon process, which requires acetic anhydride and acetic acid, derived from acetylene, lagged because of the high cost of acetylene produced by the old calcium carbide method. It was only after the development of natural gas and its pipeline network had provided a cheaper source of acetylene that the acetate process was used more extensively in the 1960s. Acetate plants were built in areas with access to natural gas, such as the Volga valley (Engels), Lithuania (Kaunas), and Armenia (Kirovakan). In 1965 cellulosic fibers, mainly viscose rayon, accounted for 80 percent of Soviet man-made fibers, while real synthetic fibers made up 20 percent of the total output. They included mainly kapron, the Soviet polyamide equivalent of nylon, which entered commercial production in the late 1940s. The production of its raw material, caprolactam, is associated with ammonia synthesis, and in accordance with the shifts in the ammonia industry, caprolactam plants are now situated along natural-gas pipelines (for example, Grodno in Belorussia) in addition to coal-basin sites (for example, Shchekino in the Moscow Basin, or Kemerovo in the Kuznetsk Basin). The production of other synthetic fibers is also linked to the availability of natural gas, for example, lavsan, the Soviet polyester fiber resembling dacron, and nitron, the acrylic fiber resembling orlon. Both are in their early stages of development, with initial production of lavsan at Kursk and of nitron at Saratov, and another plant under development at Mogilev, in Belorussia. For production statistics of Soviet man-made fibers, see Tables 19 and 20.

*Table 19*

Percentage Distribution of Soviet Man-Made Fibers by Types

|  | *1940* | *1948* | *1958* | *1965* |
| --- | --- | --- | --- | --- |
| Total Output | | | | |
| (thousand metric tons) | 11.1 | 11.1 | 166.0 | 407.3 |
| Percentage Distribution: | | | | |
| Cellulosics | 100 | 99.4 | 92.3 | 81.0 |
| Viscose | 90.2 | 87.6 | 83.9 | 72.3 |
| Cuprammonium | 9.8 | 11.6 | 6.9 | 4.4 |
| Acetate | — | 0.2 | 1.5 | 4.3 |
| Synthetics | — | 0.6 | 7.7 | 19.0 |
| Polyamide (kapron) | — | 0.6 | 7.2 | 16.1 |
| Polyester (lavsan) | — | — | — | 1.8 |
| Acrylic (nitron) | — | — | — | 0.7 |
| Others | — | — | 0.5 | 0.4 |

## Synthetic Resins & Plastics

The Soviet Union long lagged in the production of synthetic resins, both in quantity and in quality. Until the advent of the oil and gas era in the 1950s provided a source of cheaper and more diversified plastics than the previous coal base, the Soviet Union was not only behind the United States, but also behind West Germany, Britain, and Japan in the production of resins. Moreover, most of the output was in the form of thermosetting resins, which harden permanently under heat and cannot be reshaped. The most common of these resins were the phenolics, which could be derived relatively cheaply from coke chemicals. The pattern persisted well into the 1950s when most of the other plastics-producing nations, in addition to increasing their output substantially, shifted to the more advan-

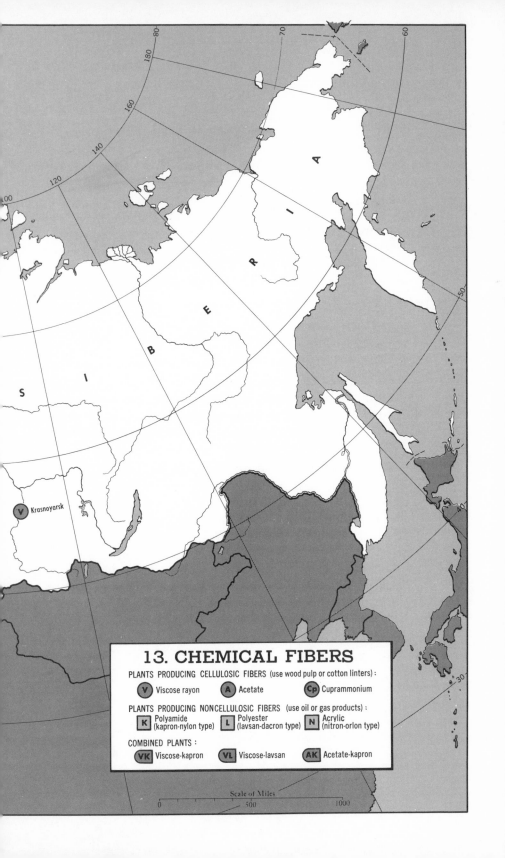

# 13. CHEMICAL FIBERS

PLANTS PRODUCING CELLULOSIC FIBERS (use wood pulp or cotton linters):

(V) Viscose rayon   (A) Acetate   (Cp) Cuprammonium

PLANTS PRODUCING NONCELLULOSIC FIBERS (use oil or gas products):

K Polyamide (kapron-nylon type)   L Polyester (lavsan-dacron type)   N Acrylic (nitron-orlon type)

COMBINED PLANTS:

(VK) Viscose-kapron   (VL) Viscose-lavsan   (AK) Acetate-kapron

Scale of Miles

0     500     1000

(V) Krasnoyarsk

S I B E R I A

*Table 20*

Regional Distribution of Soviet Output of Man-Made Fibers
(in thousands of metric tons)

| | 1940 | 1945 | 1950 | 1958 | 1960 | 1965 |
|---|---|---|---|---|---|---|
| European USSR | 11.1 | 1.1 | 23.3 | 140.5 | 168.1 | 321.8 |
| European Russia | 7.0 | 1.1 | 18.2 | 121.5 | 139.2 | 235.1 |
| Ukraine | 1.6 | — | 2.9 | 9.3 | 14.2 | 44.0 |
| Belorussia | 2.5 | — | 2.2 | 9.7 | 14.7 | 24.1 |
| Latvia | — | — | — | — | — | 10 |
| Armenia | — | — | — | — | — | 7.2 |
| Urals | — | 0.01 | 0.5 | | 4.0 | 5 |
| Asian USSR | — | — | 0.4 | | 39.1 | 80.5 |
| Siberia | — | — | — | | 33.3 | 72.5 |
| Kazakhstan | — | — | 0.1 | 4.5 | 5.0 | |
| Uzbekistan | — | — | 0.3 | 0.8 | 0.8 | |
| Total USSR | 11.1 | 1.1 | 24.2 | 166.0 | 211.2 | 407.3 |

tageous thermoplastic resins, which can be remelted and reshaped. The expansion of the oil and gas industries and related petrochemical production resulted in a substantial increase in output and diversification of the plastics industry. Among the thermosetting plastics, urea resins, with far wider color possibilities than the phenolics, went into commercial production in the mid-1950s and surpassed the phenolics in total output by 1964. The urea resins, derived from ammonia, are associated with nitrogenous fertilizer plants. The production of the thermoplastics also got under way in the early 1960s. They included the vinyl resins, especially polyvinyl chloride, whose production was increased in connection with chlorine output at Novomoskovsk (Tula Oblast), Sterlitamak (Bashkir ASSR), and Usol'ye (Irkutsk Oblast) and in acetylene-based industries, such as the chemical industry of Yerevan (Armenia). The output of polyolefins (polyethylene, polypropylene) was expanded in connection with the use of oil refinery gases (Groznyy, Salavat, Novokuybyshevsk, Novopolotsk, Gur'yev).

# PART

## Regional
## Survey

# 5

# EUROPEAN RUSSIA

## Central European Russia

As the historical and economic heart of the Soviet Union, Central European Russia, although generally poor in energy and mineral resources, has developed into one of the nation's major manufacturing areas, based on long-haul raw materials and fuels, the use of a skilled labor force, and an established industrial capacity. Low-grade local resources for energy, such as peat and brown coal, have been developed for generating power in addition to the hydroelectric potential on the upper reaches of the Volga River. However, for most of its supply of energy, the region has had to depend on long-haul Donets steam coals and fuel oil, long-distance transmission of electric power from the large stations on the lower reaches of the Volga and, more recently, long-distance transmission of crude oil and natural gas from other parts of the Soviet Union.

The only economical resource base for the development of heavy industry is the iron ore of the so-called Kursk Magnetic Anomaly, which since 1959–60 has stimulated the expansion of an integrated iron and steel industry at Tula and especially at Lipetsk. Elsewhere in the region, crude-oil and natural-gas pipelines have given rise to oil refineries as well as petrochemical and other chemical plants at scattered locations, mainly established industrial centers. The only significant local chemical raw-material base, low-grade phosphate deposits, is used as ground phosphate rock (Fig. 14).

*Fuel and Power.* The region's brown-coal basin, the Moscow Basin, centered in the Tula area, south of the Soviet capital, began its commercial production in the mid-nineteenth century, and accounted for one-fourth of Russia's total coal output in the 1870s. However, the low-grade, high-cost brown coal could not meet the competition of the bituminous coal mined in the developing Donets Basin, and output in the Moscow Basin declined sharply to less than 1 percent of Russia's total coal production on the eve of World War I.

In the early period of the Soviet industrialization drive, the Moscow Basin again became a major source of fuel for Central Russia as Soviet planners marshaled all available resources for economic development, often regardless of cost. From less than 1 million tons before the start of the first five-year plan (1928–32), the Moscow Basin output rose to 10 million tons on the eve of World War II. Rapidly recovering from damage suffered during the war, the basin continued to expand to a production of 20 million tons in 1945, 31 million in 1950, 39.5 million in 1955, and reached a peak of 47.6 million tons in 1959. Thereafter, the availability of natural gas and increasing concern for economic cost factors resulted in a gradual decline of production to 40.8 million tons in 1965, with about 90 percent of the output coming from mines in Tula Oblast. Small amounts of coal are produced in peripheral sections of the Moscow Basin, in Smolensk, Kaluga, Ryazan', and Kalinin oblasts, each of which mines only about 1 million tons a year.

Because of the distribution of coal seams in small separate lenticular deposits, each of the 100 underground mines of the Moscow Basin disposes of limited reserves, estimated to last from fifteen to twenty-five years at an average output rate of about 300,000 tons per mine. The present policy is to continue to operate existing underground mines until the reserves become depleted but not to build new mines. A production level of from 30 to 40 million tons is to be maintained through the 1970s by the construction of strip mines in the few areas accessible to surface mining. In the mid-1960s two strip mines were in operation, at Kimovsk (opened in 1958) and nearby Ushakovskiy (opened in 1963), with a combined output of about 3 million tons. Additional strip mines were under construction with a view to raising the amount of surface-mined

94

coal to 8 or 9 million tons in the 1970s. As old underground mines are shut down, new industries (metal fabrication, consumer goods, processed foods) are being introduced to provide employment.

During the period of rapid expansion in the 1940s and 1950s, Moscow Basin coal served as a power station fuel, as a railroad fuel and, to some extent, as a source of hydrogen (through the water–gas reaction) for ammonia synthesis at the Novomoskovsk chemical complex (called Stalinogorsk until 1961). However, the increasing electrification of railroads and the more efficient derivation of hydrogen for ammonia synthesis from the newly available natural gas now limit the use of brown coal mainly to power generation.

Before World War II, Moscow Basin coal generated power at two major steam electric stations: the Kashira and Novomoskovsk plants. The Kashira station was situated just east of the old town of Kashira in a new power-workers' settlement that was originally called Ternovsk, later Kaganovich (1935–57), and finally Novokashirsk, before being incorporated into Kashira proper in 1963. The Kashira station was opened in 1922 with two 6,000-kilowatt units. Subsequent expansion, from 1928 to 1932, raised the capacity to 186,000 kilowatts, including three 50,000-kilowatt units. After postwar reconstruction, the capacity was raised to 266,000 kilowatts. The Kashira plant underwent a revival in the late 1960s, with the installation of a 100,000-kilowatt experimental unit in 1966, and three 300,000-kilowatt generators in 1967–69, raising the total capacity to 1.2 million kilowatts. Three more 300,000-kilowatt units were planned for the early 1970s.

The second prewar power plant, at Novomoskovsk, went into operation in 1934 in conjunction with the opening of the ammonia-synthesis plant. The first two 50,000-kilowatt units were supplemented in 1939 by a 100,000-kilowatt generator for a total capacity of 200,000 kilowatts. During the latter part of World War II the station was expanded to 350,000 kilowatts. The capacity in 1969 was 450,000 kilowatts.

After the war two more major power stations were based on Moscow Basin brown coal; they were the Shchekino and Cherepet' stations. The Shchekino station opened in 1950 at the new power-workers' town of Sovetsk, southeast of Shchekino, a coal-mining center. By 1957, when the station was completed, it had a capacity

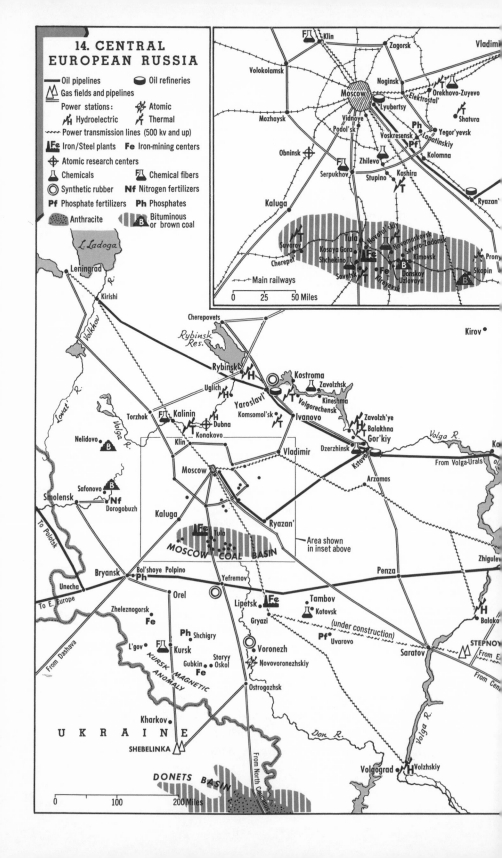

of 610,000 kilowatts. This was substantially increased in 1964–65 with the installation of two 200,000-kilowatt generators. The Cherepet' station was opened in 1953 at the new town of Suvorov, a few miles east of Cherepet' proper. The station, used for testing experimental turbines for superheated high-pressure steam, first acquired four 150,000-kilowatt units, installed by 1958. Later three 300,000-kilowatt generators raised the total capacity to 1.5 million kilowatts by the mid-1960s.

In addition to the brown-coal power stations of the Moscow Basin, the electric grid of the Central Russian region also includes peat-fueled stations east of Moscow (the Shatura power plant, with a capacity of 186,000 kilowatts, and the Orekhovo-Zuyevo plant), near Ivanovo (at Komsomol'sk), and near Gor'kiy (at Balakhna). The Central region accounts for about one-third of the Soviet Union's peat production. A 600,000-kilowatt station, which will also burn peat, was under construction near Shatura in the 1960s.

Hydroelectric power became a significant element on the eve of World War II, with the inauguration of three stations on the upper Volga River. The Ivan'kovo station, at the present atomic research town of Dubna, opened in 1937 with a capacity of 30,000 kilowatts in conjunction with the completion of the Moscow–Volga Canal. It was followed in 1940 by the 110,000-kilowatt Uglich station and the following year by the first of six 55,000-kilowatt units at the Rybinsk station. The station at Rybinsk (known as Shcherbakov from 1946 to 1957) reached its full capacity of 330,000 kilowatts in 1950. The Gor'kiy hydroelectric station, at the new town of Zavolzh'ye, upstream from Gor'kiy, began feeding power into the Central grid in 1955–56 when eight 50,000-kilowatt generating units were installed for a total capacity of 400,000 kilowatts. It was later upgraded to 520,000 kilowatts by technical improvements. The supply of the power-hungry Central region improved further when 500-kilovolt long-distance transmission lines went into operation from the Kuybyshev station in 1956 and from the Volgograd plant in 1959.

A major element in improving the energy supply was the long-distance transmission of natural gas to Moscow. The first pipelines, completed from Saratov in 1946 and from the Dashava field in the Carpathian foothills in 1950, provided gas mainly for domestic consumers in the Soviet capital. Its steam electric stations continued to

97

burn long-haul coal, mostly from the Donets Basin, totaling 7 million tons. It was only with the arrival of a more abundant flow of natural gas from the Stavropol' field in the Northern Caucasus in 1957 that most of the city's power stations were converted from coal to gas, reducing the long coal hauls and improving the air-pollution problem. Additional gas became available in 1967 with completion of a pipeline from Central Asia.

*Iron and Steel.* The resource with the greatest future is the iron ore of the Kursk Magnetic Anomaly, so called because of the disturbing effect of the underground masses of iron ore on compass needles, first observed in the eighteenth century. Explored in the 1930s and, more intensively, after World War II, the KMA, as it is commonly abbreviated, consists of two 150-mile-long zones of vast reserves of low-grade iron quartzites, with an iron content of 30 to 40 percent, overlain in some sectors by high-grade weathered iron ores containing 55 to 60 percent iron.

Heavy waterlogging of the strata containing the richer ores long discouraged development of the high-grade deposits and induced Soviet planners to give priority to the exploitation of the lower-grade quartzites. These efforts were concentrated at the new town of Gubkin (1967 population: 42,000). Flooding of an experimental mine in 1936 at the village of Korobkovo, just north of Gubkin, had suggested the prohibitive waterlogging of the rich iron ore, but the mine was reopened in 1952 to tap the deeper quartzite. It now yields about 600,000 tons of crude ore, which is being converted into about 300,000 tons of 60 percent concentrate.

The success of the experimental quartzite mine led to the start of construction of a second and larger mine, the South Korobkovo, in 1951. It went into operation in 1959, together with a concentrator with a capacity of processing up to 3 million tons of crude ore. Altogether the Korobkovo quartzite deposit yielded 1.5 million tons of iron concentrate in 1965.

Meanwhile, further exploration of the Kursk Magnetic Anomaly in the 1950s had shown that some of the rich ore deposits were accessible to open-pit operations despite waterlogging and that their operation was economical, particularly if the mining of the rich ore was combined with the use of the more abundant poor ore in the same deposit. In the mid-1950s, work got under way to strip 200 to

300 feet of overburden from two of the more accessible deposits.

The Lebedi deposit, situated three miles southeast of Gubkin and twelve miles southwest of Staryy Oskol, went into operation in 1959, and by 1965 was producing 6 million tons of direct-shipping ore with an iron content of 54 to 58 percent. During the late 1960s, work was under way at Lebedi on a great open pit to tap also the deeper lower-grade quartzite for concentration into usable ore at a mill under construction at nearby Gumny, just south of Staryy Oskol. The concentrator, when completed in the early 1970s, will be able to convert 30 million tons of crude ore a year into 15 million tons of concentrate with an iron content of up to 68 percent.

The second major iron ore development was the Mikhaylovka deposit, northwest of Kursk, where the new mining town of Zheleznogorsk (iron mountain) was inaugurated in 1958 and raised to city status in 1962. It had a population of 19,000 in 1967. The rich-ore section of the Mikhaylovka deposit went into operation in two stages: a capacity of 2.5 million tons in 1962 and an additional 2 million tons in 1965. It thus yielded 4.5 million tons of direct-shipping ore in the mid-1960s. The capacity was to be doubled by 1970. As in the Lebedi deposit, preparations were under way in the late 1960s to excavate an open pit to tap the deeper iron quartzite and to build a concentrator with a potential capacity of 30 million tons of crude ore and 15 million tons of up to 68-percent concentrate. When first developed in the late 1950s the Mikhaylovka deposit was approached by a 30-mile-long rail spur from Arbuzovo station on the L'gov–Bryansk railroad, in the southwest. In the late 1960s a more direct rail outlet from the mine to the Lipetsk steel mill was under construction between Zheleznogorsk and Orel, 65 miles to the northeast.

In the mid-1960s, the Kursk Magnetic Anomaly produced a total of 12 million tons of direct-shipping ore (10.5 million tons) and concentrate (1.5 million tons), including 7.5 million tons from the Gubkin complex (the Korobkovo quartzite and Lebedi high-grade ore mines) and 4.5 million tons from the Zheleznogorsk complex. In addition to the two major quartzite-concentration projects of 15 million tons of concentrate each, expansion of the high-grade ore capacity was under way in the late 1960s. The Zheleznogorsk complex was to be doubled, to 9 million tons, and the Gubkin complex was to be expanded to about 12 million tons by the stripping of overburden from two rich-ore sites, the South Lebedi and adjacent Stoyla open pits, with a combined capacity of 6 million tons. The two pits yielded their first ore in late 1968.

The availability of KMA iron ore resulted in major expansion of existing iron and steel centers at Tula and Lipetsk and stirred talk of the construction of a new integrated plant, for which a site has been tentatively selected at L'gov, west of Kursk. Before 1960, the Tula and Lipetsk complexes had processed iron ore mainly from small local deposits (500,000 tons a year at Tula and 300,000 tons at Lipetsk) into cast iron and had lacked any significant steelmaking capacity. As a result of the development of the Kursk Magnetic Anomaly, major expansion got under way in the 1960s at both centers, in blast furnaces and steelmaking facilities. Tula and Lipetsk each have an old prerevolutionary mill and a new plant, dating from the 1930s.

At Tula, the older plant, dating from 1895 at Kosaya Gora, south of Tula, produced about 170,000 tons of cast iron in 1940, while the newer plant, inaugurated in 1935 at Novotul'skiy, southeast of the city, yielded 260,000 tons. After 1960, the Novotul'skiy plant was expanded through the reconstruction of existing blast furnaces and the addition of new capacity to handle the flow of KMA ore while Kosaya Gora continued to use local ore, from Kireyevsk, for the production of cast iron and ferroalloys.

A similar situation exists at Lipetsk. There, an older plant, called Svobodnyy Sokol (free falcon), dating from 1897, yielded more than 100,000 tons of iron before World War II, while the newer plant, opened in 1934, produced almost 500,000 tons. The new plant, called the Novolipetsk mill, was converted to the use of KMA ore with the addition of a third blast furnace in 1962 and a fourth, with a working volume of 70,000 cubic feet, in 1967. It then produced 2.4 million tons of pig iron a year. Blast furnace No. 5, originally designed for a working volume of 95,000 cubic feet, but later expanded to 112,000 cubic feet, was scheduled to go into operation in 1970. Its capacity of 2.3 million tons of pig iron almost doubled the capacity of the plant. Electric furnaces and a continuous casting unit opened at the Novolipetsk plant in 1959 and an oxygen converter shop in 1966. The construction of coking facilities gave rise to a nitrogenous fertilizer plant in 1965, deriving hydrogen for ammonia synthesis from coke gases. The older Svobodnyy Sokol plant continued to use iron ore from the local deposit at Syrskiy, southwest of Lipetsk, with an output of about 300,000 tons of ore in the middle 1960s. The Lipetsk ferroalloys plant dates from 1945.

*Chemical Industries.* Chemical industries of the region, reinforced since the late 1950s by oil and natural gas pipelines as well as other resource-based developments, are widely scattered and will be discussed oblast by oblast.

In Moscow Oblast, chemical fibers are produced at Klin, where viscose-rayon production, begun in 1931, was supplemented after World War II by kapron, the Soviet equivalent of nylon, and at Serpukhov, where manufacture of acetate rayon began in 1953–54. Both fiber plants supply the important textile industry of the Moscow area. The Moscow industrial complex also includes some of the Soviet Union's oldest plastics factories, including the Karbolit plant of Orekhovo-Zuyevo, producing phenolic resins, and Zhilevo (polystyrene, polyester), north of Stupino. The Rastorguyevo coke plant at the new town of Vidnoye, south of Moscow, produces gas and chemicals from Donets Basin coking coal. The large superphosphate complex at Voskresensk, opened in 1931, produces concentrated fertilizer from long-haul Kola apatite and from sulfuric acid derived from Urals pyrites, and ground phosphate rock from nearby mines at Lopatinskiy, to the northeast, and at Fosforitnyy, to the east. The total output of these phosphate mines, named for the nearby city of Yegor'yevsk, was 500,000 tons of ground rock in the mid-1960s.

A small oil refinery, opened in 1938 in the southeast Moscow suburb of Lyubertsy, was expanded after it was reached in 1963 by a crude-oil pipeline from the Tatar fields via Gor'kiy and Ryazan'. A catalytic reforming unit was opened at the Moscow refinery in 1965.

The Podol'sk chemical–metallurgical plant, south of Moscow, is an important element of the Soviet Union's nonferrous and rare metals industries, particularly in research and development. Originally designed as a plant for the recovery of secondary nonferrous metals, the Podol'sk mill was inaugurated in 1949 (construction began in 1940 but was interrupted by World War II). In the 1950s, when new applications in electronics and the nuclear and space fields brought various rare metals to the fore, the Podol'sk plant became a key experimental development center. It was the first Soviet plant, in 1954–55, to produce titanium dioxide pigment, titanium sponge metal and ingot on a commercial scale. It also developed methods in the metallurgy of other rare metals, including columbium and tantalum.

In Ryazan' Oblast, the capital of Ryazan' expanded in population from 136,000 in 1956 to 322,000 in 1968 as a result of industrial development, including oil refining and chemical fibers. The oil refinery, which opened with its first atmospheric distillation unit in 1960, was reached the following year by a crude-oil pipeline from the Tatar fields via Gor'kiy. It added thermal cracking in 1961 and catalytic cracking in 1967. A second primary distillation unit, opened in 1968, doubled the refinery's straight-run capacity. The chemical fibers are produced at a large viscose rayon plant, opened in 1960.

The growing industry of the Ryazan' petrochemical complex is to be served with electric power by a 1.8-million kilowatt coal-fueled station under construction at Bestuzhevo, 40 miles south of Ryazan', on the lower Pronya River, a tributary of the Oka. This power plant, to be equipped with six generators of 300,000 kilowatts each, will burn surface-mined brown coal from nearby pits in the eastern wing of the Moscow Basin around Skopin. The lower Pronya power station is to be linked by a 220-kilovolt power line to Ryazan' and a 500-kilovolt line to Moscow.

In Tula Oblast, the principal chemical center at Novomoskovsk (opened in 1933; 1968 population: 126,000), is based on ammonia synthesis, but covers a wide range of other chemicals. Having long derived its hydrogen from Uráls coke and, to some extent, from Moscow Basin brown coal by the water–gas reaction, the Novomoskovsk complex was converted to natural gas in 1958, when it was reached by the first pipeline from the Stavropol' gas field in the Northern Caucasus. In the mid-1960s the plant produced 15 percent of Soviet ammonia. Since the arrival of gas, the fertilizer department has been shifting increasingly toward the production of more concentrated nitrogenous fertilizers such as urea and complex fertilizers (e.g., ammonium phosphate). The share of simple ammonium nitrate in the production of nitrogenous fertilizers dropped from 75 percent in 1958 to 55 percent in 1965. A chlorine–caustic department, using brine from a nearby salt deposit, went into operation in 1963. The latest addition is an organic synthesis department producing polyvinyl chloride, a thermoplastic resin, and raw materials for the manufacture of lavsan, the polyester fiber resembling dacron. The Novomoskovsk plant also produces argon and crypton, the inert gases, as by-products of the fractional distillation of liquid air used to make nitrogen for ammonia synthesis.

A second nitrogen-based chemical center is Shchekino (1968 population: 56,000). Its chemical industry originally used gas derived from the underground gasification of brown coal. This relatively inefficient process was superseded by natural gas in the 1950s. In addition to hydrogen for ammonia synthesis, the Shchekino chemical complex also uses natural gas for the production of methyl alcohol and formaldehyde. A caprolactam unit, making the raw material for kapron, opened at Shchekino in 1966. It supplies a kapron mill producing tire cord and silk that went into operation in 1970 at nearby Guskino.

Tula Oblast includes the synthetic-rubber center of Yefremov, in operation since 1933. Long dependent on grain alcohol for the production of butadiene, the constituent of the original butadiene–sodium rubber of the 1930s, the Yefremov plant was converted in the mid-1960s to the production of the advanced polybutadiene rubber, using petroleum-base raw materials.

A second synthetic-rubber plant, in operation since 1932 at Voronezh, provides the basis of an integrated rubber-fabricating industry in that industrial center, including the manufacture of tire cord and automobile tires. The synthetic-rubber plant at Voronezh was the first of the old Soviet plants to complete its conversion, in 1949–56, from the use of grain alcohol for manufacture of the old butadiene–sodium rubber to petroleum-based rubber, first styrene–butadiene, and later polybutadiene. At Novovoronezhskiy, south of Voronezh, is one of the Soviet Union's nuclear power stations, of the pressurized water, water-moderated type. A first unit with an electrical generating capacity of 210, 000 kilowatts opened in 1964, and through technical improvements was subsequently expanded to 240,000 kilowatts. A second unit of 375,000 kilowatts was added in 1969. The Novovoronezhskiy station is to be further expanded in the 1970s with the installation of two 440,000-kilowatt units and would then become the Soviet Union's largest nuclear power plant with a combined electrical capacity of 1.5 million kilowatts.

In Tambov Oblast, in addition to an aniline-dye plant opened in 1949 at Kotovsk, south of Tambov, a superphosphate complex opened in 1968 at Uvarovo, in the southeastern part of the oblast. It uses Kola apatite for the production of double superphosphate. Elsewhere in the Central Region south of Moscow, ground phosphate rock is being produced at Shchigry, east of Kursk, with a capacity of 500,000 tons a year, and at Bol'shoye Polpino, near Bryansk, with a capacity of 1.5 million tons a year.

At Kursk, the Soviet Union's first synthetic-fiber mill producing lavsan went into operation in 1960. The production of the polyamide fiber, kapron, was added in 1964–65.

In Smolensk Oblast, a power and chemical complex arose after the mid-1950s in the Safonovo-Dorogobuzh area. The Dorogobuzh steam electric station using coal mined at Safonovo, a western outlier of the Moscow brown-coal basin, went into operation in 1957 at Verkhnedneprovskiy, southeast of Safonovo. In the early 1960s, as the brown-coal industry began to decline, new employment was provided for Safonovo with the construction of a plastics plant, which opened in 1963. A natural-gas pipeline completed in 1965 from the Bryansk gas distribution center to Dorogobuzh provided a new fuel for the power plant and a raw material for ammonia synthesis and a nitrogenous-fertilizer plant that opened in the same year. A 220-kilovolt power transmission line completed in 1964 between the Dorogobuzh and Cherepet' stations linked the Smolensk power system to the Central Russian grid.

In Kalinin Oblast, too, a new power-generating complex has arisen, based on natural gas. The first of eight 300,000-kilowatt units planned for the 2.4-million kilowatt plant at Konakovo went into operation in 1964, the eighth in 1969. The Konakovo station is linked with Moscow by a 750-kilovolt power line, the first AC line of such a high voltage completed in the Soviet Union. In the city of Kalinin, a chemical fiber plant has gone through several technological stages since first opened in the 1930s. The original equipment, producing rayon by the cuprammonium process, was moved during World War II to Kustanay, in northern Kazakhstan. In the postwar period the Kalinin mill used the viscose process, later supplemented by the production of nitron, the Soviet acrylic fiber.

In the sector northeast of Moscow, a chemical plant at Vladimir has long been producing cellulose acetate for acetate rayon plants in the Soviet Union; and an old aniline-dyes plant opposite Kineshma, on the left bank of the Volga River, was set up as a separate city of Zavolzhsk in 1954 (1967 population: 15,000).

At Yaroslavl', a synthetic-rubber and rubber-fabricating complex was supplemented in the early 1960s by a new oil refinery linked by pipeline with the oil fields of the Tatar ASSR (via Gor'kiy). The first atmospheric distillation unit at Yaroslavl' was inaugurated in 1961, followed by thermal cracking in 1962 and catalytic reforming in 1964. A second primary distillation still was added in 1968. Refinery by-product gases are used to produce carbon black at Yaroslavl' since 1962. The original synthetic-rubber plant in the city opened in 1932 and, like others in Central European Russia, used grain alcohol for the manufacture of the butadiene component of butadiene–sodium rubber. With the conversion to petroleum-based synthetic rubber, Yaroslavl' now uses the by-products of its new refinery for rubber production. Both the synthetic rubber and the carbon black are used locally for the manufacture of automobile tires.

The Gor'kiy industrial area also acquired a major oil refinery based on Tatar crude oil, when the first pipeline from Almet'yevsk, center of the Tatar fields, was completed in 1957. The refinery is situated at Kstovo, a new town inaugurated in that year southeast of Gor'kiy, with a population of 43,000 in 1967. The refining complex continued to expand through the 1960s. A third atmospheric distillation unit was inaugurated in 1962 and a catalytic reforming unit in 1965. Hydrogen obtained as a by-product of reforming is used to upgrade the high-sulfur diesel oil through desulfurizing. Such a hydrogen treatment unit opened at the Kstovo refinery in 1965.

The Gor'kiy area includes Dzerzhinsk, one of the Soviet Union's oldest and most diversified chemical centers, with a population of 201,000 in 1967. Dating from World War I and having undergone substantial expansion, Dzerzhinsk produces a wide range of chemical products, including alkalies and chlorine, synthetic resins and plastics materials, all on the basis of long-haul raw materials. The arrival of natural gas from the Stepnoye field near Saratov in the late 1950s further diversified the product range and made it more economical. The new town of Zavolzh'ye, at the Gor'kiy hydro station (1967 population: 26,000), produces engines for the Gor'kiy automobile industry.

In Kirov Oblast, the construction of a large peat-fed power plant east of Kirov in the mid-1950s gave rise to the new town of Kirovo-Chepetsk (1967 population: 43,000) (Fig. 15), and development of a wood-processing industry south of Kirov in the same period is reflected in the new town of Novovyatsk (1967 population: 25,000). Kirov itself has a tire plant dating from 1943. Northeast of Kirov are the upper Vyatka phosphate deposits of Rudnichnyy, at the end of a rail branch opened in 1931. It produces about 300,000 tons of ground phosphate rock (in terms of 19 percent $P_2O_5$).

A major power-generation center was under construction in the late 1960s in Kostroma Oblast. It is situated southeast of the city of Kostroma, on the right bank of the Volga River at the mouth of the Shacha. The new town of Volgorechensk was inaugurated on the site in 1964. The ultimate capacity of the steam electric station, which will burn fuel oil and natural gas, will be 4.8 million kilowatts. The first four 300,000-kilowatt generators were installed in 1969 and 1970; they were to be followed by 500,000-kilowatt units and later perhaps 1.2-million-kilowatt units.

## North European Russia

The northern part of European Russia is characterized by widely separated resource complexes, many of which serve to supply Leningrad's manufacturing industries. Characteristic of the pattern of resource development is the iron and steel center of Cherepovets, which uses iron ore from the Kola Peninsula, 900 miles away, and coking coal from Vorkuta, 1,100 miles distant, to produce pig iron, steel ingots, and rolled steel products for the machine-building industries of Leningrad. Vorkuta also supplies most of the region, including Leningrad, with steam coals. The apatite of the Kola Peninsula is the principal raw-material source for the Soviet Union's superphosphate plants, including one in Leningrad. The Kola Peninsula is also one of the nation's producers of nickel–copper–cobalt ores. The aluminum industry of North European Russia is based on bauxite of Boksitogorsk and increasingly on nephelite, a coproduct of apatite, with alumina production at Boksitogorsk, Pikalevo, and Volkhov, and aluminum production at Volkhov, Nadvoitsy, and Kandalaksha (Fig. 15).

### THE LENINGRAD AREA

Resource development around Leningrad has involved mainly the provision of fuels and energy for the city's industries. Until the late 1950s peat was a major source of energy, with more than 2 million tons of peat a year providing 70 percent of the fuel burned by the area's power stations. The remaining 30 percent were made up by long-haul fuel oil and steam coals. The arrival of natural gas from the North Caucasus in 1959 changed the fuel structure substantially by providing virtually all the fuel used by domestic consumers in the Leningrad metropolitan area and replacing some of the long-haul coal as power station fuel. Among fuels that are expected to lose importance as a result of the availability of the more economical natural gas is the oil shale from four underground mines of the town of Slantsy. Originally developed before World War II, in 1934, oil-shale production was greatly expanded in the 1950s, rising from about 350,000 tons in 1950 to 4.1 million tons in the mid-1960s. Like the Estonian oil shale, of which the Slantsy deposit is an easterly extension (Slantsy means "shales" in Russian), the Slantsy shale is distilled to yield shale gas and chemicals. The gas was piped to Leningrad via a branch joining the pipeline from Kohtla-Järve to Leningrad.

About 50 percent of the electric power is derived from hydroelectric stations. These installations are situated on the Vuoksa River near Svetogorsk on the Finnish border; on the Volkhov River at Volkhov; on the Svir' River at Svir'stroy and Podporozh'ye; and on the Narva River at Narva, on the Estonian border. The Enso and Raukhiala stations at Svetogorsk (the former Enso) on the Vuoksa have a capacity of 100,000 kilowatts each and were acquired from Finland in 1940 together with the Karelian Isthmus. The Volkhov station, one of the first hydroelectric plants of the Soviet Union, went into operation in 1926 with a capacity of 58,000 kilowatts; after reconstruction in 1944, it had eight generating units of 8,000 kilowatts each for a total capacity of 64,000 kilowatts. On the Svir' River, the Lower Svir' station at Svir'stroy went into operation in 1933–35 with a capacity of 100,000 kilowatts and was linked in 1934 to Leningrad by the Soviet Union's first 220-kilovolt power transmission line. The Upper Svir' station, at Podporozh'ye, went into operation in 1952 with a capacity of 160,000 kilowatts. The largest peat-fed power station serving Leningrad proper is the No. 8 station at Kirovsk, on the Neva River, with a capacity of 312,000 kilowatts.

A substantial addition to the energy complex of the area is the new oil refinery of Kirishi, 65 miles southeast of Leningrad, which opened in 1966. It was reached in 1969 by a crude-oil pipeline from the Tatar-Bashkir fields, via Gor'kiy and Yaroslavl'. The refinery's fuel oil is to provide the basis of a large steam electric station, under construction in the late 1960s, with a capacity of about 1.35 million kilowatts. The refinery is also to be linked with Leningrad by a pipeline for refined products. Kirishi was formally inaugurated as a city in 1965, when it had a population of 20,000. It is expected to grow to 50,000 by 1970.

The aluminum industry was originally based on bauxite from Boksitogorsk. The Soviet Union's first alumina and aluminum plant opened at Volkhov in 1932, followed by a second alumina plant at Boksitogorsk in 1938. After World War II, when technology for using nephelite from the Kola Peninsula had been developed, the Volkhov alumina production was converted to the use of nephelite in 1949. A second alumina plant using nephelite was opened in 1959 at Pikalevo, site of limestone deposits required for the nephelite–alumina process. Pikalevo, which became a new city in 1954, had a population of 20,000 in 1967. The bauxite-based alumina plant at Boksitogorsk (1967 population: 22,000) resumed operations in 1953 after its wartime destruction, but its local bauxite reserves, at least those easily accessible, were approaching depletion in the mid-1960s. Attention therefore focused increasingly on the development of a second major bauxite source in Northern European Russia, the so-called North Onega deposits, situated in the northern Onega River valley near Plesetsk (Arkhangel'sk Oblast). The largest and most promising of these deposits, associated with karst limestone and situated near the surface for open-pit operation, is on the Iksa River, a left tributary of the Onega, west of Plesetsk. Development work began in 1968. The North Onega bauxite may be

108

converted into alumina at the Boksitogorsk plant, whose capacity would be made idle by depletion of the local deposit. The alumina-producing facilities of Northern European Russia, including the nephelite-based plants at Volkhov and Pikalevo and the bauxite-based plant at Boksitogorsk, send their output to aluminum-reduction shops at Volkhov; at Nadvoitsy in Karelia (opened in 1954) and at Kandalaksha, in the Kola Peninsula (in operation since 1951). The chemical industry in the area was long concentrated at Leningrad itself. There the Neva superphosphate plant, originally based on phosphate shipments from overseas, was converted to the use of domestic Kola apatite in 1931–32. Leningrad also is a major producer of plastics and synthetic resins (the Okhta chemical plant) and of plastic fabricated articles, of tires and other rubber products (although it has no synthetic-rubber plant of its own), paints and allied products. During the chemical expansion program of the early 1960s, the production of superphosphate was also introduced in 1964 at the aluminum plant of Volkhov, where the fluorine component of Kola apatite was used for the manufacture of synthetic cryolite and aluminum fluoride, needed in the aluminum-reduction process.

A phosphate rock deposit at Kingisepp, containing ore with an average of 6 to 7 percent $P_2O_5$, was mined on a commercial scale beginning in 1963. Though of low grade, the ore can be easily upgraded to a 32-percent $P_2O_5$ phosphate by beneficiation. The Kingisepp installation, known as Fosforit (phosphorite), consists of two beneficiation plants, each with a capacity of 840,000 tons of ground phosphate rock (in terms of the standard 19 percent $P_2O_5$ content). The first plant was opened in December, 1963, and the second in June, 1965. In the late 1960s they were producing about 1.6 million tons of standard phosphate rock. The beneficiated product of the Kingisepp mine (with 32 percent $P_2O_5$) is of sufficiently high grade to be used in the manufacture of superphosphate in combination with apatite concentrate from the Kola Peninsula.

Another chemical complex, based on the newly available natural gas, is an ammonia-synthesis plant under construction in the late 1960s at Novgorod, an ancient city served by the natural-gas pipeline from the Northern Caucasus to Leningrad. The plant opened in 1967 with completion of a methanol (methyl alcohol) unit. It completed ammonia and urea installations in 1969. The industrial

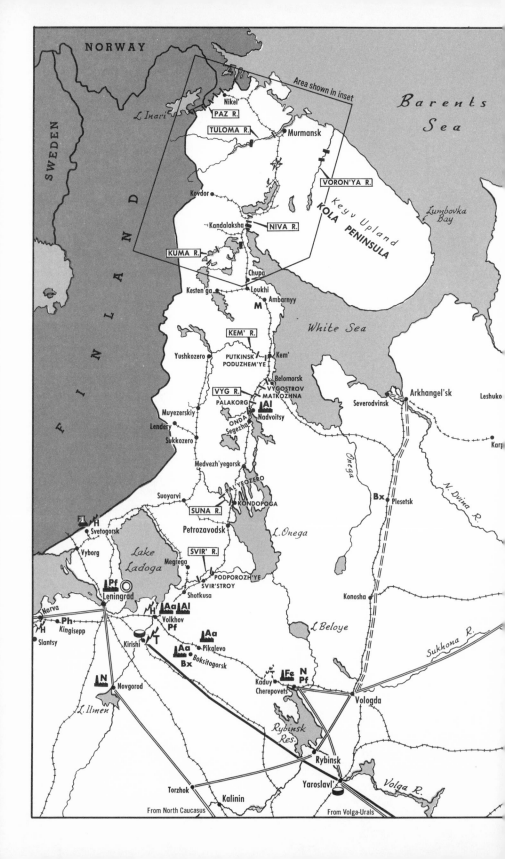

NORWAY

*L. Inari*

SWEDEN

FINLAND

Nikel'

**PAZ R.**

**TULOMA R.**

Murmansk

Kovdor

Kandalaksha

**NIVA R.**

**KUMA R.**

Chupa

Kesten'ga

Loukhi

Ambarnyy

M

*White Sea*

**KEM' R.**

Yushkozero

PUTKINSK
PODUZHEM'YE

Kem'

Belomorsk

**VYG R.**

VYGOSTROV
MATKOZHNA

PALAKORG

Al

Muyezerskiy

ONDA
Segezha

Nadvoitsy

Lendery

Sukkozero

Medvezh'yegorsk

Suoyarvi

L. YEOZERO

KONDOPOGA

**SUNA R.**

Petrozavodsk

*L. Onega*

Svetogorsk

H

*Lake
Ladoga*

Vyborg

Megrega

**SVIR' R.**

PODPOROZH'YE
SVIR'STROY

Pf

Leningrad

Shotkusa

Narva

Ph

H

Kingisepp

H

Volkhov

Aa

Al

Pf

T

Slantsy

Kirishi

Aa

Pikalevo

Aa

Bx

Boksitogorsk

N

Novgorod

*L. Ilmen*

Kaduy

Fe

N

Pf

Cherepovets

*L. Beloye*

Konosha

Vologda

Torzhok

Kalinin

From North Caucasus

*Rybinsk
Res.*

Rybinsk

Yaroslavl'

*Volga R.*

From Volga-Urals

*Barents
Sea*

VORON'YA R.

*Keyv Upland*
**KOLA PENINSULA**

*Lumbovka
Bay*

Area shown in inset

Arkhangel'sk

Leshuko

Severodvinsk

Karp

*Onega*

Bx

Plesetsk

*N. Dvina R.*

*Sukhona R.*

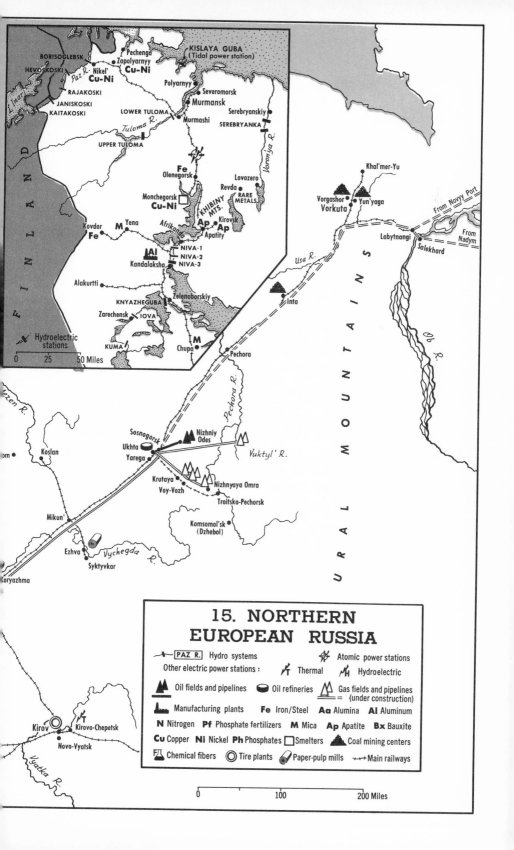

# 15. NORTHERN EUROPEAN RUSSIA

**Legend:**

- ⊢ PAZ R. Hydro systems
- Other electric power stations:
- ⚡ Atomic power stations
- ⟟T Thermal
- ⟟H Hydroelectric
- ▲ Oil fields and pipelines
- ● Oil refineries
- △ Gas fields and pipelines (under construction)
- ▲ Manufacturing plants
- **Fe** Iron/Steel
- **Aa** Alumina
- **Al** Aluminum
- **N** Nitrogen
- **Pf** Phosphate fertilizers
- **M** Mica
- **Ap** Apatite
- **Bx** Bauxite
- **Cu** Copper
- **Ni** Nickel
- **Ph** Phosphates
- ☐ Smelters
- ▲ Coal mining centers
- ⚗ Chemical fibers
- ◎ Tire plants
- ⬭ Paper-pulp mills
- ⊢⊢⊢ Main railways

**Map labels (upper inset):**

KISLAYA GUBA (Tidal power station)
BORISOGLEBSK
Pechenga
Zapolyarnyy **Cu-Ni**
HEVOSKOSKI
Nikel' **Cu-Ni**
Paz R.
L. Inari
RAJAKOSKI
JANISKOSKI
KAITAKOSKI
Polyarnyy
Severomorsk
Murmansk
Severomorsk
Serebryanskiy
LOWER TULOMA
Murmashi
SEREBRYANKA
Tuloma R.
Voronya R.
UPPER TULOMA
**Fe** Olenegorsk
Lovozero
Revda
RARE METALS
Khal'mer-Yu
Monchegorsk **Cu-Ni**
KHIBINY MTS.
**Ap** Kirovsk
Vorgashor
Yun'yaga
Vorkuta
Kovdor **Fe**
**M** Yena
Afrikanda
**Ap** Apatity
Labytnangi
Salekhard
From Novyy Port
From Nadym
**Al**
NIVA-1
NIVA-2
NIVA-3
Kandalaksha
Usa R.
Alakurtti
Zelenoborskiy
Inta
KNYAZHEGUBA
Zarechensk
IOVA
Ob R.
**M**
KUMA
Chupa
Pechora

Hydroelectric stations
0   25   50 Miles

FINLAND

**Map labels (lower/main):**

Mezen R.
Koslan
Sosnogorsk
Nizhniy Odes
Ukhta
Yarega
Vuktyl' R.
URAL MOUNTAINS
Krutaya
Voy-Vozh
Nizhnyaya Omra
Troitsko-Pechorsk
Mikun'
Komsomol'sk (Dzhebol)
Ezhva
Vychegda R.
Syktyvkar
Koryazhma
Kirov
Kirovo-Chepetsk
Novo-Vyatsk
Vyatka R.

0   100   200 Miles

expansion associated with the chemical complex raised Novgorod's population from 60,000 in 1959 to 107,000 in 1967.

## KARELIA

In Karelia, resource development has mainly involved the construction of hydroelectric stations on the republic's rapid-strewn rivers along which a large number of lakes serve as natural reservoirs. Power stations, with a total generating capacity of 600,000 kilowatts, fall into three clusters or systems: the Suna River system, in the south, around Kondopoga; the Vyg River system, in the center, between Segezha and Belomorsk; and the Kem' River system, in the north.

The stations of the Suna system, including the 28,000-kilowatt Kondopoga station (opened in 1928) and the 22,000-kilowatt Pal'yeozero station (opened in 1954), serve the Kondopoga–Petrozavodsk area, linked since 1959 with the Leningrad power grid via the Svir' River system. The Vyg system, with a total capacity of 230,000 kilowatts, was built since the mid-1950s. Its five stations include the 80,000-kilowatt Onda station at Kamennyy Bor, completed in 1956, and the 60,000-kilowatt Matkozhna station, opened in 1953, which provides power to the nearby Nadvoitsy aluminum reduction plant. The Vyg power system was connected with the Suna and Svir' grids in 1965 by a 220-kilovolt line. The newest series of hydroelectric stations was under construction in the late 1960s on the Kem' River, where five stations are planned to have a total capacity of 250,000 kilowatts. The first in the series, the 84,000-kilowatt Putkinsk station, went into operation in 1967, followed by the construction of the 45,000-kilowatt Poduzhem'ye station at the Vochazh rapids above the town of Kem'.

On the northern border of Karelia, with Murmansk Oblast, the Kovda-Kuma system, consisting of three stations with a total capacity of 300,000 kilowatts, serves both Murmansk Oblast and adjoining parts of Karelia where muscovite sheet mica is recovered from pegmatite deposits. The pegmatite district, with mining centers at Chupa and Ambarnyy, also yields quartz crystal and ceramic-grade feldspar.

Expansion of the timber industry has been associated with the construction of the West Karelian Railroad, running north of

Suoyarvi parallel to the Leningrad–Murmansk line. Work on the railroad began in the mid-1950s, and the first 125-mile-long line, via Sukkozero to Lendery, was completed in 1959. An additional 120-mile-long section, running northward from Sukkozero via Muyezerskiy to Yushkozero, went into operation in 1964.

## THE KOLA PENINSULA

Like Karelia, the Kola Peninsula, which is coextensive with Murmansk Oblast, depends largely on hydroelectric power for its industrial energy. Hydroelectric stations generated about 70 percent of the total electricity output of 6 billion kilowatt-hours in the mid-1960s, with the principal power systems on the Kovda River, on the border with Karelia; on the Niva River, which flows south out of Lake Imandra to the White Sea at Kandalaksha; on the Tuloma River, flowing northeast to Murmansk Bay; and on the Paz River, the outlet of Lake Inari on the border between the Soviet Union and Finland and Norway.

The first unit on the Kovda River was the Knyazheguba hydroelectric station, opened in 1955–56, with four generators totaling more than 100,000 kilowatts. The town of Zelenoborskiy developed at the station site. The second plant, the 80,000-kilowatt Iova station, went into operation in 1960–61 at the new settlement of Zarechensk. The third station in this series, the Kuma station, situated across the border in Karelia, opened in 1962–63.

Of the three stations on the Niva River, the first to be put into operation was the Niva-2 plant, with a capacity of 60,000 kilowatts, installed in 1934–38. The plant was rebuilt after World War II, and the Niva-3 station, with a capacity of 150,000 kilowatts, was completed in 1949. Three years later the Niva series was finished with the construction of the smaller Niva-1 station (26,000 kilowatts). The Niva system provided electric power for the early electrification of the Murmansk–Kandalaksha railroad, the industrial development of the apatite center of Kirovsk, and the aluminum reduction plant that opened in 1951 at Kandalaksha. Construction on this aluminum plant began in 1939, was interrupted by World War II, and resumed in 1949. Four reduction shops, placed in operation between 1951 and 1953, process nephelite-based alumina from Volkhov and, since 1959, from Pikalevo.

The Tuloma hydroelectric system consists of two stations: the 37,500-kilowatt Lower Tuloma station, inaugurated in 1937 at Murmashi, and the 228,000-kilowatt Upper Tuloma station, opened in 1964–65 at the outlet of Lake Notozero. The Upper Tuloma plant, consisting of four 57,000-kilowatt units, was built by a Finnish concern.

Finnish and Norwegian workers also constructed a series of smaller stations along the boundary stream known as Paz in Russian, Patsjoki in Finnish, and Pasvik in Norwegian. The three stations along the Finnish border are: the 30,000-kilowatt station at Yaniskoski (Janiskoski), opened in 1950–51; the 40,000-kilowatt station at Rayakoski (Rajakoski), in 1955; and the 11,000-kilowatt station at Kaytakoski (Kaitakoski), in 1959. A larger station on the Norwegian part of the river, the 52,000-kilowatt Borisoglebsk station, went into operation in 1963. Work was under way in the late 1960s on the 45,000-kilowatt station of Khevoskoski (Hevoskoski), between the Borisoglebsk and Rayakoski installations. Another major hydroelectric project, on which work began in 1960, involves the construction of two stations, Serebryanka I and Serebryanka II, each with a capacity of more than 100,000 kilowatts, on the Voron'ya River, which flows north from Lake Lovozero to the Barents Sea, 60 miles east of Murmansk. When completed in the 1970s the Serebryanka stations may provide the electric power for development of remote mineral deposits in the interior of the Kola Peninsula. They include, in particular, vast deposits of kyanite in the Keyv uplands, the principal east-west watershed of the peninsula. Kyanite, an aluminum silicate, is widely used in the manufacture of high-alumina refractories and represents a potential raw material for the production of aluminum and aluminum alloys through electrothermal reduction.

In view of the approaching exhaustion of potential hydroelectric sites in the Kola Peninsula and the absence of local mineral fuels, other types of energy are being developed in the area. The peninsula has been selected for the construction of one of the 880,000-kilowatt central nuclear power stations of the pressurized water type, adopted as a standard in Soviet atomic energy development on the basis of the performance of the Novovoronezhskiy station. The Kola nuclear power station will have two 440,000-kilowatt reactors, each operating two 220,000-kilowatt generators. The station, under construction south of Murmansk, will help raise the electrical generating capacity of the Kola Peninsula from about 1.5 million kilowatts in the late 1960s to 2.5 million kilowatts sometime in the 1970s.

The Kola Peninsula has also been selected for Soviet experimentation and development of tidal power. An experimental installation went into construction in 1962 in a fjord-like inlet known as Kislaya Guba, near the fishing port of Port Vladimir. The first of two 400-kilowatt generators went into operation at the station at the end of 1968. If its performance justifies the use of tidal stations, the Soviet Union is expected to proceed next with a 320,000-kilowatt station at Lumbovka Bay, on the north shore of the Kola Peninsula, 200 miles southeast of Murmansk.

The earliest development of mineral resources was the exploitation of the rich apatite deposits in the Khibiny Mountains. There, large reserves of apatite, a calcium phosphate that serves as the principal raw material for the Soviet Union's superphosphate industry, are associated with nephelite, a complex sodium–potassium–aluminum silicate that yields alumina, potash, and soda.

Apatite mining began in 1930 after a 14-mile-long spur had been laid from the rail junction of Apatity, on the Leningrad–Murmansk railroad, to the future mining town of Kirovsk. A concentrator opened at Kirovsk in 1931 (with a second stage added in 1934) converted the raw ore, containing 20 to 25 percent $P_2O_5$, into an apatite concentrate of 39.5 percent phosphorus pentoxide. The nephelite, containing 20 to 30 percent alumina, was at first discarded in tailings, but was increasingly used after World War II when the first plant for the conversion of nephelite concentrate into alumina went into operation in 1949 at Volkhov. At first, the ore was mined mainly underground at Kukisvumchorr, just north of Kirovsk, and by 1939 the Kirovsk apatite complex converted 2.5 million tons of raw ore into 1.5 million tons of apatite concentrate. In the 1950s, after the prewar production level had been restored, output more than doubled, partly as a result of the opening in 1954 of a new deposit near Kirovsk known as Yukspor. By 1960 the Kirovsk complex was mining 8.5 million tons of crude ore, which yielded 3.8 million tons of apatite concentrate at ANOF-1, as the first apatite–nephelite beneficiation factory was known by its Russian initials.

Meanwhile, in the late 1950s, the development of a second mining and beneficiation complex began nearer the rail junction of Apatity, to the west of Kirovsk. It included the Rasvumchorr deposit, which in contrast to the Kirovsk complex was exploited through surface mines, and a second concentrator, the ANOF-2. A new urban center developed, first designated informally as Novyy Gorod (new town), later officially as Molodezhnyy (youth town, for its youthful population). In addition to the apatite concentrator, the new center also included the large Kirovsk steam electric station, which burns Pechora long-haul steam coals and generates several hundred thousand kilowatts of electric power, and the science research institutes of the Kola branch of the Soviet Academy of Sciences. Officially inaugurated in 1959, Molodezhnyy and Apatity (situated just to the southwest) were combined in 1966 into the new enlarged city of Apatity, with a population of 38,000. The older Kirovsk had a population of 46,000 by this time. The ANOF-2 concentrator went into operation in 1963, and within two years reached a capacity of 11 million tons of crude ore and 5 million tons of apatite concentrate. In the mid-1960s all the mines and the two concentrating plants of the Kirovsk–Apatity area produced about 18 million tons of crude ore, half from surface mines, and about 8 million tons of apatite concentrate.

About half of the total apatite output (4.5 million tons in 1967) was exported, much of it through the port of Murmansk. The other half, representing 75 percent of the Soviet Union's phosphatic raw material consumption, moved south by rail and waterway to nearly all the superphosphate plants of the country. In the late 1960s a mechanized rail–water transshipment port was under development at Perguba, just south of Medvezh'yegorsk in Karelia, to modernize the transfer of apatite and nephelite shipments from the railroad to the White Sea–Baltic waterway. The transshipment port is expected to reduce transport costs by shifting an increasing share of apatite and nephelite hauls to waterways. Nephelite shipments, in particular, are expected to increase in conjunction with plans of constructing nephelite-based alumina plants elsewhere in European Russia, for example, in the Ul'yanovsk area and elsewhere along the Volga River, where the limestone required for the nephelite–alumina process is available.

While the Kola Peninsula is primarily a raw material producer when it comes to apatite and nephelite, the area's nickel–cobalt–copper industry represents an integrated system from mining to the output of finished metals.

The complete cycle is represented by the Severonikel' (Northern Nickel) smelter and refinery opened in 1938 at Monchegorsk near a mine that has since become largely depleted. The smelter was dismantled at the onset of the German invasion of the Soviet Union in 1941, and its equipment was used in part to construct the smelter at Noril'sk in northern Siberia. But the Monchegorsk complex was rebuilt and expanded after the war and is one of the Soviet Union's principal nickel producers. In addition to cobalt and copper, it yields gold, silver, the platinum-group metals, tellurium, and selenium. The second nickel complex, Pechenganikel' at the town of Nikel', was acquired from Finland at the end of World War II with the annexation of the Pechenga district. The Pechenga complex, whose mine is also approaching depletion, does not have a complete metallurgical cycle. Its end-product is a matte, an intermediate material that is then sent to Monchegorsk for further refining. The exhaustion of the Monchegorsk and Pechenga deposits led to further exploration and the discovery and development of a third nickel complex at the Zhdanov deposit, east of the town of Nikel'. The development of the new deposit, where the town of Zapolyarnyy arose, was facilitated by the construction of a 115-mile-long railroad (opened in 1960) linking the Pechenga district with the Murmansk main line. The Zhdanov mine and concentrator began operations in 1965. Its end-product is a pelletized concentrate that is shipped to Monchegorsk for further processing. Some of the Zhdanov pellets are converted into matte at the Pechenga smelter before going on to Monchegorsk for electrolytic refining. As the center of the nickel industry of the Kola Peninsula, Monchegorsk had a population of 53,000 in 1967.

The development of an iron ore base supplying the new iron and steel complex at Cherepovets (Vologda Oblast) began in the mid-1950s. It involved the joint use of iron ore from two deposits, Olenegorsk, which yields an acidic ore, and Kovdor, whose basic ore helps to neutralize the Olenegorsk ore. Both ores have an average iron content of 31 percent and are beneficiated to a concentrate of about 62 percent iron. The optimal mixture in the Cherepovets blast furnaces is one-third Kovdor ore and two-thirds Olenegorsk ore. The Olenegorsk mine and concentrator opened in 1955, together with completion of the first blast furnace at Cherepovets, but the development of the Kovdor complex lagged and its operation did not begin until 1962. The exclusive use of Olenegorsk ore in the first few years required large inputs of limestone at Cherepovets raising costs and reducing blast furnace efficiency until the Kovdor basic ore became available. In the mid-1960s, Olenegorsk converted 8.5 million tons of crude ore to 3.5 million tons of concentrate, and Kovdor converted 6 million tons of crude ore to 2.4 million tons of concentrate. Some of the Olenegorsk ore was being exported because of its proximity to the port of Murmansk. While the location of the Olenegorsk iron ore mine near the Murmansk main line required the construction of only a short rail spur, a 70-mile-long railroad had to be constructed to open up the Kovdor deposit. In 1967 Olenegorsk had a population of 20,000 and Kovdor about 15,000.

The Kovdor district opens prospects for the development of minerals other than iron ore. Kovdor ore also contains apatite and baddeleyite (zirconium oxide), which were at first discarded as tailings. However, a pilot plant opened in 1965 to extract apatite and baddeleyite concentrates from the tailings. A few miles from the Kovdor iron mine is the Soviet Union's largest deposit of vermiculite, a mica-like mineral that has the unusual property of swelling to as much as 20 times its original volume when heated. Though widely used in the United States, mainly as an insulating and fire-resistant building material, vermiculite is little known in the Soviet Union. A pilot beneficiation plant with a capacity of 3,500 tons opened at Kovdor in 1964, and a larger mill with a capacity of 56,000 tons of concentrate was under construction in the late 1960s. Fire resistant asbestos-vermiculite products were being manufactured at the mica-processing factory of Kolpino, the southeast suburb of Leningrad.

Mica, too, is mined in the Kovdor district. Associated with the vermiculite is a type of mica known as phlogopite, with uses in the electronic and electrical industries. Another type, muscovite, has been mined since the 1930s at Yena, on the railroad east of Kovdor. The muscovite mica is found in feldspar-bearing pegmatite dikes capable of yielding a potash feldspar, used as flux in making glasses and fine ceramic products. An open-pit mine and a crushing and concentrating plant for feldspar were under construction in the late 1960s. The pegmatite dikes may also contain minerals of such valuable metals as beryllium, columbium and tantalum.

One of the Soviet Union's principal commercial deposits of columbium and tantalum, associated with rare earths of the cerium group, is operated in the Lovozero complex of alkaline rocks, east of the apatite-producing area of Kirovsk. Mining of the columbium–tantalum mineral, known as loparite, began on a commercial scale in 1951 at the newly established mining town of Revda, on the north side of the Lovozero massif. Concentrates from the Revda mill move by highway to the railroad station of Olenegorsk on the main Murmansk line.

Columbium is also associated with titanomagnetites at the Afrikanda deposit, west of Apatity. An attempt was made in the 1950s to develop the deposit. A concentrator went into operation at Afrikanda in 1957 but, because of technological problems, had to be converted to the processing of nickel sulfide ores the following year.

### KOMI ASSR

Two major resource complexes, both involving the production of fuels, stand out in the Komi ASSR. They are the bituminous coal basin in the valley of the Usa River, a tributary of the Pechora, and oil and natural-gas deposits in the Ukhta area.

Mining at Vorkuta, within the Arctic Circle, began on a small scale in 1934, but large-scale operations had to await the construction of the Pechora railroad, which was completed provisionally in 1941 on the eve of the Soviet Union's entry into World War II. (Permanent operation did not begin until 1950.) During the war, the Pechora coal basin played an important role in supplying northern European Russia, as output rose to 3.3 million tons by 1945. The basin was further expanded during the postwar period as a source of steam coal for Leningrad, Arkhangel'sk, Murmansk, and other industrial centers of the region, reaching 14.2 million tons by 1955.

Since the opening of the iron and steel plant at Cherepovets in that year, production of the Pechora basin has leveled off at about 17 to 18 million tons a year, as new mine construction was limited to coking coals and many uneconomical shafts were closed. Among new coking coal mines opened in the basin were Khal'mer-Yu, 35 miles northeast of Vorkuta, where a mine with an annual capacity of 600,000 tons began operations in 1957, and Yun'yaga, just northeast of Vorkuta, where a 1.2-million-ton mine opened in 1964. Although the 12 million tons of coal produced in 1965 by the eighteen underground mines of the Vorkuta area were of coking quality, only about 5 million tons were actually used for coking purposes at the Cherepovets mill. The rest of the coking-grade coal, as well as 6 million tons of steam coals produced by seven mines in the Inta area of the Pechora basin, were used for power generation in Northern European Russia. Significant expansion of the coking coal production in the Vorkuta area appears to be hampered by the high cost of mining under sub-Arctic conditions and the absence of a direct rail outlet to the iron and steel industry of the Urals. The most promising deposit for expansion is the Vorgashor deposit, 10 miles northwest of Vorkuta, where a mine with a capacity of 4.5 million tons was under construction in the late 1960s.

The population of the city of Vorkuta proper was 65,000 in 1967, but the entire urban district, including suburban mining settlements, had a population of 150,000. Inta had a population of 51,000 in 1967. A new mine with a capacity of 1.5 million tons of steam coals was inaugurated at Inta in 1965, but in general its development is leveling off because of the absence of coking coal in its deposit.

The history of the oil and natural-gas deposits of the Ukhta area goes back to 1929 when drilling first uncovered commercial quantities of both fuels. However, as in the case of Pechora coal, the development effort began only during World War II. During the 1950s crude-oil production in the Ukhta area was less than 1 million tons, including an unusually heavy, viscous crude oil (now nearing depletion), mined at Yarega, southwest of Ukhta, and lighter crude oils associated with the natural-gas deposits. Both the heavy crude oil, which yielded low-temperature lubricants and asphalt, and the lighter crude oil were processed at a small refinery built in Ukhta in 1947–49. After the discovery in 1959 of a larger oil deposit in the West Tebuk area, 40 miles east of Ukhta, production rose from 1.1 million tons in 1960 to 2.2 million in 1965. In the mid-1960s, Ukhta crude oil began to move by rail to the newly completed refineries of Kirishi, near Leningrad, and Ryazan'. A production goal of 6 million tons was set for 1970, mainly from the West Tebuk deposit, where the oil town of Nizhniy Odes (Lower Odes) was inaugurated in 1964. A crude-oil pipeline from Ukhta to the Yaroslavl' refinery is planned for the early 1970s.

Similarly, the natural-gas industry of Ukhta, long of local importance, was undergoing major expansion in the late 1960s. Beginning in World War II, natural gas produced in the area of Krutaya and Voy-Vozh, in the upper reaches of the Izhma River, 35 miles southeast of Ukhta, was used for the production of carbon black at small furnaces in the gas fields. The carbon-black industry was expanded in the 1950s with the construction of more modern installations at Sosnogorsk (called Izhma until 1957; 1967 population: 23,000), just northeast of Ukhta on the railroad. Some of the natural-gas deposits discovered in the area in the late 1940s and early 1950s, such as the deposits around Nizhnyaya Omra, were found to be helium-bearing. Helium was beginning to be in demand as a pressuring agent in liquid-fueled missiles and space vehicles and was probably recovered from these Komi fields in gas liquefaction plants. Almost all the natural-gas production, fluctuating around 1 billion cubic meters a year in the 1950s, was used for the manufacture of carbon black, and the Komi ASSR accounted for about 40,000 tons, or half of the Soviet Union's total production of carbon black. Since then the expansion of the natural-gas industry elsewhere and the construction of additional carbon-black plants has reduced the Komi share.

The discovery of what was thought to be a major gas deposit in 1956 at Dzhebol, on the Pechora River south of the mouth of the Ilych, led to plans for the construction of a pipeline south to the Berezniki-Perm' area of the southern Urals. However, subsequent exploration of the deposit showed that earlier reserve estimates had been exaggerated and the project was abandoned. A road still leads southward from Troitsko-Pechorsk to a place called Komsomol'sk-on-the-Pechora, which was to have been the new center of the Dzhebol gas field.

It was not until the mid-1960s that a deposit with gas reserves large enough to justify long-distance transmission was discovered in the Ukhta area. This is the Vuktyl deposit, on the Vuktyl River, a small right tributary of the Pechora, 115 miles east of Ukhta. A 40-inch pipeline to Ukhta, opened in 1968, feeds into a 48-inch trunk system running from Ukhta through Kotlas and Rybinsk to Torzhok, a gas-distribution center on the Moscow-Leningrad pipeline system. The Ukhta-Torzhok pipeline, completed in 1969, is to be part of a trunk system feeding natural gas from major fields in northwest Siberia to European Russia. The development of the Vuktyl deposit is expected to raise natural-gas production in the Komi ASSR from its 1965 level of 0.6 billion cubic meters to a level of 8 to 10 billion by 1970.

The Ukhta area is also a potential producer of high-grade titanium ore. A deposit of titanium-bearing minerals has been discovered in Middle Devonian sandstones just below the depleted viscous petroleum deposit of Yarega. The titanium deposit, consisting mainly of leucoxene, could be tapped through the three mines already built to extract the Yarega oil. An experimental concentrator operated in 1963–64 converted the Yarega titanium ore into a high-grade concentrate containing 80 percent titanium oxide. Such a high-grade product could be used for the manufacture of pigment and metal without going through the usual intermediate titanium slag stage required of lower-grade concentrates.

Electric power output in the Komi ASSR has been limited to heat and power stations at Vorkuta and Ukhta, burning Vorkuta coal. The water-power potential of the Pechora and Vychegda rivers has not been utilized. However, plans were made in the late 1960s for the construction of a 1.5-million kilowatt hydroelectric station at Ust'-Izhma, on the Pechora River at the mouth of the Izhma, a left tributary. There was also a proposal for a 1.2-million kilowatt steam electric station at the town of Pechora.

A basic industry of national significance is the timber industry, reflected in new railroad construction and the building of one of the Soviet Union's major wood-processing complexes. In 1966 a railroad was completed between Mikun' and Koslan, opening up untapped timber reserves in the upper reaches of the Mezen' River. It is to be extended to Yertom. The same area is being approached from the major timber port of Arkhangel'sk by a railroad under construction in the late 1960s to Karpogory and Leshukonskoye. New timber stands are also to be made accessible by the construction of a railroad between Ukhta and Troitsko-Pechersk, which will at the same time serve the natural-gas fields along the way. Not directly related to the timber industry were a railroad spur completed in 1950 between the Vorkuta area and the lower reaches of the Ob' at Labytnangi, opposite Salekhard, and a branch, opened in 1960, connecting Syktyvkar, the Komi capital, to the main Pechora line. It is at Ezhva, a northern suburb of Syktyvkar, that a major timber-processing complex went into operation in 1968–69 with its first wood pulp and paperboard. It will process 2.5 million tons of wood a year and yield a wide range of products, including plywood, pressboard, and printing paper. A similar complex, a large pulp and paper mill, also opened in 1961 at Koryazhma, east of Kotlas, in adjoining Arkhangel'sk Oblast.

CHEREPOVETS COMPLEX

One of the elements giving territorial unity to the resources of North European Russia is the iron and steel complex of Cherepovets, where a major chemical industry was being added in the late 1960s. Cherepovets was selected after World War II as the site of a steel industry that would use Kola iron ore, Vorkuta coking coal, and Leningrad scrap metal to produce the steel products for Leningrad's large engineering industry. Operating practice showed that the long hauls required for Kola iron ore (900 miles) and Vorkuta coal (1,100 miles) raised the cost of pig iron at Cherepovets substantially above the cost at other Soviet iron and steel plants, situated nearer coal or iron ore sources. However, the production of steel ingots and rolled products was considered to be more economical in view of the availability of large amounts of scrap metal.

Ground for the complex was broken in 1949 and the first blast furnace began operations in 1955, followed the next year by No. 2. Steel production began in 1958 with the completion of the first open-hearth furnaces. A third and larger blast furnace, with a working volume of 70,000 cubic feet and an annual capacity of 1.5 million tons, was added in 1962, and a still larger furnace, with a

123

working volume of 95,000 cubic feet and a capacity of 1.7 million tons, was completed in 1969. In the mid-1960s, the first three blast furnaces produced about 3 million tons of pig iron a year.

In the first ten years of operation, the chemical component of the Cherepovets complex was limited to ammonia synthesis from coke-oven gases and the production of ammonium sulfate fertilizer. Natural gas became available in 1961 by completion of a pipeline from the Stepnoye field near Saratov via Gor'kiy and Ivanovo, but the gas was used primarily as a fuel in blast furnaces and open-hearth furnaces to reduce coke requirements. However, with the prospects of greater availability of natural gas at Cherepovets, particularly from the newly discovered Vuktyl field near Ukhta and the large reserves in northwest Siberia, construction was under way in the late 1960s on a major nitrogenous fertilizer complex that could derive hydrogen for ammonia synthesis from natural gas. Cherepovets has also been selected as the site of a double-superphosphate plant, producing high-analysis fertilizers from Kola apatite. The potentialities of recovering sulfur from natural gas for the manufacture of sulfuric acid may have been a factor in the site selection.

As a result of the development of the iron and steel industry, the population of Cherepovets rose from its prewar level of 32,000 to 92,000 in 1959 and 165,000 by 1967. Further increases can be expected as a result of the construction of chemical enterprises. The growing industries are to be supplied with additional power by a 1.2-million-kilowatt peat-fueled electric station under construction in the late 1960s on the Suda River near Kaduy, 25 miles west of Cherepovets. The start of operation was planned for 1971.

## The Volga Region

The Volga region, which in this discussion includes the Volga valley south of Kazan' and the lower reaches of the Kama River, is the Soviet Union's principal oil-producing province, with a total output of 174 million tons in 1965, or 72 percent of the Soviet total. Three of the Volga's political subdivisions—the Tatar ASSR, Bashkir ASSR, and Kuybyshev Oblast—have since the late 1950s outdistanced the output of the Baku fields, which had been the leading producer in the Soviet Union until 1956. The region has relatively small reserves of dry gas, but produces substantial amounts of gas as a by-product of oil reservoirs.

A significant aspect of resource development along the Volga has been the construction of some of the Soviet Union's largest hydro-electric stations, notably at Togliatti (formerly Stavropol'), near Kuybyshev, and at Volzhskiy, near Volgograd (formerly Stalingrad). The hydroelectric stations, besides transmitting surplus power to Moscow and the Urals, have attracted energy-oriented industries such as aluminum and chemicals, while the development of oil and gas resources has given rise to an important petrochemical industry in the region (Fig. 16).

### BASHKIR ASSR

The first oil was found in the region in commercial quantities in 1932 at Ishimbay, and a small oil refinery began operations there in 1936. While the centers of crude-oil production shifted repeatedly within the republic as old deposits were depleted and new fields went into operation, Ishimbay became the core of the refining and petrochemical complex of Sterlitamak–Ishimbay–Salavat in the 1950s. The development of crude-oil output at Ishimbay was followed by the discovery of oil at Tuymazy in 1937. The growth of production led to the construction of a second refinery, which opened in 1938 at Ufa, the republic's capital. By 1940, Bashkiria produced 1.5 million tons of crude oil a year.

Intensive exploration for oil during World War II led to the expansion of the Tuymazy field, where the new oil city of Oktyabr'-skiy was founded in 1946. The area boomed in the 1950s as the population of Oktyabr'skiy grew to 75,000 and crude-oil output in the Bashkir republic rose from 5.8 million tons in 1950 to 23.4 million tons in 1958. About 60 percent of the total production was contributed by the Tuymazy–Oktyabr'skiy area.

The increased production of natural gas associated with the oil output led to the construction of a natural-gasoline plant (opened in 1954) and a carbon-black plant at Tuymazy. To process the increasing flow of crude oil, the Ishimbay refinery had been expanded in 1945 and a second refinery, the Novo-Ufa (New Ufa) refinery, was opened in the republic's capital in 1957. Gas from the Tuymazy field was also used to fuel a newly built power station at Urussu, just across the border in the Tatar ASSR.

Crude oil production declined in the Tuymazy field after the late 1950s, and industry at Oktyabr'skiy shifted to the manufacture of consumer goods (apparel, footwear, china) to provide employment as the population remained at the 70,000 to 80,000 level.

Meanwhile the center of oil production shifted to progressively newer areas. In 1954–55, oil was struck in the Belebey–Aksakovo field, 50 miles south of Tuymazy. Natural-gas reserves at Shkapovo, south of Aksakovo, were deemed sufficiently large to warrant construction of pipelines to Tuymazy, for the production of carbon black, and to Magnitogorsk, for use in the iron and steel plant. A natural-gasoline plant was opened at Shkapovo itself in 1961. The Belebey area boomed in the late 1950s, replacing the Tuymazy area as the leading oil producer in the Bashkir ASSR.

In the early 1960s, the center of production shifted once again, this time to the Arlan area in the northwest, where the oil town of Neftekamsk (1967 population: 30,000) arose. The Arlan area, which adjoins the new producing fields in the southern part of Perm' Oblast, was linked by pipelines with Ufa and Salavat, a new petrochemical center. In the late 1960s the Arlan field accounted for a fourth of Bashkiria's total oil production, which in 1965 was 43.5 million tons and in 1967 47.8 million tons. The 1970 plan was 49 million tons. A 2.4-million kilowatt electric power station, designed to burn high-sulfur fuel oil from the Bashkir deposits, was under construction in the late 1960s at Karmanovo, on the Buy River, 15 miles northeast of Neftekamsk. The first of the planned eight 300,000-kilowatt generating units went into operation in 1968. Continuing exploration in the central section of Bashkiria uncovered new productive fields at Chekmagush, 50 miles northwest of Ufa, and in the immediate vicinity of Ufa itself.

In the late 1960s, crude oil development began in the southeast Udmurt ASSR, just across the Kama River from Bashkiria's Arlan-Neftekamsk oil field. The first Udmurt producing area, at Arkhangel'skoye, was scheduled to yield 100,000 tons in 1969.

As noted earlier, refining and petrochemical industries are concentrated at Ufa (1968 population: 724,000), and in the Sterlitamak–

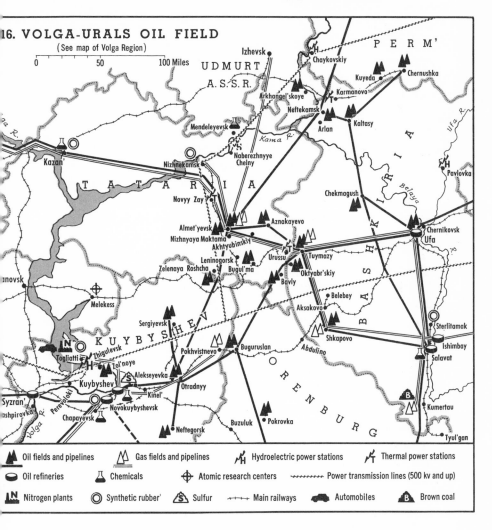

## 16. VOLGA-URALS OIL FIELD
(See map of Volga Region)

| Legend | | | |
|---|---|---|---|
| Oil fields and pipelines | Gas fields and pipelines | Hydroelectric power stations | Thermal power stations |
| Oil refineries | Chemicals | Atomic research centers | Power transmission lines (500 kv and up) |
| Nitrogen plants | Synthetic rubber' | Sulfur | Main railways · Automobiles · Brown coal |

Ishimbay–Salavat complex. The refining industry of Ufa is situated in the northeastern part of the city, where the independent urban entity of Chernikovsk existed from 1944 to 1956 before being reincorporated into Ufa. In addition to two refineries, opened in 1938 and 1957, Ufa has a petrochemical complex that began operations in 1956 with the production of synthetic alcohol from refinery ethylene. A second section, opened in 1960–61, contained units for the manufacture of methylstyrene, a component of one of the main

Soviet general-purpose synthetic rubbers; polyethylene, a major thermoplastic; and butyl alcohol, used in organic synthesis and as a solvent. A herbicide unit was added in 1963, and a pilot plant producing a new synthetic rubber, the ethylene–propylene terpolymer, opened in 1967.

Sterlitamak, the oldest of the three-city complex, 75 miles south of Ufa, is also Bashkiria's second largest city (1967 population: 162,000). Dating from the middle of the eighteenth century, Sterlitamak was a regional processing center of farm products in the 1930s when the oil era dawned. During World War II it was selected as the site of a major soda–cement plant, using local salt and limestone. Salt brines move to the plant by pipeline from the Yarbishkadak deposit, 8 miles south of Sterlitamak, and limestone is carried by cableway from the nearby mountain Shakhtau. The production of caustic soda and chlorine from the electrolysis of salt began in 1944; soda-ash production, by the ammonia–soda process, was inaugurated in 1951, and cement was first produced in 1952.

In the same year construction began on a synthetic-rubber plant that was to produce butadiene-methylstyrene rubber. Production began in 1960, using methylstyrene from Ufa, and the following year an additional unit was opened, deriving butadiene locally through dehydrogenation of butane. In 1963 the Sterlitamak synthetic-rubber plant acquired the Soviet Union's first unit for the manufacture of isoprene rubber, a synthetic equivalent of natural rubber. In an expansion of its original industry based on salt and limestone, Sterlitamak opened a second caustic soda and chlorine plant in the early 1960s to produce carbide-based acteylene, hydrochloric acid, polyvinyl chloride, and other vinyl resins.

In addition to Ishimbay (1967 population: 53,000), with its oil refinery dating from 1936, the petrochemical cluster also includes the new city of Salavat, 15 miles south of Sterlitamak. Construction of this city began in 1950, and by 1967 it had a population of more than 98,000. Salavat is the principal source of electric power for the tri-city cluster, from a steam electric station opened in 1952 and expanded continuously through the 1950s, and from a second thermal power plant, opened in 1966. In addition to an oil refinery dating from the mid-1950s, Salavat has a large petrochemical industry, whose product range includes ethylene-base and phenol-base chemicals. In 1961 an ammonia-synthesis plant was opened, obtaining its hydrogen as a by-product of ethylene production and of the new caustic-chlorine plant at Sterlitamak.

Although most of Bashkiria's electric power supply is based on the burning of fuel oil and natural gas, auxiliary sources of energy were placed in exploitation in the 1950s. A hydroelectric station with a capacity of 160,000 kilowatts was opened in 1959–60 at Pavlovka, on the Ufa River, 50 miles northeast of Ufa. In 1949 an open-cut brown-coal mine opened in the South Urals coal basin near Yermolayevo, at the end of a railroad built southward from Ufa through Sterlitamak. The brown coal was used to fuel a large power station at the new mining city of Kumertau, just north of Yermolayevo. Kumertau (1967 population: 39,000) also has a coal-briquetting plant. The open pit at Kumertau produced 6.7 million tons in 1965. The railroad was extended 45 miles southward across the border of Orenburg Oblast in the mid-1950s to tap an additional brown-coal deposit at Tyul'gan, with a potential additional capacity of 3 to 4 million tons. But, with the general shift to oil and gas, the Tyul'gan open pit was not developed.

## TATAR ASSR

The Tatar ASSR, a late starter among Soviet petroleum producers, yielded its first commercial oil in significant amounts in the late 1940s, but boomed to first place by 1956 and has held that position ever since. Although the first oil was struck at Bavly, in the southeastern part of the republic, just across the border from the Bashkir field of Tuymazy–Oktyabr'skiy, it was the discovery of the Romashkino field (at Almet'yevsk) in 1948 that was the determining factor in Tatar oil expansion. Unlike Bashkiria, where centers of oil production shifted through the years, the Romashkino field has retained its predominance, and the new oil city of Almet'yevsk reached a population of 74,000 in 1967.

With no refinery of its own, Almet'yevsk sends crude oil to refineries at Perm' and Kstovo (near Gor'kiy) through pipelines completed in 1957. The line to the Gor'kiy area was supplemented during the early 1960s by a second line and was extended to refineries at Yaroslavl' and Kirishi, in the north, and at Ryazan', in the center. A third crude-oil line to the Gor'kiy area was laid in the late

1960s. Almet'yevsk is also the main source of crude oil moving through the Friendship Pipeline to Eastern Europe, and, through a connection with the Bashkir pipeline system, helps feed the Siberian oil pipeline.

Major new urban centers related to the oil development in the Tatar republic are Leninogorsk (1967 population; 42,000), south of Almet'yevsk; Zelenaya Roshcha, to the southwest; and Aktyubinskiy and Aznakayevo, to the east. The old town of Bugul'ma, dating from 1781, also benefited from the oil boom, as its population rose from about 30,000 in the 1940s to 74,000 by 1967.

Total crude-oil production in the Tatar ASSR rose from less than 1 million tons in 1950 to 13.2 million in 1955, 28.5 million in 1958, and 76.5 million in 1965. It was 93 million in 1968; the 1970 plan was 100 million tons. The processing of petroleum products is limited to a large natural-gasoline plant at Nizhnyaya Maktama, just southeast of Almet'yevsk. The natural-gasoline plant, sometimes called the Minnibayevo plant (for a nearby village), processes casinghead gases from the Tatar fields with helium as a by-product, and accounts for the production of 45 percent of the Soviet Union's liquefied petroleum gases.

A liquefied-gas line, opened in 1964, supplies an organic-synthesis plant at Kazan', which produces acetone, phenol, ethylene, and the raw material for polyester fibers. A second products pipeline from the Minnibayevo natural-gasoline plant was completed in 1967 to Nizhnekamsk (1967 population: 38,000), a new petrochemical center under construction on the Kama River north of Almet'yevsk. A synthetic-rubber plant, one of the first units to be completed at Nizhnekamsk in 1969, will produce isoprene rubber. Subsequent units in the Nizhnekamsk chemical complex are planned to manufacture automobile tires (expected in 1972), plastics and fertilizers.

In addition to a large steam electric plant that went into operation at Nizhnekamsk in 1967, the electric power needs of the area are being met by a major oil-burning power station at Novyy Zay, halfway between Almet'yevsk and Nizhnekamsk. The station, named for the nearby town of Zainsk, began operations in 1963 with its first 200,000-kilowatt unit. By 1966 six units had been installed for a capacity of 1.2 million kilowatts. Two more 200,000-kilowatt units were to be added in the late 1960s, with a capacity of 2.4 million kilowatts to be reached in the 1970s. In addition, the Nizhne-Kama (Lower Kama) hydroelectric station of 1,080,000 kilowatts is planned on the Kama River at Naberezhnyye Chelny. Work on the site was officially begun in 1963, but lagged through the 1960s, apparently because of lack of funds and because of concern that the reservoir might flood as yet unexplored oil lands.

West of the Tatar ASSR, a hydroelectric station is planned on the Volga River, 15 miles below Cheboksary. The 1.4-million kilowatt site was scheduled to go into construction in 1969, with the first generating units expected in 1974. In anticipation of the availability of low-cost electric power, the Cheboksary area was selected in the early 1960s for the construction of a chemical complex producing aniline dyes, chlorine compounds, and ammonium sulfate. The new chemical town, which will also house the dam-construction workers, is Novocheboksarsk, with a population of 24,000 in 1967.

### KUYBYSHEV OBLAST

In Kuybyshev Oblast, the Soviet Union's third largest petroleum-producing region since 1959, oil was first struck in 1936–37 near Syzran', followed by a strike at Zol'noye (east of Zhigulevsk) in 1942. In that year the first refinery was completed at Syzran'. A second refinery began operations at Kuybyshev in 1945. However, crude-oil output remained low, rising from 1.3 million tons at the end of World War II in 1945 to 3.5 million tons in 1950 and 7.3 million tons in 1955.

It was in the second half of the 1950s that the development of large new fields placed the oblast in the forefront of Soviet producers. The first big strike was in 1955 in the Mukhanovo field, 50 miles east of Kuybyshev, where the new town of Otradnyy developed, reaching a population of 43,000 in 1967. By that time the Mukhanovo field accounted for 40 to 50 percent of the oblast's total crude-oil production, which rose from 16.3 million tons in 1958 to 33.4 million tons in 1965. It remained steady at about 34 million tons in the late 1960s. A natural-gasoline plant went into operation at Otradnyy in 1962, and was expanded in 1964, to process casinghead gas from the Mukhanovo field.

A second major oil deposit was discovered in 1958–59 in the area of Kuleshovka, 50 miles southeast of Kuybyshev, and gave rise to the new oil town of Neftegorsk. A natural-gasoline plant went into operation there in 1967. A third oil-field development took place in the mid-1960s in the Sergiyevsk field, north of Otradnyy. Two pipe-lines carried oil from Orlyanka, center of the Sergiyevsk field, to Otradnyy.

The availability of crude oil, both from Kuybyshev Oblast itself and from the adjoining Tatar ASSR, combined with the completion of the great hydroelectric dam near Kuybyshev on the Volga, stimulated the development of a major oil-refining and petrochemical industry with centers at Novokuybyshevsk, a southwest suburb of Kuybyshev, and Togliatti. The Kuybyshev power station was originally planned before World War II just north of the city, where the Volga River hairpin bend breaks through the easternmost outlier of the Zhiguli Mountains. Subsequent surveys showed, however, that a reservoir formed at that site would risk undermining the limestone karst of the Zhiguli range. The dam site was therefore moved farther upstream, to a point between the present communities of Togliatti, on the north shore, and Zhigulevsk (called Otvazhnyy until 1949), on the south shore. Construction of the dam began in 1950, and the first generating unit was placed in operation in late 1955. By the end of 1957 all twenty units had been installed, giving the power station a total capacity of 2.3 million kilowatts. High-voltage power lines, operating first at 400 and later at 500 kilovolts, were completed westward to Moscow in 1956 and eastward to the Urals in 1958.

The head created by the filling of the Kuybyshev reservoir is to be used by a second hydroelectric station that was being designed in the late 1960s for Perevoloki, on the narrow isthmus separating the reservoir from the southern branch of the Volga River's hairpin bend. The Perevoloki station, which is to have roughly the same generating capacity as the Kuybyshev dam, would include a system of locks shortening the north–south Volga water route by eliminating the bend past Kuybyshev.

The filling of the reservoir backed up by the Kuybyshev power station required the moving of many populated places, including the old Volga River town of Stavropol', dating from the eighteenth century. It was relocated on a plateau above the dam and developed as a new industrial center, adopting the name of Togliatti (for the late Italian Communist party leader) in 1964. The new city had a population of 61,000 in 1959 and more than doubled within the span of eight years, reaching 143,000 in 1967. Rapid further growth was expected.

The first installation related to the petrochemical complex was the Togliatti synthetic-rubber plant, which went into operation in 1961. At first it produced general-purpose styrene–butadiene rubber according to the same technological scheme as the Sterlitamak plant, which had opened in the Bashkir ASSR the previous year. The first section of the Togliatti plant used methylstyrene from a synthetic alcohol plant at Novokuybyshevsk and produced butadiene through dehydrogenation of butane. In 1964 and 1968 two more units were added to the Togliatti synthetic-rubber plant, to produce isoprene rubber.

Another component of the Togliatti chemical industry is a nitrogen-fixation plant that went into operation in 1965. The Togliatti plant derives hydrogen for ammonia synthesis from gas piped from the Otradnyy natural-gasoline plant. Natural-gas supplies were expanded with the completion in 1969 of a branch of the Central Asia–Central European Russia pipeline from the pumping station of Mokrous, east of Saratov, to Togliatti. Further industrial development of Togliatti is associated with the construction of a 600,000-unit automobile plant that will produce Fiats.

Petrochemical production is expected to be concentrated increasingly at Novokuybyshevsk (1967 population: 107,000) rather than at Togliatti, which has no oil-refining capacity of its own. Novokuybyshevsk arose in the early 1950s with the construction of an oil refinery, the second in the area. Refinery gases and liquid petroleum gases from natural-gasoline plants at Otradnyy and at Zol'noye, northwest of Kuybyshev, provide raw materials for a synthetic-alcohol plant that went into operation at Novokuybyshevsk in 1957. A second section, opened four years later, produces phenol, acetone, and methylstyrene, the synthetic-rubber component. Polyethylene production was added in 1962–63. A butadiene unit opened at Novokuybyshevsk in 1967, and it was deemed more economical to locate additional synthetic-rubber capacity at Novokuybyshevsk instead of Togliatti, 80 miles away around the Volga River bend.

Southwest of Novokuybyshevsk is the old center of a chemical-defense industry, Chapayevsk (1967 population: 87,000), specializing in explosives. A significant component of the chemical industries of the complex is the native sulfur deposit of Alekseyevka, just east of Kuybyshev, for which a treatment plant was inaugurated in 1965. Another basic element in the chemical industries is elemental phosphorus, derived from phosphate rock (mainly from the Karatau deposits of southern Kazakhstan) in a plant opened in 1963 at Togliatti. In addition to making elemental phosphorus, an important industrial chemical and military material, by the thermal reduction of phosphate rock with coke and sand in electric furnaces, the phosphorus plant also produces fertilizers and other phosphorus compounds.

In addition to an oil refinery dating from 1942, Syzran' (1967 population: 169,000) acquired a carbon-black plant in 1963, fed by hydrocarbon liquids and gases from the refinery. On the southern outskirts of Syzran', an oil-shale deposit at Kashpirovka has been mined since 1918, supplying a shale distillery (opened in 1935) and a steam electric station (opened in 1944). The mine yields about 1.2 million tons of oil shale a year. The most valuable of the oil-shale chemicals produced at the Syzran' distillery is thiophene, a volatile sulfur compound, used in the manufacture of ichthamnol, an antiseptic and emollient.

ORENBURG OBLAST

In the eastern part of Kuybyshev Oblast, an oil and gas field straddles the border with Orenburg Oblast in a Permian deposit discovered in 1937–38. Production developed during World War II, when one of the first gas pipelines in the area (opened in 1943) carried both natural gas and oil-field gas to Kuybyshev and furnished raw material for a carbon-black plant at Pokhvistnevo. The population of Pokhvistnevo rose as a result of this industrial development from 6,500 in 1939 to 23,000 in 1959, but then leveled off. The early oil-producing center of Orenburg Oblast was Buguruslan, which doubled in population from 21,000 in 1939 to 42,000 in 1959. But until 1960 oil and gas production in Orenburg Oblast was negligible: about 0.5 million cubic meters of gas and less than 1 million tons of crude oil. However, continued exploration in the 1960s uncovered more promising deposits south and southeast of Buguruslan. The large Pokrovka oil deposit was linked by a pipeline to the main transmission system at Otradnyy, and a new oil field went into operation in 1968 at Sorochinsk. Crude oil production rose rapidly to 2.6 million tons in 1965 and to 4.3 million tons in 1967. An increase to as much as 15 million tons is expected in the 1970s. Exploration for natural gas also yielded a major deposit near Krasnyy Kholm, southwest of the city of Orenburg. It was reported in 1968 to have reserves of several hundred billion cubic meters, placing it in the category of the largest Soviet natural gas deposits. Production was planned to start in 1969.

SARATOV OBLAST

Saratov Oblast is significant mainly for natural-gas fields rather than crude-oil production. Oil output from fields around Saratov city, first utilized in the late 1940s, and across the Volga River in the Sovetskoye area, developed in the late 1950s, reached a peak of 3 million tons in 1958–60, but declined to 1.3 million by 1965. Even before the discovery of oil, Saratov was selected as the site of a large oil refinery because of its favorable transport situation. The refinery, opened in 1934, was the largest in the Soviet Union before World War II. It processed crude oil from Baku, which was shipped at first along the Volga River and later by a pipeline completed in 1944 between Astrakhan', the Caspian oil terminal, and Saratov. With the increase in crude-oil production in the Tatar fields in the 1950s, Saratov switched from Baku crude oils to Tatar crude oils. The shortage of refinery capacity in the Volga region made it also necessary to reverse the oil flow along the Saratov–Astrakhan' pipeline, sending crude oil from the Volga region for refining at the Groznyy and Baku refineries. In conjunction with Saratov refinery gases, a synthetic-alcohol plant went into operation in 1957. A catalytic cracking unit opened in 1967 at the Saratov refinery (Fig. 17).

Natural gas was first developed during World War II around Saratov city, and the first long-distance gas pipeline, Saratov–Moscow (520 miles), was inaugurated in 1946. The original gas fields, at Yelshanka, Kurdyum, and Peschano-Umet, yielded up to 1 billion cubic meters a year in the mid-1950s. The Stepnoye gas deposit, explored after 1955 on the right bank of the Volga, across from Saratov, had greater reserves than the right-bank fields and

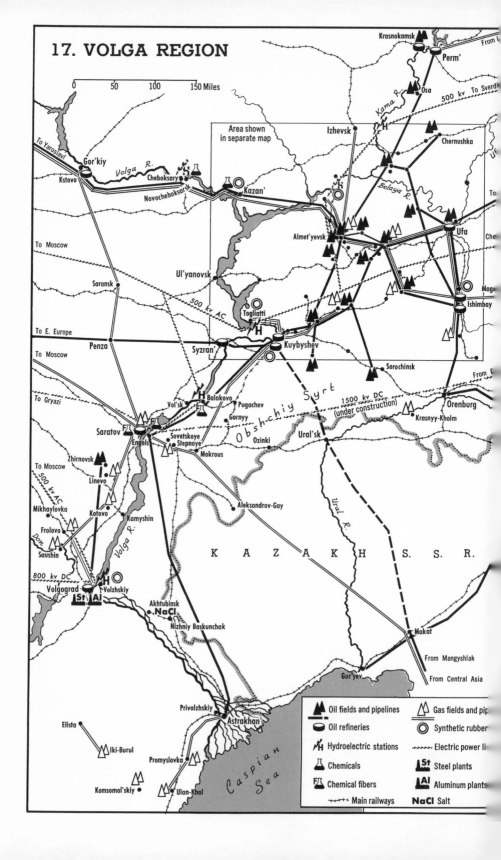

# 17. VOLGA REGION

0   50   100   150 Miles

Krasnokamsk
From
Perm'
Osa
500 kv To Sverd
Kama R.
Chernushka
Izhevsk
Area shown
in separate map
Belaya R.
Gor'kiy
To Yaroslavl
Volga R.
Kstovo
Cheboksary
Kazan'
Novocheboksarsk
Almet'yevsk
Ufa
Che
To Moscow
Ul'yanovsk
Ishimbay
Saransk
500 kv AC
Togliatti
To E. Europe
Penza
Syzran'
Kuybyshev
To Moscow
Sorochinsk
To Gryazi
Vol'sk
Balakovo
Pugachev
Obshchiy Syrt
1500 kv DC
(under construction)
Orenburg
Gornyy
Krasnyy-Kholm
Saratov
Sovetskoye
Engels
Stepnoye
Ozinki
Ural'sk
From
Zhirnovsk
Mokrous
To Moscow
Linevo
500 kv AC
Aleksandrov-Gay
Mikhaylovka
Kotovo
Kamyshin
Frolovo
Ural R.
Don R.
Saushin
K   A   Z   A   K   H       S.   S.   R.
800 kv DC
Volgograd
Volzhskiy
St  Al
Akhtubinsk
NaCl
Nizhniy Baskunchak
Makat
From Mangyshlak
From Central Asia
Gur'yev
Elista
Privolzhskiy
Iki-Burul
Astrakhan'
Promyslovka
Komsomol'skiy
Ulan-Khol
Caspian
Sea

| | |
|---|---|
| 🗻 Oil fields and pipelines | ⛰ Gas fields and pip |
| ⬭ Oil refineries | ◎ Synthetic rubber |
| ♯H Hydroelectric stations | ∿∿ Electric power li |
| ⚗ Chemicals | St Steel plants |
| FⱵ Chemical fibers | Al Aluminum plants |
| +++ Main railways | NaCl Salt |

served as the gas source for a pipeline of 735 miles to Gor'kiy and Cherepovets (built 1959–61). By 1965 natural-gas production in the oblast rose to 6.2 billion cubic meters, of which 55 percent came from Stepnoye. However, output began to decline in the late 1960s. The availability of gas led to the conversion of Saratov steam electric stations from solid fuels to gas. The stations had been based on steam coals from the Donets Basin and on oil shale from the Savel'yev deposit (mining town of Gornyy) and Ozinki deposits, 150 to 170 miles east of Saratov, in the low hills known as the Obshchiy Syrt. As a result of the conversion of the power plants, the oil shale mines were closed in 1955–57.

The power supply of the Saratov manufacturing complex was improved in the late 1960s with completion of the Saratov hydroelectric station on the Volga River. The station, situated at the town of Balakovo, 80 miles northeast of Saratov, went into construction and the first generating units began operation in late 1967. Because of the low head provided by the Volga River, the station uses relatively small turbines. It will have tweny-one units of 60,000 kilowatts each and two 45,000-kilowatt units, for a total capacity of 1.35 million kilowatts by 1970.

In the early 1960s the area acquired several chemical fiber plants. Acrylonitrile, derived from ethylene and other petroleum products of the Saratov refinery, became the raw material of a plant opened in 1963 at Saratov to produce nitron, the Soviet acrylic fiber. A chemical-fiber plant opened in 1960 at Engels, across the Volga River from Saratov, makes acetate rayon from Siberian wood pulp and gas-based acetylene as well as kapron, the Soviet polyamide fiber, derived from long-haul caprolactam. A third fiber plant, opened in 1962 at Balakovo, produces viscose rayon from Siberian wood pulp for use in tire cord. Balakovo was reached by a railroad from Pugachev in 1965 and, of the major cities in the oblast, recorded the most rapid population growth in the 1960s, from 36,000 in 1959 to 85,000 in 1967.

### VOLGOGRAD OBLAST

Volgograd Oblast, where oil and gas were first struck in the mid-1940s around Frolovo in the small Archeda field, began to develop its hydrocarbon resources commercially in the 1950s. The

Frolovo–Volgograd gas pipeline opened in 1953, followed in 1957 by a second transmission line from the Saushin deposit, on the Don River south of Frolovo. However, the early gas fields had relatively small reserves. Production increased more rapidly in the 1960s with development of the largest deposit in the oblast, the Korobki field, 110 miles north of Volgograd, which was linked by pipeline with the Volgograd area in 1963. By 1965 the Korobki field contributed 5 billion cubic meters of the oblast's total gas production of 6.6 billion cubic meters. A natural gasoline plant began operations in 1966 at Kotovo, center of the gas field, with a population of 17,000 in 1967. Natural gas has partly replaced fuel oil, coal, and coke at the Red October steel mill of Volgograd and at the city's steam electric stations. Some gas is also piped northward into the transmission system centered on Saratov. Oil production in Volgograd Oblast has been associated with the gas fields. The Korobki field first yielded crude oil in 1951. But the main oil-producing center is Zhirnovsk, in the north, from where oil is piped to a new refinery in Volgograd, opened in 1957. The oblast produced 6.2 million tons of crude oil in 1965.

Subsequent industrial development of Volgograd was related to a large extent to the low-cost hydroelectric power of the Volga River dam on the northern outskirts of the city. Construction of the dam began in 1950, initially as part of a major water-management project that included the proposed Volga–Ural River canal and several irrigation systems. These projects, part of Stalin's ambitious plan for the "transformation of nature," were abandoned after his death in 1953, and construction of the Volgograd dam also stagnated for several years for lack of funds. The power project was finally completed, with the installation of twenty-two generators of 115,000 kilowatts between 1958 and 1961, for a total installed capacity of 2.53 million kilowatts. The station was linked to the energy-deficient Moscow area by two 500-kilovolt lines, completed in 1959 and 1961.

In addition it attracted power-oriented industries to the Volgograd area. The first was an aluminum plant, opened in 1959 on the right bank of the Volga River, near the dam. With a second section added in 1960 and a third in 1962, the aluminum plant is believed to have a capacity of about 200,000 tons. It uses partly Hungarian alumina, returning finished aluminum to Hungary (70,000 tons in 1968).

On the left bank of the Volga, meanwhile, the new city of Volzhskiy has arisen in conjunction with the dam project, reaching a population of 67,000 by the time the power project went into operation in 1959, and 114,000 in 1967. Among the industries at Volzhskiy is an isoprene synthetic-rubber plant, which went into operation in 1966, using liquefied petroleum gases from the Kotovo natural-gasoline plant as raw materials. The isoprene rubber and local kapron cord are used in a tire plant, opened in 1964.

The Volgograd complex also produces the carbon black needed for rubber fabrication, using natural gas and oil refinery by-products. The carbon-black plant, opened in 1965, is part of a growing petro-chemical complex developing around the oil refinery on the southern outskirts of Volgograd, south of the Volga–Don Canal.

### ASTRAKHAN' OBLAST

In Astrakhan' Oblast, in the lower reaches of the Volga, the development of mineral resources is limited to the salt deposits of Lake Baskunchak, one of the principal sources of common salt in the Soviet Union, and natural-gas deposits of local significance near the city of Astrakhan'. Lake Baskunchak produced 3.9 million tons of salt in 1964. This represents 29 percent of the Soviet Union's total salt output and 70 percent of the lake salt. The principal consuming industries are chemicals (1.6 million tons) and fish processing (0.7 million tons). The Baskunchak salt operation is seasonal in char-acter, being limited to the summer, when excavators can operate on the salt surface of the lake, and the Volga River provides a low-cost transport route. The salt is mined and ground at the settlement of Nizhniy Baskunchak (Lower Baskunchak), on the lake, and is shipped either by rail from the nearby station of Verkhniy Baskun-chak (Upper Baskunchak) or from the Volga River terminal of Akhtubinsk.

Natural gas is produced at Promyslovka, 60 miles southwest of Astrakhan', and a pipeline was completed in 1959. A second pipeline from Ulan-Khol to Astrakhan' opened in 1967. Among industries using the new gas fuel is a pulp and paperboard mill at Privolzh-skiy, across the river from Astrakhan', that uses reeds of the Volga delta marshes as raw material. The mill began operations in 1962.

# The Northern Caucasus

The mineral resource base of the Northern Caucasus, including the Lower Don region, was long limited to the eastern wing of the Donets Basin, with its anthracite mines, the declining oil fields of Maykop and Groznyy, and metal ores in the higher reaches of the Caucasus, including the important molybdenum and tungsten deposit of Tyrnyauz. In the 1950s, however, the region, notably Krasnodar and Stavropol' krays, emerged as one of the Soviet Union's major sources of natural gas, feeding the fuel to central European Russia and Transcaucasia and using it as a power station fuel and chemical raw material within the Northern Caucasus. At the same time new oil discoveries, raising crude output from 6.5 million tons in 1955 to 20.7 million in 1965, helped revive the petroleum industry and eliminated the need for long hauls of crude oil from other parts of the Soviet Union to fill the capacity of refineries at Groznyy (Fig. 18).

## EASTERN DONETS BASIN

The eastern wing of the Donets Basin, in Rostov Oblast, accounts for about 17 percent of the basin's coal output. The southwestern part of the Rostov coal basin, around the old mining centers of Shakhty and Novoshakhtinsk, produces anthracite, which is used as a power station fuel at major steam electric stations in the two cities, and has also been found suitable as a substitute for metallurgical coke after calcination (heat treatment). Some coking coals and other bituminous coals are mined in the northeastern part of the basin, near the right bank of the Northern Donets River. There, the new mining towns are situated, notably Gukovo, which rose from a population of 9,000 in 1939 to 68,000 in 1967, and Donetsk (the former Gundorovka), which was founded at the end of World War II and reached a population of 39,000 by 1967. Total coal production in Rostov Oblast was 32 million tons in 1965, of which 3.6 million tons represented coking coals. Most of the output, about 70 percent, was shipped out of the oblast for use in power stations.

Energy supplied by culm-burning power stations was supple-

mented in the early 1950s by hydroelectric power from the Tsimlyansk dam on the Don River. The dam, forming the large
Tsimlyansk Reservoir, was completed in the summer of 1952 in
conjunction with the opening of the Volga–Don Canal between
Volgograd on the Volga and Kalach on the Don. Four electric
generating units, installed in the Tsimlyansk plant in 1952–54, have
a combined capacity of 164,000 kilowatts.

Adjoining the dam are two new towns of 15,000 to 20,000 population, the smaller Tsimlyansk, an agricultural processing center, on
the right bank, and the larger Volgodonsk, a chemical center, on
the left bank. Volgodonsk uses paraffin from the Groznyy oil refinery in the manufacture of fatty acids.

The development of the natural-gas fields to the south has introduced gas as an industrial raw material in the manufacturing center
of Novocherkassk. A chemical plant, producing polymers from
Stavropol' gas, began production in 1964. However, the industries of
Novocherkassk also reflect the proximity of the anthracite coal of
the nearby Donets Basin. Culm is used as the principal fuel at a
2.4-million-kilowatt power station inaugurated at Novocherkassk in
1965. Half the design capacity was achieved in 1968 when the
fourth of eight 300,000-kilowatt generators was installed.

Other primary industries in Rostov Oblast are a viscose-rayon
plant at Kamensk-Shakhtinskiy (opened in the mid-1950s) and two
steel plants: Taganrog, which produces open-hearth steel and rolled
products, mainly pipe; and Krasnyy Sulin, which has rolling facilities
only.

## STAVROPOL' AND KRASNODAR KRAYS

Natural-gas development in the Northern Caucasus dates
from the late 1950s. The largest field and the first to be developed
(in 1956) is the North Stavropol' field, which produced 14.5 billion
cubic meters a year by 1965 and was thus one of the largest natural-
gas producers in the Soviet Union. The Stavropol' field is linked to
Moscow by a system of transmission mains, including a 28-inch
pipeline opened in 1956 and a 32-inch line completed the following
year. A group of gas deposits in northern Krasnodar Kray also feeds
gas into the transmission system since 1959, when a third pipeline
(of 40-inch pipe) was inaugurated to Serpukhov, south of Moscow,

on a gas-pipeline system circling the Soviet capital. (In the same year Krasnodar gas reached Leningrad through a 28-inch pipeline from Serpukhov via Kalinin, Torzhok and Novgorod.) The early northern Krasnodar gas fields are the Leningradskaya field, which dates from the late 1950s and yielded 2 to 3 billion cubic meters a year through the 1960s, and Kanevskaya, with about half the output of the Leningradskaya field. Two newer fields are: Starominskaya, which opened in 1962 and yielded more than 2 billion cubic meters a year in the mid-1960s, and Berezanskaya, which began production in 1963 and produced 4.6 billion cubic meters in 1965. A fifth major Krasnodar gas field is situated 10 miles north of Maykop. Slow to develop in the early 1960s, it reached an output of 5.8 billion cubic meters in 1965, thus exceeding all the other Krasnodar gas fields.

The Stavropol' field also serves as a source of natural gas for power stations and industrial plants to the south along the northern piedmont of the Caucasus and even in Transcaucasia, where natural-gas reserves at Karadag (near Baku) are limited and approached depletion in the late 1960s. A pipeline from Stavropol' reached Groznyy in 1959 and was extended through Ordzhonikidze across the Caucasus range to Tbilisi in 1963. It was followed by a second, parallel, cross-mountain line in 1966. Total natural-gas production of the Northern Caucasus in 1965 was 37 billion cubic meters, or a third of the Soviet total, with 15 billion coming from Stavropol' and 22 billion from the Krasnodar field. Most of the output moved northward to Central European Russia, and only about 4 billion cubic meters was transmitted southward to the Caucasus.

In addition to long-distance transmission, the region's natural-gas resources are used in local power plants and chemical enterprises. The principal consumer is the new chemical and power-generating center of Nevinnomyssk, south of Stavropol'. A gas-fueled steam electric station opened there in 1960 followed two years later by a nitrogenous fertilizer plant that derives hydrogen for ammonia synthesis from gas. The power station was at first equipped with small generators and had a capacity of only 100,000 kilowatts by 1962, but an expansion program begun in 1964 envisaged a capacity increase to 1 million kilowatts. The first three 150,000-kilowatt units were installed in 1964 and 1965. The fertilizer plant, which acquired a second section in 1965, produces a wide range of nitrogen-based chemicals. The gas available at Nevin-nomyssk is also used (since 1968) as a source of acetylene for the manufacture of plastics and chemical fibers. Nevinnomyssk, a sleepy agricultural market town until the mid-1950s, had a population of 63,000 in 1967. In Stavropol' itself, natural gas serves as raw material for a carbon-black plant opened in 1958. The population of Stavropol' increased from 123,000 in 1956 to 177,000 in 1967.

The petroleum industry of the Northern Caucasus, substantially revived by the discovery of new oil deposits in the 1950s, is focused on two refining areas: Krasnodar–Tuapse and Groznyy. The oldest fields in the Krasnodar area are the so-called Maykop fields, southwest of Maykop, with producing centers at Neftegorsk, Apsheronsk, and Khadyzhensk. Before World War II, crude-oil production was 2.3 million tons in this district. After the war, additional important deposits were discovered as exploration proceeded westward along the foothills of the Caucasus toward the lower reaches of the Kuban' River. The largest of the deposits is Anastasiyevskaya–Troitskaya near Slavyansk, west of Krasnodar. In 1965 this district accounted for half of the Krasnodar crude-oil production of about 6.1 million tons. (Output in 1955 was 3.9 million tons.)

The oil is refined at Krasnodar and Tuapse, two cities that are to be linked by a new direct railroad under construction since 1968. The oil refinery at Tuapse was dismantled in 1942 during World War II and reinstalled at Krasnovodsk in Central Asia. After the war a refinery was built again at Tuapse, going into production in 1949. The sulfurless crude oil of the Krasnodar fields yields high-grade refined products, a large part of which is exported through the Black Sea terminals of Tuapse and Novorossiysk. Natural gas from the oil fields is processed at a natural-gasoline plant at Afipskiy, just southwest of Krasnodar, opened in 1963 and expanded two years later.

### GROZNYY PETROLEUM DISTRICT

In the eastern part of the Northern Caucasus is the Groznyy oil-producing province, which has been in commercial production since 1893 in the Starogroznenskiy (Old Groznyy) field, northwest of the city. By 1913 the Novogroznenskiy (New Groznyy) field went into operation, 25 miles east of Groznyy. After having reached

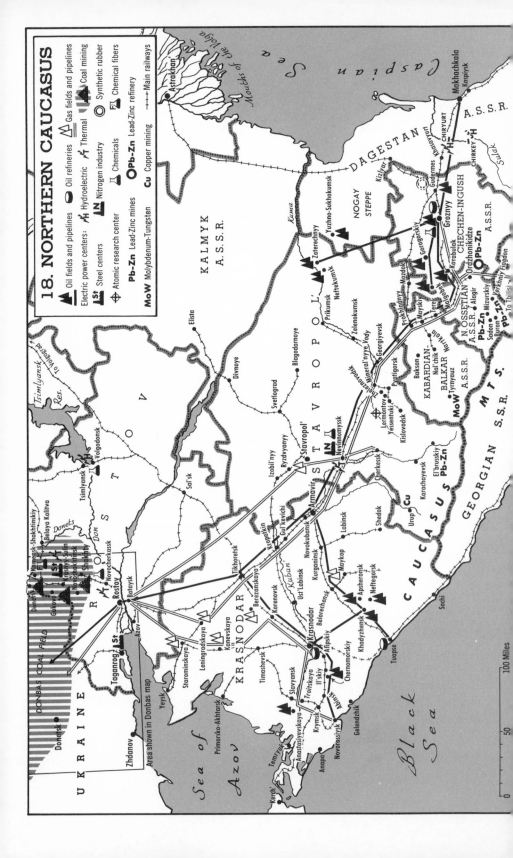

a peak of almost 8 million tons of crude oil in 1931 output declined despite the addition of a new deposit at Malgobek in 1933 and dropped to 2.3 million tons in 1940.

To keep the large refining capacity of the Groznyy plants busy, a pipeline was built in 1936 from the Caspian Sea terminal of Makhachkala to move Baku crude oil to the Groznyy refineries. Local crude-oil production remained low after World War II, and by the mid-1950s was 2 to 3 million tons. Crude oil was hauled all the way from the Volga–Urals fields, where rapid growth of production had far surpassed the construction of refining capacity.

In the late 1950s, however, new discoveries in the Groznyy area marked the beginning of a new period of expansion. The new finds were in Cretaceous and Jurassic rocks below the Tertiary formations that had been exploited in the past. The principal new deposits were discovered west of Groznyy around Karabulak and Malgobek. The new oil town of Karabulak was connected by a crude-oil pipeline with Groznyy in 1961, and a natural-gasoline plant opened at Karabulak in 1965, supplying liquefied petroleum gases to the Groznyy petrochemical industry.

The second oil-bearing area was discovered in the 1950s in the arid Nogay Steppe south of the lower Kuma River, in a zone about 100 miles north of Groznyy. There the oil town of Zaterechnyy was founded in 1956 in the Ozek-Suat field, Neftekumsk in 1961 in the Kamysh-Burun field, and Yuzhno-Sukhokumsk in 1963. Pipelines supplied additional crude oil to the Groznyy refinery, and, at Neftekumsk, a second natural-gasoline plant went into operation in 1964.

As a result of these discoveries, the total output of the crude-oil fields focused on Groznyy rose from 2.8 million tons in 1955 to almost 15 million tons in 1965. This included the Chechen-Ingush ASSR around Groznyy proper, where production rose to 9 million tons. Zaterechnyy and Neftekumsk, politically in Stavropol' Kray, accounted for 4.6 million tons, and the Yuzhno-Sukhokumsk strike helped raise the crude-oil output of Dagestan ASSR, previously a few hundred thousand tons, to 1 million. By 1968 the entire district produced 23 million tons.

Increased crude-oil output spurred plans for the construction of new pipelines out of the Groznyy district. One pipeline, 300 miles long, opened in 1969 to connect the rejuvenated Malgobek field with an existing pipeline system at Tikhoretsk for export via the Black Sea terminal of Novorossiysk. Another pipeline was expected to carry Groznyy crude oil to a proposed refinery in the Lisichansk–Severodonetsk area of the Donets Basin. The Groznyy refinery was also expanded with the addition of a catalytic cracking unit in 1967.

Meantime a petrochemical complex developed at Groznyy. The first section of a phenol and acetone plant opened in 1954, with a second section following in 1960. A synthetic alcohol plant was also constructed in two stages and went into production in 1958 and 1964. Polyethylene has been produced at Groznyy since 1962. A synthetic-rubber plant that would utilize the new abundance of hydrocarbon raw materials was under construction at the late 1960s at Gudermes, 30 miles east of Groznyy.

Electric power for the growing Groznyy industry has been provided by fuel oil and natural gas. A substantial hydroelectric power development is under way on the Sulak River, to the east in neighboring Dagestan. A hydroelectric plant of 72,000 kilowatts was completed in 1961 at Chiryurt, where the Sulak River debouches from the last Caucasus gorge just south of the Makhachkala–Groznyy railroad. Construction began in 1963 on the Chirkey plant farther upstream, which will have a 750-foot-high dam and is planned to generate 1 million kilowatts of energy (four generators of 250,000 kilowatts each). The availability of low-cost power is expected to attract energy-oriented industries to the area.

### METAL RESOURCES

Metal ore resources are relatively limited in the Northern Caucasus, although new deposits are under development. One of the most significant resources is the molybdenum–tungsten deposit of Tyrnyauz in the Baksan River valley of the Kabardian-Balkar ASSR. Initially opened in 1940, the concentrator was destroyed in World War II, and rebuilt in 1945, with several expansions through the 1950s and 1960s. The molybdenum concentrate is treated by a hydrometallurgical process at a mill opened in 1961 at Nal'chik, where excess molybdenum is also extracted from the tungsten concentrate. The operation yields valuable by-products such as bismuth.

Small lead–zinc deposits in the upper Ardon River valley in the North Ossetian ASSR provided the basis for a smelter founded in Ordzhonikidze in 1904. The plant was modernized in the early 1930s, and began producing electrolytic zinc in 1934. In subsequent years, additions were built to extract valuable by-products of zinc ores such as gold and silver, cadmium, germanium, and indium. The local mines at Sadon, Verkhniy Zgid, and Buron, with a concentrator at Mizurskiy, all in the Ardon valley, were inadequate to supply the capacity of the Ordzhonikidze refinery, and concentrates were hauled long distances from as far away as Kazakhstan and the Urals. In the early 1960s, the local zinc–lead ore supply was expanded with the completion of a new concentrator in the upper Fiagdon valley, just east of the Ardon. The Ordzhonikidze smelter also processes lead–zinc ore from a mine at Elbrusskiy (called Magaro until 1957), in the upper reaches of the Kuban' River, in the Karachay-Cherkess Autonomous Oblast.

A major metal ore site under development in the 1960s was a large copper deposit at Urup, in the upper course of the Urup River. A concentrator opened in 1968 was said to have a capacity of 1 million tons of crude ore a year.

# 6

## TRANSCAUCASIA

### Azerbaydzhan SSR

The development of resources in the Azerbaydzhan SSR has been dominated by the recovery of the petroleum industry of Baku from a decline during World War II and by the emergence of the republic as the principal supplier of electric power and natural gas for Transcaucasia as a whole (Fig. 19).

Commercial oil production in the Baku fields dates from the 1870s, and at the·turn of the century the area was for a time the world's principal petroleum producer. Within the Soviet oil industry, Baku retained a preeminent position until World War II, when output dropped sharply as the exploration of new reserves failed to keep pace with exhaustion of oil wells, and attention began to be directed to new oil-bearing provinces between the Volga River and the Urals. In 1940, Azerbaydzhan produced 22.2 million tons of crude oil, or 71 percent of the Soviet Union's total. After having dropped to 11.5 million tons in 1945, oil output in the republic slowly recovered and approached the 1940 level in the late 1960s. In 1968, Azerbaydzhan produced 21.1 million tons of oil, but by this time the development of the Volga–Urals fields had eclipsed the republic as a major oil producer, and it accounted for only 7 percent of the Soviet Union's total.

The postwar recovery of the fields was made possible largely through the drilling of deeper wells to reach new deposits on land and through the exploration and exploitation of offshore deposits. Although this tended to increase the cost of crude-oil production, the low sulfur content of the Baku crude oils, compared with the high-sulfur crude oils of the Volga–Urals region, greatly simplified refining processes and yielded high-grade antiknock gasoline, lubricating oils, and other refined products that were competitive despite the high cost of the crude oil. Furthermore the geographical situation of the Baku fields, linked by pipelines with ship terminals at Batumi on the Black Sea coast, was more favorable for export than the location of the Volga–Urals fields, deep inland in European Russia.

Oil production in the Baku fields was long concentrated on the Apsheron Peninsula, around the south coast city of Baku. The old fields were situated northeast of Baku, between Sabunchi and Surakhany, and southwest of Baku, in the area of Bibi-Eybat. Despite deeper drilling to reach new horizons, these fields yielded less than a third of the total Azerbaydzhan production in the 1960s.

Offshore production began on a small scale in the late 1930s north of Artem Island, off the east coast of the Apsheron Peninsula, from which there is a causeway, but began to rise rapidly after the start of operations in 1951 in the reef area known as Neftyanyye Kamni (oil rocks), 25 miles east of the peninsula, on the Caspian coastal shelf. A 150-mile-long system of causeways has been built in the offshore field, connecting drilling rigs with the mainland and accommodating an oil-workers' town above the surface of the Caspian Sea. Neftyanyye Kammi remained the principal offshore producer in the 1950s, helping to raise the share of offshore oil in the total Azerbaydzhan production to 30 percent by 1957.

The offshore development program advanced another step in 1960 with the completion of a causeway linking Peschanyy Island, off the south coast, with the Apsheron Peninsula. This stimulated exploitation of the Peschanyy offshore field, situated about 10 miles south of the island. In the late 1960s the offshore development effort was concentrated southwest of the peninsula in the Kobystan district in an oil-bearing structure extending southeast from the Sangachaly area on the coast past Duvannyy Island to Bulla Island, 10 miles offshore. The structure yielded 1.5 million tons of oil in 1967 and was expected to account for about 3 million by 1970. About 55 percent of the republic's oil production originated in offshore wells in 1967.

While oil production extended offshore, new fields were also being developed inland. The first major producer outside the Apsheron Peninsula was the Siazan' field, 60 miles northwest of Baku, discovered in 1933. A more promising series of deposits was explored in the early 1950s in the lower valley of the Kura River, at whose mouth the Neftechala field has been producing since the 1930s. The lower Kura deposits, situated on the left bank in the Shirvan Steppe, first produced at Kyurov-Dag and Mishov-Dag, two hill ranges just northeast of the Kura River town of Ali-Bayramly, where the headquarters of the new Shirvan oil-field administration was established in 1956. Subsequent exploration led to production in 1964 from the Kyursangya structure in the Shirvan Steppe, 15 miles southeast of Ali-Bayramly. So promising are the deposits of the lower Kura valley that an oil refinery was planned for the area as part of the five-year plan 1966–70.

Until the discovery of a natural-gas and condensate deposit at Karadag, 20 miles southwest of Baku, gas production was mainly casinghead gas recovered as a by-product of crude-oil output. Together with crude oil it reached a high point in 1940, with 2.5 billion cubic meters, declined during the war, and recovered to only half the prewar level by the early 1950s. Commercial operation at the Karadag deposit began in 1956, when the first pipeline was laid to a power plant in Belyy Gorod (white city), the oil refinery district of Baku. The following year Karadag gas was made available for a 450,000-kilowatt steam power plant at Sumgait, a satellite industrial city, 20 miles northwest of Baku, and in 1958 a gas pipeline reached the 319,000-kilowatt Severnaya (northern) power station on the northeast shore of the Apsheron Peninsula.

Although Karadag gas also represented an important chemical raw material, its immediate importance was as a power station fuel replacing high-sulfur oil shipped from the Volga–Urals fields and even coal from the Ukraine's Donets Basin. Until the availability of natural gas, it was more economical to burn long-haul fuels in the Baku power plants than to use the valuable local low-sulfur fuel oil, which could be used to greater advantage in cracking units to yield gasoline.

As a result of the discovery of the Karadag field, the significance of gas as a power station fuel rose from 20 percent of all fuels in 1955 to 78 percent in 1958, with a corresponding decline in the use of fuel oil. In addition to serving power stations in the Baku area, the gas was also supplied to Tbilisi and Yerevan, in the neighboring republics of Georgia and Armenia, via a pipeline constructed in 1959–60. Of the total 1960 Azerbaydzhan gas output of 5.8 billion cubic meters, 4.5 billion was natural gas (of which 3.1 billion, or 70 percent, came from Karadag) and 1.3 billion was casinghead gas from the oil fields.

However, the Azerbaydzhan reserves of natural gas were limited and approached depletion in the late 1960s. The Karadag deposit was down to an annual output of 0.7 billion cubic meters by 1965 and other deposits, such as Zyrya, on the Apsheron Peninsula east of Baku, and Kalmas, in the lower Kura district southwest of Karadag, were inadequate to compensate for the decline. As natural-gas output declined through the 1960s to about 2 billion cubic meters a year, an effort was made to make fuller use of the oil-field gas. By 1965, oil-field gas accounted for 50 percent of all gas compared with 25 percent in 1960. But even the prospects of increasing gas output from the oil fields were limited by the level of oil production.

In the light of this situation, the prospects of obtaining natural gas from Iranian fields under an accord signed in 1966 assumed increasing importance in the late 1960s. A 44-inch pipeline from the Iranian fields at Saveh, southwest of Teheran, was under construction in the late 1960s. It enters Azerbaydzhan at Astara and was to connect with the existing Karadag–Tbilisi–Yerevan transmission system at Kazi-Magomed. The depleted deposits of Karadag, Kalmas, and others were to serve as storage reservoirs for the Iranian gas. Longer-range plans for the import of Iranian gas envisaged a second entry point at Dzhulfa and ultimately a reversal of the gas flow in the Stavropol'–Ordzhonikidze–Tbilisi transmission system across the Caucasus so that Iranian gas would replenish the North Caucasus supplies for Central European Russia.

The plans for the arrival of Iranian gas also seemed to assure a continuing raw-material supply for gas processing plants in the Baku area. A plant for the manufacture of natural gasoline and liquefied petroleum gases was opened at the Karadag gas field in 1961. Another natural-gasoline plant was completed in 1963 at the

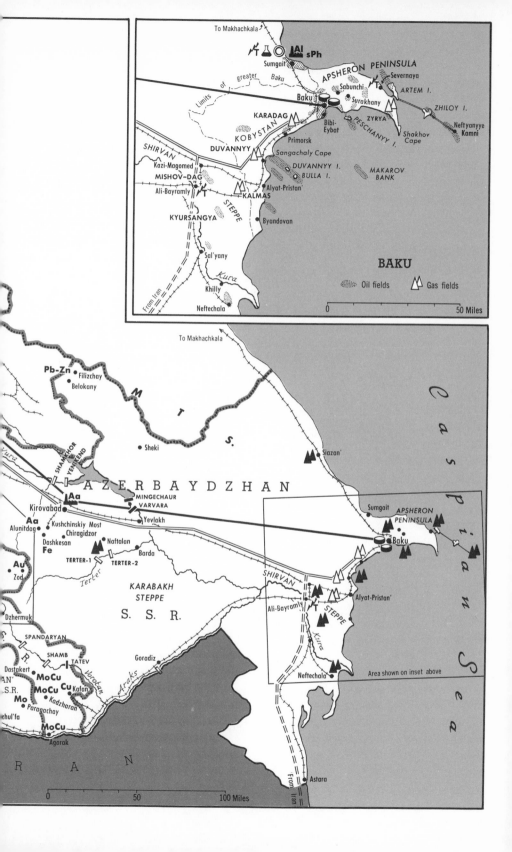

## BAKU

To Makhachkala

Sumgait

**APSHERON PENINSULA**

Al sPh

Severnaya

Sabunchi          T.

Baku

Surakhany          ARTEM I.

Limits of greater Baku

**KARADAG**

ZYRYA

Bibi-Eybat          PESCHANYY I.

ZHILOY I.

**KOBYSTAN**

Shakhov Cape

Neftyanyye Kamni

**DUVANNYY**

Primorsk

Sangachaly Cape

**SHIRVAN**

Kazi-Magomed

**MISHOV-DAG**          STEPPE

Ali-Bayramly          T

**KALMAS**

DUVANNYY I.          MAKAROV BANK

BULLA I.

Alyat-Pristan'

**KYURSANGYA**

Byandovan

Sal'yany

Kura

Khilly

Neftechala

Oil fields          Gas fields

0                    50 Miles

To Makhachkala

**Pb-Zn**          Filizchay

Belokany

M

T

S.

Sheki

Siazan'

SHAMKHOR

YENIKEND

**Aa**

**A Z E R B A Y D Z H A N**

MINGECHAUR

VARVARA

Sumgait          **APSHERON PENINSULA**

Kirovabad

Yevlakh

Baku

**Aa**

Kushchinskiy Most

Alunitdag

Chiragidzor

Dashkesan

Naftalan

**Fe**

TERTER-1          Barda

TERTER-2

**SHIRVAN**

**Au**          **KARABAKH STEPPE**

Zod

Terter

Ali-Bayramly          STEPPE          Alyat-Pristan'

T

Dzhermuk

**S. S. R.**

**SPANDARYAN**

**SHAMB**          TATEV

Goradiz

Neftechala

Dastakert

**MoCu**          Kafan

Area shown on inset above

**MoCu**          **Cu**

**Mo**          Kadzharan

Paragachay

chul'fa

**MoCu**

Agarak

Astara

R          N

0          50          100 Miles

From Iran

C a s p i a n   S e a

Siazan' oil and gas field, followed by the opening of a pipeline to Sumgait the following year. Natural gas also provided the raw material for carbon-black manufacture at Karadag.

Like the related deposits at Cheleken and Nebit-Dag in Turkmenia, across the Caspian Sea, the oil-well brine of Azerbaydzhan has also provided the basis for the extraction of iodine and bromine. In 1958, the republic accounted for 70 percent of the Soviet Union's iodine, from plants at Surakhany, near Baku, and Neftechala. Additional iodine and bromine plants were planned at Karadag and at Khilly, near Neftechala.

Until the early 1950s, Azerbaydzhan's electric power supply derived mainly from oil-fueled electric stations in the Baku area. In 1953 the completion of the Mingechaur hydroelectric project, under construction since the end of World War II, drastically changed the power situation in the republic. The Mingechaur dam and reservoir, a multipurpose project, not only began to feed electricity into the republic's grid from six generators with a combined capacity of 360,000 kilowatts, but also provided a water source for irrigation canals extending into the Shirvan Steppe, on the left bank of the Kura River, and the Karabakh Steppe, on the right bank. The small Varvara station, of 16,500 kilowatts, was added on the Kura River just below Mingechaur in 1956. The Mingechaur power stimulated the installation of energy-oriented industries, such as aluminum production, in the Baku area, and turned Azerbaydzhan into an electric power supplier for neighboring Georgia and Armenia via a 330-kilovolt transmission line. This trend was further accented with the completion of a 600,000-kilowatt gas-fueled power station at Ali-Bayramly in 1962–63. The station, the first of the open-air installation type in the Soviet Union (without a powerhouse), was expanded in the late 1960s to a capacity of 1.05 million kilowatts, using 150,000-kilowatt units. It transmits power westward to the Kirovabad area via a 330-kilovolt line opened in 1968.

Hydroelectric power projects under construction during this period were the 75,000-kilowatt Terter No. 2 station, on the Terter River (the 50,000-kilowatt Terter No. 1 station is planned farther upstream), and a Soviet–Iranian power station on the Araks River at Goradiz. This project, with a capacity of 44,000 kilowatts, including one 22,000-kilowatt station on each bank, was scheduled for completion in 1970. A larger project, the 350,000-kilowatt Shamkhor station on the Kura River, above the Mingechaur reservoir, was in the design stage. It is to be followed later by the 150,000-kilowatt Yenikend plant, just downstream. As a result of electric power development after completion of the Mingechaur project, power generation in Azerbaydzhan doubled from 5 billion kilowatt-hours in 1955 to 11.2 billion in 1967. Almost 15 percent of the total supply was transmitted to Georgia and Armenia.

The availability of cheap hydroelectric power attracted an aluminum industry even before a local raw-material base was developed. The first stage of a reduction plant, using long-haul alumina from the Urals, went into operation at Sumgait in 1955. The second stage, bringing the plant up to full capacity estimated at more than 50,000 tons, was opened in 1959. It required additional alumina shipments from the Leningrad district and even Hungary. The prospective local raw-material source was the large Zaglik alunite deposit at Alunitdag, near Dashkesan, southwest of Kirovabad. It was to be the first attempt in world practice to derive commercial alumina from alunite, a hydrous potassium aluminum sulfate, which would also yield potash and sulfuric acid as by-products. The Alunitdag mine, connected by a cableway with the railhead at Kushchinskiy Most, began operations in 1964. Construction of the alumina plant had begun in 1958, but technological and construction problems long delayed completion. The plant did not go into operation until early 1966, when it produced its first alumina and sulfuric acid. A potassium sulfate unit opened in 1968. The Kirovabad plant was designed to produce 200,000 tons of alumina at full capacity for reduction plants at Sumgait, Yerevan, and Volgograd.

In addition to the alunite deposit, the Dashkesan mining district also represents the iron ore supply for Transcaucasia's modest iron and steel industry, a source of cobalt, and of pyrites for the manufacture of sulfuric acid (before the alunite process was developed). The magnetite deposit at Dashkesan has been mined since 1954 as an ore source for blast furnaces at the Rustavi iron and steel plant in Georgia, 110 rail miles away. More than 2 million tons of crude ore containing 40 percent iron were being produced annually in the 1960s from two open-cut mines. Concentration yielded 1.4 million tons of usable ore with an iron content to 55 percent for shipping to Rustavi. Cobalt associated with the magnetite deposit has been mined since the nineteenth century. The pyrite deposit of Chiragidzor, east of Dashkesan, has also been worked since before the Russian Revolution.

Other minor mining operations are found in Nakhichevan' ASSR, an autonomous republic that is separated from the rest of Azerbaydzhan by Armenian territory. The Gyumushlug mine, in the northwest, was worked by Arabs for silver in the sixth and ninth centuries, and now yields lead–zinc concentrate. The Paragachay mine, in the southeast, has yielded molybdenum ore since 1948. It is related to the more significant copper–molybdenum deposits in the Kadzharan area, just across the border in Armenia. The 1966–70 five-year plan called for development of a newly explored complex metallic deposit at Filizchay, north of Belokany, on the slopes of the main Caucasus range in the northern part of Azerbaydzhan. The Filizchay deposit contains zinc, lead, copper, gold, and a variety of valuable rare metals. A mercury deposit was also under development at Shorbulag, in the upper reaches of the Terter River.

Virtually all the primary industries based on recent resource development have been concentrated in the new industrial city of Sumgait, which had a population of 104,000 in 1967. Its construction began in 1944 around a small chlorine-caustic chemical plant, and four years later it was established as a separate city. In addition to the aluminum plant, opened in 1955, Sumgait has a steel-pipe rolling plant and a synthetic-rubber plant, both in operation since 1953; a superphosphate plant, opened in the early 1960s; as well as petrochemical and basic chemical (chlorine and caustic soda) installations.

The Sumgait steel mill, which was producing 800,000 tons of steel ingots and more than 600,000 tons of rolled products (75 percent is steel pipe) in the mid-1960s, uses local scrap and long-haul pig iron from the Ukraine. Until 1957 not even the steel-mill operations at Sumgait were integrated as the plant sent ingots to mills in Georgia for rolling into billets suitable for pipe manufacture back in Sumgait. However, the completion of a blooming mill and billet mill in 1957 eliminated the irrational cross-hauling between Sumgait and the Georgian mill of Rustavi. The installation of new open-hearth furnaces and a second 10-inch pipe mill in 1959–60 doubled the original plant capacity of 400,000 tons of ingot steel and more than 200,000 tons of pipe. Sumgait produces 40 percent of the oil pipe needed in Azerbaydzhan, the rest coming from Rustavi.

The Sumgait synthetic-rubber plant was one of the first Soviet installations to produce synthetic ethyl alcohol from oil refinery gases and to use synthetic alcohol in the manufacture of butadiene, one of the main constituents of general-purpose synthetic rubber. Synthetic-alcohol production began at Sumgait in 1952, and the synthetic-rubber unit was completed five years later. A butane unit opened in 1960 made it possible to produce butadiene directly from the by-products of petroleum refining. In addition to the general-purpose butadiene–styrene rubber, Sumgait also produces special types, such as butyl rubber, since 1962. The general-purpose rubber is used primarily in a tire plant, with a capacity of about 1 million tires a year, opened in the Kishly area of Baku in 1959. With the production of carbon black at Karadag, needed to impart toughness to rubber products, the Baku–Sumgait area thus possesses an integrated rubber manufacturing and fabricating industry.

Until the start of operations at the Sumgait superphosphate plant, sulfuric acid was being produced at a small plant in Baku with a capacity of 30,000 tons of acid. The acid department of the Sumgait superphosphate plant, which opened in 1961, added a capacity of 180,000 tons of acid. Operation of the superphosphate section, with an ultimate capacity of 800,000 tons of fertilizer, began in 1963.

Since the original chlorine–caustic plant opened in World War II, the chemical industry of Sumgait has been diversified. The chlorine plant uses salt from Kuuli, near Krasnovodsk, across the Caspian Sea, and from a deposit near Nakhichevan' for the production of caustic soda, chlorine products, detergents, and various farm chemicals. A petrochemical industry is under development, and one of its first components, an ethylene unit, opened in 1967.

## Georgian SSR

Georgia's principal resource on a Soviet national and even on an international level is the manganese deposit of Chiatura, which contributes about one-third of the Soviet Union's manganese ore and is one of the world's largest manganese producers. On a regional level, within Transcaucasia, Georgia's resource development has been focused on the exploitation of an important hydroelectric potential, notably along the mountain rivers of western Georgia.

The Chiatura deposit, situated on a plateau of 1,500–2,000 feet elevation, dissected by the Kvirila River and its tributaries, has been exploited since 1879. Before World War I it accounted for half of the world's manganese trade. Chiatura's output in 1913 was 966,000 tons. After a decline in the early Soviet period, production rose from 389,000 tons to 1.45 million in 1940 and 1.87 million in 1941. The dislocation of the Soviet economy during World War II resulted in another decline, to 850,000 by 1945. In the postwar period, production recovered rapidly to 1.8 million tons of usable ore in 1950 and 3.0 million in 1960.

Mining operations were long focused on high-grade primary oxides, which made up 46 percent of the reserves and required little beneficiation beyond simple crushing, screening, and washing. To prevent early depletion of the high-grade ores as demand for manganese rose, greater attention was given after the mid-1950s to the mining of lower-grade carbonate ores, which made up 40 percent of the reserves and required concentration. Carbonate mines opened in 1957–58 at New Itkhvisi (Russian: Novyy Itkhvisi; Georgian: Akhali Itkhvisi) and in 1960 at Darkveti. The concentrate obtained from beneficiation mills at these mines was used primarily for the production of manganese dioxide needed in battery manufacture and for other chemical purposes, although some of the carbonate concentrate also went for metallurgical uses. A further step in the program to make use of low-grade materials that were previously wasted was the completion in 1962 of a large central concentrator for the flotation of so-called fourth-grade ores and slimes.

The conversion of the Chiatura mining operations from the high-grade oxides to the lower-grade carbonates was associated with a decline of the amount of usable ore produced. Output dropped from 3 million tons in 1960 to 2.6 million in 1966 and 1.7 million in 1968. At the same time the amount of crude ore mined increased sharply because of the greater reliance on low-grade ores. In 1960, when the exploitation of carbonate ores was still in its early stages, the volume of crude ore was only somewhat greater than the output of usable ore. In 1966, when carbonate ores represented a substantial share of mine production, it required 5.6 million tons of crude ore to yield the 2.6 million tons of usable ore after concentration.

Transportation of the manganese ore was improved in 1957 with the inauguration of an electrified broad-gauge spur from the main line at Zestafoni to the Chiatura mines. Previously the mines were accessible only by a narrow-gauge line, requiring transshipment at Shorapani on the main line. Part of the manganese ore moves directly to the port of Poti, on the Black Sea, for export or for shipment to the Ukraine through the port of Zhdanov. Since 1933, part of the ore has been smelted at the Zestafoni ferroalloys plant, which produces ferromanganese and other manganese ferroalloys for use in the steel industry. In addition to blast furnaces and electric furnaces at Zestafoni, an electrolysis shop for the production of manganese metal opened in 1958. The plant was further expanded in the late 1960s.

Georgia has its own small iron and steel industry, based on the provision of iron ore from the Dashkesan mine in adjoining Azerbaydzhan, and coke from Georgian coals. But the limited production capacity and reserves at Dashkesan and the poor coking quality of Georgian coals have required the use of additional long-haul pig iron and as much as 1.5 million tons of coking coal from the Donets Basin. The iron and steel industry is thus a high-cost operation and no expansion is planned. The plant, built in the 1940s at the new city of Rustavi, southeast of Tbilisi, began steel production in 1950 and pig-iron smelting in 1954. In the mid-1960s it was producing 1.4 million tons of steel ingots from eight open-hearth furnaces (the last of which was placed in operation in 1957) and only 800,000 tons of pig iron from two blast furnaces. Forty percent of its rolled products, totaling 1 million tons, consist of steel pipe for the Azerbaydzhan oil industry. Rustavi meets 60 percent of the pipe requirements and Sumgait 40 percent.

Of almost greater significance for Transcaucasia has been the development of a chemical industry at Rustavi, based at first on coke chemicals and, after the completion of natural-gas pipelines from the Baku area in 1959 and the Northern Caucasus in 1963, on the use of the transmitted gas. The basis for the chemical industry at Rustavi was laid in 1956 with the start of production of coke-based ammonia and nitrogenous fertilizers for Georgia's tea, citrus and wine growers. Fertilizer output reached more than 400,000 tons in the mid-1960s and was to be doubled under the five-year plan 1966–70 through the addition of urea-fertilizer production.

A related component of the chemical industry of Rustavi is a synthetic-fiber complex that produces tire cord and fabrics from kapron. The production of the basic raw material, caprolactam (derived from ammonia), began in 1963, followed in the next year by the production of kapron yarn and in 1965 by tire cord. The Rustavi chemical complex also includes the production of potassium permanganate and other manganese chemicals from Chiatura ore.

Georgia's mineral industries produce a number of unusual materials with specific applications in the Soviet industry. They include talc (used mainly in ceramics and paints), from a mine at Tsnelisi, southwest of Tskhinvali, in the South Ossetian Autonomous Oblast; and barite and gumbrin. Georgia's barite, obtained mainly in the Madneuli area, southwest of Tbilisi, and at Iri (between Oni and Kvaisi), in the upper Rioni valley, accounts for 70 percent of the Soviet Union's total output. It has a variety of uses, including well-drilling muds for the petroleum industry and in the manufacture of lithopone, a white pigment. A lithopone plant at Kutaisi is one of Georgia's oldest chemical plants. Near Kutaisi is the deposit of gumbrin, a bentonite-like clay named for its mine, Gumbra, that is used as a catalyst and bleaching or filtering agent in petroleum refining. Georgia is also virtually the only place in the Soviet Union with deposits of andesite, an acid-resistant lava that is used as dimension stone or as a crushed cement additive in the chemical industry.

Nonferrous metals production has thus far been restricted to the small Kvaisi mine, which has been supplying lead and zinc concentrate since the late 1940s to Ordzhonikidze. However the 1966–70 five-year plan called for development of a large complex ore deposit at Madneuli, southwest of Tbilisi, containing copper, lead, and zinc, in addition to barite. Barite has been moving out of Madneuli since 1966, when an electrified rail spur was completed from the railroad station of Marneuli, south of Tbilisi. A pilot plant for the concentration of the open-cut copper–lead–zinc ore went into operation in the same year, and full-fledged construction on a concentrator was scheduled to begin in 1969 at Kazreti, near the Madneuli deposit. The copper concentrate was expected to be smelted at the nearby Alaverdi smelter, across the border in Armenia.

Until the 1960s Georgia's principal electric power supply for industrialization was a series of small hydroelectric stations built since the late 1920s. Among the earliest hydropower plants of the Soviet Union were the 36,000-kilowatt Zemo-Avchala station, just above Tbilisi, on the Kura River, opened in 1927, and the first 48,000-kilowatt station on the Rioni River, completed in 1933 to supply electricity to the energy-consuming ferroalloys plant at Zestafoni. A third prewar plant (16,000 kilowatts), on the Adzharis-Tskhali River, supplied power to the city of Batumi. In 1940, about 70 percent of Georgia's power output of 742 million kilowatt-hours was generated by hydroelectric installations.

The development of the republic's water-power potential continued after World War II. On the Khrami River, one hydroelectric station (113,000 kilowatts) was opened in 1947 and a second plant (110,000 kilowatts), farther downstream in 1963. On the Rioni River, two Gumati stations, with a combined capacity of 66,500 kilowatts, were opened in 1956–58 north of Kutaisi, and a third, the Ladzhanuri station (112,000 kilowatts), was completed in 1960 in a project that involved the diversion of water from the nearby Tskhenis-Tskhali River through a tunnel to the Rioni.

However, Georgia's early hydroelectric stations proved inadequate to sustain the growing industrialization of the republic. Because they had been built in the vicinity of urban centers, they lacked large storage reservoirs and were generating electricity on a relatively low head of water. Power generation on the streams, most of them fed by glaciers in the high Caucasus, was moreover subject to heavy seasonal fluctuations, with a high-water stage during the glacier melting period of spring and summer and a low-water stage in autumn and winter.

The average hydroelectric plant generated power 3,500 hours a year compared with 5,500 hours at steam power stations. Only a few hydroelectric stations such as the Khrami stations and the Tkibuli (80,000 kilowatts) and Shaori (40,000 kilowatts) stations, opened on the Tkibuli River in 1955–56, had storage reservoirs that enabled them to generate power all year round, especially in the autumn-winter low-water stage. Increasing reliance had to be placed on a system of coal-fed power stations built at the coal-mining centers of Tkvarcheli and Tkibuli as well as other cities. This trend was further accentuated in the 1960s after the arrival of natural gas, a far cheaper and economical power station fuel than the costly Georgian coal.

Construction began on a large thermal power station at Gardabani, southeast of Rustavi. The first of six 160,000-kilowatt units was installed at the plant, known as the Tbilisi regional power station, in 1963, and a fifth in 1968. The last one was to be installed by 1970, bringing the capacity up to the designed 960,000 kilowatts, or again as much as the entire electric power generating capacity of Georgia in 1960. In the late 1960s, Georgia's steam electric stations thus accounted for two-thirds of all power generation.

At the same time, however, plans are being made to make more effective use of the republic's hydroelectric potential by construction of large power stations with ample storage reservoirs for year-round operation. The largest of these stations, the Inguri plant, on the river of the same name, at Dzhvari, 20 miles upstream from Zugdidi, is planned to have a capacity of 1.6 million kilowatts. Construction began in 1961 on the site, which will have an archtype dam 900 feet high, one of the highest in the Soviet Union. The first 265,000-kilowatt units were to be installed by 1970, giving power to major centers via a 500-kilovolt transmission line. The construction of the 1-million-kilowatt Tobari station farther upstream on the Inguri is envisaged for the 1970s. Other hydroelectric plans include three stations of the Vartsikhe complex, with a combined capacity of 200,000 kilowatts, on the Rioni River below the Rioni power station, and the 350,000-kilowatt Namakhvani station, also on the Rioni, above the two Gumati stations. A third planned project is the 130,000-kilowatt Zhinvali station, on the Aragvi River, north of Tbilisi.

Georgia's small coal deposits have been unable to meet the needs of the republic, much less of the rest of Transcaucasia, which has no coal reserves of its own. In most years, Georgia has had 1.5 million tons of Donets Basin coal, mostly coking grades, shipped in to supplement its own production.

The oldest coal-mining center is Tkibuli, northeast of Kutaisi, with an annual output of about 1.4 million tons from three mines. Tkibuli has been in exploitation since the mid-nineteenth century. Its coal, though subbituminous and not suitable for coking, has been mixed with the coking coal of Tkvarcheli and the Donets Basin for use in the Rustavi blast furnaces. The Shaori deposit, adjoining Tkibuli, was under development in the late 1960s. The Tkvarcheli deposit, northeast of Ochamchire, has been mined since the mid-1930s. It produced about 1 million tons a year in the mid-1960s from six small mines.

As a supplementary power station fuel, a lignite deposit has been mined since the 1930s at Vale, near Akhaltsikhe, close to the Turkish border. Its output was 170,000 tons in 1965.

Coal production, which amounted to 625,000 tons in 1940, rose after World War II to a high point of 3 million tons in 1958, but declined during the 1960s after the coming of natural gas. It ranged around 2.5 million tons in the mid-1960s.

Industry has thus become heavily dependent on the use of piped natural gas both for power generation and as a raw material for the chemical industry. The first gas line was completed in 1959, from the newly developed field at Karadag, near Baku. Because of the limited reserves of the Karadag deposit, this supply was supplemented by a pipeline from the Stavropol' field of the Northern Caucasus, which reached Georgia in 1963 from Ordzhonikidze across the main Caucasus range along the route of the Georgian Military Highway. A second parallel pipeline from the Northern Caucasus was completed in 1966. Georgia consumed 1.5 billion cubic meters in 1965 and expected to double this consumption with the planned arrival of Iranian gas.

This discussion of the Georgian fuel industry would be incomplete without consideration of the Batumi oil refinery. Batumi is the Black Sea terminal for exports of Baku oil, having been linked with this oil-producing district by pipeline since 1906. The Batumi refinery, a relatively small installation, went into operation in 1929. A second Baku–Batumi pipeline was added two years later to keep it supplied with crude oil and to provide another outlet for Baku's exports. A third pipeline was reported under construction in the 1960s. Batumi's output of refined products long emphasized kerosene as a household fuel. However, the increasing electrification of rural areas and the advent of natural gas in cities has reduced the market for kerosene. Accordingly the Batumi refinery was expected to stress the production of fuel oils, which were burned increasingly at steam electric stations in combination with natural gas.

## Armenian SSR

Armenia's contribution of resources to the Soviet economy has involved a substantial part of the nation's copper and, particularly, molybdenum concentrate, associated with copper. In addition, Armenian industry, having long relied almost entirely on the generation of cheap hydroelectric power, has attracted a number of energy-oriented activities, such as the reduction of aluminum, the production of synthetic rubber, and other power-consuming chemical processes. Projects for the development of resources in the coming years include the exploitation of a newly developed gold-lode deposit, expected to become one of the Soviet Union's principal sources of gold, and the development of a new type of raw material, nephelite syenite, for the production of alumina and a wide range of by-products.

Overshadowing Armenia's resource development has been the problem of the most effective use of the waters of Lake Sevan, a natural mountain reservoir of 550 square miles that dominates the republic as a tempting source of water for irrigation and power generation.

The first Sevan plan, proposed in 1910 and adopted by Soviet planners in the 1930s, called for the draining of the shallower southeastern part of the lake to reduce the loss of water through evaporation (which was 92 percent of the outgo) and thus make available more runoff for irrigation and a system of hydroelectric stations along the lake's outlet, the Razdan River (formerly called Zanga). The drainage project, over a period of fifty years, would have lowered the lake's level by 150 feet, reducing its area to about 80 square miles (one-seventh of the original area) in the deeper northwestern portion. After the fifty-year period, a new balance between inflow and precipitation on the one hand, and outflow and evaporation on the other hand, was to have been assured in the reduced water body, making more water available for economic uses. To make use of the artificially increased outflow during the fifty-year period, a system of hydroelectric stations was to be built along the Razdan River. Eight stations were to be built over a period of fifteen years, with a total capacity of more than 600,000 kilowatts.

The first station, Kanaker (88,000 kilowatts, later raised to 102,000 kilowatts), just north of Yerevan, was completed in 1936 after six years of construction, and gave rise to energy-oriented industries, such as the production of acetylene from calcium carbide for the manufacture of synthetic rubber. World War II interrupted the construction of additional power stations along the Razdan, and for years Lake Sevan was being drained at the increased outflow rate without the expected payoff in hydroelectric power generation. It was only after twelve years had passed after the construction of the Kanaker station that the second power plant, the Ozernaya or Sevan station (34,000 kilowatts), was completed in 1949 at the actual outlet tunnel from the lake. Other stations followed. The Gyumush plant, the largest in the series, with 224,000 kilowatts, was inaugurated in 1953; Arzni, below Gyumush, with a capacity of 70,000 kilowatts, was completed in 1956–57; Atarbekyan (80,000 kilowatts), above Gyumush, in 1959; and the Yerevan station (44,000 kilowatts), the sixth, in 1962.

By this time, however, a set of unforeseen circumstances had led to a revision of the original Sevan plan, and the last two power plants along the Razdan River were canceled.

In the twenty-five years that had elapsed since the start of the lake drainage project, almost one-third of its water had run off at the increased outflow rate, and the level of the lake had dropped by about 40 feet. As the shoreline retreated, it was found that unexpected additional measures would be required to make use of the former lake bottom. Certain parts would require a system of drainage canals to prevent waterlogging, and other parts would require irrigation, which would reduce the inflow into the lake and thus upset the planned water balance. The resulting drop in the water table also produced increased erosion on the slopes of the ranges enclosing the Sevan basin. These additional factors would have raised the cost of the drainage project by 50 percent over the original estimates.

In addition, it became evident in the 1950s that the transmission of newly discovered natural gas from Azerbaydzhan and the Northern Caucasus as well as the availability of surplus electric power in these areas would no longer make Armenia dependent entirely on the Razdan hydroelectric system for power generation. The combination of undesirable consequences in the natural environment of the lake as a result of the proposed drainage and the expectation of changes in the energy supply for Armenia's economy led to a fundamental revision of the Sevan project in 1961.

Under the revised plan, Lake Sevan is to be preserved as a far larger body of water than was envisaged by the original project. The drop of the lake level is to be halted at about 60 feet below the original level, preserving a lake with 86.5 percent of the original area and 56 percent of the original volume of water. The smaller evaporation from the reduced area would make additional water available for runoff through the Razdan River, amounting to 170 million cubic meters a year compared with the 66 million cubic meters of outflow of the original natural lake.

But this increased outflow was far short of the 700 million cubic meters envisaged under the earlier plan and of the 500 million cubic meters regarded as a minimum to serve existing irrigation systems and power stations along the Razdan River. To make up the difference, the new Sevan plan called for an increase in the lake's intake (and, consequently, its outflow) through the diversion of water from adjoining watersheds, notably the Arpa River basin, south of the lake. A diversion tunnel from the upper Arpa River was to carry 300 million cubic meters of water a year to Lake Sevan. Construction of the 30-mile-long tunnel was under way in the late 1960s from a reservoir on the Arpa, just below the mineral-springs resort of Dzhermuk, northward through the Vardenis mountain range to the south shore of Lake Sevan.

Even before completion of the Arpa–Sevan diversion project and the achievement of a new water balance in the Sevan basin, expected in the early 1970s, the yearly outflow rate from the lake through the Razdan River has been gradually cut back since 1961, with a corresponding reduction in hydroelectric power generation, as natural gas and electric power from Azerbaydzhan became available. Until that time Armenia had been dependent entirely on the hydroelectric power of the Razdan River. The republic's power output rose steadily after World War II, as one station after another was completed in the system, generating electricity at full capacity as the outflow rate from the lake was increased to an average of more than 1,200 million cubic meters a year during the 1950s. Hydroelectric power output rose from 450 million kilowatt-hours in 1945 to 950 million in 1950, 2.2 billion in 1955, and reached a peak of 2.77 billion in 1961 (90 percent from the Razdan system).

The previous year both a natural-gas pipeline and a 220-kilovolt power transmission line (later raised to 330 kilovolts) were completed from Akstafa in Azerbaydzhan, inaugurating a new era in Armenia's electric power industry. As Azerbaydzhan power began to be transmitted to Armenia at a rate of about 1 billion kilowatt-hours a year and new gas-fueled power plants began operations, the Razdan River discharge from Lake Sevan was gradually reduced from 1,450 million cubic meters in 1961 to 600 million cubic meters in 1965. Electric power generation along the Razdan, accordingly, was more than halved during this period, from 2.5 billion kilowatt-hours in 1961 to 1.2 billion in 1965.

The first gas-fueled heat and power plant of Armenia to go into construction was at Kirovakan, the chemical center. It began operations in 1964, with installation of the first of four 12,500-kilowatt units, and reached its full capacity of 50,000 kilowatts in 1966. Meanwhile construction on a much larger gas-fueled heat and power station had started in Yerevan in 1960, and the first three units of 50,000 kilowatts each were installed there in 1963. Two more 50,000-kilowatt units and two 150,000-kilowatt units were added in 1964–66, bringing the total capacity to 550,000 kilowatts. The Yerevan station accounted for somewhat less than half of the republic's generating capacity, but, because of the reduced output of the Razdan hydroelectric stations, produced about three-fourths of the total electricity in the mid-1960s.

An even greater thermal power-generating center was under development in the late 1960s at the town of Razdan (called Akhta until 1959), where a major alumina–cement–chemical complex was being built on the basis of nearby nephelite syenite deposits. The immediate heat and power needs of the construction project were met in 1966–67 by the construction of a station with two 50,000-kilowatt units. Two more 100,000-kilowatt generators were to be added there by 1970. But for longer-range requirements construction was under way on a 1.2-million-kilowatt thermal station at Razdan. The first three 200,000-kilowatt generators were planned to go into operation in the early 1970s.

Although the importance of hydroelectric power has greatly declined as a result of the cutback of the Razdan system, additional water-power projects are under way or contemplated elsewhere in the republic, notably on the Vorotan River in the southeastern panhandle. Three stations are planned on the Vorotan, which, because of dropping 9,000 feet over a course of 120 miles, is eminently suitable for power generation. Construction of the first of three stations, the Tatev plant, with a capacity of 157,000 kilowatts from three turbines, began in 1961 and was to go into operation in 1969. A Shamb station, with a capacity of 160,000 kilowatts, and the 88,000-kilowatt Spandaryan plant, with a regulatory storage reservoir, are planned further upstream. Another prospective hydroelectric development is the 185,000-kilowatt Shnokh project, in the Debed River valley, northeast of Alaverdi, the copper-smelting center.

However, despite these projects, Armenia will be heavily dependent on energy and fuel imports in the foreseeable future. Gas requirements by 1970 are estimated at 5 billion cubic meters, to be supplied by Azerbaydzhan (one-third) and the Northern Caucasus (two-thirds). There are also plans for the construction of a pipeline from Iranian gas fields. Because of the continuing energy deficit, the Yerevan area has been selected as a potential site for a nuclear power plant with a capacity of 880,000 kilowatts.

Mineral resource development focuses on copper–molybdenum deposits in the Zangezur mountains of the southeastern panhandle. This district has been a center of mining activity since the Middle Ages, particularly around Kafan, where copper is associated with lead–zinc ores. Although the Kafan mines were modernized and a new concentrator was opened in 1934 and a second in 1967, attention shifted increasingly to the copper–molybdenum deposits, especially after World War II, as the demand for molybdenum in special alloy steels increased.

The production centers are situated roughly in a north–south line extending northward from the Araks River (on the Iranian border) parallel to the boundary of the Nakhichevan' ASSR on the west. The largest center, Kadzharan (1959 population: 11,300), is situated 15 miles west of Kafan, the railhead. Kadzharan (formerly known as Pirdoudan) began operations in 1952, at first in underground mines. Since 1959 its ores are being extracted entirely from more economical open-cut mines. The northernmost mining center, Dastakert (1959 population: 2,350), is reached by a 15-mile-long road southward from Sisian, and has also been in operation since the early 1950s. The newest copper–molybdenum mining center is Agarak (1959 population: 1,639), which went into operation in 1963. Agarak is the southernmost of the three, near the railroad that runs among the Araks River and the Iranian border, and ships its concentrate through Karchivan station.

In addition to the copper concentrate, which accounts for 15 to 20 percent of the value of output, and the molybdenum concentrate, which makes up 80 to 85 percent of the value, the ores of Kadzharan, Dastakert, and Agarak also yield a number of valuable by-products, such as rhenium, selenium, and tellurium. The molybdenum concentrates have thus far been sent out of Armenia to processing plants elsewhere in the USSR, but the 1966–70 five-year plan called for the construction of a molybdenum-products plant at Kirovakan to process the growing output of molybdenum concentrate and recover the valuable by-products associated with it.

Armenia's copper concentrates are processed within the republic, at Alaverdi, another old copper-mining district, where a smelter has been in operation since before the Soviet regime. It resumed production in 1926 and has been expanded over the years, adding converters for the production of blister copper in 1936, the first electrolytic installation for copper refining in 1948, and the second in 1961. The Alaverdi smelter was expanded and modernized in the 1960s to accommodate an increasing supply of copper concentrates from various mines in Transcaucasia, to eliminate the discharge of byproduct gases and thus improve the recovery of rare, disseminated metals from slimes and flue dusts. In view of the relatively higher cost of long-haul coal and other fuels and the lower cost of electric power, smelter capacity was expanded through the construction of electric furnaces instead of the conventional fuel-burning reverberatory furnaces.

The expansion of the smelter was made necessary in part by the resumption of large-scale mining operations at the nearby copper mine of Shamlug and the complex-ore (copper, lead, zinc) mine of Akhtala. These mines yielded silver and copper as early as the ninth century, but their high-grade ores became depleted in modern times. However, the discovery of large new (though lower-grade) ore bodies in the 1940s revived interest in these mines, particularly in view of their proximity to the Alaverdi smelter. After the intricate beneficiation technology required for the newly discovered ores had been tested at a pilot installation opened at Akhtala in 1954, construction began on a large new concentrator that would process the Shamlug copper ore in one section and the complex Akhtala ore in another. The copper section began operations in 1967.

The modernization of the Alaverdi smelter also led to more efficient production of sulfuric acid from sulfur recovered from smelter gases. The by-product gases had been used partly by an old sulfuric acid plant opened in 1942. Beginning in 1945 the acid was used in combination with long-haul Kola apatite concentrate to produce ordinary superphosphate. By 1960 the Alaverdi copper and chemical complex was producing 60,000 tons of sulfuric acid and 100,000 tons of superphosphate. In the mid-1960s, the sulfuric-acid plant was reconstructed, using the contact method, which yielded a more concentrated and purer acid than the lead-chamber method employed in the 1942 installation. The new plant also assured fuller utilization of smelter gases (previously only 30 to 35 percent were used). The first contact unit was opened in 1967 and the second in 1968, with two more due by 1970. The new plant, when completed, will have a capacity of about 150,000 tons. The production of simple superphosphate was interrupted in 1964 in conjunction with reconstruction of the sulfuric-acid process. It remained doubtful whether the long hauls required for Kola apatite made it economical to produce ordinary superphosphate in Armenia.

The gold-lode deposit that is expected to make Armenia one of the Soviet Union's principal gold producers is situated in the Zod area, east of Vardenis (formerly Basargechar), near Lake Sevan. The deposit is near Zod Pass, at the junction of two ranges that surround the Sevan basin—the Sevan (or Shakhdag mountains on the north and the Zangezur (or East Sevan) mountains on the east.

After a pilot-plant phase at Zod itself, a mill to recover the gold by flotation is planned at the town of Ararat, some distance from Lake Sevan, to avoid pollution. The Zod mine may be linked to the treatment plant by a railroad along the north shore of Lake Sevan that would also serve Shorzha, site of a large deposit of dunite, a magnesium silicate used as a refractory material.

The aluminum plant at Kanaker, a northern suburb of Yerevan, has used long-haul Urals alumina since it went into operation in 1950 after six years' construction. In 1959 the plant added a wirebar mill and in 1961 a foil-rolling installation, establishing an integrated fabricating industry that also includes a cable plant at Yerevan.

The development of a local raw-material source for alumina production lagged because of technological problems in processing the nephelite syenite, not used elsewhere as a commercial source of alumina. The Tezhsar deposit of nephelite syenite is found on the southern slopes of the Pambak Range, on a tributary of the Marmarik River. A 15-mile-long railroad will take the rock to a processing plant at Razdan, where it will be treated with limestone in kilns, with an ultimate capacity of 1.2-million tons of cement. In addition to alumina and cement, the nephelite syenite is expected to yield a variety of chemical by-products, including soda ash, potash, and yerevanite, a special glass. Construction began in 1960, and in the first stage (opened in 1969) a 600,000-ton kiln started producing cement only, using limestone from the town of Ararat.

Armenia's chemical industry, which arose in 1927 on the basis of the processing of calcium carbide, using local limestone deposits, was converted to the use of natural gas in the mid-1960s. The industry is centered in Yerevan and Kirovakan, each with a distinctive series of chemical products.

The Yerevan industry has been based on acetylene, obtained by the reaction of water on calcium carbide. Acetylene, through the intermediate vinylacetylene, was used after 1940 at a newly constructed synthetic-rubber plant in making chloroprene, a valuable rubber that does not require sulfur for vulcanization. Acetylene, supplied by the synthetic-rubber plant to another Yerevan plant known as Polyvinylacetate, yielded acetic acid, which in turn has been used in the manufacture of cellulose acetate on a large scale since 1963. Acetylene and acetic acid are also the basis for the manufacture of vinyl acetate and the whole group of vinyl resins. Chloroprene rubber is not used for tires, and a tire plant inaugurated in Yerevan in 1943 (with a capacity of 1.2 million tires a year) has used synthetic rubber from other plants in the USSR as well as imported natural rubber.

While the Yerevan chemical industry was based on the acetylene cycle, the industry at Kirovakan used the cyanamide process, a nitrogen-fixation method using calcium carbide. The Kirovakan chemical plant opened in 1932 with the production of calcium carbide from limestone. In successive expansion programs, it added the manufacture of cyanide salts in 1941, ammonia and nitrogenous fertilizers in 1949–51, artificial corundum in 1959, dicyandiamide and its derivative, melamine resin, in 1960, and acetate rayon (using cellulose acetate from Yerevan) in 1962.

Yerevan's chemical industry was converted partly to the use of natural gas in 1966, and the following year 40 percent of the synthetic rubber was to be manufactured from acetylene derived from natural gas instead of calcium carbide. Also in 1967, Kirovakan's ammonia production switched from the cyanamide process to the use of natural gas, and a urea unit opened the following year. The changeover from calcium carbide to natural gas as a raw material for the Armenian chemical industry resulted in substantial electric power savings and in generally more economical processes than the antiquated and power-consuming calcium-carbide method.

Armenia's industrialization program, particularly the development of the Razdan valley, was promoted with the completion of a railroad from Yerevan to Lake Sevan in 1960. There are plans for extending it to a junction with the Transcaucasian main line at Akstafa. The segment between Akstafa and Idzhevan was under construction in the late 1960s.

# 7

# THE UKRAINE
# AND MOLDAVIA

The existence of the Soviet Union's principal coking coal, iron ore, and manganese mining districts in the Ukraine has made that republic the nation's leading producer of iron and steel products, associated with coke-based chemicals. The iron and steel industry had its beginnings in the 1880s, when the center of iron smelting began to shift from the old charcoal reduction plants of the Urals to the newly developed technology based on the use of coking coals. In the late nineteenth and early twentieth centuries, when primitive smelting technology required a greater weight of coal and coke than iron ore to produce a ton of pig iron, iron and steel plants tended to be situated near coal mines or, at most, half way between the coal and the iron ore.

Two clusters of iron and steel plants thus arose, a larger grouping in the Donets Basin, where the coal was mined, and a smaller grouping along the Dnieper River, between the coal and the Krivoy Rog iron ore. In the 1930s, the Dnieper group expanded substantially as the availability of cheap hydroelectric power from the first Dnieper dam stimulated industrial development, and by 1940, pig iron output was almost evenly divided between the two clusters. In addition the first blast furnace was opened at Krivoy Rog itself in 1934, and a new seaboard iron and steel plant opened in 1933 at Mariupol' (called Zhdanov after 1948), using Kerch' iron ore from across the Sea of Azov. After World War II, expansion has been concentrated at these two newer centers, particularly at Krivoy Rog, whose iron and steel plant, the largest of the Ukraine, was planned to reach a pig iron capacity of 8.5 million tons by 1970.

Petroleum production, negligible until the mid-1950s, increased rapidly in the 1960s after the discovery of new deposits in the old producing area of the Carpathian foothills and in the newly developed area on the left bank of the Dnieper River. But gains in crude-oil output were overshadowed by the discovery of one of the Soviet Union's largest natural-gas deposits, at Shebelinka, south of Khar'kov, which produced about one-fifth of the country's natural gas in the mid-1960s. Natural-gas deposits were also developed in the Carpathian piedmont. The Ukrainian electric power industry, long dependent on coal-burning stations and the single Dnieper hydroelectric plant, was expanded after the mid-1950s through the use of natural gas and the construction of a whole series of hydro-electric stations along the Dnieper River. Natural gas also stimulated the development of a chemical industry, previously based mainly on coke chemicals. Other chemical raw materials include potash deposits in the Carpathian foothills; newly discovered deposits of native sulfur, also in the Carpathian area; and the salt-rich brine of the Sivash, a lagoon between the Crimea and the mainland. Buried sand deposits in two areas of the Ukraine have also become the Soviet Union's principal sources of titanium and zirconium.

Ukrainian resource development for heavy industry will be discussed here in terms of major industrial concentrations: the Donets Basin, with its coal mines, iron and steel production, electric power, and diversified chemical industry based on coke, salt, limestone, and natural gas; the Khar'kov complex, with the Shebelinka natural-gas field; the Dnieper riverside complex, with iron and steel, hydroelectric power, and energy-oriented industries; the Krivoy Rog iron ore basin, with its expanding iron and steel industry and the Nikopol' manganese basin; the Kremenchug oil-refining and petro-chemical complex; the Crimean brine-based chemical industry; and the southwestern Ukraine, with the oil, gas, potash, and sulfur resources of the Carpathians.

## The Donets Basin

The Donets Basin, though situated largely within the Ukrainian SSR, also extends eastward into Rostov Oblast of the Russian SFSR, with about five-sixths of the total coal production in the Ukraine and one-sixth in Rostov Oblast. In 1965, out of a total Donbas coal output of 206 million tons, 174 million originated in the Ukrainian section and 32 million in the Rostov section. (The resource development of the Rostov section is discussed under the Northern Caucasus.) Of the total reserves of the Donets Basin, 30 percent is anthracite, mainly in the south and southeast; 28 percent is high-volatile bituminous coal, in the northwest, suitable for gas production; 25 percent is low- and medium-volatile bituminous coal, suitable for coking and found mainly in the southwest and west; and 17 percent is semianthracite, mainly in the north and northeast.

Commercial production, beginning in the 1820s, was at first limited largely to anthracite, used mainly as a steamship fuel on the Black Sea. After 1880, the rise of an iron and steel industry based on the use of coke and the general development of industry led to the mining of coking coals and other bituminous coals, reducing the share of anthracite in the basin's total output to a lesser share, ranging from 20 to 40 percent. (Coal output in Rostov Oblast, situated in the eastern part of the basin, consists mainly of anthracite.)

Total coal production of the Ukrainian part of the Donets Basin reflected the industrial growth of the Soviet Union as a whole. From 22.8 million tons in 1913, output rose to 83.4 million tons in 1940. After recovering from destruction of mines in World War II, which set production back to 30.3 million tons in 1945, coal output in the Ukrainian Donbas rose to 77 million tons in 1950, doubled to 158 million tons by 1960, and reached 174 million tons in 1965.

The Ukrainian Donbas falls into four coal-mining administrations: Donbassantratsit and Luganskugol' (*ugol'* = coal) in Lugansk Oblast, and Artemugol' and Donetskugol' in Donetsk Oblast. The principal mining centers of each administration, with type of coal mined, are: *Donbassantratsit*: Antratsit, Krasnyy Luch, and Sverd-lovsk (anthracite), and Krasnodon (bituminous); *Luganskugol*: Kommunarsk and Kadiyevka (bituminous); *Artemugol*: Thorez (until 1974 called Chistyakovo), Snezhnoye, and Shakhtersk (an-thracite), and Gorlovka (bituminous); *Donetskugol*: Donetsk, Makeyevka, Selidovo, and Krasnoarmeysk (bituminous) (Fig. 20).

As the upper coal seams have been exhausted, notably around Gorlovka, Donetsk, and Makeyevka, coal production has been main-tained through the construction of deeper mines and expansion of the mining area, particularly toward the west. The development of the so-called Western Donbas in Dnepropetrovsk Oblast began in the mid-1950s. The first mine, known as the Zapadno-Donbasskaya (Western Donbas) No. 1, opened to production in 1963 with an annual capacity of 600,000 tons at the new mining town of Pershotravensk (called Shakhterskoye before 1960), 25 miles southeast of Pavlograd. The second, known as Ternovskaya No. 1, with a capacity of 900,000 tons, went into operation in 1964 at Ternovka, 10 miles east of Pavlograd. A third, Voskhod No. 2, also with a capacity of 900,000 tons, raised the total mining capacity of the new district to 2.4 million tons by 1965. A fourth mine, the Western Donbas No. 4, under construction since 1959, yielded its first coal in late 1968. Eight other coking–coal mines, with a total capacity of 14 million tons, were said to be under construction in the late 1960s, including the No. 6/42 mine with a capacity of 2.4 million tons near Pavlograd. Also under construction was a central coal-washing plant, with a capacity of 5 million tons of coal a year. The coking coal resources of the Western Donbas are at relatively shallow depths, 600 to 1,200 feet, and have the advantage of being nearer the iron and steel industry of the Dnieper valley than the more easterly mines of the Donbas. To provide a direct rail outlet for the coal, a railroad from Krasnoarmeysk to Pavlograd was completed in the early 1960s, and then extended via Novomos-kovsk to the Dneprodzerzhinsk dam on the Dnieper River by 1967.

The coal of the Donets Basin serves as the fuel for a network of electric power stations that generate about half of the total elec-tricity of the Ukraine. Many of the steam electric stations use fine anthracite material recovered at low cost from culm and silt banks laid down in the early days of anthracite mining. Since the construction of the first coal-based stations in the 1920s, the capacity of generators and stations has steadily increased.

The first major station, the Shterovka power plant (in Russian: Shtergres), began operations in 1926 with a generating capacity of 20,000 kilowatts, and was expanded to 152,000 kilowatts by World War II. It was rebuilt with a capacity of 178,000 kilowatts after having been destroyed during the war. The town of Shtergres, which grew up around the station, 5 miles southwest of Krasnyy Luch, on the Mius River, was renamed Miusinsk in 1965. A second prewar power station, the Zuyevka power plant (in Russian: Zugres), 7 miles east of Khartsyzsk, on the Krynka River, went into operation in 1931, with two 50,000-kilowatt generating units, and reached a capacity of 300,000 kilowatts by World War II. After the war it was rebuilt by 1947. A third power station, at Kurakhovo, 25 miles west of Donetsk, went into operation with a 50,000-kilowatt generator just before the German attack on the Soviet Union in 1941; it was dismantled and moved eastward, and reinstalled in 1946 with subsequent additions in capacity.

A second stage of electric power development involved the construction of two major steam electric stations in the early 1950s. The Mironovskiy station, on the upper Lugan' River, halfway between Artemovsk and Debal'tsevo, went into operation in 1953, reaching a capacity of 500,000 kilowatts in 1957. The Slavyansk station, on the Northern Donets River, northeast of the city of the same name, went into operation in 1954, reaching a capacity of 300,000 kilowatts in 1957. It was expanded in 1968 through addition of the Soviet Union's first 800,000-kilowatt generating unit. A second such unit was to follow.

In the late 1950s, two further power stations were built. The first 100,000-kilowatt unit of the Lugansk station, at Schast'ye (Happiness), on the Northern Donets, north of Lugansk, went into operation in 1956. By 1958 seven such generators had raised the capacity to 700,000 kilowatts. This first stage was followed by the installation of four 200,000-kilowatt units in 1961–63, raising the total capacity to 1.5 million kilowatts. It was further increased to 2.3 million in the late 1960s. The second major Donbas station under development during this period was Starobeshevo, situated at Novyy Svet (New Light), on the Kal'mius River, 17 miles south-

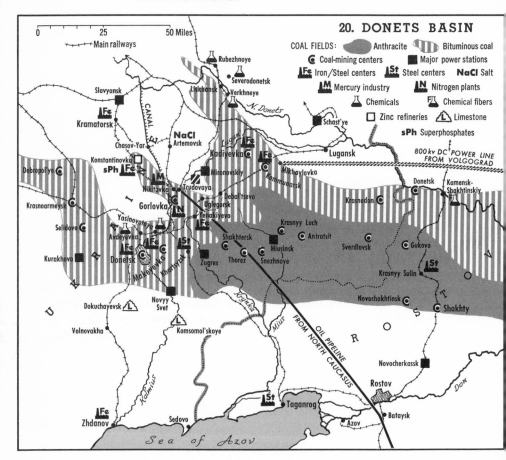

## 20. DONETS BASIN

COAL FIELDS: Anthracite | Bituminous coal
- **C** Coal-mining centers | Major power stations
- **Fe** Iron/Steel centers | **St** Steel centers | **NaCl** Salt
- **M** Mercury industry | **N** Nitrogen plants
- Chemicals | **FI** Chemical fibers
- Zinc refineries | **L** Limestone
- sPh Superphosphates

800 kv DC POWER LINE FROM VOLGOGRAD

OIL PIPELINE FROM NORTH CAUCASUS

Sea of Azov

east of Donetsk. It opened in 1958. After three 100,000-kilowatt units had been completed the following year, a new series of 200,-000-kilowatt units began to be installed, raising the capacity to its final design of 2.3 million kilowatts by 1967. The principal new power project in the late 1960s was the construction of the Uglegorsk station, on the upper Lugan' River, with a designed capacity of 3.6 million kilowatts. Four 300,000-kilowatt units were to be installed in the early 1970s, followed by three 800,000-kilowatt units.

The Donbas power grid was linked with the Dnieper grid and the Rostov grid on the eve of World War II to form the Southern power system, expanded in the late 1950s to include the Khar'kov and Volgograd grids, and in 1966 the power system of the Western

Ukraine. In addition to conventional alternating-current lines linking the Donbas with Volgograd via the Tsimlyansk hydroelectric station on the Don River, an experimental direct-current 800-kilovolt line was opened between the Donbas substation at Mikhaylovka, just northeast of Kommunarsk, and the Volgograd hydroelectric station in October, 1962.

The iron and steel industry consists of several integrated plants dating from before the Soviet period that have been substantially expanded and modernized since World War II. The oldest plant, at Donetsk (called originally Yuzovka, for a Scottish industrialist Hughes, and later, until 1961, Stalino), dates from the 1870s. Others, with their founding dates, are at Yenakiyevo (1895), Makeyevka (1899), Kramatorsk (1897), and Kommunarsk (1896; originally called Alchevsk and later, until 1961, Voroshilovsk). All were expanded by the construction of new blast furnaces and steel making capacity in the 1950s and 1960s, with the largest increases at the Kommunarsk, Yenakiyevo, and Makeyevka plants.

However, the most important iron and steel complex has grown up at Zhdanov, south of the Donets Basin proper, on the Sea of Azov, where the old Il'yich plant dates from 1897, and the new Azovstal' plant from 1933. At the Il'yich plant a new blast furnace (replacing an older one) opened in 1957, and three additional blast furnaces, Nos. 3, 4, and 5, were opened in 1958, 1963, and 1965. The No. 5 furnace has a working volume of 2,300 cubic meters (80,000 cubic feet), with an annual smelting capacity of 1.37 million metric tons. At the Azovstal' plant, three blast furnaces were built before World War II. Two other large furnaces were added in 1958 and 1959.

While the Il'yich plant at Zhdanov, like the blast furnaces in the Donets Basin proper, uses iron ore from the Krivoy Rog basin, the Azovstal' plant has been oriented toward the use of high-phosphorus ore from the Kerch' Peninsula of the Crimea, situated across the Sea of Azov from Zhdanov. The Kerch' 40-percent ore consists of a powdery oolitic limonite, mined in open pits, washed to remove excess silica, and sintered to form a 45-percent self-fluxing agglomerate. This is shipped in a hot state by barge across the Sea of Azov to Zhdanov. There a high-phosphorus pig iron is produced in the blast furnaces of the Azovstal' mill. When converted to steel, this pig iron yields a basic slag rich in phosphorus that can be utilized as fertilizer.

The Kerch' operations include two deposits with open pits having a combined capacity of about 10 million tons of crude ore and a concentrator producing about 6 million tons of usable ore (as of 1966). The pits in the Kamysh-Burun deposits, at the mining town of Arshintsevo on the southern outskirts of the city of Kerch', were the first to resume production, in 1951, after wartime destruction. They have a capacity of 4 million tons of crude ore. The Chernomorskiy (Black Sea) pits Nos. 1 and 2 opened in 1958 and 1965 in the El'tigen deposit, just south of Kamysh-Burun. They yield about 6 million tons of crude ore a year. An uneconomical integrated iron and steel plant at Kerch', which used local ore, was destroyed during World War II and has not been rebuilt.

In 1966 the Donets Basin accounted for 18.5 million tons out of the Ukraine's total pig iron production of 35.2 million tons. Donetsk Oblast, with the large mills at Zhdanov, Donetsk, Makeyevka, and Yenakiyevo, and smaller integrated mills at Konstantinovka and Kramatorsk, produced 15.2 million tons of pig iron. Lugansk Oblast contributed 3.3 million tons. Most of it was produced at the integrated plant of Kommunarsk. The rest came from blast furnaces of the smaller Almaznaya plant at the city of Kadiyevka, where a ferroalloys plant equipped with electric furnaces also went into operation in 1962.

The Donets Basin is well supplied with fluxes and refractories for the iron and steel industry. The principal sources of limestone and dolomite are Dokuchayevsk, 20 miles south of Donetsk, and Komsomol'skoye, 30 miles southeast of Donetsk, while the main refractory-producing center is Chasov-Yar, 10 miles west of Artemovsk.

The chemical industry of the basin has been based traditionally on the use of coke chemicals, derived from coke-oven gases, and salt and limestone deposits in the Slavyansk–Artemovsk area. In addition to the iron and steel centers, coke–chemical plants are found at Gorlovka, where hydrogen derived from coke-oven gases is used in ammonia synthesis in a nitrogenous fertilizer plant dating from the mid-1930s. New coke–chemical plants were opened in 1953 at Yasinovataya, and in 1963 at Avdeyevka, both 10 miles north of Donetsk. At Slavyansk, an old prerevolutionary soda plant producing soda ash and chlorine-caustic soda was supplemented by a new, larger plant on which construction was begun in 1938, interrupted by World War II, and completed in 1946.

A major chemical complex is found in the Lisichansk area. The city's southern suburb, Verkhneye, is the site of the Donsoda plant, another soda producer, dating from before the Revolution and expanded during the Soviet period; and the city of Rubezhnoye, north of Lisichansk, across the Northern Donets River, is one of the Soviet Union's largest producers of aniline dyes, dating from World War I. In the 1950s, a new chemical complex developed in the Lisichansk area, at Severodonetsk, northeast of Lisichansk, across the Northern Donets. The Severodonetsk plant was under construction before the outbreak of World War II, but at the beginning of hostilities its equipment was evacuated eastward. Reconstruction was resumed in 1948, and operations began in 1951 with the production of nitric acid and ammonium nitrate from Gorlovka coke-based ammonia. Two years later Severodonetsk began its own ammonia production from Donets coke gases. After the arrival of natural gas by pipeline from the Shebelinka field in 1958, the Severodonetsk complex converted partly from coke chemicals to the use of hydrocarbons. The product range at Severodonetsk (which rose in population from 33,000 in 1959 to 74,000 in 1967) includes caprolactam (since 1962), used for the manufacture of kapron fiber, and acetylene-based chemicals, including acetic acid, acetic anhydride and, since 1968, vinyl acetate, used in the production of vinyl resins and other plastics. There are plans for the construction of a major oil refinery at Severodonetsk, based on crude oil from the expanded fields around Groznyy in the Caucasus.

A superphosphate plant at Konstantinovka is associated with a local zinc smelter and refinery, using Kola Peninsula apatite and by-product sulfuric acid derived from the smelter's sulfuric gases. Before World War II, the Konstantinovka zinc refinery (opened in 1930) processed long-haul zinc concentrates by the retort distillation method, employing coke as a reducing agent. After the war, the plant reopened in 1951 after having been converted to the electrolytic reduction method.

The Donets Basin has the Soviet Union's oldest mercury mine

and mill at Nikitovka, a northern suburb of Gorlovka, which was the country's main producer of mercury before World War II. Since then production has been supplemented by the mercury mines of Central Asia, but Nikitovka has also expanded, with a second mill opening in 1968.

Relatively low precipitation (about 20 inches a year) in the Donets Basin, combined with a highly permeable subsoil and heavy demands for industrial water, has required the construction of aqueducts from outside the area. A canal from the Northern Donets River, northeast of Slavyansk, to Donetsk was opened in 1957–58. There are plans for the construction of another aqueduct, rising in the Dneprodzerzhinsk reservoir on the Dnieper River and extending eastward past Lozovaya along the watershed between the Northern Donets River in the north and the Samara River, a Dnieper tributary, in the south.

## Khar'kov Complex

In the Khar'kov manufacturing complex, northwest of the Donets Basin, the principal resource development has been the opening up of the Shebelinka natural-gas deposit, one of the largest in the Soviet Union. The deposit, on the right bank of the Northern Donets, 35 miles southeast of Khar'kov, was discovered in 1949 and went into operation in 1956 with the construction of its first pipeline to Khar'kov. Other pipelines followed: to Dnepropetrovsk (1957), Krivoy Rog (1959), Odessa (1963) and on to Kishinev; to Belgorod, Bryansk and Moscow in 1959; and to join the pipeline system running from the Northern Caucasus to Moscow and Leningrad in 1961.

As the pipeline system expanded, gas production at Shebelinka increased from about 5 billion cubic meters in 1958 to 26 billion cubic meters in 1965. Locally the Shebelinka field gave rise to the gas-workers' town of Chervonyy Donets (Ukrainian, = red Donets), founded in 1959; a natural gasoline plant, which went into operation the following year; and a large gas-fueled electric power station, which began to generate electricity in 1960. The power plant, situated at Komsomol'skoye, near Zmiyev, across the Northern Donets from the Shebelinka field, is designed for an ultimate capacity of 2.4 million kilowatts. The first section of six 200,000-

kilowatt units was completed in 1966; the second section, of four 300,000-kilowatt units, was installed in the late 1960s (Fig. 21).

The Shebelinka deposit, already one of the Soviet Union's largest, was supplemented in 1965 with the discovery of another major gas deposit at Yefremovka, 20 miles west of Shebelinka. Production began there is 1967 and was expected to reach 6 billion cubic meters by 1970 with the completion of a 40-inch pipeline connecting the new field with Kiev.

The chemical industry of the Khar'kov area is represented by the complex at Sumy, northwest of Khar'kov. The Sumy plant began as a manufacturer of superphosphate in 1954, passing through several stages of expansion in the 1960s. The sulfuric acid produced at Sumy from Urals pyrites for the production of superphosphate has also been used since 1963 for the manufacture of titanium dioxide pigment by the sulfate process. The raw material for the pigment manufacture is ilmenite from the buried sand deposits of Irshansk and Vol'nogorsk.

## The Dnieper Riverside District

The Dnieper riverside industrial district, comprising the cities of Dneprodzerzhinsk, Dnepropetrovsk, and Zaporozh'ye, arose in the 1880s with the construction of iron and steel plants halfway between the iron ore of the Krivoy Rog basin and the coking coal of the Donbas. The Dneprodzerzhinsk plant, whose eight prewar blast furnaces were supplemented by four more in 1951–56, was the Ukraine's largest producer of pig iron until the expansion of the Krivoy Rog plant in the 1960s. Steelmaking capacity was also substantially increased at Dneprodzerzhinsk; a twentieth open-hearth furnace began production in 1959. The Petrovskiy iron and steel mill at Dnepropetrovsk, with a pig iron capacity of 1 million tons before World War II, was also expanded during its reconstruction after the war.

At Zaporozh'ye, large-scale industrial development got under way after the first Dnieper hydroelectric station began producing power in 1932. The first blast furnace at the Zaporozhstal' mill went into operation in 1933 and a third in 1938, giving the mill a total pig iron capacity of 780,000 tons on the eve of World War II. Additional blast furnaces were constructed after the war, raising pig-iron output to 3.5 million tons by 1966. Energy-oriented industries that opened in Zaporozh'ye during the 1930s included an electric-steels plant (1932), a ferroalloys plant (1933), an alumina and aluminum plant (1933–34), and a magnesium plant (1935).

Before World War II the Zaporozh'ye alumina–aluminum plant used bauxite from deposits at Boksitogorsk, east of Leningrad, and the Urals. In 1940 it produced about 40,000 tons of alumina, one-third of the total Soviet output, and 36,000 tons of aluminum, out of a total Soviet aluminum output of 60,000 tons. Some alumina had to be shipped to Zaporozh'ye to supplement the local production. After the war, aluminum capacity was reopened in 1949 and alumina capacity in 1955. Pending the completion of its own alumina-making facilities, the plant shipped in alumina by rail from the Urals. The raw material for the alumina after 1955 was Greek bauxite shipped in by sea. The average annual volume of bauxite deliveries from Greece suggests an output of about 200,000 tons of alumina, enough to make 100,000 tons of aluminum. In a diversification program, the plant has also been producing high-purity silicon (since 1958) and germanium for use in semiconductor devices. It also recovers vanadium from bauxite as a by-product of the alumina process.

The Zaporozh'ye magnesium plant reopened in 1956 after wartime destruction, but by that time the growing uses of titanium and the discovery of titanium-bearing sands in the Ukraine reoriented by the plant toward production of titanium metal by the magnesium reduction process. The production of magnesium metal was largely limited to the process requirements. At first the titanium plant used Urals ilmenite concentrate, which was smelted in electric furnaces to yield pig iron and titanium slag for further processing. Since 1960 the plant has been supplied with titanium-bearing materials from the Ukraine's own sand deposits, notably the Vol'nogorsk concentrator. The new abundant supply raised the production of titanium fourfold by 1965. During this period, the plant produced only sponge metal. Ingots, obtained by melting the sponge in arc furnaces, were planned to go into production in the late 1960s.

The first Dnieper hydroelectric station, at Zaporozh'ye, in operation since 1932, initially with a capacity of 558,000 kilowatts, was destroyed in World War II, but was rebuilt in 1947–49 to a total of 648,000 kilowatts (nine units of 72,000 kilowatts each). There are plans for raising the station's capacity to 1.5 million kilowatts through the installation of additional generators on the left bank of the Dnieper River (the original powerhouse is situated on the right bank).

In the 1950s the Dnieper industrial district acquired an even larger electric power source with the construction of the Pridneprovsk gas-fueled power station, situated on the southeast outskirts of Dnepropetrovsk, on Chapli, a former island in the Dnieper River, subsequently connected with the left bank. The station, the Soviet Union's largest steam power installation, fed by Shebelinka gas, was built in three stages: six 100,000-kilowatt units (the first in 1954); four 150,000-kilowatt units, yielding a total capacity of 1.2 million kilowatts by August, 1961; followed by four 300,000-kilowatt units, for a total capacity of 2.4 million kilowatts by 1967.

A second major steam electric station was planned to go into construction in the late 1960s in the Dnieper riverside district. The station, known as Novodneprovsk (New Dnieper), was originally designed to have a generating capacity of 3.2 million kilowatts, consisting of four 800,000-kilowatt units. A later revision of the design provided for a twin of the Uglegorsk station under construction in the Donets Basin, with four 300,000-kilowatt units and three 800,000-kilowatt units, for a total capacity of 3.6 million kilowatts. Construction was scheduled to begin in 1969 on the Kakhovka reservoir, southwest of Zaporozh'ye near the village of Ivanovka.

In addition to the original Dnieper dam at Zaporozh'ye, two more hydroelectric stations were built in the Dnieper district. The Kakhovka station, at Novaya Kakhovka, has a relatively small generating capacity, six units of 57,200 kilowatts each, installed in 1955–56, for a total capacity of 343,200 kilowatts, but created a large reservoir backing up to Zaporozh'ye and providing a source of industrial water and irrigation in the semiarid southern Ukraine. In the late 1950s and early 1960s, an irrigation trunk canal was built southward from Novaya Kakhovka to the Crimean isthmus, with a western branch into the steppe south of Kherson. A canal from the Kakhovka reservoir to the Krivoy Rog iron basin was completed in 1960.

The second new hydroelectric station, just above Dneprodzerzhinsk, generates power through eight 44,000-kilowatt units, installed in 1963–64, for a total capacity of 352,000 kilowatts. Its reservoir is being studied as a potential water-supply source for the Donets Basin via a canal that would run along the watershed between the Orel' and Northern Donets rivers in the north, and the Samara River in the south.

An additional energy source for the Dnepropetrovsk area is a small gas field discovered in 1962–63 at Pereshchepino, 40 miles north of Dnepropetrovsk. A pipeline, serving the pipe-manufacturing center of Novomoskovsk along the way, was opened in 1966, supplying 700 million cubic meters of gas a year.

Thirty miles west of Dneprodzerzhinsk, in the valley of the Samotkan' River, a Dnieper tributary, is one of two major Ukrainian centers for the mining and concentrating of heavy-mineral sands containing titanium, zirconium, and hafnium. The mining town of Vol'nogorsk, founded on the site, was inaugurated as a workers settlement in 1958 and was raised to the status of city in 1964. Since commercial production of ilmenite, rutile, and zirconium concentrates began in 1960, the Vol'nogorsk concentrator has been supplying titanium-bearing materials to the Soviet Union's principal titanium metal plants—Zaporozh'ye, on the Dnieper; Berezniki, in the Urals; and Ust'-Kamenogorsk, in eastern Kazakhstan.

Another mineral development project in the Dnieper riverside district is the iron-ore mining complex of Belozerka, on the south shore of the Kakhovka reservoir. The deposit, explored in 1957–58, was found to contain high-grade ores, including 66 percent ore suitable for direct use in open-hearth steel furnaces, and 58-percent ores for smelting in blast furnaces. The first stage of an underground-mining complex, with a capacity of 7 million tons, was scheduled to go into operation in 1969. The miners' town of Dneprorudnyy was inaugurated in 1963, and a railroad branch to the prospective mining complex was completed in 1965.

## The Krivoy Rog Basin

The Krivoy Rog iron ore basin, west of the Dnieper riverside district, has become the Soviet Union's principal source of iron

ore since it went into commercial production in the 1880s in conjunction with the use of Donbas coal. By the turn of the century,
the Krivoy Rog basin was yielding more iron ore than the Urals,
which until then had been the leading metallurgical area based on
the use of charcoal. The Krivoy Rog basin contains both high-grade
ores, with an iron content of 55 to 60 percent, which account for
20 percent of the proven reserves and are accessible mainly through
underground mines, and low-grade iron quartzites, with a metal
content of 30 to 37 percent, which constitute most of the reserves
and are partly accessible through open-pit mining. Until 1955 the
basin yielded only high-grade ores from underground mines, mainly
from the central sector between Krivoy Rog city and the town of
Terny, 15 miles to the northeast, along the right bank of the
Saksagan' River. Production rose from 4.5 million tons in 1928, at
the start of the Soviet industrialization drive, to 18.9 million in
1940. After World War II, iron ore mining recovered the prewar
level in 1950 and then virtually doubled to 37 million tons by 1955.

In the meantime, however, the exhaustion of the highest-grade
ores (60 percent iron) at relatively shallow depths required the
construction of increasingly deeper (and more costly) mines, where
the average metal content of the high-grade ores dropped to 55
percent. These factors, combined with the development of a technology for enriching the poorer ores available through open-pit
mining, led to a new phase in the development of the basin. In this
phase the extraction of high-grade ores was kept to a level of 40 to
45 million tons, and further expansion of iron ore production was
achieved through the development of open-pit mining of iron
quartzites and concentrators that raise the metal content of the ores
from an average of 35 percent to 62 to 65 percent.

Within the ten-year period 1955–65, five large concentrators with
associated open-pit mines went into operation: the Southern plant,
6 miles south of Krivoy Rog city, on the right bank of the Ingulets
River, which went into operation in 1955, with additional sections
opened in 1960 and 1965; the New Krivoy Rog plant, 5 miles southeast of Krivoy Rog, on the left bank of the Ingulets, opened in 1959
and expanded in 1966; the Central plant, 10 miles northeast of
Krivoy Rog, on the right bank of the Saksagan', opened in 1961,
with additional sections added in 1962 and 1964; the Northern

plant, 17 miles northeast of Krivoy Rog, at the town of Terny, opened in 1964; and the Ingulets plant, 20 miles south of Krivoy Rog, on the left bank of the Ingulets River, opened in 1965.

In the mid-1960s, as a result of these developments, the Krivoy Rog basin produced about 110 million tons of raw ore, including about 44 million tons of direct-shipping ores of 55 percent iron content and about 66 million tons of iron quartzites of 35 percent metal content, which were converted into about 34 million tons of 62 to 65 percent concentrate. During the five-year plan of 1966–70, with the construction of the second stages at the Northern and the Ingulets concentrators, the production of concentrates from quartzites was expected to rise to about 45 million tons. Technical improvements were envisaged to raise the iron content of all the concentrate to 65 percent, and part of the concentrate at the Central concentrator was converted to pellets for more efficient blast-furnace use.

The expansion of the basin through the use of surface-mined quartzites since 1955 has been associated with an expansion of the Krivoy Rog iron and steel mill into the Soviet Union's second largest metallurgical plant (after Magnitogorsk). Although iron smelting at Krivoy Rog dates from 1892, the modern plant has developed only since the 1930s, when three blast furnaces were constructed there. These were rebuilt by 1951 after their wartime destruction, and a fourth blast furnace was added in 1958. This was followed at a rapid rate by the opening of the No. 5 furnace in 1960, No. 6 in 1961, and No. 7 in 1962. The eighth, with a working volume of 95,000 cubic feet and a capacity of 1.7 million metric tons a year, was completed in 1967, bringing the total pig iron capacity of the Krivoy Rog plant to about 7 million tons a year. The No. 9 blast furnace, of the same size as No. 8, was scheduled to begin operations in 1970, raising total production to 8.5 million tons of pig iron.

In addition to an old electric plant dating from the 1930s, the increasing power needs of the area have required the construction of a second power plant, with a designed capacity of 2.4 million kilowatts. The first of eight 300,000-kilowatt units opened in 1965 at this station, which is situated at Zelenodol'sk, 6 miles south of Apostolovo, near the canal from the Kakhovka reservoir that supplies the increasing water needs of the Krivoy Rog basin. The sixth generator was scheduled to be installed in 1969.

Special mention must be made of a major uranium deposit at the northern end of the Krivoy Rog basin, at Zheltyye Vody and Terny. The uranium is associated with magnetite iron ore in Precambrian metamorphic rocks. The Zheltyye Vody deposit was originally mined for its iron ore alone. In conjunction with the discovery and development of the uranium component of the deposit in the 1950s, the mining settlement (originally known as Zheltaya Reka [yellow river]) was raised to the status of city and renamed Zheltyye Vody (yellow waters). In 1967 the new uranium center had a population of 41,000 compared with the old iron-mining settlement's population of 6,500 in 1939. The town of Terny, also associated with an iron–uranium mine, was founded in 1957 and rose to a population of 27,000 by 1967. It was merged with Krivoy Rog in 1969.

A major element of the Ukrainian iron and steel industry is the Nikopol' manganese basin, which supplies about two-thirds of the Soviet Union's manganese. Commercial production in the basin began in the 1880s and for a long time was limited to underground mining of high-grade oxides at Marganets, in the eastern part, 15 miles northeast of Nikopol'. In 1940 the basin produced almost 40 percent of the Soviet Union's manganese output, with 60 percent coming from the Chiatura mines of Georgia. After World War II, mining in the Nikopol' basin was expanded substantially through the mining of lower-grade carbonate ores in strip mines. The first open pit went into operation in 1952 in the western part of the basin at Ordzhonikidze, 20 miles northwest of Nikopol'. By 1965, about 70 percent of the 10 million tons of crude ore of the Nikopol' basin was mined in open pits.

The high-grade ores mined in the past required little beneficiation beyond crushing, screening, and washing. The increasing reliance on lower-grade ores required more thorough concentration, including flotation and magnetic separation. The first modern concentrator, the Bogdanovka mill, opened at Ordzhonikidze in 1959. It was followed in 1961 by the Grushevka mill at Marganets and in 1964 by the Chkalovsk mill, 10 miles northwest of Nikopol'. Each had a capacity of 2.4 million tons of crude ore. A larger concen-

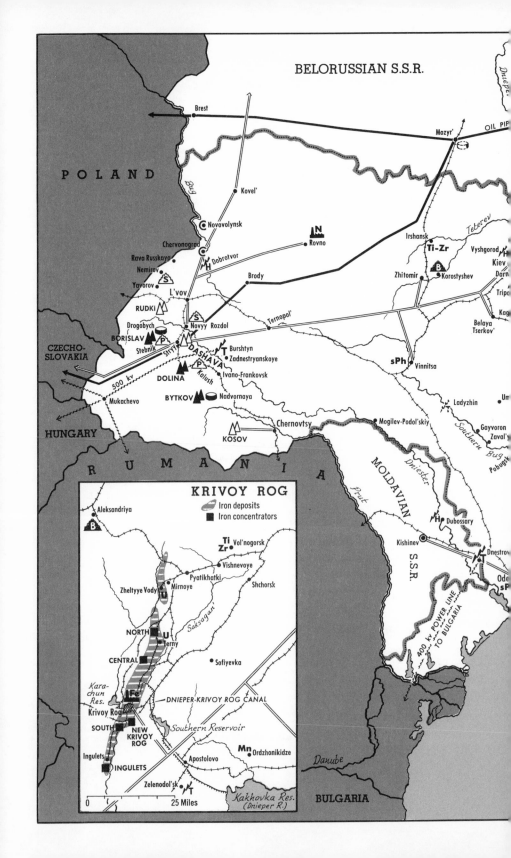

BELORUSSIAN S.S.R.

POLAND

Brest

Mozyr'

OIL PIP

Kovel'

Novovolynsk

Chervonograd

Rava Russkaya

Nemirov

Yavorov

L'vov

RUDKI

Drogobych

BORISLAV

Stebnik

DASHAVA

DOLINA

BYTKOV

Mukachevo

KOSOV

HUNGARY

CZECHO-
SLOVAKIA

500 kv

Strvi

Kalush

Nadvornaya

Dobrotvor

Brody

Novyy Rozdol

Burshtyn

Zadnestryanskoye

Ivano-Frankovsk

Ternopol'

Rovno

Irshansk

Zhitomir

Korostyshev

Ti-Zr

Vyshgorod

Kiev

Darn

Tripo

Kag

Belaya
Tserkov'

sPh

Vinnitsa

Ladyzhin

Un

Gayvoron

Zaval'

Pobugsk

Chernovtsy

Mogilev-Podol'skiy

Southern Bug

MOLDAVIAN

Dnester

Prut

Kishinev

Dubossary

Dnestrov

S.S.R.

Ode

sP

Teterev

Dnieper

RUMANIA

400 kv POWER LINE
TO BULGARIA

Danube

BULGARIA

KRIVOY ROG

Iron deposits
Iron concentrators

Aleksandriya

Vol'nogorsk

Ti
Zr

Vishnevoye

Pyatikhatki

Shchorsk

Zheltyye Vody

Mirnoye

Saksagan

NORTH

Terny

CENTRAL

Sofiyevka

Karachun
Res.

DNIEPER-KRIVOY ROG CANAL

Krivoy Rog

Southern Reservoir

SOUTH

NEW
KRIVOY
ROG

Ingulets

INGULETS

Apostolovo

Mn
Ordzhonikidze

Zelenodol'sk

Kakhovka Res.
(Dnieper R.)

0                    25 Miles

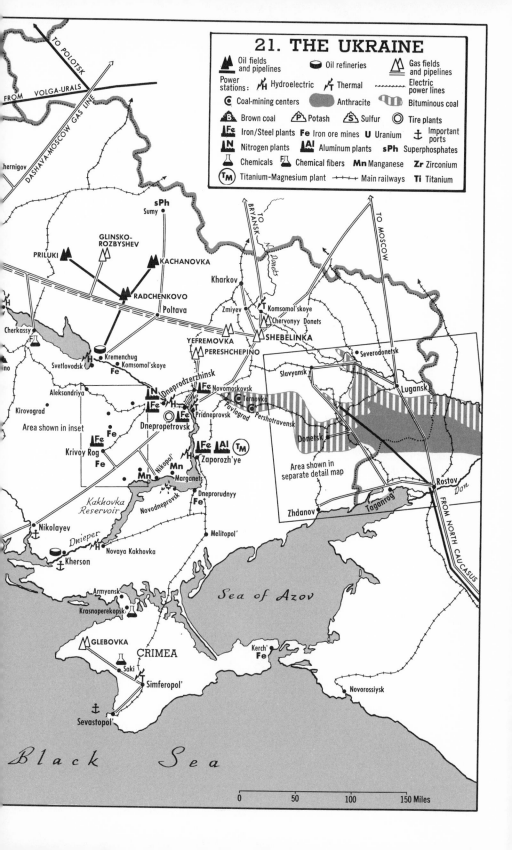

## 21. THE UKRAINE

Oil fields and pipelines    Oil refineries    Gas fields and pipelines

Power stations:   **H** Hydroelectric    **T** Thermal    Electric power lines

**C** Coal-mining centers    Anthracite    Bituminous coal

**B** Brown coal    **P** Potash    **S** Sulfur    Tire plants

**Fe** Iron/Steel plants   **Fe** Iron ore mines   **U** Uranium    Important ports

**N** Nitrogen plants    **Al** Aluminum plants    **sPh** Superphosphates

Chemicals    Chemical fibers    **Mn** Manganese    **Zr** Zirconium

**TM** Titanium-Magnesium plant   +——+ Main railways    **Ti** Titanium

TO POLOTSK

FROM VOLGA-URALS

DASHAVA-MOSCOW GAS LINE

hernigov

TO BRYANSK

TO MOSCOW

**sPh** Sumy

GLINSKO-ROZBYSHEV

PRILUKI    KACHANOVKA

RADCHENKOVO

Poltava

Kharkov

Zmiyev    **T** Komsomol'skoye

Chervonyy Donets

YEFREMOVKA    SHEBELINKA

PERESHCHEPINO

Severodonetsk

**H**

Cherkassy    Kremenchug

no    Svetlovodsk    **H**   Komsomol'skoye   **Fe**

Slavyansk    Lugansk

Aleksandriya    **N**   Dneprodzerzhinsk   **Fe** Novomoskovsk

Kirovograd    **Fe**   **H**   Ternovka    **C**

Area shown in inset    **Fe**   Dnepropetrovsk   Pridneprovsk   Pavlograd   Pershotravensk

Krivoy Rog    **Fe**    **Fe**   Donetsk

**Fe**   **Al**   **TM**

Zaporozh'ye

**H**

**Mn** Nikopol'   **Mn**   Marganets

Dneprorudnyy   **Fe**

Area shown in separate detail map

Kakhovka Reservoir   Novodneprovsk

Nikolayev    Dnieper    **H**   Novaya Kakhovka

Melitopol'

Zhdanov    Taganrog    Rostov

Don

FROM NORTH CAUCASUS

Kherson

Armyansk

Krasnoperekopsk

Sea of Azov

GLEBOVKA    CRIMEA    Kerch'   **Fe**

Saki

Simferopol'

Novorossiysk

Sevastopol'

*Black Sea*

0    50    100    150 Miles

trator, the Pokrovka mill, with a capacity of 6 million tons of crude ore, was under construction in the late 1960s near Ordzhonikidze. The total output of usable manganese ore in 1965 was 4.7 million tons, of which half was high-grade ore requiring little beneficiation and half lower-grade ore subject to more thorough concentration. Much of the output of the basin was converted into ferromanganese at ferroalloys plants at Zaporozh'ye and Nikopol' (opened in 1966).

## Kremenchug Complex

North of the Krivoy Rog basin, on the Dnieper River, is the diversified Kremenchug industrial complex, comprising hydroelectric power, petrochemicals and oil refining, an open-pit brown coal mine, and a northern outlier of the Krivoy Rog iron basin. Recent industrial growth was spurred by the construction of a hydroelectric station on the Dnieper River, eight miles above the city. Twelve 57,200-kilowatt generators, making a total capacity of 686,400 kilowatts, were installed in the Kremenchug station in 1959–60. The new power station town, originally called Khrushchev, absorbed the old Ukrainian town of Novogeorgiyevsk in 1961 and was renamed Kremges (for Kremenchug Hydroelectric Station) in 1962 and finally Svetlovodsk in 1969 (1967 population: 30,000).

The Kremenchug oil refinery, situated east of the city, on the left bank of the Dnieper River, went into operation in 1966. The refinery, largest in the Ukraine, was originally planned to process crude oils from the Tatar fields, to be transported to Kremenchug via a branch of the Friendship pipeline. However, the discovery of oil deposits in the Dnieper–Donets depression on the left bank of the Dnieper River reoriented the refinery toward use of local crude oils. A crude-oil line, opened in 1966, collects the output of the various deposits and pipes it to the Kremenchug refinery. Two major producing districts have arisen in the Dnieper–Donets depression since production began in the late 1950s: the Chernigov district, centered on Priluki southeast of the city of Chernigov, and the Poltava district. The Chernigov district, with the principal producing fields at Priluki and nearby Gnedintsy and Lelyaki, yielded more than 40 percent of the Ukraine's total crude oil output in 1967, or 4.7 million out of 11 million tons. The Poltava district, with the principal producers in the Radchenkovo field around Gogolevo, east of Mirgorod, and the Kachanovka field, west of Akhtyrka in adjoining Sumy Oblast, yielded about 3 million tons. The rest of the oil came from the western Ukraine.

Various uses are made of natural gas associated with the oil fields. A natural-gasoline plant is in operation at the Kachanovka field. A natural-gas line opened in 1967 from the Glinsko-Rozbyshev field in the Poltava district to Kiev, and a carbon-black plant was inaugurated at Kremenchug in 1965. The industrial development of Kremenchug is reflected in its population growth in the 1960s. After having been virtually stagnant at the 90,000 level (in 1939–59) it rose by 50 percent, to 136,000, in 1967.

The iron ore deposit is situated 10 miles east of Kremenchug, on the left bank of the Dnieper River, and consists of relatively small reserves of high-grade ore (60 percent iron), found underground in waterlogged strata, and much larger reserves of low-grade quartzites (35 percent iron), accessible through open-pit mining. A mining and concentrating complex, similar to those in the Krivoy Rog basin, began operations in 1969 at the mining town of Komsomol'-skoye (founded in 1961, when construction began). At full capacity the concentrator is designed to convert 15 million tons of crude ore into 6.7 million tons of concentrate with an iron content of 64 percent.

The open-pit brown coal mines are situated at Aleksandriya, south of Kremenchug. In operation since the 1950s the Aleksandriya mines are the principal component of the Ukraine's Dnieper brown-coal basin, with a total output of 10.8 million tons in 1965. About 8 million originated in the five Aleksandriya strip mines. The brown coal, of low heating value and high ash content, is briquetted and used in local power plants.

To meet the growing water needs of the iron and steel industry of the Krivoy Rog basin, plans were made in 1968 for the construction of a canal that would run from the Kremenchug reservoir south through the Aleksandriya coal basin and along the upper Ingulets River to the Krivoy Rog area.

Farther upstream along the Dnieper River, industrial development is being promoted in part by the construction of hydroelectric stations and steam electric plants as well as expansion of the chemical industry. A growing chemical center is Cherkassy, on the south bank of the Kremenchug reservoir. A cellulosic-fiber plant opened there in 1961, with a second section added two years later, and a nitrogenous fertilizer installation, using natural gas, went into operation in 1965 with an ammonia unit. Urea and ammonium nitrate units were being added in the late 1960s. As in Kremenchug, the population of Cherkassy mounted as a result of the new industrialization, from 85,000 in 1959 to 128,000 in 1967. An auxiliary energy source southwest of Cherkassy is the open-pit coal mine of Vatutino (formerly called Yurkovka), which has been producing 2 million tons a year since the early 1950s.

## The Kiev Region

Near the upper head of the Kremenchug reservoir, another Dnieper hydroelectric station is under construction near Kanev. The plant, with a designed capacity of 420,000 kilowatts, was scheduled to go into operation by 1970. Another hydroelectric station was inaugurated in late 1964 north of Kiev, at the town of Vyshgorod. The Kiev station was originally designed to consist of a 326,000-kilowatt station in the Dnieper River and a 200,000-kilowatt station of the pumped storage type on the right bank. However, the original capacity of 16,300 kilowatts per turbine was raised to 18,500 kilowatts, and when the installation of the 20 units of the river-bed station was completed in 1968, its capacity was 370,000 kilowatts instead of the planned 326,000. Installation of the pumped-storage turbines was to follow.

The generating capacity of these Dnieper hydroelectric stations is small compared with the 1.8-million kilowatt steam electric station under construction on the Dnieper River at Tripol'ye, 25 miles southeast of Kiev. This station is to be the principal power producer of the Kiev district, linked by high-voltage transmission lines with the power grids of the western and southern Ukraine. The station site is connected by a 20-mile-long rail spur with the main line at Kagarlyk. A first 300,000-kilowatt generator was to be installed in late 1969.

The Kiev industrial district, given over mainly to manufacturing, includes two chemical fiber installations. One, at Darnitsa, the left-bank suburb of Kiev, is a viscose-rayon plant, opened in 1959. The other is a polyamide-fiber complex at Chernigov, which began operations in 1962. The initial stage, expanded in 1963 and 1964, produces kapron (a type of nylon manufactured from caprolactam) and a second stage makes anid (another type of nylon manufactured from adipic acid and hexamethylenediamine). Both fibers are used for tire cord. The development of the synthetic-fiber industry raised the population of Chernigov from 90,000 in 1959 to 139,000 in 1967.

West of Kiev, resource developments include a small open-pit brown-coal mine at Korostyshev, in operation since the early 1950s, with a capacity of 700,000 tons, and the dredging of heavy-mineral sands, yielding titanium and zirconium ores, around Irshansk, on the Irsha River. In contrast to the Vol'nogorsk operation in the Dnieper riverside district, the Irshansk operation yields titanium-bearing materials mainly for the manufacture of titanium dioxide pigment rather than titanium metal. The first concentrator at Irshansk went into operation in 1960 and a second in 1965. A third was under construction in the late 1960s. The ilmenite concentrate is shipped to Sumy for manufacture into pigment and will also supply a second pigment plant, to open in 1970 at Armyansk, in the Perekop Isthmus of the Crimea.

South of Irshansk, the city of Zhitomir has been selected as the site of a polyamide fiber plant producing kapron, under construction in the late 1960s. Another new chemical center is Rovno, where a nitrogenous fertilizer plant, deriving hydrogen from natural gas, opened in late 1968 with its first ammonia unit. South of Zhitomir is the older chemical center of Vinnitsa, with a superphosphate fertilizer plant dating from the pre-Soviet period. The Vinnitsa plant has been pioneering in the Soviet production of more advanced fertilizers, such as triple superphosphate and complex fertilizers containing nitrogen, phosphorus, and potassium.

Increasing industrialization of the right-bank Ukraine southwest of Kiev has led to the selection of Ladyzhin, southeast of Vinnitsa, on the Southern Bug River, as the site of a 1.8-million kilowatt steam electric station. It was under construction in the late 1960s, with the first 300,000-kilowatt unit due in 1971. A hydroelectric project is under consideration on the Dniester River at Mogilev-Podol'skiy, with a capacity of 800,000 to 900,000 kilowatts.

Among extractive industries on the Bug River southeast of the Ladyzhin power complex is the open-pit graphite mine of Zaval'ye, one of the Soviet Union's two producers of natural graphite, and a nickel smelter under construction in the late 1960s. The nickel plant, at Pobugskoye, northwest of Pervomaysk, will produce ferro-nickel in electric furnaces from a local nickel silicate deposit.

## Western Ukraine

In contrast to the scattered pattern in the right-bank Ukraine southwest of Kiev, resource development projects have been concentrated in the Carpathian area of the western Ukraine. There the old nineteenth-century oil field of Borislav, with two small refineries at nearby Drogobych, has been declining since its peak production of 1 million tons in 1913. It was superseded in the early 1950s by new fields at Dolina and Bytkov, near Ivano-Frankovsk (called Stanislav until 1962). West Ukrainian oil output thus rose from the stagnant level of 250,000 tons in the 1940s at Borislav to about 1 million tons by 1958 and 3 million by 1967. The increased output of crude oil stimulated expansion of a small re-finery at Nadvornaya, near Bytkov, where a paraffin unit was added in 1964 to process the paraffin-rich crude oil of the new field. The availability of casinghead gas at Dolina also led to the construction of two natural-gasoline plants, the second of which opened in 1966.

Natural-gas development in the Carpathians began with the opening of the Dashava field, east of Stryy, in the 1920s while the area was part of Poland. Dashava was linked by pipeline with the manufacturing city of L'vov, and a second pipeline was added in 1941 after the area had passed to the Soviet Union. Long-range transmission of Dashava gas began in 1948 when a pipeline was completed to Kiev, with an extension to Moscow in 1951. Another pipeline, running northward from Dashava, reached Minsk in 1960 and Vilna and Riga the following years. In the meantime the rela-tively small gas reserves at Dashava were supplemented by the exploration of larger fields nearby between Stryy and Rudki, 30 miles to the northwest. The oldest of these fields, at Ugersko, began production in 1946 and yielded 1.5 to 2 billion cubic meters a year through the 1950s and 1960s. The Bil'che-Volitsa field, opened in 1949, reached an annual output of more than 2 billion cubic meters in the mid-1960s. The third field, at Rudki, went into production in 1957 and yielded more than 3 billion cubic meters a year in the mid-1960s. Total production of the west Ukrainian gas fields was 6 billion cubic meters in 1965, compared with the 26 billion cubic meters of the Shebelinka field near Khar'kov. In conjunction with the casinghead gases of the Dolina–Bytkov oil fields, the gas fields of the western Ukraine also supply Czechoslovakia through a pipe-line, known as the Brotherhood transmission system, opened in 1967. Another foreign consumer is Austria, which began to receive west Ukrainian gas under an agreement signed in 1968. A smaller gas field of the western Ukraine, at Kosov, was linked with Cher-novtsy in 1960.

The chemical resources of the Carpathians are mainly potash and native sulfur. Potash mines at Kalush and Stebnik, in operation since the nineteenth century, have averaged an output of 300,000 tons a year in recent decades, accounting for less than 10 percent of the Soviet Union's total potash production. By the 1960s their limited sylvite (potassium chloride) reserves were near depletion and steps were taken to make use of more abundant kainite and langbeinite (potassium sulfate) reserves. A new mine with a ca-pacity of 1.4 million tons of raw ore opened at Stebnik in 1966, and a mill concentrates the potash component of kainite to twice the average content of 12 percent $K_2O$ in the natural salt. Since 1963 potassium sulfate has been extracted from langbeinite at a new mill in Kalush, which has been further supplied with potassium-bearing salts from the adjoining Dombrovskiy open-pit operation, inaugurated in 1967. A Kalush chemical–metallurgical plant, which was opened in 1965, produces potassium and magnesium com-pounds derived from the complex salts.

The native sulfur deposit, on the left bank of the Dniester, north of Zhidachov, was discovered in the 1950s, and has become the Soviet Union's principal source of sulfur. The sulfur beds, with a sulfur content of up to 25 percent, are being mined in open pits since production began in 1959 in the drained marshy floodplain of the Dniester River. The new mining town of Novyy Rozdol (New Rozdol) was inaugurated in the same year. The Rozdol operation was further expanded in 1964.

A second major sulfur producer went into operation in 1968 at Yavorov, 30 miles west of L'vov. The new mining town, first tentatively called Yantarnyy (amber), was renamed Novoyavorovskoye in 1969. In contrast to the open-pit operation at Rozdol, the Yavorov deposit is being mined both in an open-pit and by the hot-water process, in which steam under pressure is pumped through a drill hole to melt the sulfur in place so that it can be carried to the surface by compressed air. The process, known as the Frasch process, is used to produce most of the native sulfur in the United States. Frasch-process mines are also planned at a later stage at a third deposit near Nemirov, 15 miles north of Yavorov.

Energy for the industrial development of the Carpathian area and the L'vov manufacturing district is supplied by two coal-fueled power stations burning bituminous steam coals from the L'vov–Volhynian basin. This basin, on the Polish border, began to be developed in 1949 and the first underground mine went into production in 1954. The northern part of the basin in Volyn' (Volhynian) Oblast has its center at Novovolynsk (1967 population: 37,000); the southern part, in L'vov Oblast, is centered on Chervonograd (1967 population: 35,000). Total output rose to 3.9 million tons in 1960 and 9.6 million tons in 1965, when eighteen underground mines were in operation.

The first power station, which opened in 1955 at Dobrotvor, is fed by a 40-mile-long pipeline carrying coal slurry from the Novovolynsk mines. Dobrotvor was at first equipped with relatively small generators, but later acquired two 150,000-kilowatt units, raising its capacity to 700,000 kilowatts by 1964. The second power station, near Burshtyn, went into operation in 1965 with 200,000-kilowatt generating units. Nine were installed by 1969 and the station was scheduled to reach its design capacity of 2.4-million kilowatts in 1970. The Dobrotvor and Burshtyn stations will then consume 90 percent of the total output of the L'vov–Volyn' basin. In addition to supplying the western Ukraine, the two power plants also transmit electricity to Eastern Europe. Through a major substation at Mukachevo, the Western Ukraine feeds electricity into Czechoslovakia, Hungary, and Rumania over 400-kilovolt lines. In 1966 the Soviet Union delivered 1.4 billion kilowatt-hours over this system. The Dobrotvor station is also linked with Zamosc (Poland) over a 220-kilovolt line opened in 1968.

## The Black Sea Coast & Crimea

Along the Black Sea coast, primary industries include oil refineries at Odessa and Kherson. Originally based on Baku crude oil shipped from Batumi across the Black Sea, the refineries also processed crude oil from the newly developed fields in the Dnieper–Donets depression before the Kremenchug refinery opened. Odessa also has an old superphosphate plant dating from before the Soviet period.

A distinctive resource area is developing around the Sivash, a brine-laden lagoon separating the Crimea from the Ukrainian mainland. Until the late 1960s the brine had been used mainly as a source of bromine, extracted by a thirty-year-old plant at Krasnoperekopsk, on the Perekop Isthmus. Several projects were under construction or planned on the isthmus during the 1966–70 five-year plan. One was a soda plant, also situated at Krasnoperekopsk, that would use the sodium chloride component of the Sivash brine; another was a magnesia plant, based on the magnesium salts of the lagoon. At Armyansk, on the isthmus north of Krasnoperekopsk, a plant for the manufacture of titanium pigments was to open in 1970. Though based on titanium-bearing materials from the heavy-mineral sands of Irshansk, west of Kiev, and Vol'nogorsk, west of Dneprodzerzhinsk, the pigment plant was located on the Sivash so that sulfuric acid used in the sulfate process of pigment manufacture could be discarded into the lagoon.

Elsewhere in the Crimea, the Sasyk lagoon on the west coast has furnished brine for a chemical plant at Saki since World War I for the manufacture of bromine and magnesium compounds. A small gas field, developed at Glebovka, in the Crimea's western Tarkhankut Peninsula, began production in 1966, providing fuel by pipeline to power stations at Saki, Simferopol', and Sevastopol'.

## Moldavian SSR

Devoid of significant mineral resources outside of building materials, Moldavia has been important mainly for its agricultural production, specializing in wine, tobacco, fruits, vegetables, and food-processing industries.

Energy was supplied to the Moldavian economy from small, inefficient stations until the construction of a 40,000-kilowatt hydroelectric plant in 1954 at Dubossary on the Dniester River. The expansion of a small steam electric station at Kishinev, opened in 1951, raised its total capacity to 57,000 kilowatts by 1961.

However, both of these power plants were dwarfed by a 1.2-million kilowatt station, the Moldavian regional power plant, which went into operation in 1964 at Dnestrovsk (the former Nezavertaylovka), 25 miles southeast of Tiraspol'. The station, which uses Donets anthracite culm to generate power through six 200,000-kilowatt units installed in 1964–67, is situated on a dammed reservoir of the Kuchurgan River, a left tributary of the Dniester. It transmits its power over a 330-kilovolt line (completed in 1968) to Kishinev, Bel'tsy, and other towns in northern Moldavia. The station is to be further expanded in the early 1970s, when it will begin transmitting electric power to Bulgaria over a 400-kilovolt line under construction in the late 1960s through Rumanian territory.

Moldavia was reached by a natural-gas pipeline from Shebelinka in 1966, but the gas was being used mainly as a household fuel. If the full capacity of the pipeline (700 million cubic meters a year) is utilized, natural gas may serve in the future as the raw material for a proposed nitrogenous fertilizer plant.

# 8

# BELORUSSIA

Until the early 1960s, the development of resources for heavy industry in Belorussia was limited to peat, which provided two-thirds of the fuel burned by the republic's power stations. Belorussia's principal industries, working for the national market, were metal fabricating (truck assembly, tractors, machine tools), electrical goods and electronics, woodworking (plywood, matches), and linen goods. In the 1960s the republic acquired an important chemical industry, based both on natural gas, brought in from the Dashava fields starting in 1960, and on crude oil, transmitted by pipeline from the Tatar oil fields. Newly developed potash deposits provided another chemical raw material. In the late 1960s Belorussia received about 3 billion cubic meters of natural gas a year. As a result of the associated changes in the fuel budget, the share of peat declined from 67 percent in 1960 to 37 percent in 1965 and 25 percent in the late 1960s.

Before World War II, Belorussia's peat-based power stations were generally small and isolated, serving their immediate surroundings. The largest electric plant, with an installed capacity of 32,000 kilowatts, went into operation in the mid-1930s at Orekhovsk, 13 miles north of Orsha. The power plant, then known as the Belorussian regional power station (abbreviated in Russian as Belgres) because it was the dominant electric supplier in the republic, used peat from the nearby Osintorf peatworks. The Orekhovsk–

Osintorf complex accounted for about one-fourth of Belorussia's total power output of 500 million kilowatt hours in 1940.

After having recovered its prewar level in 1949, the power industry proceeded on a major expansion program and the construction of a unified grid. The peat-fed Smolevichi power station, with a capacity of 100,000 kilowatts, was built in the mid-1950s at Zhodino, 35 miles northeast of Minsk. Zhodino, a new town that was given the status of city in 1963, became a motor-vehicle production center specializing in the manufacture of heavy dump trucks with a capacity of 25 and 40 tons, used in the Soviet Union's open-pit mining operations. A 110-kilovolt power line linking the Smolevichi station at Zhodino with the reconstructed Orekhovsk power complex and with a steam electric station in Minsk became the basis of the future power grid. The Smolevichi station was to be expanded to about 600,000 kilowatts by 1970.

A second major power plant, the peat-fed Vasilevichi station, with a capacity of 150,000 kilowatts, was built in the late 1950s at Shatilki, on the Berezina River, 85 miles westnorthwest of Gomel. The station provided the power supply for a viscose fiber plant that began production at Shatilki in 1964. The town was renamed Svetlogorsk in 1961. In addition to serving the local industry, the Vasilevichi station was also linked by a 110-kilovolt line with Rechitsa and Gomel', thus giving rise to a power grid in the southeastern part of Belorussia. The Gomel and Minsk grids were also connected by a 220-kilovolt line via Bobruysk in 1960.

The next major power project, with a designed capacity of 900,-000 kilowatts, went into operation in 1961 at Beloozersk, a new town situated in the midst of peat bogs, 10 miles eastsoutheast of Bereza, which is about half way between Brest and Baranovichi. The station reached its designed capacity in 1968 with the installation of its sixth 150,000-kilowatt generating unit. As the power-producing center of southwest Belorussia, the station serves the towns of Brest, Pinsk, and Baranovichi, as well as new chemical industries in Grodno to the north and the potash-mining town of Soligorsk to the east, by 220-kilovolt transmission lines.

The principal Belorussian power project under construction in the late 1960s is on Lake Lukoml', 55 miles northwest of Orsha. The new town of Novolukoml' was inaugurated at the power station site in 1965. The predominantly oil-burning station will generate power through eight 300,000-kilowatt units for a total capacity of 2.4 million kilowatts. The first generating unit started production in 1969. The Lukoml' station is to be connected with Minsk, Mogilev, Gomel', and Vitebsk by 330-kilovolt power lines.

Although both the Beloozersk and Lukoml' stations are situated in the midst of peat bogs, peat is inadequate to fuel such large power producers economically. It is therefore supplemented by long-haul anthracite culm and steam coals from the Donets Basin, by natural gas (which reached Belorussia from the West Ukrainian fields in 1960), and by fuel oil from Belorussian refineries at Polotsk and Mozyr'.

Among the consumers of the additional power from the Lukoml' project is the new oil-refining and petrochemical complex in the Polotsk area, 55 miles to the north. The Polotsk petroleum complex was designed to use crude oil from the Tatar–Bashkir region. The first gasoline at the refinery was produced in 1963, two years before a branch of the Friendship oil pipeline was completed between Unecha and Polotsk. One of the largest refineries of the Soviet Union, the Polotsk complex serves the needs of Belorussia and the Baltic republics. The refinery is situated in the new town of Novopolotsk (1967 population: 26,000), on the left bank of the Western Dvina River, west of the old city of Polotsk. Part of the oil complex is a major petrochemical center, where the production of polyethylene began in 1968. It is to be used as a raw material by a plastics-fabricating industry developing at Borisov. The Polotsk petrochemical complex will also produce raw materials for the production of polyester fiber at Mogilev and of polyamide fiber at Grodno. It will also yield acrylonitrile, which it will use in a 50,000-ton acrylic fiber (nitron) unit. The various units producing hydrocarbon derivatives for the manufacture of man-made fibers were scheduled to go into operation in 1969–70.

A second oil refinery and petrochemical complex is planned to go into operation in the early 1970s near Mozyr', a town on the Pripet River, situated at the point where the Friendship oil pipeline forks into two branches, one running southwestward toward Czechoslovakia and Hungary, the other westward toward Poland and East Germany. Mozyr' is expected to produce carbon black for a truck-

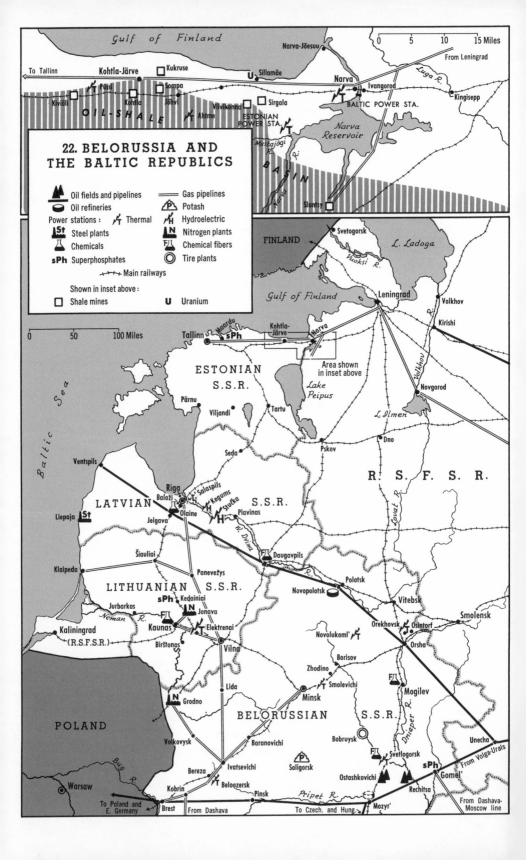

tire plant under construction at Bobruysk (for the Zhodino and Minsk truck-assembly plants) and a wide range of other petrochemical products based on the availability of abundant water and the nearby Soligorsk salt in addition to crude oil. Although both the Polotsk and Mozyr' refineries are to be oriented primarily toward the use of high-sulfur crude oils from the Tatar–Bashkir region, the discovery of higher-grade low-sulfur crude oil in the southeastern part of Belorussia in the mid-1960s may provide a substantial additional source. The first commercial crude oil, which is suitable for the production of high-octane gasoline, low-sulfur Diesel oils, and high-grade lubricants, was obtained in 1964 from wells drilled near Rechitsa, at the northwestern end of the new oil-bearing province under development on the left bank of the Dnieper River in the Ukraine. Crude-oil output rose from 40,000 tons in 1965 to 1.7 million tons in 1968, and was expected to reach 4 million tons by 1970.

In addition to petrochemicals, Belorussia's expanding chemical industry produces a variety of fertilizers and chemical fibers. The discovery of salt and potash deposits in 1949 in the Starobin area, 70 miles south of Minsk, made Belorussia the Soviet Union's second largest potential producer of potash, after the Solikamsk–Berezniki deposits in the western Urals. The development of the deposit gave rise to the new city of Soligorsk (on the site of the former village of Chizhevichi; 1967 population: 28,000). The first mining and milling complex went into operation in 1963. A second complex opened in 1965 and a third was to follow in 1970. Each had a capacity of 2 million tons of potash. By 1970 Belorussia was expected to account for 40 percent of the Soviet Union's potash production. In 1966 the republic supplied 2.2 million tons (in terms of 41.6 percent $K_2O$ equivalent), or about 30 percent of total Soviet production.

The old city of Grodno was selected as the site of Belorussia's nitrogenous fertilizer industry based on the use of natural gas from Dashava. The Grodno plant opened in 1963, at first producing ammonium nitrate and nitric acid from long-haul ammonia. Local ammonia synthesis began in 1965 after completion of the Volkovysk–Grodno branch of the Dashava–Minsk gas pipeline. The Grodno plant will also produce caprolactam, the basic ingredient of kapron, using natural gas and petrochemicals delivered by the Polotsk oil refining complex. The Grodno caprolactam unit, one of the nation's largest with a capacity of 50,000 tons, was scheduled to go into operation in late 1969.

Belorussia's superphosphate plant, situated in Gomel', began production in 1965 on the basis of apatite from the Kola Peninsula and local sulfuric acid. Within the span of a few years, Belorussia thus acquired a diversified chemical fertilizer industry producing nitrogenous, phosphate, and potash fertilizers.

In addition to producing a major share of the Soviet Union's potash, Belorussia also expected to account for 12 percent of the nation's output of chemical fibers by 1970. An old viscose-rayon mill, using wood pulp from northern European Russia, has been in operation in Mogilev since 1932, undergoing expansion in the 1950s that raised annual output from 2,000 tons in 1950 to 17,000 tons by 1961. This manufacturing capacity was doubled in 1965 with the start of operation at a second viscose-yarn mill at Svetlogorsk (the former Shatilki). In the late 1960s further expansion of the chemical-fiber industry was under way at Mogilev with the construction of a 50,000-ton mill producing lavsan, the Soviet polyester fiber resembling dacron. The Mogilev mill will be supplied by the Polotsk petrochemical complex with the two principal ingredients of polyester fiber: paraxylene, used for making terephthalic acid, and ethylene glycol.

# 9

# THE BALTIC REGION

## Lithuanian SSR

Until the arrival of a natural-gas pipeline from Dashava in 1961, Lithuanian industry was dependent for fuels on the republic's peat resources, supplemented by long-haul coal. Peat output, which was concentrated around the principal cities, Vilna, Kaunas, Siauliai, and Panevezys, rose to a peak of 2.2 million tons in 1959 before declining to 933,000 tons in 1965. The peat-fed power stations produced about 1 billion kilowatt-hours of electricity. They were supplemented by the Kaunas hydroelectric station, with a capacity of 90,000 kilowatts, completed in 1959 on the Neman River. A second plant is planned in the 1970s upstream at Birstonas, 20 miles south of Kaunas, with a generating capacity of 600,000 kilowatts.

The availability of natural gas ushered in a new era in Lithuania's industrial structure by stimulating the construction of a major gas-fueled power station and gas-based chemical industries. The power plant, known as the Lithuanian regional electric station, was built at the new town of Elektrenai, halfway between Vilna and Kaunas. The first generating section, consisting of four 150,000-kilowatt units, was installed in 1962–65, and a second section, consisting of two 300,000-kilowatt units, in 1967–68, raising the total capacity to 1.2 million kilowatts. There were plans for the installation of two additional 300,000-kilowatt units, raising the capacity to 1.8 million kilowatts in the early 1970s. The power output of the Elektrenai station, which burns fuel oil in addition to natural gas, raised the republic's total electricity production to 4.7 billion kilowatt-hours in 1967. Lithuania became a net electric power exporter, transmitting some of its electricity over 330-kilovolt lines to Minsk (since 1964) and to Riga.

Natural gas also became the raw material of a new nitrogenous fertilizer plant at Jonava, 20 miles northeast of Kaunas. The first stage of the plant, producing ammonia (on the basis of gas-based hydrogen) and ammonia water, went into operation in 1964. A second stage, with units for the production of methanol (opened 1968), ammonium nitrate, urea and urea resins was under construction in the late 1960s. Two other major chemical plants, based on raw materials hauled from outside Lithuania, were built in the 1960s. The town of Kedainiai, 25 miles north of Kaunas, was selected as the site of a superphosphate plant, using Kola apatite. The plant produces 300,000 tons of sulfuric acid, from three sections opened in 1962, 1963, and 1964, and 600,000 tons of superphosphate (since 1963). Fluorine recovered from the apatite as a by-product is used in the manufacture of aluminum fluoride, required as an electrolyte in aluminum production. The third chemical plant is an acetate rayon plant at Kaunas that went into operation in 1963, using cellulose acetate from Vladimir. The acetate yarn is used by Lithuania's knitwear industry.

The construction of an oil refinery at Jurbarkas, on the Neman River, 45 miles west of Kaunas, began in the late 1960s. It is to be fed with crude oil from the Tatar–Bashkir fields via a branch of the Friendship pipeline. After the start of operations, expected in the early 1970s, the population of Jurbarkas is planned to rise to 50,000 (it was 5,200 in 1963). After an intensive geological exploration effort starting in 1959, oil was struck in 1968 in Lithuania, at Gargzdai (just east of Klaipeda), and in adjoining Kaliningrad Oblast, but it was not immediately apparent whether significant reserves were involved.

## Latvian SSR

Of the three Baltic republics, Latvia is the only one expected to have an electric power deficit in the foreseeable future, and will continue to depend to a large extent on electricity transmission from the shale-fueled power complex of northeast Estonia and from the gas-fed electric plant at Elektrenai in Lithuania. Unlike the two other republics, Latvia relies heavily on hydroelectric power from stations along the Daugava (Western Dvina) River. Out of a total installed capacity of 1.2 million kilowatts in 1966, 900,000 kilowatts were in hydroelectric stations and 300,000 kilowatts in steam electric stations.

However, because of a highly irregular seasonal flow in the Daugava, with a low-water stage from December to February, and a high-water stage in the spring when the snow cover in the drainage basin melts, electric power output from the hydroelectric stations must be combined with production of the steam electric stations. These are concentrated in Riga, the republic's capital and principal manufacturing center, as well as other major cities, such as Liepaja, Daugavpils, Jelgava, and Ventspils. The largest steam electric stations are in Riga, including a 150,000-kilowatt heat and power plant opened in 1955.

Because of the electric power deficit, peat plays a somewhat more important role in Latvia than in the two other Baltic republics. Peat output for fuel declined from a high of 2.2 million tons in 1959 to 1.4 million tons in 1965, but in that year Latvia still produced as much peat as Lithuania (900,000 tons) and Estonia (500,000 tons) combined. In addition to two old peatworks, at Balozi and Olaine, south of Riga along the railroad to Jelgava, the Riga heat and power plant also uses peat from a new works, opened at Seda, 75 miles northeast of Riga.

Natural gas from the Western Ukraine arrived by pipeline in 1962 and has been used mainly in Riga for households as well as for an additional power station fuel. In 1965 Latvia consumed 650 million cubic meters of natural gas. In subsequent years the gas transmission system was extended to other Latvian cities, including Jelgava (1966), Broceni, a cement center, and Liepaja (1967), and Daugavpils. In the 1970s, Riga is expected to be connected by a gas pipeline via Pskov and Valday with the transmission center of Torzhok, through which West Siberian gas is to be fed into the European pipeline system.

Latvia's first hydroelectric station on the Daugava was the Kegums plant, 30 miles southeast of Riga. It was first opened in

1939–40, destroyed in World War II, and rebuilt in 1945–47. After the addition of a fourth turbine in 1953, it reached a capacity of 68,000 kilowatts.

However, Latvia's total generating capacity remained less than 400,000 kilowatts until the construction of the Plavinas hydroelectric station on the Daugava, 50 miles southeast of Riga and 15 miles below the town of Plavinas. It went into construction in 1961 and was completed in 1966, with a total of ten 82,500-kilowatt units installed at the station in 1965–66 for the designed capacity of 825,000 kilowatts. The dam-builders' settlement of Peter Stucka, founded in 1961 at the station site, became the town of Stucka in 1967. Construction was under way in the late 1960s on a third Daugava River station, the Riga hydroelectric plant, situated at Salaspils, 10 miles southeast of Riga. The Riga station is expected to have a capacity of 400,000 kilowatts. There are also plans for expanding the Kegums station to 200,000 kilowatts.

Although the Plavinas station added substantially to electric-generating capacity, the station operates only about 20 percent of the time to help cover peak power consumption periods. It thus hardly doubled the total power output of the republic, from 1.6 billion kilowatt-hours (in the early 1960s) to about 3.0 billion in 1967, when power needs were about 3.7 billion kilowatt-hours. The deficit is being made up by transmission from Estonia, via a 330-kilovolt line completed in 1960, and from Lithuania.

Latvia's oldest chemical plant was a superphosphate installation built in Riga in 1892 for use of foreign phosphate rock (from North Africa). Under Soviet rule the plant was converted to the use of Kola apatite and expanded in capacity, producing 330,000 tons of superphosphate a year in the 1960s. The plant was shut down in 1967 as an anti-pollution measure. As part of the chemical expansion program of the 1960s, the town of Daugavpils was selected as the site of a plant for the manufacture of kapron, for use in tire-cord and fabrics. The plant went into operation in 1963. The peat-producing center of Olaine, where a briquetting plant opened in 1959, also acquired a chemical industry in the 1960s. It included the manufacture of plastics, chemical reagents, and pharmaceuticals.

Latvia also has a small steel plant at Liepaja, dating from 1882, operating largely on scrap metal. After the construction of additional rolling capacity in the early 1950s, a disproportion developed at the plant between steel-ingot capacity and rolling mills, forcing the long haul of billets from the Donets Basin and the Urals. The construction of additional open-hearth furnaces in 1965–66 restored the balance, giving the Liepaja plant both a smelting and rolling capacity of about 300,000 tons a year.

Though not directly affecting Latvian resource use, mention should be made of the oil-shipping terminal of Ventspils, a major export outlet for Tatar crude oil. The first crude oil was shipped through Ventspils in 1961. The marine terminal received its crude oil in rail tank cars until a pipeline branching off from the Friendship transmission system at Unecha reached Ventspils in 1968 (via Polotsk).

## Estonian SSR

Estonia is the only one of the Baltic republics with substantial mineral resources of its own in addition to peat. They are primarily the oil-shale basin of northeast Estonia and, to a lesser extent, phosphate rock deposits at Maardu near Tallinn. Oil shale, mined since before the Soviet assumption of power in World War II, has been substantially expanded as a power station fuel and as a source of shale gas and other products of shale distillation. In connection with the increasing availability of natural gas, a cheaper fuel than the processed shale gas, greater attention is expected to be given the chemical processing of oil shale.

Oil-shale production, which amounted to 1.9 million tons in 1940 (the year in which Estonia became Soviet), dropped to 0.9 million tons by 1945 as a result of destruction of mines during World War II. In the postwar period, output rose to 3.5 million tons in 1950, 7 million tons in 1955, and 9.2 million tons in 1958. During the seven-year plan (1959–65), production increased further, to 15.8 million tons by 1965, stimulated largely by the construction of the 1.6-million kilowatt shale-fed Baltic power station, just west of Narva. Increasing power needs are expected to raise shale production to 21.5 million tons by 1970, with most of the increase from newly developed strip mines in the eastern part of the basin around Viivikonna and Sirgala. Surface mining of oil shale began on a small scale in the early 1950s and was greatly expanded in the 1960s in connection with power station needs. The first of three Sirgala strip mines, each with a capacity of 4 to 4.5 million tons, began opertions in 1962. It reached its design capacity in 1968. Two other open pits, Sirgala No. 2 and Sirgala No. 3, were under construction in the late 1960s. As a result of these projects, the share of strip mining of oil shale was planned to increase from 4 million tons (25 percent of the total 1965 output) to 9.1 million tons (42 percent of the planned 1970 output of 21.5 million tons).

The principal urban centers of the shale basin are situated in the western part among the older underground mines. They are Kohtla-Järve (1965 population: 65,000) and Kivioli (1965 population: 11,000). Shale distilleries at both towns produce shale gas, fuel oil, lubricants, gasoline, road oil, and electrode coke. A detergent-manufacturing unit was added at Kivioli in 1969.

The shale gas has been transmitted by pipelines to Leningrad (since 1948) and to Tallinn (since 1953), and in the mid-1960s Estonia produced 500 million cubic meters of gas. However, with the availability of the cheaper natural gas, the significance of shale gas began to decline in the late 1960s. Beginning in 1969, the flow in the pipeline to Leningrad was reversed and natural gas moved to Estonia. It was mixed with shale gas for household use and also served as the raw material for ammonia synthesis in a new nitrogenous fertilizer plant opened at Kohtla-Järve in early 1969.

Before the start of construction on the large shale-fed power stations in the Narva area, the principal sources of electric power were two steam electric stations at Kohtla-Järve (opened in 1949) and in its southeast suburb of Ahtme (opened in 1951), and the 50,000 kilowatt hydroelectric station at Narva, opened in 1955. These power plants were linked by 110-kilovolt lines with Tallinn and Tartu, Estonia's two principal cities and industrial centers. By 1955, Estonia's power output had risen to about 1 billion kilowatt-hours. The biggest expansion of the electric power industry got under way with the construction of the first Baltic power station, at Soldina, just west of Narva. The first generator of the station, consisting of eight 100,000-kilowatt units and four 200,000-kilowatt units, went into operation in 1959 and the last in 1966, for a total capacity of 1.6 million kilowatts. Consuming 10 million tons of shale a year, the first Baltic power station raised Estonia's electrical output to 8.6 billion kilowatt-hours in 1967. Since 1960 the republic has been a net exporter of electrical energy, transmitting power to Leningrad and Riga via 330-kilovolt lines. In 1967 about 5 billion kilowatt-hours were transmitted. A second large power station, the New Baltic (later renamed Estonian) electric plant, also with a planned capacity of 1.6 million kilowatts, was under construction in the late 1960s. The first two 200,000-kilowatt units went into operation in 1969.

The phosphorite deposit at Maardu, 10 miles east of Tallinn, has long produced ground phosphate rock from an underground mine, which yielded up to 150,000 tons a year in the mid-1950s. In 1956 the Maardu plant acquired a sulfuric-acid department and began processing long-haul Kola apatite into superphosphate. In a further expansion, a surface mine opened at Maardu in 1964, with a capacity of about 250,000 tons of phosphate rock. The Maardu complex thus produced about 900,000 tons of phosphate fertilizer in the mid-1960s, about evenly divided between local ground phosphate rock and apatite-based superphosphate.

Special mention should be made of the uranium-mining and concentrating operation at Sillimäe, a town founded in 1957 on the Baltic coast, 15 miles west of Narva. The town (1965 population: 10,000) is believed to derive uranium ores from uraniferous clays in the glint, the escarpment facing the Gulf of Finland.

# 10

# THE URALS

One of the oldest Russian mining regions, the Urals developed an iron and copper industry in the early eighteenth century, based on the use of local ores and charcoal. By 1800 the region yielded about 80 percent of Russia's iron and virtually all of its copper. It was also a major producer of precious stones, gold, and salt.

However, in the second half of the nineteenth century, the Urals' iron industry declined as a technological shift from charcoal to coke began to favor the new Ukrainian iron and steel industry, with coking coal in the Donets Basin and iron ore at Krivoy Rog. The share of the Urals in Russian pig iron production dropped from 70 percent in 1860 to 20 percent on the eve of World War I.

Under the Soviet period, the policy of industrialization promoted a revival of the iron and steel industry by combining Urals iron ore and Siberian coking coal (in the Kuznetsk Basin) in a long-haul shuttle arrangement. This Urals–Kuznetsk combination gave rise to two new steel centers, at Magnitogorsk in the Urals and at Novokuznetsk in the Kuznetsk Basin.

The revival of the Urals steel industry was accelerated during World War II, when the Ukrainian mills were occupied by the Germans, and the Soviet war effort was largely dependent on the industry of the Urals. Two new iron and steel mills arose during the war, at Nizhniy Tagil and at Chelyabinsk. The Urals–Kuznetsk combination was gradually loosened as the Kuznetsk steel industry made increasing use of Siberian iron ores and the Urals mills used coking coal from the nearer Karaganda basin in addition to the Kuzbas.

After World War II, particularly after 1950, expansion of the iron and steel industry continued at Magnitogorsk, Nizhniy Tagil, Chelyabinsk, and a fourth modern mill at Novotroitsk. As Urals iron ore reserves declined, particularly the deposit at Magnitogorsk, the Urals mills became increasingly dependent on two newly developed deposits: the Rudnyy deposit in northwest Kazakhstan, which supplied the plants at Magnitogorsk, Novotroitsk, and Chelyabinsk, and the titaniferous magnetite deposit at Kachkanar, which became the principal ore source for the Nizhniy Tagil plant.

While the Urals copper industry was gradually eclipsed by new discoveries, notably in Kazakhstan and Uzbekistan, the region developed in the 1930s into the Soviet Union's principal supplier of alumina for aluminum reduction plants. Other important metals for modern industry that are produced in the Urals are nickel, cobalt, and magnesium. The latter is derived from magnesium chloride, a component of the rich salt and potash deposits of the Solikamsk–Berezniki area of the northwest Urals. These deposits have given rise to a major chemical industry, which also includes the production of superphosphate, based on the use of pyrites and copper smelter gases, and the production of coke chemicals.

A generally fuel-poor region, the Urals has relied for its energy production on local deposits of subbituminous coals; on long-haul coals from the Kuznetsk, Karaganda, and Ekibastuz basins; on hydroelectric power; and, since the mid-1960s, on natural gas piped from the Gazli field, near Bukhara, in Central Asia, and from the Igrim field, in the lower reaches of the Ob' River, in northwest Siberia. In the future, the Urals will also be supplied with cheap power transmitted over long-distance lines from large pithead electric plants at the Ekibastuz surface coal mines of northeast Kazakhstan.

The following survey of resource development for heavy industry in the Urals is discussed in terms of major industrial clusters or complexes, centered on major mining towns, processing centers, and sources of electric power.

## Serov Complex

On the eastern slopes of the Ural Mountains, in Sverdlovsk Oblast, the northernmost cluster is the steel–aluminum–coal complex of the Serov area. Serov (called Nadezhdinsk until 1939), a city of 104,000 in 1967, arose on the site of an old ironworks founded in the 1890s. The iron and steel plant, the largest of the old Urals ironworks, had a capacity of a quarter-million tons of pig iron and steel before World War II. In 1958 a large blast furnace was added to the six smaller units.

The Serov blast furnaces, with a total capacity of about 1 million tons of pig iron, are supplied with iron ore from several small underground mines grouped in two districts, the Ivdel' district, north of Serov, and the Bogoslovsk district, west of Serov. The two mines of the northern district, at Polunochnoye and Marsyaty, each yield about 300,000 tons of crude ore a year. The mines in the Bogoslovsk district, at Rudnichnyy (Auerbakh deposit), Vorontsovka, and Pokrovsk-Ural'skiy, yield about 1.5 million tons of crude ore. In 1965 all these mines produced 2.2 million tons of crude ore, with an average content of 43-percent iron, which was converted into 1.3 million tons of usable ore. The mines were approaching depletion in the late 1960s and are to be replaced by the newly developed North Peschanka deposit, between Rudnichnyy and Vorontsovka, west of Serov. North Peschanka, which began operations in 1968, will yield 5 million tons of crude ore (from two 2.5-million-ton shafts) when full capacity is reached in the early 1970s.

A ferroalloys plant associated with the Serov iron and steel plant began operations in 1958 and was expanded in 1961–62. At first it produced a variety of ferroalloys, including ferrochromium, ferrosilicon, and ferromanganese. Some of the manganese came from Polunochnoye, north of Serov, where manganese began to be mined in World War II to make up for the loss of the occupied Nikopol' mines of the Ukraine. After the war the Polunochnoye mine continued to yield from 30,000 to 40,000 tons of ore a year from underground workings. The other manganese mine, at Marsyaty, was shut down after its wartime operation. In the future the Serov ferroalloys plant is expected to specialize in ferrovanadium, based on the growing output of the vanadiferous titaniferous magnetite deposit of Kachkanar.

The aluminum industry of the Serov area is concentrated in two centers: a bauxite-mining complex at Severoural'sk (1967 population: 26,000) and an alumina–aluminum complex at Krasnotur'insk (1967 population: 61,000). Bauxite mining has been under way since 1934 at the Krasnaya Shapochka (Red Ridinghood) deposit at Severoural'sk. In the 1940s operations were extended to two nearby deposits at Kal'ya, 12 miles north, and Cheremukhovo, 20 miles north. Despite the need for underground mining and a flooding problem in the karst limestone surrounding the bauxite deposits, production has steadily increased in the postwar period, rising from about 700,000 tons of bauxite at the end of World War II to about 3.5 million tons in the mid-1960s. As the principal supplier of aluminum ore of the USSR, Severoural'sk ships its bauxite to major alumina plants at Krasnotur'insk and Kamensk-Ural'skiy, which in turn supply alumina to aluminum reduction plants in Siberia near low-cost sources of electric power. Some of the alumina is reduced to aluminum at Krasnotur'insk and Kamensk-Ural'skiy. The Krasnotur'insk mill began to produce alumina in 1943 and aluminum two years later.

Energy for aluminum reduction and other industries in the Serov complex is provided by local brown-coal mines and, since 1966, by natural gas from the Punga deposit of Western Siberia. Brown coal is mined at Karpinsk (1967 population: 41,000; in operation since 1936) and Volchansk (1967 population: 22,000; opened in 1944). The combined production of brown coal in 1965 was 21 million tons, with each deposit contributing half from three strip mines. The deposit at Karpinsk is expected to become depleted in the early 1970s and at Volchansk in the early 1980s. The brown coal serves as fuel at steam electric stations attached to the Krasnotur'insk aluminum plant and the Serov iron and steel mill. The two power plants are linked by a 220-kilovolt transmission line.

On the higher slopes of the Urals, west of Serov, are platinum placer mines that were the world's principal source of platinum during the nineteenth and early twentieth century. The center of this platinum-mining industry is Kytlym. However, since the 1940s the Urals placers have been superseded to a large extent by platinum-group metals obtained as a by-product of the smelting of copper-nickel ores of Noril'sk in northern Siberia. In contrast to the Urals output, which is high in osmium and iridium, but low in palladium, the production of the Noril'sk district is distinguished by a high palladium content.

## Nizhniy Tagil Complex

The Nizhniy Tagil iron and steel plant, which was inaugurated in 1940, is the center of another industrial complex that includes the old iron mines of Nizhniy Tagil and Kushva, the new iron mines of Kachkanar, the copper-chemical industry of Krasnoural'sk, and the steam electric station of Nizhnyaya Tura as the principal power producer.

Nizhniy Tagil, with a population of 379,000 in 1968, is one of the largest industrial cities of the Urals. Unlike Magnitogorsk, it also has an important steel-fabricating industry (railroad car-building plant) in addition to primary iron and steel production. The city arose on the site of an early eighteenth-century ironworks, which yielded about 100,000 tons of pig iron before World War II. A modern iron and steel plant, inaugurated in 1940, has a capacity of 4 to 5 million tons of pig iron. It consists of six blast furnaces opened in 1940 (two units), 1944, 1952, 1959, and 1969. The No. 6 furnace, inaugurated in 1969, has a working volume of 95,000 cubic feet and an annual capacity of 1.7 million tons. Open-hearth furnaces at Nizhniy Tagil were supplemented in 1963 by large oxygen converters.

Until the early 1960s the plant was supplied with ore mainly from deposits exploited since the early eighteenth century at Nizhniy Tagil and at Kushva. The Vysokaya mine at Nizhniy Tagil produced almost 6 million tons of crude ore in 1965 and the nearby Lebyazh'ye mine, 1.2 million tons. The 1965 output of the Goroblagodat' mine at Kushva was 5 million tons. The combined crude-ore output of 12 million tons of the entire district was converted into 6 million tons of usable ore. Until the 1950s production from these mines was entirely from open pits. But as the surface deposits were depleted, underground mining became increasingly important and, in the mid-1960s, accounted for half of the total output. Although these mines have a relatively high iron content, the average iron content

218

of the ore mined declined after the 1950s from 40–45 to 30 percent as the higher grade surface deposits became depleted; moreover, the reserves are small.

The need for an additional iron ore source led to the development of the Kachkanar deposit of vanadium-bearing titaniferous magnetite, consisting of vast reserves of very low-grade ore (17 percent iron). Despite the low metal content, Soviet economic planners felt that a large-scale operation in open pits and easy concentration of the ore, which is low in sulfur and phosphorus, would make its mining economical. A major asset of the Kachkanar ore is its vanadium content. Development of the deposit began in 1958; a 25-mile-long railroad spur was built northward from Aziatskaya station (on the Kushva–Chusovoy railroad), and the first stage of the mining and concentrating complex went into operation in 1963. In 1966 its capacity was doubled to 16.5 million tons of crude ore, converted into 2.7 million tons of concentrate with an iron content of 62 percent and a vanadium content of 0.5 to 0.68 percent. Although the Kachkanar ore contains 9 percent ilmenite and some platinum, the relatively low content of these metals does not justify separate recovery because the increased concentration costs would make the entire operation uneconomical. The third section, raising the total capacity to 25 million tons of ore, opened in 1969. Further expansion in the 1970s was to increase output to 33 million tons of ore and 5.4 million tons of concentrate. The concentrate moves to the Nizhniy Tagil plant, where vanadium pig iron is processed in oxygen converters to yield steel and vanadium slag. The slag, which contains 15 percent vanadium, is then transported to Chusovoy, across the Urals divide in Perm' Oblast.

Chusovoy, after Serov the second largest of the old Urals ironworks, specialized after 1936 in the production of ferrovanadium and vanadium steels. Until the opening up of the Kachkanar deposit, the Chusovoy plant was supplied only by the vanadiferous titaniferous magnetite deposits of Kusa, west of Chelyabinsk, and Pervoural'sk, west of Sverdlovsk. The Kusa mine, with higher-grade ore, ships to Chusovoy both an iron–vanadium concentrate (48 percent iron and 0.68 percent vanadium) and a separate titanium concentrate (41.6 percent); the lower-grade Pervoural'sk ore yields only the iron–vanadium concentrate.

The Nizhniy Tagil complex also contains the copper smelter

opened in 1931 at Krasnouralsk (1967 population: 40,000) and an associated superphosphate plant, using smelter gases for the production of sulfuric acid. The Nizhnyaya Tura steam electric station, opened in 1950, burns brown coal from Karpinsk and Volchansk.

## Sverdlovsk Complex

Several major mining centers and processing plants (copper, aluminum, gold, asbestos) are grouped around Sverdlovsk, the leading industrial city of the Urals and the heart of the southern complex of Sverdlovsk Oblast. Unlike Serov and Nizhniy Tagil to the north, Sverdlovsk has no integrated iron and steel industry, and is significant primarily for its manufacturing (heavy machinery). Primary industries are clustered around Sverdlovsk within a radius of 50 to 60 miles.

Copper is represented by two smelters: Kirovgrad (1967 population: 23,000), to the north, dating from before the Soviet period; and Revda (1967 population: 57,000), to the west, which began operations in 1940. Kirovgrad derives 60 percent of its copper from scrap, but also uses locally mined ore, notably from Levikha, to the northwest. The Sredneural'sk plant in Revda receives its ore from the copper-mining center of Degtyarsk (1967 population: 24,000), to the southeast. Since 1963 the Sredneuralsk' smelter also derives sulfuric acid from pyrites and uses the acid in the manufacture of superphosphate fertilizer. The two smelters send their blister copper for electrolytic refining to Verknyaya Pyshma (1967 population: 35,000), where a refinery was opened in 1934.

The alumina–aluminum center in the Sverdlovsk district is Kamensk-Ural'skiy (1967 population: 161,000). Originally founded on a small local bauxite deposit in 1939, it soon became dependent on bauxite shipments from the larger reserves of Severoural'sk. Kamensk-Ural'skiy ships most of its alumina to other reduction centers near cheap power sources in Siberia.

Just northeast of Sverdlovsk is the gold-lode mining center of Berezovskiy, which has been in production for two centuries. Berezovskiy (1967 population: 35,000) produces most of its gold from six underground mines, but also operates a dredge for placer deposits. Some of the lode gold ore is concentrated for smelting at copper smelters. The higher-grade lode gold is treated in a local mill, and the resulting sulfide concentrate is shipped to copper smelters for further treatment. The lower-grade ore is shipped directly to the smelters as a flux material (because of the high silica content of the quartz gangue), with recovery of the gold content at the smelter.

The asbestos center of Asbest (the former Bazhenovo), east of Sverdlovsk, has been the nation's principal chrysotile asbestos producer since the late nineteenth century. Asbest had a population of 74,000 in 1967. The asbestos is mined in three large open pits arranged along a north–south axis east of the city. In the mid-1960s the pits yielded 15 million tons of fiber-bearing rock, or about 1.5 million tons of unmanufactured fiber, of which a third was the shortest fiber grade used in asbestos-cement products.

South of Sverdlovsk is Polevskoy (1967 population: 54,000), a chemical center producing synthetic cryolite and other fluorine-base chemicals from fluorspar hauled from Kalanguy (Eastern Siberia) and other mines.

The city of Rezh (1967 population: 30,000), northeast of Sverdlovsk, is a nickel smelter that was converted from an old ironworks in 1936. The smelter, which was modernized in the early 1960s, ships its matte to Verkhniy Ufaley, in Chelyabinsk Oblast, for electrolytic refining.

The large electric power requirements of the Sverdlovsk industrial complex are met by several major steam electric stations in the area. The largest are the Sredneural'sk power plant, at Sredneural'sk (1967 population: 16,000), just west of the copper refinery of Verkhnyaya Pyshma, and the 1.6-million-kilowatt Verkhniy Tagil plant, 45 miles northwest of Sverdlovsk. In addition to brown coal from deposits in the Chelyabinsk area and long-haul coal from Ekibastuz, the fuel needs of the area are met by fuel oil and, since 1963, by natural gas from the Gazli field near Bukhara in Central Asia. Electric power is also transmitted by high-voltage lines from the Kuybyshev hydroelectric station on the Volga River (a 500-kilovolt line opened in 1959) and from two stations on the Kama River: the Kama station at Perm' (two 220-kilovolt lines; the first inaugurated in 1955) and the Votkinsk station at Chaykovskiy (a 500-kilovolt line, opened in the early 1960s).

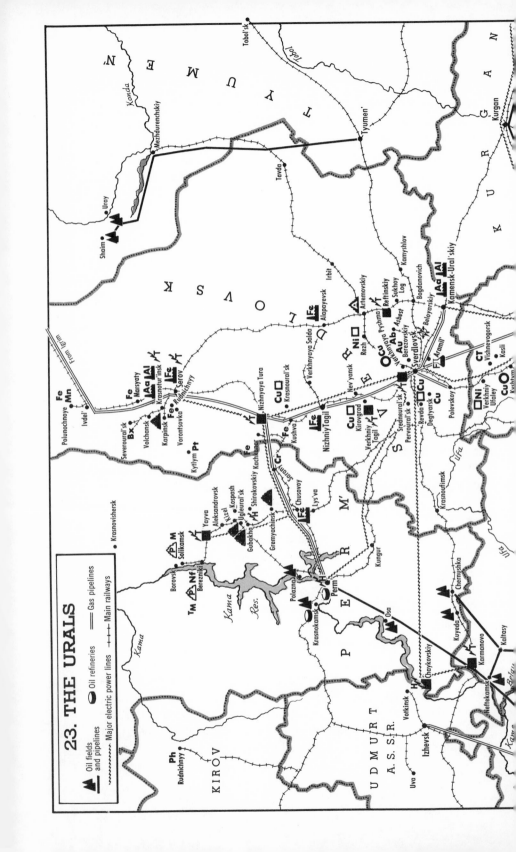

## 23. THE URALS

Oil fields and pipelines
Oil refineries
Gas pipelines
Major electric power lines
Main railways

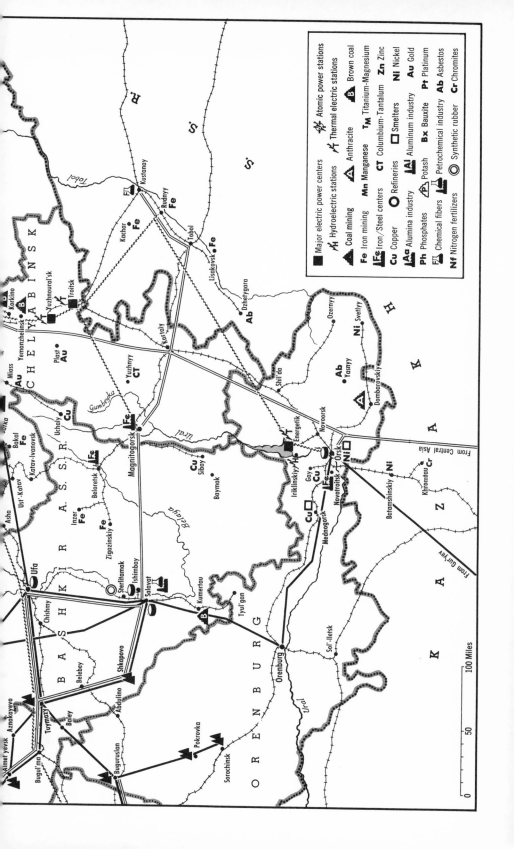

One of the Soviet Union's atomic power plants, using a boiling-water–graphite reactor and superheating of steam in the reactor, is in operation at Beloyarskiy, 30 miles east of Sverdlovsk. The first reactor, with a 100,000-kilowatt electrical capacity, went into commercial operation in 1964, and a second reactor of 200,000 kilowatts in 1968. The third unit will be a 600,000-kilowatt breeder reactor.

A new steam electric station at Reftinskiy, under construction in the late 1960s on the Reft River, east of Sverdlovsk, is to be equipped with 300,000-kilowatt generating units in its first stage, designed for both natural gas and Ekibastuz coal.

The small Yegorshino–Bulanash coal basin, northeast of the Reft River, has its center at Artemovskiy (formerly called Yegorshino; 1967 population: 38,000). It consists of an anthracite mine, with a capacity of 150,000 tons a year, and three bituminous coal mines at Bulanash, to the southeast, with a combined capacity of 900,000 tons a year. In 1965 this basin produced about 1 million tons.

## Chelyabinsk Oblast

Chelyabinsk, the capital of Chelyabinsk Oblast, in addition to being the center of a major industrial cluster, is also the site of one of the Urals' modern iron and steel mills. It began production in World War II, with the completion of the first electric steel furnaces in 1943 and the first three blast furnaces in 1944–45. A fourth blast furnace was added in 1955. During the 1940s and early 1950s, the Chelyabinsk mill mainly used iron ore from the Bakal mine, 190 rail mines to the west. But the enriched surface limonite (with 45 to 50 percent iron), accessible in open pits, was approaching exhaustion after two hundred years of mining, requiring increasing use of the deeper primary siderite ore, with an average iron content of 30 to 35 percent. In 1965 about 15 percent of the total Bakal output of 5 million tons of usable ore was mined underground. However, increasing mining of siderite through deep shafts was expected to shift the bulk of Bakal production from limonite to siderite in the early 1970s. In contrast to the high-grade limonite, the siderite requires preliminary enrichment by roasting.

With the availability of the newly developed Rudnyy ore of northwest Kakakhstan, beginning in 1957. Chelyabinsk became one of its principal consuming plants. Pig iron output topped 3 million tons after the 61,000-cubic-foot No. 5 furnace was inaugurated at Chelyabinsk in 1958. For steelmaking, Chelyabinsk has relied mainly on electric furnaces, but an oxygen-converter shop was under construction in 1967. The electro-metallurgical orientation of the complex is also evident in the presence of a ferroalloys plant, opened in 1931 and expanded in 1954–55 by addition of special ferro-molybdenum and ferrotungsten shops; an electrode plant, in operation since 1934; and a zinc refinery, opened in 1935.

About 50 miles northwest of Chelyabinsk is the twin-city copper complex of Karabash (smelter) and Kyshtym (electrolytic refinery), dating from before the Revolution. Beyond Kyshtym is the nickel smelter of Verkhniy Ufaley, completed in 1933 to process local nickel ores associated with the weathering of ultrabasic rocks, notably serpentine. Nearby pegmatite deposits in the Vishnevyye Gory (Cherry Mountains) are one of the Soviet Union's principal source of tantalum and columbium, two rare metals that became important only in the nuclear and space age because of their high heat resistance. The mining center, named for the mountains, is the town of Vishnevogorsk, founded in 1949 (1959 population: 9,100).

West of Chelyabinsk, along the main railroad crossing of the Urals, is a string of old mining centers that have been converted into manufacturing towns in the Soviet period: Miass (motor vehicles), Zlatoust (special steels, tools and dies, and watches), Kusa (boilers, with titaniferous magnetite mine at nearby Magnitka), Satka (low-phosphorous foundry pig iron based on Bakal ore, magnesite, and chromite refractories), Ust'-Katav (streetcar building), and Asha (pig iron based on Bakal ore, and wood chemicals).

Energy for the industries of the Chelyabinsk cluster is supplied partly by the brown coal of the Chelyabinsk basin, with the principal mining centers at Kopeysk (1967 population: 166,000), Korkino (83,000), and Yemanzhelinsk (36,000). The basin produced 23.7 million tons of coal a year in 1965, including 7.8 million from strip mines. The largest power plant based on Chelyabinsk brown coal, with a capacity of 1 million kilowatts, is situated at Yuzhnoural'sk (1967 population: 30,000), 50 miles south of Chelyabinsk. The power station went into operation in 1952–53 with four 50,000-kilowatt generators. It added four 100,000-kilowatt units in the mid-1950s and two 200,000-kilowatt units in 1960–61. A second major power plant, this one fueled with long-haul coal from Ekibastuz, is situated at Troitsk (1967 population: 86,000), a rail junction 75 miles south of Chelyabinsk. Like the Yuzhnoural'sk station, the Troitsk power plant was also built in several stages with increasingly large generators. It received three 100,000-kilowatt units in 1960–61 and four 300,000-kilowatt units in 1965–67, raising the total capacity to 1.5 million kilowatts. A 500,000-kilowatt generator was to be added in the late 1960s.

One of the Urals' two major gold-lode deposits, the Kochkar' deposit, is situated west of Yuzhnoural'sk. In operation since the mid-nineteenth century, it is being exploited through twelve underground mines yielding quartz ores associated with pyrite and arsenopyrite. The mining town of Plast, center of the Kochkar' deposit, had a population of 25,000 in 1967.

## Magnitogorsk

Magnitogorsk, the Soviet Union's largest iron and steel center, did not attract subsidiary manufacturing or form the nucleus of a major urban cluster after its founding in the early 1930s, largely because of its poor transport situation. The city developed at the end of a rail spur, leading 85 miles west from the rail junction of Kartaly. Although plans were announced calling for the construction of a westward outlet across the Ural Mountains, they have been shelved for the time being. The original plan, announced in the mid-1950s, called for a railroad from Magnitogorsk via Beloretsk and Sterlitamak to Abdulino (on the Ufa–Kuybyshev main line). The railroad reached Beloretsk in 1958, thus completing a 65-mile-long section of the entire proposed 335-mile-long line. A more northerly route was proposed in the early 1960s, to take the railroad from Beloretsk to the Ufa–Kuybyshev main line at Chishmy, but no further construction has been reported. Pending the completion of a westward outlet, Magnitogorsk is linked with European Russia via Chelyabinsk in the north and Orsk in the south.

The iron and steel plant arose on the basis of a local iron ore deposit in Magnitnaya Gora (Magnet Mountain), for which the city was named, and coking coal from the Kuznetsk Basin and, later, Karaganda. The first pig iron at Magnitogorsk was produced in 1932 and the first steel in 1933, as part of the shuttle arrangement under which Magnitogorsk ore moved to the Novokuznetsk iron and steel mill and Kuznetsk coking coal to Magnitogorsk. As Novokuznetsk gradually expanded its local iron ore supply, especially in World War II and after, shipments of Magnitogorsk ore to Siberia declined. However, a high rate of consumption (more than 15 million tons of crude ore a year in the 1950s and 1960s) led to a rapid exhaustion of the Magnitnaya deposit, particularly of the higher-grade oxidized ore (50 percent iron) that overlies the lower-grade sulfide ore (42 percent iron and a high sulfur content). Since 1960 Magnitogorsk has depended increasingly on ore from the newly developed Rudnyy deposit, 200 miles to the east, in northwest Kazakhstan.

Magnitogorsk emerged from World War II with six blast furnaces, No. 6 having been completed in 1943. Additional blast furnaces were built in the early 1950s (Nos. 7 and 8), 1964 (No. 9), and 1966 (No. 10). The last two furnaces have annual capacities of 1.2 million tons, suggesting a total pig iron capacity of 9 million tons in 1966. Steelmaking capacity was about 6 million tons in 1958 and 10 million tons in 1966.

In addition to being linked by rail to Beloretsk, where an old ironworks has been converted to steel wire and cable manufacture, Magnitogorsk is also the outlet for concentrates of the Sibay copper-zinc open-pit mine, 65 mail miles to the south. Sibay, which is situated in the Bashkir ASSR, was reached by the railroad in 1954; a concentrator went into operation five years later. A second Bashkir open-pit copper and zinc mining center is Uchaly, which started shipping concentrates in 1958 over a newly completed 60-mile-long railroad spur (southward from Miass). East of Magnitogorsk, in the basin of the Gumbeyka River, is another area where rare metals (columbium, tantalum) are mined. The settlement of Yuzhnyy arose there in 1961.

## Orsk Complex

At the southern end of the Urals lies the industrial cluster centered on Orsk, a regional processing center that developed particularly after World War II. An old refinery was built in 1936 to process crude oil from Baku (transported by pipeline from the Gur'yev water terminal on the Caspian Sea). As output of the Emba field (near Gur'yev) increased, the Orsk refinery processed crude oil from that field. Since 1961, when a pipeline from Ishimbay was completed, Orsk added Bashkir crude oil to its input. Finally, with the development of Mangyshlak crude oil in the mid-1960s, the flow over the Gur'yev–Orsk line again became a significant element. A synthetic-alcohol plant, using Orsk refinery gases, went into operation in 1955.

The South Urals nickel–cobalt refinery at Orsk was opened in 1939 to process nickel oxide ores from the nearby Akkermanovka deposit. After World War II, the smelter became increasingly dependent for ores on the Kimpersay nickel–cobalt deposit at Batamshinskiy, 45 miles south of Orsk, in Kazakhstan. Finally, in the mid-1960s, yet another potential raw-material source was added, with the development of the Buruktal nickel–cobalt deposit at Svetlyy, 105 miles east of Orsk. Svetlyy, reached by railroad from Dombarovskiy in 1964, has a metallurgical plant of its own, with a reduction roasting shop and electric furnaces producing ferronickel.

Just west of Orsk is the city of Novotroitsk (1967 population: 82,000), where an integrated iron and steel plant developed in the 1950s. Construction on the plant began just before World War II, with a view to processing a naturally alloyed iron ore high in nickel and chromium. However, the war delayed construction, and the first 300,000-ton blast furnace producing chromium–nickel pig iron was completed only in 1955, with the first oxygen converters following in 1956 and the first open-hearth furnace two years later. A second 300,000-ton blast furnace opened in 1958 and a third, with a capacity of 1 million tons a year, in 1963. While the two smaller blast furnaces continue to use the local alloyed iron ore, of which 2 million tons a year are being mined, the third blast furnace smelts long-haul iron concentrate from the Rudnyy iron-mining complex in Kazakhstan. A chromium-chemical plant opened in Novotroitsk in 1963, using local chemical-grade chromite.

The copper industry in the area is represented by the Mednogorsk smelter, which began operations in 1939 on the basis of local Blyava copper–sulfide deposits. Formerly mined underground, Blyava ore is being extracted in an open pit since 1955. The raw-material base of the Mednogorsk smelter was greatly expanded with the opening up of the Gay deposit, north of Orsk. The Gay deposit, described as the largest in reserves in the Urals and the richest in copper content (up to 8 and 10 percent), was discovered in 1950. It was reached by a railroad spur in 1958 and the first ore, mined underground, started moving to the Mednogorsk smelter in 1961. Two years later an open pit went into operation on the site. The mining town of Gay had a population of 30,000 in the mid-1960s.

Another recent development is the opening of the Kiyembay (Kiimbay) asbestos deposit at the new mining town of Yasnyy, 25 miles northeast of Dombarovskiy. The asbestos complex, with a designed capacity of 500,000 tons of fiber-bearing rock, will produce short nonspinning grades of chrysotile fiber. The first fiber-bearing rock moved to the Dzhetygara mill in 1966.

With local fuel sources limited to a small anthracite mine at Dombarovskiy, Orsk has been dependent on long-haul coal and fuel oil for its power needs. Since 1963, natural gas from the Gazli field near Bukhara has also been used. A major power-producing center began to arise in the late 1950s at Iriklinskiy, 30 miles north of Orsk. A dam on the Ural River, completed in 1955, created a reservoir to regulate the highly uneven stream flow and thus assure a year-round water source. In 1958–59 four small hydroturbines were installed at the Iriklinskiy dam, for a total capacity of 30,000 kilowatts, to ease the power shortage of the Orsk area and the newly developed copper centers of Sibay and Gay. However, in view of the limited hydroelectric potential of the Ural River, the Iriklinskiy reservoir was chosen as the site for the construction of a major steam electric station with a capacity of 2.4 million kilowatts that would burn fuel oil and natural gas. A 30-mile-long railroad spur from Novoorsk, on the main line, was completed in 1966 to a new power station settlement called Energetik. The first of a series of 300,000-kilowatt generating units opened in 1969. The station was linked by a 500-kilovolt transmission line with the iron-mining complex at Rudnyy and a 220-kilovolt line with Orsk.

## The Western Urals

Resources on the western slopes of the Urals include the salt and potash deposits of the Berezniki–Solikamsk area; the Kizel–

Gubakha basin of bituminous coal, and the oil-refining and chemical complex of Perm'–Krasnokamsk, with the hydroelectric stations on the upper Kama River. Some diamond dredges operate in the Krasnovishersk district.

The Berezniki–Solikamsk district is made up of the cities of Solikamsk (1967 population: 88,000) and Berezniki (134,000), which form the twin centers of an urban district with a population of about 250,000.

Saltworks were established on the upper Kama River as early as the fifteenth and sixteenth centuries, when the Russians first settled the western slopes of the Ural Mountains. In two clusters of saltworks, in the area of the present Berezniki and Solikamsk, salt brine was produced from underground deposits. The area was reached by a railroad in the 1870s, and soon thereafter Russia's first ammonia–soda plant, using natural brines, began production at Berezniki. As coal mining developed at Kizel, coal gradually replaced firewood as the fuel used for evaporation of the brines.

However, in both Berezniki and Solikamsk, a modern chemical industry dates largely from the Soviet period. On the basis of the deposits of sylvinite (potassium chloride) and the associated carnallite (hydrous potassium-magnesium chloride), the Soviet Union's first modern potash plant opened in Solikamsk in 1934, after five years' construction, followed in 1936 by a magnesium plant, which made use of electrolysis of the magnesium chloride component of the local deposits. Two rare metals, cesium and rubidium, with potential applications in ion engines for space flight and in thermionic converters for changing heat directly into electricity, are produced as by-products of carnallite at Solikamsk.

Not directly related to the potash–magnesium industry is the large paper and pulp mill at Borovsk, a northern suburb of Solikamsk. The mill at Borovsk, which existed as a separate city in 1949–59, produces about a fourth of the Soviet Union's newsprint. The paper mill went into operation in 1941.

At Berezniki, the first Soviet chemical development was the completion in 1932 of a nitrogenous fertilizer plant, deriving hydrogen for synthetic ammonia production from water gas (obtained from Gubakha coke). An additional source of hydrogen for ammonia is the by-product hydrogen obtained from caustic soda and chlorine production. Nitric acid, a product of the nitrogen industry, in turn is used in making aniline dyes. In the late 1950s about a third of the Soviet Union's aniline dyes were made in Berezniki. During World War II a second magnesium plant opened in Berezniki (in 1943), using equipment evacuated from the Zaporozh'ye magnesium plant in the Ukraine. In 1960–62 the Berezniki magnesium plant was converted to the production of titanium sponge by the magnesium reduction process. A second section opened in 1968.

In addition to the old prewar potash mill at Solikamsk, a mill opened at Berezniki in 1954–55 and was expanded to more than twice its size in 1963. In the mid-1960s the mines in the Solikamsk–Berezniki area yielded about 10 million tons of crude sylvinite ore with an average of 15 percent $K_2O$, or 3.4 million tons of standard potash fertilizer (41.6 percent $K_2O$). A second potash plant, with a capacity of 5.5 million tons of fertilizer, was scheduled to open at Berezniki in late 1969, and a third mill was under construction.

The large amounts of electrical and steam energy required for the chemical industry of the Solikamsk–Berezniki area have been provided by a number of steam electric plants fueled with Kizel coal, the largest being the Berezniki thermal electric plants Nos. 2 and 4. The No. 4 station, opened in 1932, was further expanded in the late 1930s and again in 1952. The new power station in the area is the Yayva electric plant, 15 miles east of Berezniki, where the first 150,000-kilowatt unit was installed in 1963, and a capacity of 600,000 kilowatts was reached by 1965.

The Kizel coal basin, the oldest in the Urals, has been exploited since the early nineteenth century. In the mid-1960s it was yielding coal at the rate of 10 million tons a year from twenty-seven underground mines. Although high in sulfur and ash content, Kizel coal is rich in volatile matter and is, therefore, a useful chemical raw material in addition to being a power station and railroad fuel. In combination with low-ash Kuznetsk coal, it yields a coke suitable for the smelting of nonferrous metals but not for pig iron. In addition to the old coal-mining cities of Kizel and Gubakha, new centers arose in World War II at Kospash, Ugleural'sk (called Polovinka until 1951), and Gremyachinsk.

Power-generating and coke–chemical enterprises are concentrated at Gubakha, site of the Urals' first large power station, the Kizel steam electric plant, opened in 1924. To supplement the coal-based power, a small hydroelectric station (28,000 kilowatts) was opened at Shirokovskiy on the Kos'va River, just east of Gubakha, in 1947. Its reservoir serves as a water source for the Kizel basin, where many streams are highly polluted by mine waters.

A major industrial complex has developed around Perm', the regional manufacturing center, and its western satellite city, Krasnokamsk. A highly diversified industrial city, Perm' combines metal-fabricating industries with chemical enterprises (aniline dyes). A superphosphate plant, in operation since 1924, now uses Kola apatite and Urals pyrites. Krasnokamsk arose in 1936 around a paper and pulp mill. Shortly thereafter oil was struck nearby, and a small oil refinery went into operation at Krasnokamsk in 1943. With the development of the Tatar oil fields in the 1950s, Perm' was selected as the site of a large refinery. A pipeline, 275 miles long, was laid from Almet'yevsk, and the refinery went into operation in 1958–59.

The large energy requirements of the Perm'–Krasnokamsk complex (1967 population: 850,000), were long met by coal-burning steam electric stations, notably the Zakamsk No. 5 station, between Perm' and Krasnokamsk, and the Perm' No. 6 station. In the early 1950s a dam was built across the Kama River on the northeast outskirts of Perm', and between 1954 and 1958 a total of twenty-four power-generating units of 21,000 kilowatts each were installed in the spillway powerhouse, for a total capacity of 504,000 kilowatts. In addition to improving the power supply of the Perm' area, the new hydroelectric station was also linked by two 220-kilovolt lines with Sverdlovsk. A second major power dam on the Kama River was completed in the early 1960s downstream from Perm'. Known as the Votkinsk hydroelectric station, it is actually situated at the new town of Chaykovskiy, 20 miles south of the old metalworking center of Votkinsk. The capacity of the Votkinsk station, originally designed for 500,000 kilowatts, was later revised to 1 million kilowatts, with ten 100,000-kilowatt units installed between 1961 and 1963. Like the Kama station at Perm', the Votkinsk plant was linked by a power transmission line with Sverdlovsk, but with a potential difference of 500 kilovolts. A large silk mill, using synthetic fibers, went into operation at Chaykovskiy in 1965, and a synthetic-rubber plant was under construction in the late 1960s.

Meanwhile the old oil field in the Krasnokamsk–Polazna area was overshadowed in the early 1960s by the development of new deposits at Kuyeda and Chernushka, on the northern margin of the Bashkir fields. Before the development of the new deposits, crude oil production in Perm' Oblast was about 3 million tons a year. The new development raised output to 9.7 million tons in 1965 and 15 million in 1968. The fields not only were able to meet the crude-oil requirements of the Perm' refinery, but provided a surplus for transmission to other areas, reversing the original flow in the Perm'–Almet'yevsk pipeline.

# 11

# SIBERIA

## Western Siberia

Until the early 1960s, the development of mineral resources for heavy industry in Western Siberia was centered almost entirely in the Kuznetsk Basin, one of the Soviet Union's principal coking coal producers. There, coal mining gave rise to a coke–chemical industry; a zinc refinery, using the distillation method to recover the metal from long-haul ores, was inaugurated in Belovo in 1930; and an integrated iron and steel plant began operations in 1932 at Novokuznetsk. During World War II this city also gained a ferro-alloys plant and an aluminum reduction plant, based on Urals alumina, and in the mid-1960s a second integrated iron and steel plant, the so-called Western Siberian plant, began operations in the Novokuznetsk area. About this time, a vast new resource area, the oil and gas province of the Ob' basin began to be developed, yielding its first commercial crude oil in 1964 and natural gas by pipeline to the Urals in 1966.

### THE KUZNETSK BASIN

Commercial coal output in the Kuznetsk Basin started at the turn of the century, when mines at Anzhero-Sudzhensk, at the northern extremity of the basin, began to yield steam coals for the newly completed Trans-Siberian Railroad. Anzhero-Sudzhensk remained the principal producer until the early 1930s, when coal mining was expanded southward in the Kuznetsk Basin in deposits of coking coals. The principal mining centers that developed during the 1930s were Leninsk-Kuznetskiy (which had a population of about 150,000 in the mid-1960s), Kiselevsk (150,000), Prokop'yevsk (300,000), and Osinniki (75,000). By the start of World War II, the coal output of the Kuznetsk Basin was 22.6 million tons, including 6 million tons of coking coal.

In the meantime an iron and steel plant developed at Novokuznetsk (called Stalinsk from 1932 to 1961). It was to be based on local coking coal and on iron ore deposits in the Gornaya Shoriya district, adjoining the Kuznetsk Basin in the south. However, in the 1930s, when the new Urals iron and steel center of Magnitogorsk was dependent on Kuzbas coking coal, the iron and steel mill at Novokuznetsk was temporarily part of a long-haul shuttle arrangement by which Kuzbas coking coal was shipped westward to the Urals, and Magnitogorsk iron ore moved eastward to the blast furnaces at Novokuznetsk.

By 1940, when the first two blast furnaces at Novokuznetsk were producing 1.5 million tons of pig iron a year, only one-fifth of the more than 3 million tons of usable ore required originated in the Gornaya Shoriya mines. The first iron ore mines in this area, whose name means "Shor mountain country," for a local Tatar people, were in the Temirtau area, 45 miles south of Novokuznetsk. The ore mined at Temirtau and especially at Odrabash was of low grade and had to be beneficiated at the nearby Mundybash concentrator (crude-ore capacity: 2.6 million tons). During World War II, the railroad was extended southward to the Tashtagol area, 75 miles from Novokuznetsk, where a mine with a larger iron content (46 percent) went into operation in 1944, raising the share of local ore in the Novokuznetsk blast furnaces to 32 percent by 1945.

After the war, both the local iron ore supply and the smelting capacity at the iron and steel mill were expanded, and by the mid-1950s 80 percent of the ore needs were met by the Gornaya Shoriya mines, including the Shalym and Sheregesh mines in the Tashtagol area. Some of these ores required beneficiation, and a larger, 5.8-million-ton concentrator, more than double the capacity of the old Mundybash concentrator, was opened in 1956 at Abagur, on the southeast outskirts of Novokuznetsk.

## 24. KUZNETSK BASIN

- ━━━ Oil pipelines
- ═══ Gas pipelines under construction
- ∿∿∿ ⊶⊶ Major electric power lines (under construction)
- 🜨 Coal mining
- ⋏ Hydroelectric stations
- ⋏ Thermal electric stations
- Fe Iron/Steel plants
- Fe Iron ore
- Mo Molybdenum
- Al Aluminum ores
- Al Aluminum plants
- Aa Alumina plants
- Chemical fibers
- Chemicals
- Nf Nitrogen fertilizers
- PbZn Lead-Zinc
- O Refineries
- ◎ Synthetic rubber
- Au Gold
- Ab Asbestos
- ┼┼┼ ╍╍╍ Main railways (under const.)

0                    50 Miles

To Belyy Yar
From Myt'dzino
Chulym
T O M S K
Yuksa
Asino
Achinsk
Aa
Al O F Krasnoyarsk
Tomsk
Mariinsk
Itatskiy
Bogotol
Arga Hills
Mazul'skiy
B
T
Divno-gorsk
KRASNOYARSK HYDRO STATION
Bolotnoye
Tayga
Anzhero-Sudzhensk
B
Berezovskoye
Nazarovo
Yurga
Topki
Barzas
Berezovskiy
Nf
Kemerovo
Berikul'skiy
Au
Goryachegorsk
Uzhur
Chulym
Yenisey
Toguchin
K E M E R O V O
Belogorsk
Al
Novosibirsk
Akademgorodok
Berdsk
Iskitim
Leninsk-Kuznetskiy
S I B I R S K
Zn O
Belovo
Inskoy
W. SIBERIAN STEEL PLANT
Mo
Sorsk
Chernogorsk
Minusinsk
Gur'yevsk
Salair
Pb
Zn
Artyshta
Fe
Usa
Abakan
K R A S N O Y A R S K
Kiselevsk
Abagur
Podobass
Mezhdurechensk
Tom'
Biskamzha
Prokop'yevsk
Fe Al
Myski
T
Vershina Tei (Teya)
Fe
Novokuznetsk
Osinniki
Askiz
Mayna
Kaltan
T
SAYAN HYDRO STATION SITE
F Chemical fibers
Barnaul
Novoaltaysk
Mundybash
Temirtau
Gornaya
Sheregesh
Fe
Shalym
Tashtagol
Fe
Abaza
Fe
Shoriya
Biysk
Biya
Aleysk
Ob'
Gorno-Altaysk
A L T A Y
Katun'
W E S T E R N  S A Y A N  M T S.
Highway
T U V A
Ab Ak-Dovurak
A. S. S. R.
M O N G O L I A

However, further expansion of the iron and steel industry of the Kuznetsk Basin made it necessary to look outside the Gornaya Shoriya area for additional iron ore sources. Not only was a fifth blast furnace opened at Novokuznetsk in 1960, raising the mill's pig iron capacity to 3.5 million tons a year, but construction was started on a second iron and steel mill, the West Siberian plant, on the right bank of the Tom' River, 10 miles northeast of Novokuznetsk. The first blast furnace at the West Siberian mill began operations in 1964 after seven years' construction, and the second (70,000 cubic feet) in 1967. A third blast furnace (100,000 cubic feet) was due in 1970.

Planned pig iron production of the two mills in 1967 was 5.5 million tons. The Gornaya Shoriya mines supplied only about half of the usable ore needs in the year. The rest came from two mines in the adjacent Khakass Autonomous Oblast (Krasnoyarsk Kray), at Abaza, which went into production in 1957, and Teya, opened in 1965, and from the more distant Korshunovo mine, opened in 1965, east of Bratsk, in Irkutsk Oblast. The first steel-making capacity at the West Siberian plant (oxygen converters and blooming mill) opened in 1968.

The development of the iron and steel industry in the Kuznetsk Basin has been accompanied by rapid expansion of coal mining, especially coking coals. From 36.8 million tons in 1950, total coal production rose to 75.3 million tons in 1958 and 97 million in 1965, including 37.5 million tons coking coal. Although geology does not favor open-pit mining, an effort has been made since the late 1940s to extract more coal from surface deposits. By 1965 surface mines yielded 22.4 million tons, and the 1970 goal was 30 million tons. Among the new coal-mining centers that arose since the 1950s are Mezhdurechensk (1967 population: 79,000), in the upper Tom' valley east of Novokuznetsk, and Berezovskiy (1967 population: 31,000). The Mezhdurechensk area contains the new Siberga and Krasnogorsk strip mines, and the Berezovskiy area the Chernigovskiy open pit.

Because of the high quality of the Kuznetsk coals and relatively lower mining costs compared with the Donets Basin, the Kuznetsk Basin markets its coal in almost half of the territory of the USSR, from central European Russia to Eastern Siberia. More than half of the total coal mined in 1965, or about 50 million tons, was shipped out of the Western Siberian region. Half of these shipments were made up of high-quality steam coals and half of coking coals, which traveled mainly to the Urals.

The abundance of coking coals laid the basis for a coke–chemical industry at the city of Kemerovo, where the first coke ovens started production in 1934. The fifth and last series of ovens was completed in 1943. By-product coke gases are used for aniline dyes and yield hydrogen for ammonia synthesis at a nitrogen fertilizer plant that began operations in 1938. Another chemical complex, added in 1962, produces caprolactam, the raw material for kapron. A second stage was opened in 1968, and a third under construction in the late 1960s was expected to make Kemerovo the Soviet Union's largest producer of caprolactam. A kapron mill was due in 1970.

The aluminum reduction plant at Novokuznetsk was opened in 1943 with equipment evacuated from Volkhov, near Leningrad, but the first section of the plant was not completed until 1956. It expanded considerably during the 1959–65 seven-year plan, and became one of the largest aluminum producers of the Soviet Union. Since the opening of the alumina plant at Pavlodar (Kazakhstan) in 1964, Novokuznetsk has received its alumina from the new source instead of the Urals. The additional alumina supply further stimulated expansion, and an eleventh electrolysis shop, of larger capacity than each of the previous ten units, was opened in 1965.

The zinc reduction plant at Belovo, the only Soviet plant still using the distillation method of zinc recovery, was opened in 1930 to process lead–zinc ores from the Salair district to the west. However, the small reserves became rapidly depleted and Belovo now refines concentrates from other Siberian mines, as far east as Tetyukhe on the Sea of Japan. The Salair district now yields mainly gold, silver, and barite.

Like other industrial districts, the Kuznetsk Basin has acquired large steam electric stations since the 1950s. The first was the South Kuzbas power plant, with a capacity of 500,000 kilowatts, built in 1950–54, at Kaltan, just south of Osinniki. It was followed by the Tomusa station, at Myski, 25 miles east of Novokuznetsk. The station, named for the Tom' and Usa rivers, went into operation in 1958 and reached its design capacity of 1.3 million kilowatts in 1965 with five 100,000-kilowatt and four 200,000-kilowatt units. It obtains its coal from the mines of Mezhdurechensk, situated at the confluence of the Tom' and Usa rivers. A third major coal-fed power plant was built at Inskoy, an eastern suburb of Belovo. Opened in 1964, the Belovo station reached its design capacity of 1.2 million kilowatts in 1968 with the sixth 200,000-kilowatt unit. The Kuznetsk Basin power plants are linked by 220-kilovolt lines with Novosibirsk, Tomsk, and Barnaul, and, since 1967, by a 500-kilovolt transmission line with the Krasnoyarsk hydroelectric station.

Novosibirsk and Barnaul are essentially manufacturing centers, but also include some primary industries. Novosibirsk is the site of the Soviet Union's largest tin smelter, processing concentrates from Eastern Siberia and the Far East. Barnaul has a large chemical fiber plant, producing both kapron (since 1960), based on caprolactam from Kemerovo, and viscose rayon (since 1963) from Siberian wood pulp. A tire-retreading plant opened in Barnaul in 1963, later acquired a carbon-black unit, and now manufactures tires.

### THE OIL AND GAS INDUSTRY

The discovery of commercial oil deposits in the late 1950s and early 1960s marked the start of a new era for the vast swampy forest of the Ob' and Irtysh river basins. Oil was struck in the Shaim area on the upper Konda River in 1959; in the Megion area on the middle Ob' in 1961, and farther downstream in the Ust'-Balyk area in 1962.

The Shaim field was the first to be developed. The first crude oil began moving by barge in the summer of 1964 down the Konda River and then up the Irtysh to the Omsk refinery, and the following year the completion of a 250-mile-long 30-inch pipeline provided a more direct outlet for Shaim crude oil to Tyumen', where it was transferred to rail tank cars. In 1967 the Shaim area was also reached by a new railroad from Tavda, originally envisaged mainly as a timber carrier. The principal center of the Shaim district is the oil workers' town of Uray, founded in 1965.

The oil fields on the middle Ob' River, somewhat slower to develop, have far greater reserves than the Shaim district. Early development centered on the Ust'-Balyk field, 30 miles southwest of the old Siberian town of Surgut. A new oil workers' town, Nefteyugansk, arose in the field in 1964 and was raised to the status of city in 1967, when its population was 15,000. In that year the Ust'-Balyk field was linked to the Omsk refinery by a 650-mile-long 40-inch pipeline, extending through Demyansk, Vagay, and Abat-skiy. It also carries crude oil from the West Surgut field, opened in 1965, and from the Pravdinsk field, 100 miles southwest of Surgut, opened in 1968. Surplus crude oil is fed into the Trans-Siberian pipeline for refining at Angarsk.

The middle Ob' oil fields are to be linked with the outside world both by a railroad and a high-voltage power transmission line. The 400-mile-long railroad from Tyumen' reached Tobol'sk in 1967, and construction toward Surgut was continuing in the late 1960s. The power line, designed for 500 kilovolts, was completed in 1969 to transmit electricity from Tyumen' to the oil district. A 1.2-million kilowatt steam electric station is planned at Surgut for the 1970s.

The third major oil district, farther upstream along the Ob' River, has its centers at the oil towns of Megion and Nizhnevartovskiy, both founded in 1964. The Samotlor oil pool, discovered around Lake Samotlor, 20 miles north of Nizhnevartovskiy, emerged as one of the largest oil accumulations of the USSR, with a potential annual output of 100 million tons. Commercial production began in 1969 when Samotlor oil began to flow through a 30-inch pipeline connecting the Nizhnevartovskiy area (and adjoining parts of Tomsk Oblast) with the previous pipeline terminal in the Ust'-Balyk field.

Crude oil production in Tyumen' Oblast, including the Shaim, Surgut, and Nizhnevartovskiy districts, rose from its first shipments of 200,000 tons in the summer of 1964 to 1 million in 1965, 3 million in 1966, and 12 million in 1968. Long-range plans call for 25 million tons of crude oil by 1970 and 70 million by 1975. According to these calculations the Western Siberian oil fields would replace the Volga–Urals province about 1980 as the Soviet Union's principal producing region.

Another Western Siberian oil field, the Sosnino–Sovetskoye field (discovered in 1964), is administratively part of Tomsk Oblast. There production began in 1966, and the following year the new oil workers' town of Strezhevoy was founded near Aleksandrovskoye, on the right bank of the Ob' River. The new field, situated on the border between Tyumen' and Tomsk Oblasts, yielded 220,000 tons in 1967 and 400,000 tons in 1968. Production increased more rapidly, to 2 million tons, after completion of the oil pipeline to Ust'–Balyk in 1969. The output goal for the early 1970s was 5 million tons. In the long run a second outlet for Tomsk crude oil is planned via a 800-mile-long 48-inch pipeline through Anzhero-Sudzhensk to a new refinery planned near Krasnoyarsk. During the late 1960s a railroad was under construction from the lumber-milling center of Asino, northeast of Tomsk, northward to Belyy Yar, on the Ket' River, a right tributary of the Ob'. Some railroad planners envisage the lumber railroad as part of a future line connecting Tomsk with Surgut, thus linking up with the Tyumen'–Surgut railroad and forging a link between Tomsk and Tyumen' through the Ob' and Irtysh valleys.

The Omsk refinery, the focal point of the new oil development of Western Siberia pending the construction of additional refineries, was opened originally in 1955 to refine crude oil transported by the Trans-Siberian pipeline from the Tatar–Bashkir fields. The development of the Siberian fields is expected to stimulate an expansion of the refining capacity at Omsk and a reorientation of the refinery from the use of Volga–Urals crude oils to the new Siberian sources. A synthetic-rubber factory that was supposed to use refinery gases as raw material was opened in 1964 to supply rubber for a tire plant completed in Omsk six years earlier. (The rubber and tire complex also includes a carbon-black plant, opened in 1959.) However, because of a shortage of petrochemical capacity at the Omsk refinery, the synthetic-rubber plant had to ship in two-thirds of its butane requirements, for the butadiene component of rubber, from the Bashkir petrochemical plants, and other petrochemicals, such as propane and propylene, from Sumgait in the Baku district. Heat and power for the Omsk petrochemical complex are supplied by a 250,000-kilowatt electric station, Omsk No. 4, opened in 1965.

While Western Siberia's development of oil resources thus focuses on the Omsk refinery, the newly developed natural gas resources are oriented westward toward the fuel-poor Urals and European Russia. Significant gas resources were discovered in the 1950s on the west bank of the lower Ob' River after an initial strike at

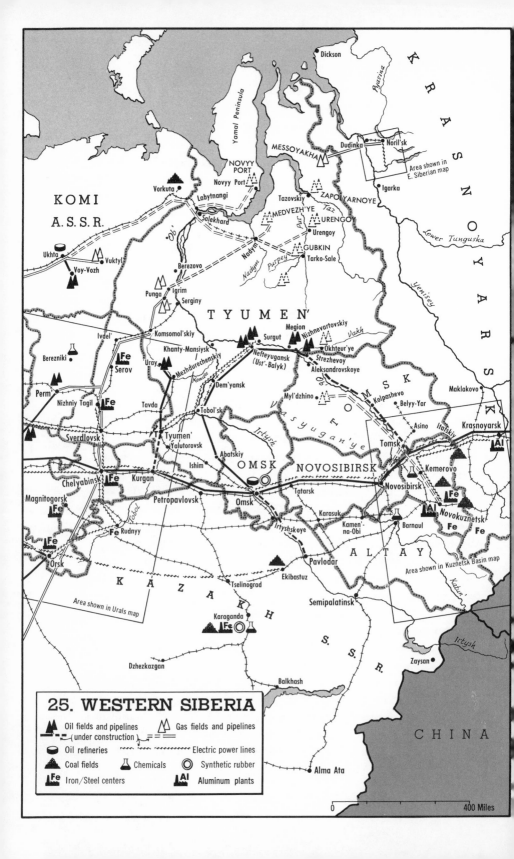

# 25. WESTERN SIBERIA

Oil fields and pipelines
— under construction
Oil refineries
Coal fields
Fe Iron/Steel centers

Gas fields and pipelines
Electric power lines
Chemicals
Synthetic rubber
Al Aluminum plants

0                    400 Miles

KOMI A.S.S.R.

KRASNOYARSK

TYUMEN'

TOMSK

OMSK

NOVOSIBIRSK

ALTAY

KAZAKH S. S. R.

CHINA

Dickson
Dudinka
Noril'sk
Igarka
Area shown in
E. Siberian map
MESSOYAKHA
Tazovskiy
ZAPOLYARNOYE
NOVYY PORT
Novyy Port
Labytnangi
Salekhard
MEDVEZH'YE
URENGOY
Urengoy
GUBKIN
Tarko-Sale
Vorkuta
Ukhta
Vuktyl
Voy-Vozh
Berezovo
Punga
Igrim
Serginy
Komsomol'skiy
Khanty-Mansiysk
Surgut
Megion
Nizhnevartovskiy
Okhteur'ye
Strezhevoy
Aleksandrovskoye
Nefteyugansk
(Ust'-Balyk)
Ivdel'
Berezniki
Perm
Serov
Fe
Uray
Mezhdurechenskiy
Dem'yansk
Myl'dzhino
Kolpashevo
Belyy-Yar
Maklakovo
Nizhniy Tagil
Fe
Tavda
Tobol'sk
Asino
Tomsk
Itatskiy
Krasnoyarsk
Al
Sverdlovsk
Tyumen'
Yalutorovsk
Abatskiy
Ishim
OMSK
NOVOSIBIRSK
Kemerovo
Novosibirsk
Chelyabinsk
Fe
Kurgan
Petropavlovsk
Omsk
Tatarsk
Karasuk
Al
Novokuznetsk
Magnitogorsk
Fe
Fe Rudnyy
Irtyshskoye
Kamen'-na-Obi
Barnaul
Fe
Fe
Orsk
Fe
Pavlodar
Area shown in Kuznetsk Basin map
Dzhezkazgan
Tselinograd
Ekibastuz
Semipalatinsk
Karaganda
Fe
Zaysan
Area shown in Urals map
Balkhash
Alma Ata

Yamal Peninsula
Ob'
Nadym
Pur
Taz
Purpey
Nadym
Tarko-Sale
Vakh
Konda
Irtysh
Vasyugan'ye
Tobol
Tobol
Irtysh
Kuban'
Irtysh
Pyasina
Lower Tunguska
Yenisey

Berezovo in 1953. Plans were made for the construction of a transmission main to the Urals. The pipeline was originally intended to tap the Igrim gas field, 60 miles south of Berezovo, but as the design of the pipeline was in progress, another gas field, at Punga, 40 miles south of Igrim, was discovered in 1963 and this became the terminal of the pipeline. The 455-mile-long 40-inch pipeline, with a capacity of 10 billion cubic meters a year, went into operation in 1966 from Punga to Serov and Nizhniy Tagil. The pipeline carried 5.2 billion cubic meters of gas to the Urals in 1967. It was extended to the Igrim field in 1968 and was expected to reach its design capacity by 1970.

The gas reserves tapped by this initial pipeline in the late 1960s are small compared with the huge gas reservoirs discovered in remote river basins of northern Tyumen' Oblast in 1964–66. These are the Medvezh'ye deposit, in the Nyda River basin; the Urengoy deposit, west of Urengoy on the Pur River; the Zapolyarnoye deposit, south of Tazovskiy, on the lower Taz River; the Gubkin deposit, near Tarko-Sale; and the Novyy Port deposit, in the Yamal Peninsula, on the west shore of the Ob' Gulf.

The town of Nadym was envisaged as the regional collecting center for the gas fields and consideration was being given to rebuilding the Salekhard–Nadym railroad. (This was part of the Salekhard–Igarka line under construction by forced labor in the early 1950s, but abandoned after Stalin's death in 1953.) Priority in development was given to the Medvezh'ye field, and work began in 1969 on the first pipeline project, a 48-inch transmission main linking Medvezh'ye via Nadym and Kazym with the present pipeline terminal at Punga for onward transmission to the Urals. Later in the 1970s two 100-inch pipelines are to carry the natural gas from the northwest Siberian fields to European Russia and possibly to other countries of Europe. Plans called for the output of 270 billion cubic meters by 1980, 50 for the Urals and 220 for European Russia.

Other natural gas deposits, in the eastern part of the West Siberian plain, were envisaged as sources of transmission lines to the Kuznetsk Basin. At first the Okhteur'ye deposit on the Vakh River was considered a likely terminal for a pipeline, but the discovery of the Myl'dzhino field in 1964, with larger reserves and closer to the consuming centers, shifted attention to the gas prospects of the

Vasyugan'ye swamps, in which Myl'dzhino is located. In the late 1960s plans were being made for the construction of a gas transmission main from Myl'dzhino to the Kuznetsk Basin, Novosibirsk, and other industrial centers of Western Siberia.

Even before oil and gas development in the Ob' basin prompted the construction of railroads specifically to gain access to the prospective producing areas (the Tyumen'–Surgut and the Salekhard–Nadym lines), other feeder lines were being built into the Western Siberian forests to open up new lumbering areas. In addition to the Asino–Belyy Yar line, envisaged in the late 1960s as ultimately extending to the oil fields of the middle Ob' valley, these feeder railroads included the Tavda–Sotnik line, extending 120 miles northward to the Konda River near the Shaim oil deposit. The railroad was completed in 1967, reaching the Konda River at the new town of Mezhdurechenskiy, 15 miles upstream from the original terminus of Sotnik. Another feeder railroad, also opened to traffic in 1967, runs 230 miles from Ivdel', in the northern Urals, to the Ob' River at Serginy. Construction was under way in the late 1960s on a branch of this railroad, extending 150 miles northward from the upper Konda River to the Severnaya Sos'va (Northern Sos'va), where the Igrim gas field is situated.

In contrast to Eastern Siberia, relatively little progress has been made in Western Siberia in developing hydroelectric power. Only one major water-power plant is in operation, at Novosibirsk, on the Ob' River, with a total installed capacity of 400,400 kilowatts. The plant, built in the southern outskirts of Novosibirsk, created a reservoir that extended 110 miles upstream to Kamen'. Construction of the Novosibirsk hydroelectric station begin in 1951; the first of seven 57,200-kilowatt generators was installed in late 1957, and the last in March, 1959. Discussion of additional hydroelectric development in the Ob' basin was dominated in the 1960s by the problem of the controversial Lower Ob' project, which would have a generating capacity of 6 to 7 million kilowatts, at a site just above Salekhard. The project, which was favored by the electric power interests as a source of electricity for the Urals, was opposed by others because its vast lowland reservoir would flood valuable farmlands, interfere with the development of other resources (such as oil, gas, and timber), and cause adverse effects in the regional water balance, climate, and soils.

# Eastern Siberia

Of all the Soviet economic regions, Eastern Siberia is best endowed with cheap fuel and energy resources. The most economical fuels are vast reserves of brown coal that can be extracted cheaply by open-pit methods and used at large pit-head power stations. Out of the region's total coal production of about 47 million tons in 1965, 73 percent consisted of surface-mined brown coal, most of which was used in local power stations. In addition to the cheap steam coals, Eastern Siberia has a large hydroelectric generating potential along the Yenisey River and its major tributary, the Angara River, which flows out of Lake Baykal. The development of this waterpower potential began in the 1950s and, together with coal-fed steam power, attracted energy-oriented industries such as aluminum reduction.

## KRASNOYARSK COMPLEX

The region's most promising source of electric power based on cheap brown coals is the Kansk–Achinsk coal basin, in Krasnoyarsk Kray, extending along the Trans-Siberian Railroad east and west of Krasnoyarsk city. The first major open-cut mine in this area was the Irsha–Borodino pit, which yielded its first coal in 1950. Designed for ultimate expansion to a capacity of 25 million tons of coal a year, this surface mine, 10 miles southeast of the Trans-Siberian Railroad town of Zaozernyy, produced about 7 million tons of coal in the mid-1960s. Pending construction of pit-head power stations, the coal was being shipped to steam electric plants in the industrial centers of Krasnoyarsk and Kansk. A second major open-cut mine, designed for ultimate expansion to 16 million tons, began operations in 1953 at Nazarovo, south of the industrial city of Achinsk. It produced about 7 million tons of coal a year in the mid-1960s, and was burning most of its output at the Nazarovo power station, the first major steam power plant of the Kansk–Achinsk basin.

Construction of the power station began in 1951, and the first of six 150,000-kilowatt generating units began producing electricity in 1961. By 1965, the station's capacity was 900,000 kilowatts. The installation of three 500,000-kilowatt units beginning in 1968 was to expand the capacity to 2.4 million kilowatts by the early 1970s. The Nazarovo station was the principal source of electric power for the industries of Krasnoyarsk until the completion of a long-distance 500-kilovolt transmission line in late 1963 from the Bratsk hydroelectric station on the Angara River. In addition to expansion of coal output at Nazarovo and Irsha–Borodino, there were long-range plans for opening even larger surface mines with pit-head power stations at Berezovskoye, 35 miles west of Nazarovo, and at Itatskiy, on the Trans-Siberian Railroad, just across the border of Kemerovo Oblast, which is considered part of Western Siberia. The Berezovskoye open pit was being designed for a capacity of 55 million tons.

The brown-coal energy base of the Krasnoyarsk area is supplemented by the hydroelectric power of the Krasnoyarsk station, at the new dam-builders' town of Divnogorsk, 20 miles west of Krasnoyarsk, on the Yenisey River. Under construction since the mid-1950s, the Krasnoyarsk station was the largest being built in the Soviet Union. In repeated design changes, its planned generators were raised from a capacity of 300,000 kilowatts to 500,000 kilowatts each in 1959, and the total planned capacity was raised in 1967 from 5 million kilowatts to 6 million. The first two 500,000-kilowatt units went into operation in late 1967 and by early 1970 ten generators had been installed for a capacity of 5 million.

The principal energy-oriented power consumer of the Krasnoyarsk territory's industrial cluster is an aluminum plant that went into operation in 1964 on the northeastern outskirts of Krasnoyarsk city. Designed to be one of the Soviet Union's largest reduction plants, it will have a total capacity of 400,000 tons when all twenty sections are in operation. Pending completion of an alumina plant at Achinsk, based on the processing of nephelite syenite, the Krasnoyarsk aluminum plant had been using alumina from the Urals and from the newly completed alumina plant at Pavlodar.

Construction of the 800,000-ton Achinsk plant, which is expected to supply the growing Siberian aluminum industry with alumina, was long delayed by changes in design and raw-material sources. When construction of the complex began in the mid-1950s, Achinsk was to use nephelite concentrate from a deposit at Goryachegorsk, 110 rail miles southwest of Achinsk. However, in the late 1950s, while development was already under way at Goryachegorsk, a higher-grade deposit of nephelite syenite was discovered on the Kiya-Shaltyr' River, 35 miles farther to the southwest, on the opposite slope of the Kuznetsk Alatau mountain range. Work at Goryachegorsk was halted and, in 1960, a development project got under way on the Kiya-Shaltyr', where the mining settlement of Belogorsk was inaugurated two years later. The new nephelite center began shipping commercial ore to Achinsk in 1968 when the railroad was extended from its previous railhead at Shush station, near Goryachegorsk. Pending completion of the rail line, small amounts of ore were trucked to the old railhead for use in a pilot plant at Achinsk, which opened in 1964 to test technological processes to be used on a large scale when commercial alumina production finally began in 1969. The nephelite is being sintered with limestone in four 600-foot rotary kilns to yield alumina, cement, soda, and potash.

A limestone quarry, with an initial capacity of 2 million tons of rock, was opened in 1964 southwest of Achinsk, in the Arga hill range. The limestone is quarried at Mazul'skiy, a former manganese-mining town, whose reserves are depleted after having played an important role in supporting the Siberian iron and steel industry with manganese during World War II. Pending the start of alumina production in the late 1960s, rotary kilns already installed at Achinsk were being used to produce cement from the Arga limestone. The first stage of a cement plant with a planned capacity of 5 million tons began operations in 1965.

Another consumer of electric power at Krasnoyarsk is a chemical industry based on the utilization of ethyl alcohol obtained by the hydrolysis of wood cellulose from wood wastes. The wood-hydrolysis industry arose in the Krasnoyarsk area in World War II as a source of industrial alcohol. In the 1950s, this alcohol became the source of butadiene, one of the constituents of general-purpose synthetic rubber, and a plant producing synthetic rubber was opened in 1956 at Krasnoyarsk. It was expanded in 1963. Together with a tire-cord factory (opened in 1960), processing wood-based viscose rayon, the rubber plant formed the basis for the construction of a tire plant (also opened in 1960) with a capacity of 2 million tires a year.

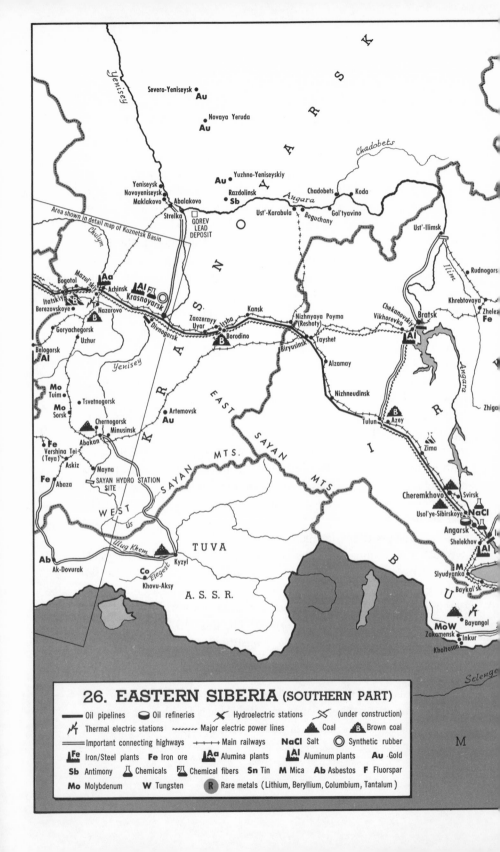

## 26. EASTERN SIBERIA (SOUTHERN PART)

Severo-Yeniseysk • **Au**

Novaya Yeruda •
**Au**

*Chadobets*

Yuzhno-Yeniseyskiy
**Au** •
Chadobets   Koda

Yeniseysk •
Novoyeniseysk •        Razdolinsk
Maklakovo • Abalakovo    • **Sb**       *Angara*
*Area shown in detail map of Kuznetsk Basin*    Ust'-Karabula • Boguchany  Gol'tyavino    Ust'-Ilimsk •
Strelka •    GOREV
*Chulym*         LEAD         ○                           *Ilim*
             DEPOSIT

Rudnogors •

Bogotol •  *Mazul'skiy*  **Aa**                                              Khrebtovaya •
Itatskiy•  **B**  Achinsk  **Al** F    Kansk        Nizhnyaya Poyma   Chekanovskiy   Bratsk   Zhele
Berezovskoye •     Krasnoyarsk ◎  Zaozernyy         (Reshoty)   Vikhorevka   **Al**    **Fe**
        **B** Nazarovo  Divnogorsk  Uyar  Ilsha                     Tayshet
Goryachegorsk •                    Borodino  **B**          Biryusinsk              *Angara*
Belogorsk •  Uzhur            *Yenisey*                     Alzamay

**Al**                                                                              Zhiga

**Mo** •
Tuim                                    Nizhneudinsk
**Mo** •   Tsvetnogorsk •
Sorsk          Artemovsk •                        Tulun  **B**
     Chernogorsk     **Au**                              • Azey
**Fe** •  Minusinsk                                       Zima
Vershina Tei  Abakan                                                      Cheremkhovo   • Svirsk
(Teya) •                                                                    Usol'ye-Sibirskoye **NaCl**
Askiz •                                                                    Angarsk
**Fe** •   Mayna •                                                          Shelekhov •
Abaza    SAYAN HYDRO STATION
         SITE                                                                        **Al**

**Ab** •                      TUVA                                                    **M**
Ak-Dovurak   *Us*   Kyzyl                                                  Slyudyanka •
        *Ulug Khem*  **Co**                                               Baykal'sk •
          Elegest •
          Khovu-Aksy                                                    **MoW**  • Bayangol
             A.S.S.R.                                              Zakamensk • Inkur
                                                                    Kholtoson •

### Legend

| | | |
|---|---|---|
| ▬ Oil pipelines | ◖ Oil refineries | ✕ Hydroelectric stations  ✕ (under construction) |
| ⚡ Thermal electric stations | ∼∼∼∼ Major electric power lines | ▲ Coal   **B** Brown coal |
| ══ Important connecting highways | ┼┼┼ Main railways   **NaCl** Salt | ◎ Synthetic rubber |
| **Fe** Iron/Steel plants   **Fe** Iron ore | **Aa** Alumina plants   **Al** Aluminum plants   **Au** Gold | |
| **Sb** Antimony   ▲ Chemicals   **Fl** Chemical fibers   **Sn** Tin   **M** Mica   **Ab** Asbestos   **F** Fluorspar | | |
| **Mo** Molybdenum   **W** Tungsten   **R** Rare metals (Lithium, Beryllium, Columbium, Tantalum) | | |

M

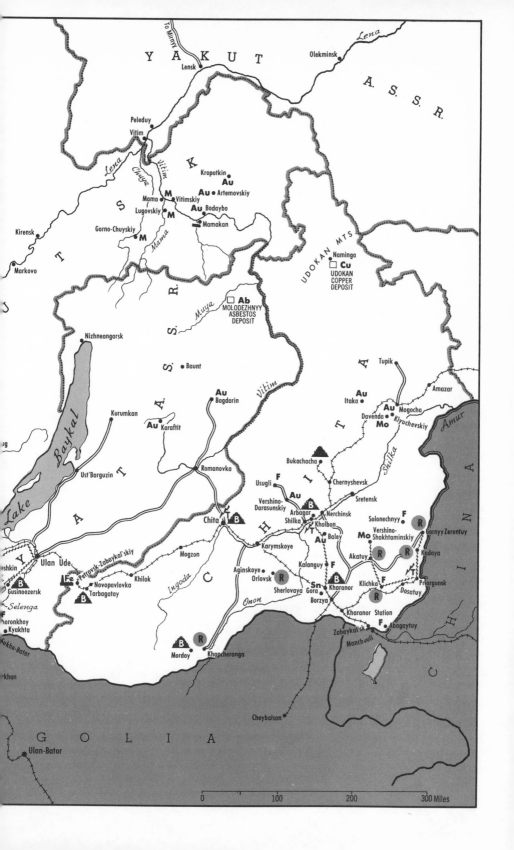

ABAKAN-MINUSINSK COMPLEX

In the southern part of Krasnoyarsk Kray, an industrial complex is forming in the Abakan–Minusinsk area. It has thus far been dependent on the old coal-mining center of Chernogorsk (1967 population: 61,000), just north of Abakan, in operation since before the Revolution. In 1965 it produced 4.7 million tons, including 1.7 million from a newly started open pit. Because of the relatively higher rank of the Chernogorsk coal, compared with the Kansk–Achinsk brown coals, mining operations are expected to be expanded in open pits, but the older underground mines are to be closed because of high costs. Consumer goods industries were under construction at Chernogorsk to absorb some of the resulting unemployment. Industrial expansion is also likely in the 1970s in the two other urban centers of the complex: Abakan (1967 population: 78,000) and Minusinsk (1967 population: 42,000).

The industrial potentialities of the area will be greatly enhanced by construction in the 1970s of one of Siberia's largest hydroelectric stations, the Sayan station, on the Yenisey River, 15 miles above the town of Mayna, where the stream emerges from a gorge through the Western Sayan Mountains. The Sayan design calls for a dam 750 feet high and a generating capacity of 6.5 million kilowatts. Earlier plans providing for twelve 540,000-kilowatt generators were changed in the late 1960s to a station of ten 650,000-kilowatt units. Access to the station site was provided in 1968 by completion of a rail spur from Kamyshta, on the South Siberian Railroad, to the proposed dam site near Mayna.

Just as the Achinsk alumina complex reaches across regional economic lines into Kemerovo Oblast to tap the nephelite deposit at Belogorsk, so the iron and steel plants of Novokuznetsk have invaded Krasnoyarsk Kray in an attempt to expand their iron ore supplies. This extension of the Novokuznetsk domain was made possible by the completion of a railroad from Novokuznetsk across the Kuznetsk Alatau to Abakan in 1959. The first iron mine shipping its ore over the new line was the Abaza mine, opened in 1957 with a planned capacity of 3 million tons a year. Pending completion of the direct line, the Abaza ore had moved to Novokuznetsk by the roundabout rail route through Achinsk and Yurga. In 1961, after completion of a 20-mile spur line from Biskamzha station, on the new railroad, a second iron ore mine, the Teya mine, went into production. This mine is associated with the workers' settlement of Vershina Tei (Teya Summit). Unlike the Abaza ore, which has an iron content of 45 percent, the 35 percent Teya ore requires concentration at the mine, which has a capacity of 5 million tons of ore a year.

Other significant development of mineral resources in the southern part of Krasnoyarsk Kray includes a molybdenum mine and concentrator and gold-lode mines. Molybdenum has been produced since 1953 at the mining and concentrating complex at the town of Sorsk (until 1966, Dzerzhinskiy), 55 miles northwest of Abakan. Sorsk (1959 population: 11,300) is served by a short rail spur from Yerbinskaya station, on the Abakan–Achinsk railroad. The gold-mining town of Artemovsk (1959 population: 13,000), 90 miles northeast of Abakan, has been in existence since 1911. Situated on the southern slopes of the Eastern Sayan Mountains, it is served by the Abakan–Tayshet railroad, completed in 1964.

### TUVA ASSR

The iron ore center of Abaza gained in stature as a transportation hub with the completion in 1969 of a highway across the Western Sayan Mountains from the Tuva ASSR. The highway provides an outlet not only for asbestos from Ak-Dovurak, 150 road miles to the south, but also for cobalt concentrate from a newly developed deposit in Tuva. The new highway supplements the old, winding Us road between Minusinsk and Kyzyl, which, running part way along the valley of the Us River, a right tributary of the Yenisey, was long the only overland route between Tuva and southern Siberia across the Western Sayan.

The Ak-Dovurak asbestos deposit, one of the largest in the Soviet Union, began production in 1964 from an open pit. The asbestos, of the chrysotile variety, yields a higher percentage of longer fibers suitable for textile uses than the Asbest deposit of the Urals. The capacity of the first stage of the Ak-Dovurak complex (the name means "white earth" in Tuvinian) is 600,000 tons of fiber-bearing rock, yielding about 30,000 tons of unmanufactured fiber. The 1967 output was 20,000 tons.

The cobalt center, where a concentrator was under construction in the late 1960s, is Khovu-Aksy, situated 50 miles southwest of Kyzyl, in the upper valley of the Elegest River. Unlike most Soviet cobalt producers, Khovu-Aksy obtains the metal from a pure cobaltite (cobalt arsenide) deposit rather than as a by-product of copper–nickel ores. The concentrate was to be treated at the nickel–cobalt smelter of Nizhniy Ufaley in the Urals.

The new extractive industries in the Tuva ASSR stimulated expansion of coal mining in the Ulug-Khem basin, west of Kyzyl. In 1965 there were two mines, an underground mine and an open pit, each producing about 150,000 tons. In the late 1960s the Kaa-Khem strip mine with a capacity of 500,000 tons was under construction seven miles from Kyzyl.

## THE YENISEYSK AREA

North of the Trans-Siberian Railroad, timber and mineral resources as well as the sites of future hydroelectric stations on the Yenisey and the lower Angara rivers are being opened up by two feeder railroads built northward from the main line. The 170-mile-long Achinsk–Abalakovo railroad, which was completed in 1963, extends from the alumina–cement city on the Trans-Siberian Railroad to a timber-processing complex under development in the Abalakovo–Maklakovo area, south of the town of Yeniseysk (1967 population: 19,000) and just below the Angara–Yenisey confluence.

In addition to opening up new lumbering areas and access to the wood-processing complex, the railroad will also serve future sites of mineral resources. The most important is the Gorev lead deposit discovered in 1956 under the stream bed of the lower Angara River. Plans in the late 1960s called for the diversion of the lower reaches of the Angara River and the construction of an open pit on the deposit. Work on the project was expected to be under way in the early 1970s. The planned diversion of the Angara River would move its confluence with the Yenisey River, now at Strelka, southward to Savinskoye, where the site for the Yeniseysk hydroelectric station is planned.

The second feeder railroad, under construction in the mid-1960s, runs 120 miles north from the Trans-Siberian station of Reshoty, where the wood–chemical center of Nizhnyaya Poyma (1959 population: 32,000) developed in the early 1950s. The feeder line was planned to open up new lumbering areas and to serve the proposed site of a hydroelectric station in the area of Boguchany on the Angara River. Here, too, the discovery of new mineral deposits forced reconsideration of water-project designs. The original site of the Boguchany station, at Gol'tyavino, 30 miles upstream, was found unsuitable in the late 1960s because the reservoir would flood newly discovered bauxite deposits in the Chadobets area. Exploration work on a new site was then moved to the Koda area, 60 miles upstream from Boguchany. Work on the Boguchany station was not expected to start until after completion of the Ust'-Ilim station in the 1970s.

A small antimony mine has been in operation since the late 1930s at Razdolinsk (1959 population: 6,400) in the lower reaches of the Angara River. The ore, mined in an underground shaft, is beneficiated to the 20 percent concentrate that is processed at a local smelter.

Since the first half of the nineteenth century the Yenisey Hills, on the right bank of the Yenisey between the Angara River and the Podkamennaya Tunguska River, have also been a significant producer of gold from placer deposits and lode mines. The centers of this gold-mining district are Severo-Yeniseysk (1959 population: 6,200), where a lode mine is in operation, and Yuzhno-Yeniseyskiy (1959 population: 2,500), a center of placer mines.

### NORIL'SK COMPLEX

A separate industrial complex in Krasnoyarsk Kray has developed around Noril'sk, north of the Arctic Circle, where an urban agglomeration approached a population of 150,000 in the late 1960s. Noril'sk arose in the mid-1930s after the discovery of a rich nickel–copper deposit containing valuable coproduct metals and of a coal deposit suitable for bunkering ships in the lower Yenisey River and along the central reaches of the Northern Sea Route. As a preliminary outlet for coal and ore, a narrow-gauge railroad was completed to the Yenisey River port of Dudinka in 1937, and the first nickel matte was obtained in 1939, when the population of Noril'sk was 13,900.

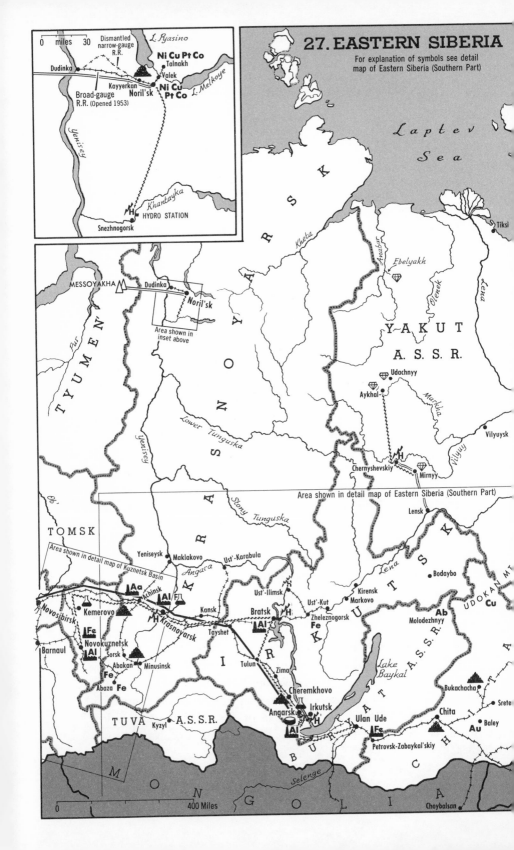

# 27. EASTERN SIBERIA

For explanation of symbols see detail map of Eastern Siberia (Southern Part)

**Inset map (top left):**

0 miles 30

Dismantled narrow-gauge R.R.

L. Pyasino

Ni Cu Pt Co

Talnakh

Dudinka

Valek

Kayyerkan

Noril'sk

Ni Cu Pt Co

Broad-gauge R.R. (Opened 1953)

L. Melkoye

Yenisey

Khantayka

HYDRO STATION

Snezhnogorsk

**Main map:**

Laptev Sea

Tiksi

K R A S N O Y A R S K

Kheta

Anabar

Ebelyakh

Olenek

Lena

MESSOYAKHA

Dudinka

Noril'sk

Area shown in inset above

Pur

T Y U M E N

Ob'

Yenisey

Lower Tunguska

YAKUT A.S.S.R.

Udachnyy

Aykhal

Markha

Vilyuysk

Viluy

Chernyshevskiy

Mirnyy

Area shown in detail map of Eastern Siberia (Southern Part)

Stony Tunguska

Lensk

TOMSK

Area shown in detail map of Kuznetsk Basin

Yeniseysk

Maklakovo

Ust'-Karabula

Angara

Bodaybo

Lena

UDOKAN MT

Novosibirsk

Kemerovo

Aa

Achinsk

Al

Fl

Kansk

Ust'-Ilimsk

H

Ust'-Kut

Kirensk

Markovo

Cu

H

Krasnoyarsk

Tayshet

Bratsk

Al

H

Zheleznogorsk

Fe

Ab

Molodezhnyy

Fe

Novokuznetsk

Sorsk

Al

Barnaul

Abakan

Minusinsk

Fe

Tulun

Zima

Lake Baykal

Bukachacha

Abaza

Fe

Cheremkhovo

Angarsk

Irkutsk

Al

H

Ulan Ude

Fe

Chita

Au

Baley

Srete

TUVA A.S.S.R.

Kyzyl

Petrovsk-Zabaykal'skiy

B U R

A T

A.S.S.R.

C H I T A

M

Selenge

N

G O L I A

Choybalsan

0          400 Miles

During World War II, when the need for nickel rose sharply, plant equipment from a nickel smelter under construction at Monchegorsk in the Kola Peninsula was moved to Noril'sk, where a nickel smelter went into operation in 1942. In the same year a steam power plant, based on local coal, began producing electricity from a first stage with a capacity of 25,000 kilowatts. However, by 1944, the city's population was still only 30,000.

It was mainly after the war that Noril'sk underwent its greatest development. In 1944 a cobalt plant went into operation, and in 1950 a large copper smelter replaced a smaller copper plant dating from the war period. To accommodate the growing traffic, the 70-mile-long railroad between Noril'sk and Dudinka was converted to broad gauge in 1953, and electrification of the line began by 1960. In association with the metallurgical plants, a small chemical industry developed, based in part on sulfuric acid derived from copper smelter gases.

As new mineral resources were developed in the Soviet Union after World War II, the importance of the Noril'sk ore remained not so much in its nickel and copper components, for the content of these metals in the ore was lower than in comparable ores of the Kola Peninsula and the southern Urals. Moreover the harsh Arctic conditions of the Noril'sk area greatly increased operating costs. The main value of the Noril'sk deposits lay rather in a wide range of valuable by-products, including platinum-group metals, particularly palladium and platinum, and selenium and tellurium, obtained during the electrolytic refining of copper. Titanium and vanadium have also been listed among the components.

In the 1940s most of the mining operations were concentrated into two open pits, at Medvezhiy Ruchey (Bear Creek) and Ugol'nyy Ruchey (Coal Creek), just southwest of the city of Noril'sk. Because surface deposits were becoming depleted, the large underground mine of Zapolyarnyy opened in 1951 in the same area to tap deeper ore horizons that were beyond the reach of the open pits. The greater importance of underground mining reduced the share of surface-mined ore from 90 percent in 1950 to 60–70 percent in the late 1950s and in the 1960s.

The available ore reserves were greatly expanded in 1961 with the discovery of the Talnakh deposit, 15 miles northeast of Noril'sk, across the valley of the Noril'skaya River, which flows from Lake Melkoye to Lake Pyasino. The first section of the Mayak (Lighthouse) underground mine at the deposit went into operation in the spring of 1966, a railroad from Noril'sk to Talnakh opened the following year, and a local power station began producing electricity in late 1968. As development of the deposit proceeded, still another deposit, called Oktyabr'skoye (October) or, by its local name, Khara-Yelakh, was being explored 5 miles northwest of Talnakh. The railroad to Dudinka was being double-tracked.

Fuels and energy for the Noril'sk mining and metallurgical complex are derived from a number of sources. The city relied at first entirely on local coal mines, which also yielded coking coal for the Noril'sk smelters and steam coals for coal-burning ships on the lower Yenisey River. In 1965, the Noril'sk area produced 3.1 million tons of coal, including 2.5 million from seven underground mines and 0.6 million from a strip mine opened in the early 1960s at Kayyerkan, west of Noril'sk. About half a million tons of coking coal was used for the production of coke, but its significance is expected to decline as more electric furnaces are built for the smelting of nickel and other metals. Most of the rest of the coal is burned in the Noril'sk heat and power station, which may have a capacity of 200,000 kilowatts or more.

After the discovery of natural gas at Tazovskiy, west of Noril'sk, plans were announced in 1964 for the construction of a 400-mile 28-inch pipeline to Noril'sk. However, these plans were shelved when gas was discovered on the Messoyakha River only 170 miles west of Noril'sk. A pipeline from the Messoyakha site was under construction in the late 1960s and was scheduled to reach Noril'sk via Dudinka at the end of 1969.

The generating capacity of the Noril'sk heat and power station is to be supplemented by one of the Soviet Union's northernmost hydroelectric stations. This is the Snezhnogorsk plant on the Khantayka River, under construction since 1963 and scheduled for completion in 1970. The hydroelectric station, originally designed for five 63,000-kilowatt generators, will have seven such units for a total capacity of 441,000 kilowatts. It will supply power to Noril'sk over a 220-kilovolt transmission line.

IRKUTSK OBLAST

*Irkutsk–Cheremkhovo Complex.* This industrial district, west of Lake Baykal, arose initially on the basis of the Cheremkhovo bituminous coal basin and a rock-salt deposit at Usol'ye. In 1964, the area's raw-material base was broadened with the arrival of a crude-oil pipeline from the Tatar–Bashkir fields, and the energy supply was greatly expanded with the development of the hydroelectric potential of the Angara River beginning in the early 1950s. This in turn attracted aluminum reduction plants and other energy-oriented industries.

The output of the Cheremkhovo basin, which has been worked as a source of steam coals for the Trans-Siberian Railroad since the 1890s, was 17.8 million tons in 1965, including 14.1 million tons from seven strip mines and 3.7 million from four older underground mines. As a result of increasing electrification of the railroad, Cheremkhovo coal has been diverted to use in local heat and power stations. Approaching depletion of the Cheremkhovo basin has stimulated interest in the Azey brown coal deposit, on the Trans-Siberian Railroad, 10 miles east of Tulun, where reserves are twice as large as in the Cheremkhovo area. The development of the Azey deposit began in the early 1960s, and an open pit there yielded 1.6 million tons in 1965.

In the early postwar period, Cheremkhovo coal served as raw material for a synthetic fuels plant at the new city of Angarsk, which produced gasoline and other hydrocarbons from coal by the hydrogenation process used in Germany during World War II. In the late 1950s this process was superseded by the construction of an oil refinery at Angarsk, which began operations in 1960–61. It received crude oil from the Tatar–Bashkir fields by rail until the pipeline arrived three years later. The oil refinery, in turn, gave rise to a petrochemical complex. This includes a plastics plant (polystyrene), and a nitrogenous fertilizer plant, where a urea unit opened in 1967. The city of Angarsk, inaugurated in 1951, had a population of 183,000 in 1967.

The petrochemical industry of Angarsk is complemented by the salt-based chemical industry of Usol'ye–Sibirskoye (1967 population: 75,000). The salt deposit there has given rise to the production of caustic soda and chlorine and their derivatives. In 1965 the Usol'ye chemical complex produced 160,000 tons of caustic, or 12 percent of the total Soviet production. In addition to caustic-chlorine production, the availability of cheap electric power has stimulated other electrochemical processes based on nearby limestone deposits. They yield calcium carbide as a source of acetylene, which in turn is the raw material for a whole range of chemicals from acetic acid to chloroprene rubber.

Another major chemical complex was under construction in the late 1960s and early 1970s near the Trans-Siberian railroad town of Zima, where a new city of 250,000 population was planned on the southeast margins of old Zima. The chemical complex, based on the nearby salt deposits of Tyret' and the cheap hydroelectric power of the region, will produce chlorine, caustic soda, and their derivatives.

Construction on the Irkutsk hydroelectric station, the first on the Angara River, began just above Irkutsk in 1950. The first generator produced electricity in 1956 and the last of eight units went into operation in 1958, for a total capacity of 660,000 kilowatts. In addition to improving the electric power supply in the area in general, the new station provided the low-cost power needed for a new aluminum plant and, via a 220-kilovolt line opened in 1957, transmitted the electric power needed in the construction of the Bratsk power station, the next phase of the Angara River development.

The aluminum reduction plant served by the Irkutsk hydroelectric station was located at Shelekhov (1967 population: 27,000), a new town eight miles southwest of Irkutsk, on the Trans-Siberian Railroad. Like other Siberian aluminum plants, the Shelekhov plant was based on alumina from the Urals pending the development of the Achinsk alumina complex. Before the first conventional reduction shop was completed, the Shelekhov plant experimented in a pilot installation with the electrothermal processing of sillimanite ore from a deposit near Kyakhta, in the Buryat ASSR. However, the tests apparently did not indicate immediate commercial feasibility, and no steps were taken to develop the sillimanite deposit. The first reduction shop began production at Shelekhov in 1962, and by 1966 six sections were in operation. Two more were to be opened in the late 1960s. Aluminum wirebars are used in part in a cable-manufacturing plant added to the Shelekhov aluminum complex.

*Bratsk Complex.* A necessary preliminary to the development of the Bratsk hydroelectric, aluminum, and wood-cellulose complex was the construction of the Tayshet–Lena branch of the Trans-Siberian Railroad. This line, completed in 1954, not only helped open up timber, mineral, and power resources along the way, but also provided a new transportation route from the west into Yakutia. At its Lena River terminal of Ust'-Kut, the new port of Osetrovo was built in the mid-1950s to serve as a rail–water transshipment point and as a gateway to the Lena River basin of Yakutia.

Construction of the Bratsk dam, at the point where the branch railroad crossed the Angara River, began in 1954. As in other major hydroelectric projects, changes in design increased the number of planned generators from the original sixteen 225,000-kilowatt units to eighteen and finally to twenty under a revised design made public in 1959. The first generator went into operation in October, 1961, and within two years the first sixteen units had been installed, bringing the station's capacity to 3.6 million kilowatts.

By that time the installation of generating units had outpaced the construction of industrial consumers and long-distance transmission lines, and in the early 1960s the Bratsk power station operated at only 25 to 30 percent of its capacity. The situation changed in 1963, when three 500-kilovolt lines were placed in operation. Two parallel lines, extending 360 miles south and southeast through Tulun to the Irkutsk area, transmitted up to 1.3 million kilowatts of power, and a third line extending about 390 miles westward through Tayshet to Krasnoyarsk carried up to 700,000 kilowatts. The situation was further improved in the late 1960s with completion of a second line westward and the extension of the 500-kilovolt transmission system to Anzhero-Sudzhensk and the Kuznetsk Basin. At the same time, a major local power consumer, the Bratsk aluminum plant, began operations.

By the end of 1966 two more generating units had been installed, bringing the total to eighteen, and the installed capacity to 4.1 million kilowatts. A change of rating in the late 1960s was planned to raise the capacity of each unit from 225,000 to 250,000 kilowatts, and the total capacity to 4.5 million kilowatts. Two more generators, bringing the station's capacity to 5 million kilowatts, were to be installed when needed.

The construction of the Bratsk aluminum plant began in 1961 at Anzeba station, 20 miles southwest of the Bratsk dam. A residential settlement named Chekanovskiy was inaugurated at the plant site in 1960. The first aluminum reduction shop was opened in May, 1966, and by the end of 1967 four out of a planned twenty-four sections were in operation.

A second major industry in the Bratsk area is based on the abundant timber resources. It is one of Siberia's largest wood-pulp plants, with a capacity of 200,000 tons of viscose pulp for rayon manufacture in the tire-cord plants of Siberia and European Russia, and 200,000 tons of paperboard. It began operations in 1966.

The Bratsk urban area, created in virgin forest since the first dam builders arrived in the early 1950s, had a population of 122,000 in 1967. Industrial workers gradually replaced construction workers, who moved on in 1963 to start work on the Ust'-Ilimsk dam, the next hydroelectric project farther downstream along the Angara River. To be completed in the 1970s, it will have a capacity roughly equal to that of Bratsk, or 4.5 to 5 million kilowatts.

The construction of the Tayshet–Ust'-Kut railroad and the development of the Bratsk power complex also made possible the opening up of the Korshunovo (or Korshunikha) iron ore deposit, 85 miles east of Bratsk on the railroad to the Lena River. Originally envisaged as an ore source for an iron and steel plant projected for Tayshet, the mine supplied the ore-poor Kuznetsk Basin when the Tayshet project was shelved in the early 1960s. The mining town of Zheleznogorsk-Ilimskiy (1967 population: 17,000) was inaugurated at the ore site in 1958. The open pit on the deposit yielded its first ore, a 32 percent magnetite, in the winter of 1964–65. A concentrator converted the ore into a 62 percent concentrate for shipment to the Kuznetsk Basin via the newly completed Tayshet–Abakan railroad. The Zheleznogorsk operation reached its designed capacity of 12 million tons of crude ore and 5 million tons of concentrate in 1967.

A railroad under construction in the late 1960s from nearby Khrebtovaya station to the site of the Ust'-Ilimsk hydroelectric project provided access to a second important iron ore deposit, at Rudnogorsk, on the eastern slopes of the Ilim River valley, 25 miles east of Nizhneilimsk.

Northeast of the Lena River railhead, between Ust'-Kut and Kirensk, oil was struck near Markovo in March, 1962. The oil strike, in Lower Cambrian rocks, unusual for oil-bearing formations, gave rise to considerable publicity, but continuing geological exploration did not suggest that the deposit was of commercial significance.

*The Gold and Mica Industry.* Isolated from the rest of Irkutsk Oblast, in the northeast, is the gold- and mica-mining district of Bodaybo and Mama, on the Vitim River.

The Bodaybo gold-mining area, where production began in the 1840s from placer deposits, was known historically as the Lena Goldfields. In recent years, manual work has been replaced increasingly by the use of large dredges, which accounted for 55 percent of the total production in 1964. Lode gold is also mined underground.

Bodaybo, the supply center of the gold mines, had a population of 18,000 in 1959. It is the head of navigation on the Vitim River and receives its supplies by water from the railhead at Osetrovo. A narrow-gauge railroad links Bodaybo with the gold mines. The area long depended for electric power on small coal-fed generators and water-power installations. The power supply was greatly improved in 1961–62 with the completion of the 86,000-kilowatt Mamakan hydroelectric station, on the Mamakan River, just above its confluence with the Vitim. The Mamakan station, consisting of four 21,500-kilowatt generators, also supplies power to the mica-mining district on the Mama and Chuya rivers, west of the Vitim River.

The Mama–Chuya mica district, which produces the muscovite type of mica (potassium mica), was first exploited in the seventeenth century when thin mica sheet was widely used for windows. The mines were abandoned in the eighteenth century when the manufacture of window glass began on a mass scale. In the 1930s interest in the mica deposits revived in connection with the development of the Soviet electrical industry, in which sheet mica has wide uses as a dielectric and insulating material. The town of Mama, founded in 1932 as a workers' settlement, dates from this period. Mining activities were considerably expanded in the 1950s, possibly in connection with the exploitation of newly important minerals, such as beryl, lithium and columbite–tantalite, which are sometimes recovered along with sheet mica. The increased activity was reflected in the founding of three more mining towns in 1952 —Vitimskiy, on the Vitim River; Lugovskiy, on the Mama River, and Gorno-Chuyskiy, on the Chuya River. In the late 1960s, the Mama–Chuya district was producing 75 percent of the Soviet Union's muscovite mica.

A second mica deposit, at Slyudyanka, at the southern tip of Lake Baykal, was the principal Soviet producer of phlogopite (magnesium mica) in the 1930s. However, its small reserves became depleted and were superseded in the early 1950s by the newly developed phlogopite deposits of the Aldan district in southern Yakutia. The Slyudyanka deposit, consisting of dolomitized limestones intersected by pegmatite dikes, is still exploited for the limestone, which is used as a cement material, and may yield some of the rare metals (beryl, lithium minerals, and columbite–tantalite) that are sometimes recovered from mica deposits. The dolomitized limestone or marble has been mined since 1958 in the Pereval (Mountain Pass) mine, just southwest of Slyudyanka (1967 population: 23,000). The limestone serves as a raw material for a cement plant at Angarsk and carbide-based chemicals at Usol'ye.

Just east of Slyudyanka, on the south shore of Lake Baykal, is the controversial sulfate-pulp mill of Baykal'sk, with a capacity of 300,000 tons of pulp a year. The plant, which went into operation in 1966, was opposed by conservationist groups who feared that the mill wastes would pollute Lake Baykal.

### BURYAT ASSR

In the Buryat ASSR (known as Buryat-Mongol until 1958), the principal mineral development has been the tungsten–molybdenum center of Zakamensk in the upper valley of the Dzhida River, a left tributary of the Selenga. Founded in 1938, Zakamensk was known as Gorodok until 1959 (population: 13,600). Its concentrators process tungsten ore from the Kholtoson mine and molybdenum ore from the Inkur mine, both south of Zakamensk. A small coal-fed power station at Bayangol, to the north, supplies electricity to the mining complex.

The main coal source for power plants in Buryatia, especially the capital and manufacturing center of Ulan-Ude, is a brown-coal deposit at Gusinoozersk, 60 miles southwest. Gusinoozersk (1959 population: 12,000) produced 1 million tons in 1965, including 600,000 tons from two underground mines and 400,000 tons from an open-pit. This filled only half of Buryatia's needs, the rest being shipped in from the Cheremkhovo basin of Irkutsk Oblast and from Chita Oblast. In conjunction with the planned construction of a 1.2-million-kilowatt steam electric station at Gusinoozersk to bolster the republic's supply of electricity, there are plans for the construction of the Kholbol'dzha strip mine at Gusinoozersk, with a capacity of 2.4 million tons of brown coal.

A fluorspar mine opened in 1968 at Khoronkhoy, on the Ulan-Ude–Ulan-Bator railroad, just north of the Mongolian border. The planned 1968 output of the mine was 30,000 tons, with an increase of two to three times planned in the early 1970s.

A major asbestos deposit in the remote northern part of the Buryat ASSR attracted attention in the late 1960s. The deposit, known as Molodezhnyy (Youth), was explored in 1960–64 and was found to contain an unusually high percentage of long spinning fibers. The deposit is situated on the Mudirikan River, a right tributary of the Muya River, 35 miles southwest of the settlement of Muya. A large open-cut mine was planned on the site, on the northern slopes of the South Muya Mountains, but development was expected to be slowed by the remote location, far from means of transportation.

### CHITA OBLAST

A diversified minerals industry exists also in Chita Oblast, where mining of silver–lead–zinc ores flourished in the second half of the eighteenth century. The mines, situated in a series of parallel hill ranges between the Shilka and the Argun', two headstreams of the Amur River, declined in the late nineteenth century, when the most easily accessible high grade ores had become depleted. Only the Russian word *zavod* (mill) in local place names, such as Nerchinskiy Zavod, Gazimurskiy Zavod, and Aleksandrovskiy Zavod, suggest the early mining activities.

Under the Soviet regime, the area at first attracted attention for its gold and tin resources. Early Soviet tin-mining centers were Olovyannaya (whose name was derived from *olovo*, the Russian word for tin), which began operation in the late 1920s but soon became depleted, and Khapcheranga and Sherlovaya Gora, which were the principal Soviet tin producers in the 1930s before the centers of tin mining shifted to the Soviet Far East. The Chita Oblast tin mines also yielded tungsten ore as a by-product.

The mining complex of Khapcheranga (1959 population: 7,000), in the upper Onon River valley, was still operating in the 1960s. Though lacking rail transportation, it was linked by a good 190-mile-long highway with the railroad station of Darasun, southeast of Chita, on the Trans-Siberian Railroad. Virtually self-sufficient, the Khapcheranga complex was supplied by a small heat and power station at Mordoy, 15 miles west, where a small coal deposit is mined as fuel. Sherlovaya Gora (1959 population: 13,000), situated on the railroad to Manchuria, long derived its tin from placer deposits, but has shifted increasingly to lode mining. A new tin-lode mine opened in 1967.

Gold production is concentrated in two centers of the Nerchinsk area. The larger of the two, Baley (1959 population: 29,000), has been a source of gold since the nineteenth century, at first from placers, but since the 1930s increasingly from underground lode mines. Since 1961 most of the production comes from the Taseyevo lode mine at Taseyevo, across the Unda River from the Baley mill. At the other gold-mining center, Vershino-Darasunskiy (1959 population: 12,000), northwest of Nerchinsk, lode gold is associated with arsenic, copper, and bismuth.

Another early mineral resource exploited during the Soviet period was fluorspar, a flux in steel production and a source of fluorine chemicals. The largest of four centers producing fluorspar is Kalanguy (1959 population: 5,700), which has been in operation since the 1920s and was formally given urban status as a workers' settlement in 1939. Fluorspar is also mined at Abagaytuy, on the Chinese border, just east of the Soviet frontier station of Zabaykal'sk; at Usugli, northwest of the gold-mining center of Vershino-Darasunskiy, and at Solonechnyy, between the old mining towns of Nerchinskiy Zavod and Gazimurskiy Zavod. Unlike the other fluorspar centers, which produce from underground shaft mines, Solonechnyy operates on open-cut mine.

In the early postwar period two small molybdenum mines were developed in the oblast. One is situated in the upper reaches of the Unda River at Vershino-Shakhtaminskiy, a settlement founded in 1948, which had a population of 4,000 in 1959. The other, founded in 1951, is Davenda (1959 population: 5,000), in the northeastern part of Chita Oblast. Nearby is another gold-lode center at Klyuchevskiy (1959 population: 4,000), which operates an open pit and is third in importance among the oblast's gold producers (after Baley and Vershino-Darasunskiy). Dredges also mine several gold placers in the area.

The old mining region in the southern part of the Shilka–Argun' interfluve assumed an entirely new cast in the 1950s when the nuclear and space age began to require new minerals and metals that had previously been ignored among the resources of Chita Oblast. These metals were found either in old mine tailings or in geological formations associated with the old mining districts. Foremost of the new metals was lithium, whose compounds are used as coolants and shielding materials in nuclear reactors and in lightweight alloys for fabrication of aerospace vehicles. Lithium occurs in granite pegmatite dikes associated with the tin–tungsten formations, and since the mid-1950s, when the great upsurge in interest in lithium deposits began, Chita Oblast has been the Soviet Union's principal source of lithium minerals. Two close associates of lithium, rubidium and cesium, also occur in lithium-bearing pegmatites. These two metals have potential uses in ionic rocket engines and in thermionic converters, which transform heat directly into electricity. Other co-products of these pegmatites include beryl and tantalite–columbite.

The largest of the new mining centers, according to the 1959 census, is Klichka (population: 7,000), which was founded in 1952. Others are Kadaya (population: 3,000) and Gornyy Zerentuy (population: 3,000), both founded in 1958, south of the old mining town of Nerchinskiy Zavod. A fourth, under development in the mid-1960s, was Akatuy, near the old mining town of Aleksandrovskiy Zavod.

To serve Klichka and the other new mining centers, a narrow-gauge railroad, 110 miles long, was built in the early 1950s from Kharanor station, on the main line to Manchuria, to Dosatuy, from where roads led to the mining towns. As a source of electric power for the new mines and their mills, a steam electric station was built on the left bank of the Argun' River at Novo-Tsurukhaytuy, which was renamed Priargunsk (1959 population: 5,000) in 1962. Construction of the first stage of the power plant, begun in 1952, was completed in 1961–62, with the installation of two 12,000-kilowatt generators. In the meantime the narrow-gauge railroad had been extended 35 miles to the site of the power plant. It is fed by brown coal from the Kharanor deposit, which is adjacent to the old tin center of Sherlovaya Gora, 30 miles northwest of the rail junction of Kharanor. A small open pit, called Kukul'bey, produced 1 million tons in 1965. A large open-pit, with a capacity of 3 million tons, was under construction in the late 1960s. In addition to providing coal for the Priargunsk power station, the Kharanor deposit also supplies a power plant at Sherlovaya Gora.

The Sherlovaya Gora power plant is linked by a transmission line with another electric station, at Kholbon, which serves the Nerchinsk mining district, including the gold center of Baley. The Kholbon steam electric station burns coal from the adjacent Arbagar brown-coal mine, which produced 200,000 tons in 1965.

Three other small coal mines in Chita Oblast supply local power stations. The Bukachacha mine, which unlike the other coal centers of the oblast produces bituminous coal, had an output of 1 million tons in 1965. The Chernovskoye mines, in a western suburb of the city of Chita, produced 1.7 million tons in 1965, including 0.7 million from an open-pit. This coal was the principal fuel at the Chita steam electric station, the largest in the oblast. Finally the Tarbagatay underground mine, at Novopavlovka, produced 200,000 tons for the needs of the adjoining small steel plant at Petrovsk-Zabaykal'skiy (1967 population 29,000). An old ironworks dating from 1789, the plant now uses pig iron from the Kuznetsk Basin for the production of steel and rolled products.

Chita Oblast is a major producer of tantalum, a metal that did not assume commercial significance until the development of nuclear and aerospace industries, with their requirements for materials that retain their strength at elevated temperatures. Tantalum is also used widely in capacitators for the electronics industry. One of the

Soviet Union's principal tantalum mines and concentrators has been in operation since 1965 at the settlement of Orlovsk, 15 miles east-southeast of Aginskoye, in a Middle Jurassic granitoid intrusion. Another important tantalum deposit was reported in 1969 at Etyka, 15 miles east of the fluorspar center of Kalanguy. The Etyka site is also associated with a Middle Jurassic granitoid intrusion. Both tantalum deposits were discovered in areas where old tungsten deposits had been mined until they became depleted. Etyka existed as a workers' settlement until 1958, when its urban status was canceled after the halt of mining operations.

A long-range project for the development of mineral resources in Chita Oblast focuses on a large copper sandstone deposit explored in the late 1950s and found to be comparable in geology and size of reserves to the Central African copper belt and the Soviet deposit of Dzhezkazgan in Kazakhstan. The deposit is in the Udokan Mountains (56° 35′ N 118° 30′ E). Its development is likely to be delayed by its remote location, 200 miles from the nearest railhead, the town of Mogocha on the Trans-Siberian Railroad.

## The Soviet Far East

This region, the most remote from centers of population and economic development in European Russia, is significant as a supplier of gold, mica, tin, tungsten, and other rare metals, as well as industrial diamonds. These resources have been developed under some of the Soviet Union's most adverse climatic and other physical–geographic conditions. Although coal reserves are abundant throughout the Soviet Far East they have been exploited only to the extent needed to provide fuel for steam locomotives along the Trans-Siberian Railroad and, since the conversion to diesel traction, primarily for the generation of steam power for small electricity systems in the populated south and for the isolated mining districts in the north. In contrast to Eastern Siberia, the hydroelectric potential of the Soviet Far East is virtually untapped.

### AMUR OBLAST

The largest coal-mining center, accounting for about 40 percent of the regional output, is Raychikhinsk (1967 population:

27,000) on the lower Bureya River, in Amur Oblast. This mining complex first produced brown coal from its Kivdinskiy mine in 1931, but was substantially expanded in World War II and in the 1950s. In 1965 it produced 12 million tons of brown coal from four open-cut mines.

About one-fifth of the output is burned at a large minehead steam power station, built in the late 1950s in the suburb of Progress. It is connected since 1959 by transmission lines with Blagoveshchensk and other towns of Amur Oblast. The rest of the coal is shipped to power stations elsewhere in Amur Oblast and Khabarovsk Kray, either by rail or, during the navigation season, along the Amur River from the river terminal of Poyarkovo. In addition to the main power grid, based on Raychikhinsk and supplying the main industrial and farming areas, the oblast has a small 12,000-kilowatt power station at Ogodzha, burning coal from a small local deposit and serving the gold-mining district of the upper Selemdzha River. The district, centered on Ekimchan, has been worked for gold since the nineteenth century, but has declined in importance compared with other gold-producing areas of the Far East. The principal remaining mine is the lode mine of Tokur, north of Ekimchan.

The Amur River and its tributaries, the Zeya and Selemdzha, have a large hydroelectric potential that was jointly surveyed in the 1950s by Soviet and Chinese teams. However, the breakdown of economic cooperation between the two nations has delayed the development of the basin. The first hydroelectric station, the Zeya project, has been under construction since 1964 and is expected to go into operation in the mid-1970s with a design capacity of 1.47 million kilowatts. The power plant is under construction just north of the town of Zeya, where the Zeya River breaks through the east–west barrier formed by the Tukuringra and Soktakhan mountain ranges.

### KHABAROVSK KRAY

This territory has had one of the few bituminous coking-coal deposits of the Soviet Far East. It is the Urgal deposit on the upper Bureya River, reached by a 200-mile-long railroad running north from the Trans-Siberian Railroad at Izvestkovyy. The Urgal deposit was developed in World War II as a potential source of coking coal for the proposed Komsomol'sk iron and steel complex. However, the abandonment of blast-furnace construction at Komsomol'sk and the high operating cost of the Urgal underground mine compared with the Raychikhinsk strip mines have limited the development of the deposit. The single underground mine, at the mining town of Sredniy Urgal (Middle Urgal), produced 1.2 million tons in 1965. A highway leading north from Chegdomyn, the railhead in the Urgal area, served the Soviet Union's first molybdenum mine at Umal'tinskiy, which was worked from 1936 until its reserves were depleted in 1962.

The heavy demand for Raychikhinsk coal as a source of energy in Khabarovsk Kray will be eased in the early 1970s with the development of the Bikin brown-coal deposit, just across the border in Primorskiy Kray. A large open-cut mine was under development in the late 1960s at Nadarovka, 25 miles south of Bikin, together with construction of a minehead power plant, known as the Primorsk station. A miners' and power-workers' town known as Luchegorsk was inaugurated at the site in 1966. The Primorsk steam electric station, with a design capacity of 1.2 million kilowatts, is planned to go into operation in the 1970s. The strip mine, which is expected to produce 1.5 million tons of brown coal in the early 1970s, is to be expanded ultimately to a capacity of 12 to 14 million tons. The Primorsk station will make possible the electrification of the Vladivostok–Khabarovsk section of the Trans-Siberian Railroad and a merger of the present power grids around Khabarovsk and the southern part of Primorskiy Kray. A 220-kilovolt line, opened in 1967, joins the Luchegorsk mining and power complex with the Vladivostok grid.

The principal power-consuming centers of the kray are the cities of Khabarovsk and Komsomol'sk. Khabarovsk (1967 population: 435,000) is primarily a manufacturing and fabricating city, although it also has an oil refinery that processes both Sakhalin crude oil and long-haul oil brought by tank cars from the west. Komsomol'sk (1967 population: 209,000), is oriented to a greater extent toward primary resource development, with a steel mill and a small oil refinery in the city and new tin-mining and wood-processing plants near by. The Amurstal' steel plant, though envisaged as an inte-

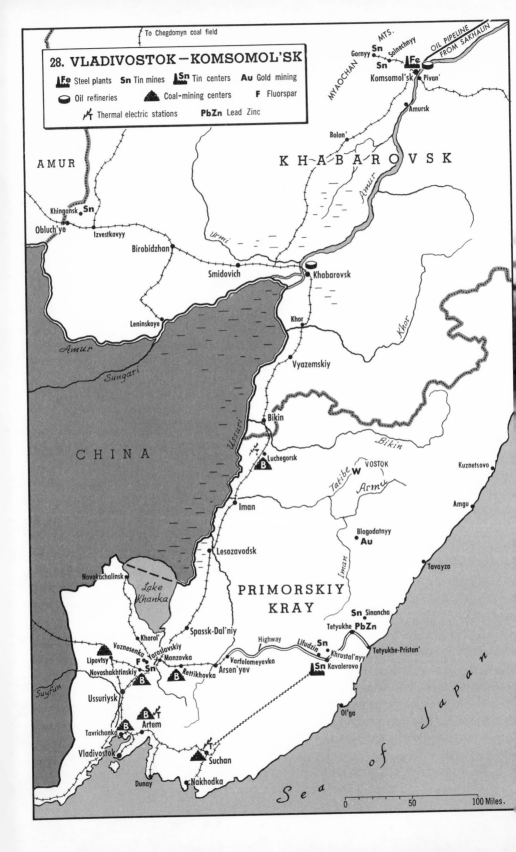

### 28. VLADIVOSTOK — KOMSOMOL'SK

**Fe** Steel plants **Sn** Tin mines **Sn** Tin centers **Au** Gold mining

**⬤** Oil refineries **▲** Coal-mining centers **F** Fluorspar

**⚡** Thermal electric stations **PbZn** Lead Zinc

To Chegdomyn coal field

MYAOCHAN MTS.
OIL PIPELINE FROM SAKHALIN

Gornyy **Sn** Solnechnyy
**Sn** **Fe** Komsomol'sk Pivan'

Amursk

Bolon'

**AMUR**

**KHABAROVSK**

Khingansk **Sn**
Obluch'ye
Izvestkovyy
Birobidzhan
Smidovich
Khabarovsk

*Urmi*

*Amur*

*Sungari*

Leninskoye

Khor

Vyazemskiy

*Khor*

**CHINA**

Bikin

*Bikin*

*Ussuri*

Luchegorsk **B**
VOSTOK
*Tatibe* **W** *Armu*

Iman

Kuznetsovo

Amgu

Blagodatnyy **Au**

*Iman*

Lesozavodsk

Tavayza

Novokachalinsk

*Lake Khanka*

**PRIMORSKIY KRAY**

**Sn** Sinancha
Tetyukhe **PbZn**

Spassk-Dal'niy
Khorol'
Voznesenka Yaroslavskiy
**F** **Sn** Manzovka
Lipovtsy
Novoshakhtinskiy **B** **B** Rettikhovka
Ussuriysk

Highway Lifudzin **Sn**
Varfolomeyevka Khrustal'nyy
Arsen'yev **Sn** Kavalerovo
Tetyukhe-Pristan'

Ol'ga

*Suyfun*

**B** **T**
Artem
Tavrichanka **B**
Vladivostok

Suchan ▲

Dunay Nakhodka ▲

*Sea of Japan*

0        50        100 Miles.

grated iron and steel complex, has been limited to steel output and the production of some rolled products, particularly tinplate, since it was inaugurated in 1943. With its limited production capacity, the plant meets only part of the steel needs of the Soviet Far East, which depends to a large extent on iron and steel products from the Urals and the Kuznetsk Basin for its steel-fabricating industries.

The tin development near Komsomol'sk is associated with the lode deposit of Solnechnyy in the Myaochan Mountains, 40 miles west of Komsomol'sk. Two mining towns arose on the deposit, Gornyy (inaugurated in 1958) and Solnechnyy (1966). Both are linked by road with Komsomol'sk. The first section of the mining and concentrating complex opened at Gornyy in 1963, and construction of a second concentrator was completed in 1969 at Solnechnyy to process the lower-grade ore of the nearby Molodezhnyy mine.

The wood-processing complex is situated at Amursk, 25 miles south of Komsomol'sk, on the left bank of the Amur River. Opened to production in 1967, the mill will specialize in the manufacture of sulfite pulp, container board, and fiberboard. Amursk has been chosen as the site of a proposed nitrogen-fertilizer plant that will use natural gas as a source of hydrogen for ammonia synthesis when a gas pipeline from Sakhalin reaches the Komsomol'sk area in the 1970s.

A recent resource development has been the exploration of gold placer deposits along the beaches of the Sea of Japan near Sovetskaya Gavan', port and railhead linked with Komsomol'sk.

An older tin-mining center in Khabarovsk Kray is situated at Khingansk (the former Mikoyanovsk) in the Jewish Autonomous Oblast. It was developed in World War II and has a small concentrator, but its reserves were approaching depletion in the late 1960s.

PRIMORSKIY KRAY

The southern section of Primorskiy Kray, also known as the Maritime Territory in English translation, has a developed electric power grid and a network of coal mines around the two principal cities: Vladivostok (1967 population: 397,000) and Ussuriysk (1967 population: 124,000). The older coal mines, all underground installations, are situated in the Vladivostok area.

They are the brown-coal mines of Artem (1967 population: 65,000), which have been in operation since 1915, and the bituminous coal mines of Suchan (1967 population: 50,000). The Artem basin produced 2.4 million tons in 1965 (3 million if the nearby Tavrichanka mine is included), and the Suchan basin, 1.9 million tons. Coal-fueled power stations at Artem and Suchan are the largest in the Soviet Far East.

Because of high underground mining costs and limited reserves in the Vladivostok area, future expansion of the coal industry is expected to come from two surface deposits in the Ussuriysk district. One is the Rettikhovka deposit, northeast of Ussuriysk, where an open-pit went into operation in 1961 and yielded 1.2 million tons in 1965. The mining town of Rettikhovka, inaugurated in 1962, lies on a spur of the Trans-Siberian Railroad running eastward to Arsen'yev and the railhead at Varfolomeyevka. The second deposit, north of Ussuriysk, is situated in the valley of the Chikheza River. The Pavlovka open-pit, with a capacity of 1.2 million tons, opened there in 1967 together with the new mining town of Novoshakhtinskiy.

The Ussuriysk district also contains a tin and fluorspar mining complex developed since the late 1950s. This is centered on the town of Yaroslavskiy, 30 miles northeast of Ussuriysk, where an open-pit and concentrator went into operation in 1958, yielding tin, lead, zinc, and silver. In the town of Voznesenka, adjoining Yaroslavskiy, a fluorspar surface mine and mill opened in 1963–64 to supply iron–steel and chemical plants of Siberia and the Urals.

An older tin-mining district is situated in the Sikhote-Alin' mountains around the Kavalerovo concentrator, 40 miles west of the port of Tetyukhe. Tin mining in the area began in World War II at Sinancha and Lifudzin, and was substantially expanded in the 1950s. Production capacity was further enhanced with the completion of a power transmission line from Suchan in 1961. Although situated near the coast, the Kavalerovo district, also called Khrustal'-nyy for one of its mines, ships its tin concentrate by truck westward to the railhead of Varfolomeyevka, from where it moves by the Trans-Siberian Railroad to the tin smelter of Novosibirsk. The port of Tetyukhe, adjoining the Kavalerovo tin district, is used mainly for the output of the lead–zinc mines of Tetyukhe. In operation since 1911, Tetyukhe smelts the lead component of the ores at a small local smelter and ships zinc concentrate for refining at Belovo, Konstantinovka, and Ordzhonikidze.

Another tin and tungsten mining district was under development in the late 1960s in the northern part of Primorskiy Kray, in the basin of the Armu and Tatibe rivers, tributaries of the Iman River. The new complex, known as Vostok (East), was to open in 1971.

### KOLYMA REGION

The most important gold-producing district of the Soviet Far East has been the upper Kolyma basin of Magadan Oblast, but since the late 1950s the gold-mining industry has shifted increasingly farther north to the Bilibino–Pevek area of the Chukchi National Okrug. Gold mining in the upper Kolyma began in the early 1930s and, until 1955–56, the industry was operated largely by the special Dal'stroy administration with the use of forced labor. A major highway was built in the 1930s from Magadan, the port city and gateway to the Kolyma gold district, and now extends to Ust'-Nera, in the upper Indigirka valley of Yakutia.

At first, the Kolyma area exploited rich, shallow placer mines that were most easily accessible, and gold production rose rapidly through the 1930s to reach a peak in 1940. In subsequent years, output declined as the rich surface deposits became exhausted and buried placers had to be mined by underground methods. As the share of underground mines increased to as much as 30 to 45 percent of the total output in the late 1940s and early 1950s, overall production declined, reaching a low point in 1956 when the use of forced manual labor ceased. The subsequent introduction of machinery made possible the removal of overburden of the buried placers and the use of surface-mining methods, thus reducing the share of underground mining. The principal present gold-mining districts are centered on the towns of Yagodnoye, on the Debin River, and Susuman, on the Berelekh River, two left tributaries of the Kolyma River, and Ust'-Omchug, near the Omchak River, a right tributary.

The relatively large power requirements of the area, where mining processes are now to a great extent electrified, for example, through the use of floating dredges, are met by a 50,000-kilowatt power station opened in 1955 at Arkagala, 30 miles northwest of Susuman. The Arkagala power station is fed by coal from mines at nearby Kadykchan, including an open-cut mine opened in 1957. Total coal output in 1965 was 1 million tons. The power plant supplies virtually the entire mining district, and is linked by 110-kilovolt lines not only with the gold centers of Susuman, Yagodnoye, and the Omchak valley, but also with the Ust'-Nera area of Yakutia by a 180-mile transmission line completed in 1958. The Arkagala power grid was connected with the city of Magadan in 1968.

The Kolyma area, in addition to the mining of gold, also was an important tin producer during the period in which forced labor was used. However, the production of tin from seventeen small lode mines and thirteen placers was judged to be uneconomical after the introduction of normal working conditions in the mid-1950s, and these mines were closed. The only producer that continued operations was Omsukchan, a tin center on an eastern spur of the main Kolyma highway. A small local power plant at Omsukchan burns coal from the Galimyy mine, 15 miles to the south.

## CHUKCHI NATIONAL OKRUG

The development of the gold and tin industry of the Chukchi National Okrug had its beginnings before World War II. Tin was discovered in the mid-1930s around Chaun Bay, where Pevek had been established as a small supply port along the Northern Sea Route. Tin mining began in 1941 at Val'kumey, just south of Pevek, from a lode mine that required concentration, and from a placer at Krasnoarmeyskiy, 40 miles east of Pevek. The mining industry of the Pevek area expanded further in the late 1950s when gold mining began in 1958 in the Komsomol'skiy placer, 70 miles southeast of Pevek. As geological exploration continued eastward along the Arctic coast, it yielded additional gold prospects, and the Plamennyy mercury deposit (68° 25' N 177° E), about 200 miles east of Pevek, which began production in 1967. To provide electric power for the mining industries in the Pevek area, a 17,000- kilowatt power station was built at the port, using coal brought in by ship. Pevek had a population of 10,000 in the mid-1960s and was raised to the status of city in 1967.

In the meantime rich placer deposits of gold began to be worked

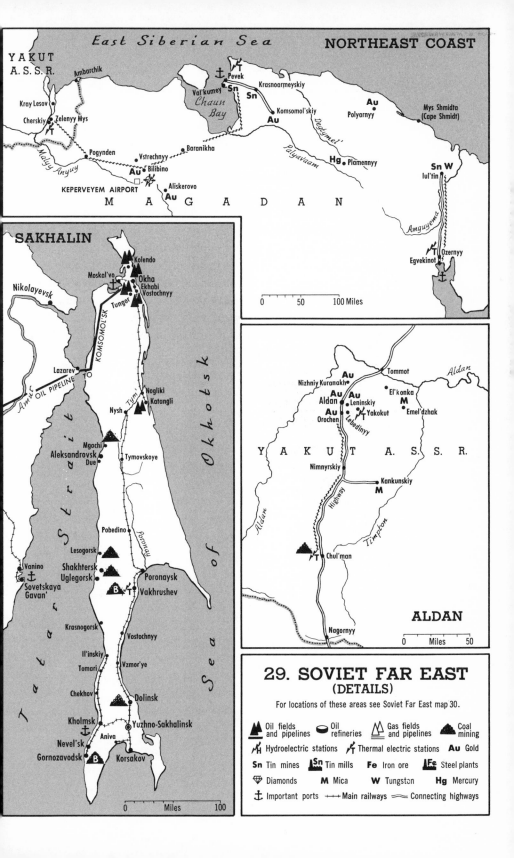

East Siberian Sea

**NORTHEAST COAST**

YAKUT
A.S.S.R.

Ambarchik

Kray Lesov

Cherskiy
Zelenyy Mys

Pogynden

Pevek
Val'kumey ⚓ ⛓T
Chaun Sn
Bay

Krasnoarmeyskiy

Komsomol'skiy
Sn Sn
Au

Au
Polyarnyy

Mys Shmidta
(Cape Shmidt)

Vstrechnyy
Baranikha

Malyy Anyuy

Au Bilibino

KEPERVEYEM AIRPORT

Aliskerovo
Au

M A G A D A N

Degtmel'

Palyavaam

Hg Plamennyy

Amguyema

Sn W
Iul'tin

Ozernyy
Egvekinot ⛓T
⚓

0    50    100 Miles

**SAKHALIN**

Kolendo

Moskal'vo ⛏H🏭
Okha
Ekhabi
Vostochnyy

Nikolayevsk

Tungor

KOMSOMOL'SK

Lazarev

Amur OIL PIPELINE TO

Nogliki
Katangli

Nysh

Mgachi
Aleksandrovsk
Due

Tymovskoye

Tym'

Pobedino

Poronay

Lesogorsk

Shakhtersk
Uglegorsk

Vanino ⚓
Sovetskaya
Gavan'

B ⛓T
Vakhrushev

Poronaysk

Krasnogorsk

Vostochnyy

Il'inskiy

Tomari

Vzmor'ye

Chekhov

Dolinsk

Kholmsk

Aniva

Yuzhno-Sakhalinsk

Nevel'sk
Gornozavodsk

B

Korsakov

Tatar Strait

Sea of Okhotsk

0    Miles    100

**ALDAN**

Nizhniy Kuranakh
Au
Aldan Au Au
Au Leninskiy
Orochen

Tommot

Aldan

El'konka
M
Yakokut
Emel'dzhak

Lebedinyy

Y A K U T    A.  S.  S.  R.

Nimnyrskiy

Kankunskiy
M

Highway

Aldan

Timpton

Chul'man
⛓T

Nagornyy

0    Miles    50

## 29. SOVIET FAR EAST
### (DETAILS)

For locations of these areas see Soviet Far East map 30.

🌋 Oil fields and pipelines    Oil refineries    Gas fields and pipelines    🏔 Coal mining

⛏H Hydroelectric stations    ⛓T Thermal electric stations    **Au** Gold

**Sn** Tin mines    **Sn** Tin mills    **Fe** Iron ore    **Fe** Steel plants

💎 Diamonds    **M** Mica    **W** Tungsten    **Hg** Mercury

⚓ Important ports    ⟝⟞ Main railways    ≈ Connecting highways in the basin of the Malyy Anyuy (Little Anyuy) River, southwest of Chaun Bay. The first mining town, Bilibino, was founded in 1960, and rapidly developed to become the principal population center of the Anyuy district, with a population of 12,000 in 1967. In 1962 two more mining towns were inaugurated, including Aliskerovo, east of Bilibino, where the district's first floating dredge was installed. To meet the electric power needs of the new mining area, a 300-mile-long power transmission line was completed from Pevek in the summer of 1965.

In the long run, however, the Anyuy district is expected to use another supply center and gateway in a new port of Zelenyy Mys, under construction to the west, on the lower Kolyma River. The new port facilities are being built in the northeastern corner of the Yakut ASSR, on the Kolyma River mouth, just north of the old village of Nizhniye Kresty (renamed Cherskiy in 1963). A floating 20,000-kilowatt power station, moored in 1969 at Zelenyy Mys, burns coal from Zyryanka. This deposit, upstream on the Kolyma River, has been producing 100,000 to 150,000 tons of coal a year from two small open-cut mines for coal-burning vessels plying the Kolyma and Indigirka rivers. A power-transmission line from Zelenyy Mys to the Anyuy gold-mining district, running via Pogynden to Bilibino, was under construction in the mid-1960s. A winter road, taking advantage of frozen ground for truck transportation, was also built between Zelenyy Mys and Bilibino during this period, and is expected to be converted ultimately to a year-round highway.

Because of the high cost of conventional power in this remote area, the Bilibino area has been selected as the site of a small atomic power plant. The first of four 12,000-kilowatt generators of the planned atomic installation is scheduled to be in operation by 1970.

A third mining district of the Chukchi National Okrug was established in the late 1950s at the base of the Chukchi Peninsula. It consists of the Iul'tin tin and tungsten mine and concentrator, opened in 1959, and the Polyarnyy gold placer, which began operations in 1963 near the settlement of Pilgyn on the Chukchi Sea. The tin center is served by a 110-mile road from the port of Egvekinot, which serves as a gateway for supplies needed by the mine and concentrator and as an outlet for the tin concentrate. A 12,000-

concentrating plant. Pending further development, Deputatskiy has been linked by a winter road, open from October until May, with the Yana River port of Ust'-Kuyga, from where tin has been shipped out via the Arctic port of Tiksi as soon as the brief shipping season opens in June. The Sogo brown-coal deposit at Tiksi yielded 100, 000 tons in 1965.

Gold is produced in three districts: the Aldan district, one of the Soviet Union's oldest producers; the Allakh-Yun district, on a right tributary of the Aldan river, in southeast Yakutia; and the upper Indigirka district, in the northeast. Placer deposits were discovered in the Aldan district in the early 1920s, and the area was reached by a highway from the Trans-Siberian Railroad town of Never or Bol'shoy Never (Greater Never) in 1931. The highway was part of the Amur–Yakutsk road, which was ultimately to provide a year-round land transport link between Yakutsk and the railroad.

In the early 1930s Aldan accounted for 20 to 25 percent of the Soviet Union's gold production, but its output level was surpassed by the newly developed Kolyma district after 1934. Like Kolyma's gold industry, Aldan's development has also passed through a number of stages. In the 1930s, rich surface placers, mainly around the town of Aldan (the former Nezametnyy) and Orochen, to the south, were worked by small-scale hand methods. Later, as the easily accessible surface deposits became exhausted and electric power became available, notably from the 7,000-kilowatt Yakokut station, near Aldan, mechanical or hydraulic equipment began to be used to work placers with a lower gold content or at shallow depths. Dredges were used particularly at Leninskiy (the former Nizhne-Stalinsk), just southeast of Aldan town. The discovery of rich lode deposits in the late 1940s opened a third stage. Concentrators were built to recover the lode gold in the Kuranakh area, north of Aldan. The additional power requirements were met by the opening in 1963, of a coal-fed power station at Chul'man, 120 miles south of Aldan, on the Yakutsk–Amur highway. Coal output from the Chul'man underground mine in 1965 was 108,000 tons, or enough for a 20,000-kilowatt power plant.

The gold industry in the Aldan area has been overshadowed to some extent by the development of mica production, especially after World War II. After the exhaustion of the old phlogopite mica mines at Slyudyanka, off the southwest tip of Lake Baykal, the Aldan district has become the Soviet Union's sole producer of this valuable variety of mica. Moreover it accounts for 80 to 90 percent of the country's total mica output, far exceeding the production of muscovite mica in the Mama–Chuya district of Irkutsk Oblast. The principal producing towns are Emel'dzhak, 30 miles southeast of Tommot, the management center of the mica industry, and Kanku (Kankunskiy), on a spur of the Amur–Yakutsk highway, 90 miles south of Tommot. Emel'dzhak has been in production since 1942, and Kanku since 1948. The raw mica, obtained about 40 percent from open pits and 60 percent from underground mines, is shipped to processing centers near now exhausted mica deposits, notably Zaozernyy and Uyar, on the Trans-Siberian Railroad between Krasnoyarsk and Kansk.

The Allakh-Yun gold district, also known as the Dzhugdzhur district for the mountains in which it is situated, has been exploited since the 1930s. Most of the production is from placers, many of them buried under glacial deposits. The management center and supply town for the mines is El'dikan, situated on the Aldan River, about 90 miles northwest from the actual placer operations. The Dzhebariki-Khaya coal mine, farther downstream on the Aldan River, produced 350,000 tons in 1965.

The gold-mining area of the upper Indigirka, centered on Ust'-Nera, a town of 11,200 in 1959, is closely linked to the Kolyma area of adjoining Magadan Oblast. It is the terminus of the Kolyma highway from the city of Magadan and obtains its electric power from the Arkagala station in the Kolyma district. Production, which began in 1942, is almost entirely from placers, the most important of which (Marshal'skiy, Razvedchik) are west of Ust'-Nera in the El'ginskiy area.

The most distinctive resource of Yakutia is its industrial diamond deposits, discovered in 1954–55. First to be developed was the more accessible deposit, a kimberlite pipe called Mir (Peace), at 62° 30′ N 114° E. A diamond-mining and milling center, Mirnyy, developed at the site, and reached a poulation of 22,000 in 1967.

Supplies for the development of Mirnyy moved from the west to the railhead and port of Osetrovo, on the upper Lena River, then downstream to Mukhtuya (renamed Lensk in 1963), which became the gateway to the diamond fields. In the first few years of operation after 1957, when the first concentrating mill opened at Mirnyy, the town was dependent on small local power generators and a winter road from the Lena River gateway. A high-voltage power transmission line from a temporary power plant at Lensk was completed in 1960, and a year-round highway was opened for traffic two years later between Lensk and Mirnyy, 160 miles north. In 1966 the Mirnyy complex reached its designed production capacity with the opening of a third concentrator.

Meanwhile the highway and power line were extended 60 miles northwest to the site of a 312,000-kilowatt hydroelectric station on the Vilyuy River. The station, next to the new settlement of Chernyshevskiy (1967 population: 12,000), was designed as the permanent source of electric power for the diamond industry and installed its four generating units in 1967-68. In the late 1960s the north–south highway and the power transmission line were extended northward for a distance of 250 miles to the second diamond district, the Alakit-Daldyn district, situated astride the Arctic Circle. Two kimberlite pipes, both larger in diameter than the Mirnyy pipe, were in process of development. The diamond center of Aykhal (66° N 111° 30′ E) began production in 1964, followed by the diamond pipe at Udachnyy (Novyy) on the Daldyn River (66° 20′ N 112° 30′ E) in 1968.

In addition to the scattered coal mines that supply electric power stations near gold, tin, and other mineral sites, fuel resources are being developed in the central part of the republic around Yakutsk. Two mines on the Lena, Kangalassy, 20 miles north of Yakutsk, and Sangar, 150 miles northwest, accounted for about one-half of Yakutia's total coal output of 1.4 million tons in 1965. A natural-gas deposit was discovered in 1956 at Tas-Tumus, at the confluence of the Vilyuy River and the Lena. A 250-mile-long pipeline from the gas field reached Yakutsk in 1967, fueling a gas-turbine power station opened in 1969. The pipeline was extended 50 miles to the Bestyakh–Pokrovsk area for use in cement and lumber plants.

### KAMCHATKA AND SAKHALIN

Two relatively isolated parts of the Soviet Far East, the Kamchatka Peninsula and Sakhalin Island, differ substantially in resource development.

Kamchatka's mineral resources are largely undeveloped. In the mid-1960s some gold placer deposits were being explored in the central Kamchatka mountain range near Mil'kovo, and there are prospects for the development of sulfur deposits in the northern part of the peninsula. Kamchatka's underground steam resources, associated with the peninsula's volcanic activity, have been the object of research as a source of commercial heat and power. An experimental 5,000-kilowatt power station using underground steam went into operation in 1965 at the Pauzhetka hot springs, near the southern tip of Kamchatka, as a source of heat and power for the nearby Ozernovskiy fish cannery. Other hot springs, near Petropavlovsk, the capital of Kamchatka, are being considered as a source of heat and power for the city, but in the meanwhile a 70,000-kilowatt steam electric station at Petropavlovsk is burning fuel oil.

In Sakhalin, fuel resources—coal, oil, and natural gas—are significant, at least on a regional level. Oil, concentrated in the northern half of the island, has been in commercial production since the 1920s. Output was at first concentrated at Okha, but in 1929 a new field at Katangli, 125 miles south of Okha, was opened to production. Later (in 1937) output began in the Ekhabi area, 5 miles south of Okha, and remained the main source until the mid-1950s, when total production was about 1 million tons. The discovery of new fields, at Tungor in 1957 and at Kolendo, north of Okha, in 1961, greatly increased production, more than doubling it within a decade to 2.4 million tons in 1965. However, despite the growth in production, Sakhalin's crude oil meets only 30 to 40 percent of the regional oil needs of the Soviet Far East.

The crude oil was shipped before World War II through the port of Moskal'vo, west of Okha. During the war (in 1943) a pipeline was built from the Sakhalin fields across the Tatar Strait at Pogibi to Sofiysk on the Amur. It was extended in 1952 to the Komsomol'sk refinery. Construction of a second parallel line began in 1963 and was completed during 1969. There are also plans for the construction of a natural-gas pipeline to Komsomol'sk from Sakhalin, where gas production was developed in the 1950s, reaching 600 million cubic meters in 1965. Half of this amount was dry gas and half oil-field gas.

Sakhalin's coal output was 4.6 million tons in 1965, mainly from sixteen underground mines near Aleksandrovsk, Uglegorsk, and

Nevel'sk, on the west coast, and near Dolinsk, on the east coast. An open-cut brown-coal mine at Vakhrushev, on the east coast, produced 0.7 million tons in 1965. It was expanded in the 1960s as a source of fuel for a large minehead power station, the South Sakhalin power plant, which began operations in 1966. One of the economic objectives in Sakhalin is the gradual completion of a unified electric power grid linking the northern and southern halves of the island.

North to south transportation has been dependent on a highway through the central valleys of the Poronay and Tym' rivers. The developed southern rail net extended as far north as Pobedino station until 1956. Construction of a northward extension was started in that year and reached Tymovskoye in 1963. The line was to be continued to Nysh in 1968 for an eventual link-up with the Okha–Katangli railroad, serving the oilfields.

# 12

# KAZAKH SSR

The development of industrial resources in the Kazakh SSR (or Kazakhstan), is best considered by regional complex in this large and diversified republic. Central Kazakhstan, with semi-desert range-grazing and some irrigated agriculture of truck produce around urban centers, contains two basic industrial complexes: the coal and steel complex centered on Karaganda and the copper complex centered on Balkhash and Dzhezkazgan. Northern Kazakhstan, the scene of the virgin-lands development program of the second half of the 1950s, includes two complexes: the Kustanay iron ore complex, which became the principal ore supplier of the Urals iron and steel industry in the 1960s; and the Pavlodar–Ekibastuz complex, with Kazakhstan's second coal basin, and aluminum, ferroalloy, and chemical industries. Eastern Kazakhstan, in the foothills of the Altay mountain system, has the republic's greatest hydroelectric potential and is the principal center of its nonferrous metals industry. Southern Kazakhstan, in addition to the manufacturing industry in Alma-Ata, the republic's capital, includes a chemical complex based on the Karatau phosphate deposits, and a nonferrous metals industry centered on the lead refinery at Chimkent. Regional development in western Kazakhstan is dominated by the growing petroleum industry of the Mangyshlak Peninsula.

## Central Kazakhstan

The Karaganda industrial complex, based on about 8 billion tons of bituminous coal reserves, mainly coking coal, is Kazakhstan's largest urban agglomeration (1967 population: 750,000), consisting of the central coal-mining city of Karaganda (498,000), its southwest coal-mining suburbs of Saran' (54,000), Abay (31,000), and Shakhtinsk (32,000), and its northern suburb of Temirtau (150,-000), with iron–steel and chemical industries.

Though discovered and exploited on a small scale in the nineteenth century, the Karaganda coal basin began to be mined on a large scale only after the arrival of the railroad from Akmolinsk (the present Tselinograd) in 1931. Production rose rapidly as Karaganda became a supply source of coking coal for the iron and steel industry of the Urals, supplementing the more distant Kuznetsk Basin. By 1940, the Karaganda industrial district had a population of 200,000 and was producing 6 million tons of coal a year. Roughly half of the output was shipped to the Urals, mostly to the steel center of Magnitogorsk. When the coal basins of the European part of the USSR were occupied by German forces in World War II and the Soviet Union had to rely on the eastern basins, production at Karaganda rose by 50 percent to 9 million tons in 1945.

Until the late 1950s coal output originated mainly from mines around Karaganda proper and in the suburban Saran' area, closest to the city. Production at Saran' began in 1946 and in the 1950s accounted for 10 to 12 percent of the total coking-coal output of the basin. Saran' was established as a separate city in 1954. During the 1960s, coal production continued to expand in a southwesterly direction from the central city into the Churubay-Nura deposit, where the new city of Abay was founded in 1961, and into the Tentek and Shakhan deposits, where the city of Shakhtinsk was established in the same year.

In 1965 the Karaganda basin produced 30 million tons of coal, of which 11 million tons was coking coal. Half the coking coal originated in the city area proper and half in the newly developed southwest suburbs. Almost all the production was from underground mines. A strip mine went into operation in 1941 during the wartime emergency in a brown-coal deposit at Mikhaylovka, a southeast suburb of Karaganda, and accounted for one-fourth of the basin's total output by 1950, but its reserves were depleted by the mid-1960s and yielded only 700,000 tons in 1965. Outside of the basin proper, a second strip mine was opened in 1957 at Kuu-Cheku, 35 miles north of Karaganda and 15 miles east of the railroad. It produced 1 million tons in 1965. Its coal is of noncoking quality, with a high ash content.

Aside from providing coking coal for the iron and steel industry of the Urals and, more recently, also in the Karaganda complex itself, the bituminous coals are used on the railroads of Kazakhstan and at the republic's principal thermal power stations. Two of these provide the electricity for the Karaganda industrial district. The Karaganda No. 1 station, at Temirtau, dates from the beginning of World War II, when it was first equipped with 13,000-kilowatt units, and reached a capacity of 271,000 kilowatts by 1956, having been expanded with three 50,000-kilowatt generators in the mid-1950s. The Karaganda No. 2 power plant, at Topar, opened in 1962 and was equipped with two 50,000-kilowatt units and five 100,000-kilowatt units to reach a capacity of 600,000 kilowatts by the end of 1965.

Coal production in the Karaganda basin has stimulated the development of other industries, primarily iron and steel at Temirtau, the northern satellite city. Temirtau, whose name means "iron mountain" in Kazakh, arose in 1945 on the site of the small village of Samarkand (not to be confused with the Central Asian city). The first industry was the small Kazakh Metallurgical Plant, built in World War II on the west shore of an artificial reservoir on the Nura River. The reservoir, known as the Samarkand reservoir, for the original name of Temirtau, became a major water supply source for the Karaganda industrial district, situated in semiarid steppe. The small wartime steel plant had no blast furnaces and used long-haul pig iron for the production of steel, which reached 400,000 tons by 1960.

The Karaganda district was selected in the 1950s as the site of one of the Soviet Union's new integrated iron and steel complexes. Although the new plant, situated in open industrial terrain between

Karaganda and the south shore of the Samarkand Reservoir, was called the Karaganda Metallurgical Plant, it became administratively part of the city of Temirtau. The first blast furnace of the new plant, with a capacity of 53,000 cubic feet, opened in 1960; the second, of 60,000 cubic feet, went into production the following year. Open-hearth steel furnaces followed in 1964. In the late 1960s the plant was producing 1.7 million tons of pig iron a year, and 800,000 tons of steel, in addition to the 400,000 tons of the old Temirtau mill. A third blast furnace, with a capacity of 95,000 cubic feet, was under construction in the late 1960s, and a fourth was planned. Oxygen converters were added for expanded steel-making capacity. A hot-sheet mill began operations in 1968 and a cold mill for automotive sheet was scheduled to open in 1969. A pipe mill for the manufacture of large-diameter steel pipe was to be added in the 1970s. The ultimate capacity of the Karaganda plant was to be 4.5 million tons of pig iron and steel each.

The iron ore source for the Karaganda iron and steel complex is the Atasu deposit at Karazhal, 150 miles southwest of Karaganda. The West Karazhal open-cut mine, with a capacity of 1.2 million tons of 55-percent direct-shipping ore, began operations in 1956, and sent its ore at first to the Urals pending completion of the first Karaganda blast furnace. A second open-cut mine, with a capacity of 1 million tons, was completed in 1961 at Bol'shoy Ktay, 10 miles east of the West Karazhal pit, to supply the second blast furnace. The completion of an underground mine with a capacity of 2.2 million tons, under construction in the late 1960s, was to double ore output to 4.5 million tons. However, other ore supplies were expected to be tapped to meet the demands of the ultimate capacity of the Karaganda iron and steel mill.

The availability of coal, relatively cheap coal-based electric power, and limestone at Topar (part of Abay city) gave rise to a chemical industry at Temirtau based on the manufacture of calcium carbide. The Temirtau chemical plant (opened in 1943) accounts for about half the commercial calcium carbide produced in the Soviet Union. The carbide–acetylene process was originally envisaged as providing the raw material for chloroprene rubber at Temirtau. However, when the synthetic-rubber plant finally opened in 1961 (it had been under construction since 1940), it utilized long-haul synthetic alcohol for the production of butadiene rubber. The production of synthetic rubber at Temirtau is tied in with the manufacture of rubber goods at Saran', where a tire-repair plant opened in 1965. Saran' is being developed as a chemical center, including the production of paints and varnishes in addition to rubber fabrication.

A 150-mile-long railroad was opened in 1965 eastward from Karaganda to the barite–lead deposit of Karagayly, just southwest of Karkaralinsk. The railroad may ultimately be extended southeastward to the Turksib main line, providing a more direct outlet to the nonferrous smelters of the East Kazakhstan district.

The principal sites for development of resources in central Kazakhstan outside the Karaganda coal and steel district are the copper operations of Balkhash and Dzhezkazgan. Dzhezkazgan has the Soviet Union's largest copper reserves, in copper sandstone deposits similar to those of the central African copper belt. Mining had its beginnings in 1928 with a primitive small operation that included the Dzhezkazgan mine, a smelter at Karsakpay, and a coal mine at Baykonur. Modern commercial output of copper ore began on a larger scale when the railroad reached the Dzhezkazgan area in 1940.

At first the copper ore was shipped without concentration to smelting centers in the Urals, but in 1954 the first concentrator opened at Dzhezkazgan, and the concentrate moved to the Balkhash smelter, which had been developed in the meantime. A second concentrator began operations at Dzhezkazgan in 1963 and was completed in 1965. A copper refining complex that would produce black copper (intermediate product), electrolytic copper, and the highly refined oxygen-free copper was under construction in the late 1960s.

The Dzhezkazgan industrial district, with a population of about 150,000, consists of the central city of Dzhezkazgan, site of the concentrators and the smelter project, situated on a reservoir dammed on the Kengir River, and two large mining settlements of 30,000 people each. One, also called Dzhezkazgan, is the site of the original small underground mine, and most of the present deep-mining operations; the other mining settlement is Nikol'skiy, where the large Zlatoust-Belovskiy open-cut mine has been worked since

1963. Current expansion is through the construction of large, high-ceilinged underground mines permitting the use of bulky mining and transport equipment. The first of three giant mechanized mines, the No. 55 mine, was opened in 1965, followed by No. 57 in 1968. The third, called No. 65, was under development in the late 1960s.

Territorially related to the Dzhezkazgan district is the manganese mine of Dzhezdy, situated on a rail spur running northwest to the foot of the Ulutau hills. The Dzhezdy deposit was developed in World War II as an emergency source of manganese for Soviet steel plants to replace the sources occupied or cut off by military operations. It declined again after the war, but was revived in the mid-1960s as a potential source of manganese for the Karaganda steel complex and for a new ferroalloys plant at Yermak, near Pavlodar. A large open-cut mine and concentrator were developed to replace the small wartime underground operation. Dzhezdy was officially known as Marganets, the Russian word for "manganese", from 1954 to 1962.

The Balkhash copper center, on the north shore of Lake Balkhash, has been in operation since 1938 and, as a result of several expansions, includes all phases of the copper manufacturing cycle, from mine through concentrator, smelter, and electrolytic refinery, to rolling mill. Based originally on the Kounradskiy open-pit mine, the Balkhash operation has shifted increasingly to the more recent Vostochno-Kounradskiy (East Kounrad) mine as the first deposit neared depletion. In the late 1960s, the raw-material base of the smelting and refining complex was further expanded with the development of a copper deposit at Sayak, 130 miles east of Balkhash. A railroad from Balkhash to Sayak was opened in 1967 and the first ore movement was expected in 1970.

In addition to copper, the Kounrad deposits have also yielded a substantial share of the Soviet Union's molybdenum, recovered at the Balkhash plant as a by-product, along with rhenium, which is a by-product of the molybdenum. Rhenium is used in tungsten and molybdenum alloys. Northwest and west of Balkhash are a number of smaller mining settlements producing rare metals. The most important are the tungsten–molybdenum center of Akchatau, founded in 1944 (1959 population: 8,500), and its subsidiary desert mining settlement to the west, Dzhambul.

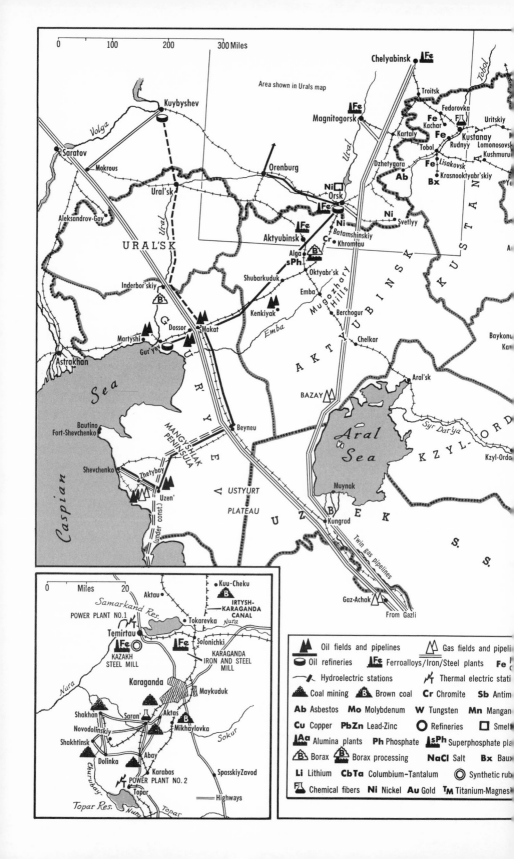

# 31. KAZAKHSTAN

Petropavlovsk  Omsk

...AKHSTAN
Irtyshskoye

...kchetav  Kzyltu
...lodarskoye
ntabrod  Aysary  L. Atansor  NaCl  Tavolzhan
Stepnyak  Au  Au  NaCl  Kalkaman  Maraldy  Kulunda
Aksu  Au  Bestobe  Pavlodar  Mikhaylovskiy  Rubtsovsk
Atbasar  Au  Akbeit  Zholymbet  Sb  Ekibastuz  Yermak  Fe
Zhaltyr'  Turgay  Maykain  Au  Shemonaikha  Leninogorsk
Tselinograd  Yermentau  Shoptykol'  Moldary  Cu  Zn  Cu  Ust'-Kamenogorsk  Zyryanovsk
znamenskiy  Maykuben  Basin  Cu  PbZn  E. KAZAKHSTAN
Osakarovka  IRTYSH-KARAGANDA  CANAL  Semipalatinsk  Area shown in inset below
Nura  Fe  Charsk  Zhangiztobe
Temirtau  Karkaralinsk  SEMIPALATINSK  L. Zaysan  Zaysan
Karaganda  PbZn  Karagayly
Area shown in inset below  Yuzhnyy  Ayaguz
Atasu
Akchatau  Aktogay  Druzhba
Cu  MoW
kol'skiy  Fe  Karazhal  Cu  Vostochno-Kounradskiy
Cu  Kounradskiy  Cu
Dzhezkazgan  Dzhambul  Balkhash  Sayak  TALDY-KURGAN
ezkazgan  Mointy  Cü  Gul'shad  Lake Balkhash
A R A G A N D A  Ili  ALMA-  Taldy-Kurgan
Tekeli  PbZn
DZHAMBUL  Iliysk  KAPCHAGAY DAM
Chu  FUTURE KAPCHAGAY RESERVOIR
...atau  Achisay  Zhanatas  Ph  Koktal  Lugovoy  Alma-Ata
Kentau  Mts.  Karatau  Ph  L. Issyk-Kul
Kentau  PbZn  Baydzhansay  sPh  Frunze
rkestan  PbZn  Ph  T  Rybach'ye
Chimkent  Ph  Dzhambul
Arys'  Pb  Lenger
ardara  Tashkent
ardara Res.  Twin gas pipelines

From Mubarek and Dzharkak

## Inset (E. KAZAKHSTAN)

To Pavlodar
Irtysh
Zmeinogorsk
PbZn  Gornyak  A  L  T  A  Y
Orlovka  Cu  Uba
CuZn  Nikolayevka  Shemonaikha
PLANNED SHUL'BA DAM  CuZn  Verkhneberezovskiy
Semipalatinsk  Pervomayskiy  CuZn  Belousovka  Leninogorsk
Cu  Glubokoye  Ul'ba  PbZn
PbZn  Ust'-Kamenogorsk
TM
Au  Serebryansk  Zyryanovsk
Auezov  UST'-BUKHTARMA  PbZn
Charsk  Ognevka  Oktyabr'skiy  Bukhtarma
Asubulak
Zhangiztobe  Georgiyevka  Belogorskiy  Li  E. KAZAKHSTAN
CbTa
SEMIPALATINSK
M t s.

Hydroelectric stations
Highways
Railways

0    40    80 Miles

Kokpekty  To Zaysan  Lake Zaysan

C  H  I  N  A

The Balkhash complex derived power from a heat and power station equipped with two 25,000-kilowatt generators, which was the largest thermal electric plant of Kazakhstan on the eve of World War II and one of the largest in the Soviet Union. The Balkhash heat and power plant was later connected with the Akchatau mining and concentrating complex and, in 1965, Akchatau was reached by a power transmission line from the Karaganda No. 2 electric station, providing a unified Karaganda–Balkhash power grid.

## Northern Kazakhstan

In northeastern Kazakhstan, in the Ekibastuz–Pavlodar–Yermak district, an important industrial complex began to be developed in the mid-1950s on the basis of cheap electric power derived from open-pit steam coals and a series of power-oriented industries.

The Ekibastuz bituminous coal basin, whose geologically confirmed reserves of 8 billion tons are roughly equal to Karaganda's, is the basic resource that gave rise to the industrial development in the area. In contrast to Karaganda's underground mines of coking coals, the Ekibastuz coal is not of coking quality and has a high ash content. However, it is a good steam coal and, being close to the surface, can be mined by economical strip-mining operations. Like Karaganda, Ekibastuz was the scene of a primitive coal industry earlier in the century, but modern development dates from the early 1950s, when the coal deposit was reached by the South Siberian Railroad, under construction between Pavlodar and Tselinograd. The No. 1 open-cut mine began operations in 1954, the No. 2 in 1959, and the No. 3 in 1963. By 1965 all three had been expanded and were yielding 14.3 million tons a year. Total output of the Ekibastuz basin approached 20 million tons in 1969. Further expansion was under way with excavation of the giant No. 5/6 pit, designed to have ultimately a capacity of 45 million tons of coal a year. The first section of this pit, with a capacity of 5 million tons a year, was scheduled to yield its first coal in 1970.

Pending the construction of large steam power plants near the mines, Ekibastuz coal has been shipped by rail to power stations in the southern Urals (Troitsk, Sredneural'sk). In 1965, 10.5 million tons out of the total output of 14.3 million was transported outside of Kazakhstan, most of it to the Urals. Long-range plans call for the construction of four gigantic pit-head power stations of 4 million kilowatts of generating capacity each. Construction of the Ekibastuz No. 1 station, to be equipped with eight 500,000-kilowatt units, began in the late 1960s. This huge block of electricity, expected to become available in the 1970s, is to be transmitted over an extra-high-voltage 1.5-million kilowatt DC line to a proposed power terminal at Gryazi, near Tambov, in central European Russia. The 1,500-mile-long transmission line is expected to provide up to 40 billion kilowatt-hours a year to the power-hungry industrial areas of the European part of the Soviet Union.

A more immediate electric power project in the Pavlodar–Ekibastuz district is the 2.4-million-kilowatt Yermak station, south of Pavlodar on the Irtysh River, where the first of eight planned 300,000-kilowatt units went into operation in 1968. In addition to feeding power to local industries, the Yermak station will be connected by conventional 500-kilovolt AC transmission lines with the Altay mining and metallurgical region of eastern Kazakhstan and, via Tselinograd, with the Kustanay area and the southern Urals. A 330-kilovolt line linking Yermak with the Altay region at Semipalatinsk opened in 1965.

The Ekibastuz power generating complex lies along the route of the 320-mile-long canal from the Irtysh River at Yermak to the expanding Karaganda industrial district. The canal, originally designed to relieve the growing water shortage in central Kazakhstan, will incidentally also meet the large water requirements of the steam electric stations of the Ekibastuz area. Though begun in the early 1960s, work on the pump-driven uphill canal project has been slow. It reached the Kalkaman area, 40 miles from the Irtysh headworks, in early 1966, and Ekibastuz, 80 miles from the Irtysh, in 1968, and the Shiderty River in 1969.

In addition to producing electric power for long-distance transmission, the Ekibastuz-based generating complex will support energy-oriented industries in the Yermak–Pavlodar area. They include a ferroalloys plant at Yermak and an aluminum plant and chemical complex in Pavlodar.

The ferroalloys plant at Yermak (1967 population: 17,000) went into operation in 1968 with a ferrosilicon section, using quartzite from a deposit at Osakarovka near Karaganda. It will also produce manganese alloys, using manganese concentrate from the expanded Dzhezdy mine in central Kazakhstan, and ferrochrome based on the chromite mines of the Aktyubinsk area.

The chemical complex at Pavlodar, under construction since 1965, will be based on the salt deposits of nearby salt lakes (Tavolzhan, to the northeast; Maraldy, east; Kalkaman, southwest), local limestone, and the by-product gases of an oil refinery to be constructed at Pavlodar. The refinery would process crude oil sent by pipeline from Omsk. The basic products of the chemical plant would be chlorine and caustic soda obtained through electrolysis of salt brine. Another product range is to be based on acetylene, to be derived from refinery gases or limestone-based carbide.

Pending completion of sufficient electric generating capacity, in view of the large power requirements of aluminum production, the Pavlodar aluminum plant limits itself for the time being to the production of alumina, the intermediate product. The raw-material source is a bauxite deposit developed in the late 1950s and early 1960s at Arkalyk, 700 rail miles to the west, in Kustanay Oblast. A rail spur from Yesil', on the main South Siberian railroad, to Arkalyk (1967 population: 30,000) was completed in 1958, and the first bauxite from an open-cut mine began moving to Pavlodar in late 1963, where alumina production began the following year. The first alumina plant at Pavlodar was completed in three stages by 1967, and a second plant was under construction in the late 1960s. To supply the second plant, a new bauxite deposit is being developed at Krasnooktyabr'skiy, 45 miles south of the rail junction of Tobol. A rail spur past the iron-mining center of Lisakovsk was under construction in the mid-1960s to Krasnooktyabr'skiy, whose reserves are said to exceed those of the Arkalyk deposit. Pending addition of its own aluminum-making capacity, the Pavlodar plant is supplementing the Urals in supplying alumina to electrolytic reduction plants in Eastern Siberia, at Novokuznetsk, Shelekhov (near Irkutsk), Krasnoyarsk, and Bratsk.

The principal resource development in Kustanay Oblast during the late 1950s and early 1960s was the opening up of an iron ore deposit at Rudnyy as a new raw-material source for the iron and steel plant at Magnitogorsk and for other steel-producing centers in the Urals. The deposit was discovered accidentally in 1949 when the erratic behavior of a compass needle in an airplane flying over the area suggested the existence of a magnetic anomaly such as might be induced by a large deposit of iron ore. Exploration of the new iron ore basin led to the identification of several deposits, including the Sokolovka and Sarbay deposits, near the new town of Rudnyy, to which priority was given in development.

The deposits consist of magnetite, with about 45 percent iron content, and reserves of 800 million tons at Sarbay and 600 million tons at Sokolovka. Both deposits begin near the surface, at depths of about 200 feet, and can be exploited in open-cut mines. Operation of the Sokolovka mine began in 1957, the year in which the new town of Rudnyy was formally declared a city. It grew to a population of about 100,000 by 1967. The Sarbay mine, six miles west of the Sokolovka operation, yielded its first ore in 1960. Expansion of both mines in subsequent years brought them up to a potential mining capacity of 26.5 million tons in 1965, including 17.5 million for the Sarbay mine and 9 million for the Sokolovka mine. Further expansion of capacity to 30 million tons was under way in the late 1960s.

Actual output at the Rudnyy iron-ore complex in 1965 was 17.2 million tons of crude 45 percent ore, which was converted through beneficiation into 11.4 million tons of usable ore, with an average metal content of 59 percent. In addition to magnetic concentration, Rudnyy ore is being dressed since 1965 in the form of self-fluxing pellets, one of the most advanced raw-material forms in blast-furnace technology. In 1968, pellets accounted for 4 million tons of the total output of 14 million tons of usable ore. Pelletizer capacity was to be doubled to 8 million tons by 1970.

The output of the Rudnyy complex is shipped 220 rail miles to Magnitogorsk over a line that was electrified in 1967, as well as to other Urals steel plants, at Novotroitsk and Chelyabinsk and, to some extent, Nizhniy Tagil.

Additional iron-ore developments are in progress in Kustanay Oblast. They include the construction of an underground mine in the Sokolovka deposit at Rudnyy and the opening up of two other iron-ore deposits, at Kachar and Lisakovsk.

The construction of the Sokolovka shaft is intended to tap the deeper portion of the deposit, where strip mining is economical only to a depth of 1,400 feet. The first section of the underground mine is to have a capacity of 5.5 million tons of crude ore, to be expanded later to 13 million tons.

The Kachar deposit, 40 miles west of Kustanay, consists of magnetite and martite ores in deep beds requiring underground mining. The ore is, however, of relatively high grade (an average of 56 percent). A 20-mile-long rail spur to the deposit was under construction in the late 1960s from Fedorovka, northwest of Kustanay, and plans called for the construction of a mine with a capacity of 21 million tons of crude ore. Completion was not expected until the mid-1970s.

Greater priority is being given to the development of the Lisakovsk deposit, where a workers' settlement inaugurated in 1967 already had a population of 5,000. The Lisakovsk deposit consists of phosphoritic limonite similar to the ores of Lorraine, with an iron content of about 36 percent, and high phosphorus and alumina content. The ore is accessible by strip-mining operations, but presents technological problems in concentration. The concentrate may be used for the production of Thomas pig iron, an intermediate product that yields phosphatic slag suitable for fertilizer when made into steel in special Thomas converters. The first stage of the Lisakovsk project, to be completed in the early 1970s, will have a capacity of 6 million tons of crude ore to be converted into 3.6 million tons of usable ore. Ultimately the Lisakovsk deposit is expected to support two gigantic mining and concentrating complexes, each with a capacity of 36 million tons of crude ore.

During the late 1950s, the development of an asbestos deposit began at Dzhetygara, site of an old depleted gold and arsenic mine. The Dzhetygara deposit contains about one-fifth of the Soviet Union's chrysotile asbestos reserves, though mostly in short fibers suitable only for nonspinning uses, such as asbestos–cement products, paper, and millboard. The asbestos project was reached by a railroad from Tobol in 1959. The first section of an open-cut mine, with a capacity of 200,000 tons of asbestos fiber, began operations in 1965. It was to be expanded to 600,000 tons in subsequent years. As a result of this development, the population of Dzhetygara doubled, from 15,000 in 1959 to almost 30,000 in 1967.

Between the two great mineral complexes of Kustanay and Ekibastuz–Pavlodar are a number of smaller, scattered mining centers, producing mainly gold from lode deposits. They include Maykain, which dates from 1937 (1957 population: 8,500), south of Ekibastuz, and several mining towns near Tselinograd: Aksu (called Stalinskiy until 1961); Bestobe and Zholymbet, each with a population of about 10,000, northeast of Tselinograd; and the smaller Akbeit, near Zhaltyr', northwest of Tselinograd. Another mine is at Stepnyak, southeast of Kokchetav. Stepnyak (1959 population: 12,700), also has a concentrator serving the other mines of the area.

## Eastern Kazakhstan

Eastern Kazakhstan, in the ranges of the Altay mountain system, is one of the Soviet Union's leading centers of lead and zinc production. The deposits extend in two roughly parallel belts running NW–SE along the right bank of the Irtysh River. In the zone near the river, the so-called Irtysh zone, the zinc deposits are associated with copper; in the Leninogorsk zone, about 40 miles from the river, the zinc deposits are associated with lead. In addition to copper, these deposits also contain a wide range of other metals, including gold and silver, cadmium, arsenic, antimony, bismuth, and a variety of rare metals, such as germanium, gallium, indium, selenium, and tellurium. Both zones have been exploited since early in the nineteenth century.

The mines in the zinc–copper zone, near the Irtysh, have focused on a smelter at Glubokoye, which originally produced lead and precious metals, but was converted to the output of blister copper in the middle 1930s. This intermediate product was then shipped to the Urals for electrolytic refining. The Glubokoye smelter has been served by two mining centers: Belousovka (1959 population: 14,000), 10 miles to the east, and Verkhneberezovskiy (1959 population: 8,500), 15 miles to the north. Including Glubokoye itself, the entire mining and smelting complex had a population of close to 50,000.

Expansion of activities in the zone during the 1960s was concerned with the recovery of gold and other valuable metals from old tailings and with the opening up of new deposits. Valuable metals contained in fumes and dust of the smelter are being recovered in the Irtysh chemical–metallurgical plant opened in the Glubokoye area in 1960.

Future development in the zinc–copper zone is expected to focus on two large deposits at the northwestern end of the mineralized belt. One is the Nikolayevka deposit, west of Shemonaikha, in East Kazakhstan Oblast; the other is the Orlovka deposit, in Semipalatinsk Oblast, just across the border from the mining settlement of Gornyak, in Altay Kray. The Nikolayevka deposit yielded lead, silver, and copper in the eighteenth and nineteenth centuries until the high-grade ores were depleted about 1870. Excavation of a major surface deposit containing copper ores with a high sulfur content began in 1964, and the first ore horizon was reached in 1968. Pending completion of the large East Kazakhstan copper–chemical plant at Ust'-Talovka, adjoining the Nikolayevka pit, the ore was being shipped to the Urals for processing.

The principal center of the Leninogorsk zone, where zinc ores are associated mainly with lead, is the city of Leninogorsk, which had a population of 70,000 in 1967. Originally called Ridder, for the discoverer of the mineral riches in the area, the town has been a mining center since the late eighteenth century. In the Soviet period, a lead smelter was opened at Leninogorsk in 1927, and expanded and modernized in 1940. The lead bullion produced by the smelter was sent to the regional metallurgical center of Ust'-Kamenogorsk for further refining and recovery of silver, gold, and other by-products. In this early period, the industry at Leninogorsk derived its electric power from three small hydroelectric stations: the 27,600-kilowatt Ul'ba plant, opened in 1934 just southwest of Leninogorsk, on the Ul'ba River; and the 5,600-kilowatt Khariuzovo plant (opened in 1927) and the 6,200-kilowatt Tishinka plant (opened in 1947), both on the Gromotukha River, a tributary of the Ul'ba, south of Leninogorsk. These small hydroelectric stations were inadequate to provide the large amounts of power required for the electrolytic reduction of zinc, and smelting operations at Leninogorsk were therefore limited to the processing of lead concentrates. However, the increasing availability of cheap power from new hydroelectric plants along the Irtysh River during the late 1950s and early 1960s led to the construction of a zinc refinery, which opened in 1966. It yields cadmium metal and sulfuric acid as by-products. The Tishinka open-cut mine, on the southern outskirts of Leninogorsk, was expanded in 1968 to supply the new zinc refinery.

The second center of the lead–zinc belt is Zyryanovsk (1967 population: 57,000). Also dating from about 1800, this mining town played a relatively minor role during the Soviet period until it was reached by a railroad from Ust'-Kamenogorsk in 1953. The improved transportation led to the construction of a large open-cut mine and concentrator, which sends lead, zinc, and copper concentrates for smelting and refining elsewhere.

In addition to the two mineral belts on the right bank of the Irtysh River, eastern Kazakhstan includes a distinctive mining district in the Kalba mountains, on the left bank. On the northeast slopes of the Kalba range, facing the Irtysh valley, tin lode deposits, associated with a variety of valuable minerals (tellurium, indium, columbium, tantalum), are mined in the Belogorskiy complex, southwest of Serebryansk. The complex includes mines and concentrators at Asubulak, dating from the mid-1950s, and at Ognevka, developed in the early 1960s. They are linked through the railroad station at Smolyanka, on the Zyryanovsk branch, with refineries at Ust'-Kamenogorsk.

On the southwestern slopes of the Kalba range, a number of gold mines, also associated with valuable rare metals, are served by roads leading from the railroad stations of Charsk and Zhangistobe. The principal development in this area is the gold-mining town of Auezov (called Bakyrchik until 1967), which rose in the early 1960s on a major lode deposit in the Kalba range, 40 road miles east of Charsk. Charsk (1959 population: 12,300), because of its gateway importance, was raised to the status of city in 1963.

Ust'-Kamenogorsk (1967 population: 212,000) is the regional metallurgical center for all this mining activity. Since first reached by rail in 1936, it has developed into the transportation hub of the entire lead–zinc industry of eastern Kazakhstan, with spurs leading northeast of Leninogorsk, southeast of Zyryanovsk, and the main rail outlet northwest toward a junction with the Turksib Railroad.

The city's industrial development dates largely from the period after World War II, when the start of hydroelectric construction on the Irtysh River provided the cheap electric power needed for electrolytic refining of nonferrous metals. The basis for the refining industry was laid even before the completion of the large stations with construction of the series of small hydroelectric plants near Leninogorsk and coal-fed steam power plants. In 1947, the city's first zinc refinery, under construction for five years, began operations, followed in 1952 by a lead refinery.

It was only at the end of 1952 that the first 85,000-kilowatt generating unit of the Ust'-Kamenogorsk hydroelectric station, in the suburb of Ablaketka, began to produce power. With the installation of its second and third turbines the following year, the station reached a capacity of 255,000 kilowatts, making it the third largest hydroelectric producer of the Soviet Union at that time, after the Dnieper station at Zaporozh'ye and the Rybinsk station on the Volga. A fourth generating unit, raising the capacity of the Ust'-Kamenogorsk station to 340,000 kilowatts, was installed in 1959, when the completion of the second Irtysh River project, the Bukhtarma dam, produced the necessary storage upstream. The Ust'-Kamenogorsk plant supplied the power needed for a second, larger, zinc refinery, which opened in June, 1955.

The power supply of eastern Kazakhstan was greatly increased in the 1960s with the completion of the Bukhtarma hydroelectric station at Serebryansk, a new town that reached a population of 17,000 by 1967. The first 75,000-kilowatt generating unit went into operation in August, 1960, and the ninth and last in November, 1966, for a total capacity of 675,000 kilowatts. This represented a substantial upscaling of the original designed capacity of six units, later (in 1957) corrected to seven units, but still exceeded in the actual construction.

The construction of the Bukhtarma hydroelectric station opened the way for the latest addition to the Ust'-Kamenogorsk refining industry with the construction of a titanium–magnesium plant, opened in 1965. The plant uses the electrolysis of magnesium chloride for the production of magnesium metal, a process requiring 8 to 9 kilowatt-hours per pound of magnesium produced, and then uses part of the magnesium as a reducing agent in converting titanium tetrachloride to titanium metal. The power requirement for the titanium reduction is 6 kilowatt-hours per pound of titanium sponge, as the metal product is called, or 15 kilowatt-hours if the recovery of the magnesium is included.

## Southern Kazakhstan

An important sector of the Kazakhstan lead–zinc industry, focused on the lead smelter of Chimkent, is found in the southern part of the republic. The smelter, the largest lead-processing plant of the USSR, was founded in 1934 to smelt the lead–zinc ores of Achisay, on the southwest slopes of the Karatau mountains. In the late 1940s, when the Achisay higher-grade ore became exhausted, mining operations shifted 15 miles west to the mines of Mirgalimsay and Kantagi, which merged to give rise to the new town of Kentau ("ore mountain" in Kazakh). This mining and concentrating center, with a population of 50,000 in the mid-1960s, became the principal ore supplier of the Chimkent smelter. Other ore sources for the smelter, which has had difficulties filling its capacity, are Baydzhansay, 70 miles north of Chimkent, and Tekeli, northeast of Alma-Ata. Chimkent also handles lead concentrates from scattered mines throughout Central Asia, yielding bismuth, cadmium, and indium as by-products. The local coal source is Lenger, 15 miles southeast on a rail spur, which produces about 400,000 tons of brown coal a year from an underground mine. In 1964 the lead smelter added a sulfuric acid unit based on sulfur from smelter gases.

In the late 1960s, Chimkent diversified its industry substantially as new energy sources became available. The city was reached by a natural-gas line from the Uzbek field of Dzharkak in 1961, and a carbon-black plant, using natural gas as a raw material, was planned. The electric power supply was improved in 1965 with the construction of a second 220-kilovolt line from Tashkent. Plans also called for construction of an oil refinery though the source of the crude oil—the Mangyshlak field or western Turkmenia—remained to be determined. The expanded use of the phosphate deposits in the Karatau range gave rise to a related chemical industry in Chimkent. A plant opened in 1966 smelts phosphate rock in electric furnaces to produce elemental phosphorus as a basis for the manufacture of detergents and other chemicals.

The source of raw material for the Chimkent phosphorus plant and, more importantly, for Dzhambul's expanding superphosphate industry, is the deposit of the Karatau mountains, discovered in 1936 and first placed in commercial production after World War II. The average grade of the Karatau phosphate rock is inferior to the high-grade apatite of the Kola Peninsula, with an average of 26 percent $P_2O_5$ for the Karatau ore compared with the 39.5 percent $P_2O_5$ contained in standard apatite concentrate. However, the Karatau rock was suitable for the production of ground phosphate, for the production of elemental phosphorus by thermal reduction, and even for the production of superphosphate by the acid treatment after the phosphate rock containing excess dolomite or other carbonates is beneficiated by a flotation process.

The first mining operation in the 70-mile-long Karatau phosphate zone began in 1946 at Chulak-Tau, where a small but relatively high-grade deposit accessible by strip mining was situated nearest to the Turksib Railroad. A 50-mile-long railroad was built from Dzhambul to Chulak-Tau, and the new mine supplied up to 700,000 tons of ground phosphate to several new superphosphate plants built in Central Asia after the war: Kokand (opened in 1946), Dzhambul (1950), Samarkand (1955), and Chardzhou (1960–61). These plants used Karatau phosphate rock in combination with Kola apatite for the production of ordinary superphosphate.

In the late 1950s, as the old Chulak-Tau surface mine became depleted, necessitating the long haul of greater amounts of Kola apatite to Central Asia, a major expansion program began in the Karatau phosphate field. An underground mine, called the Molodezhnyy (Youth) mine, was built at Chulak-Tau to tap the deeper beds of the high-grade deposit. The mine, with a capacity of 800,-000 tons of ground phosphate rock, opened in 1964. The previous year Chulak-Tau was renamed Karatau and raised to the status of a city. It had a population of 27,000 in 1967.

Meanwhile, the railroad had been extended 20 miles in 1959 beyond Chulak-Tau (Karatau) to the Aksay deposit at Koktal, where an open-cut mine with a designed capacity of 2 million tons of lower-grade ore went into operation in 1963. The Aksay phosphate, after beneficiation at a flotation plant to remove 15 to 25 percent dolomite, is suitable for the production of superphosphate fertilizer by the acid treatment. The Karatau flotation plant, in operation since 1963, yields about 1.4 million tons of concentrate a year.

But the ultimate objective of the Karatau development was the Zhanatas (Dzhanatas) deposit, the largest potential producer. The railroad was extended to Zhanatas, 70 miles northwest of Karatau, in 1964, and rock shipments began the following year. The first section of the Zhanatas surface mine has a capacity of 2.2 million tons of furnace-grade rock, suitable for the production of elemental phosphorus by the thermal reduction method. This rock moves mainly to the Chimkent phosphorus plant. Ultimately the Zhanatas operation is expected to yield 11 million tons of phosphate rock. In the late 1960s total production of usable phosphate from all the Karatau operations was 3 to 4 million tons (in terms of the standard 19 percent $P_2O_5$ content).

The Karatau development stimulated the industrialization of the city of Dzhambul, whose population rose from 64,000 in 1939 to 158,000 in 1967. The fertilizer industry, which began with the production of ordinary superphosphate in 1950, became more sophisticated. An ammonium phosphate unit opened in 1963, a new plant for the production of double superphosphate began production in late 1968. The new‑plant yields a more concentrated fertilizer by treating phosphate rock with phosphoric acid. Dzhambul was also selected as the site of one of Kazakhstan's large thermal power stations, with a designed capacity of 1.2 million kilowatts. The first 200,000-kilowatt unit opened in 1967, No. 2 in 1968, No. 3 the next year. Dzhambul was also reached in 1968 by a natural-gas line from the Mubarek field of Uzbekistan.

A potential energy-oriented industrial complex may arise around the Kapchagay hydroelectric station on the Ili River north of Alma-Ata. The construction of the station, in the Kapchagay gorge 7 miles downstream from the old Turksib Railroad town of Ili, had been discussed since the 1950s, but was not included in any development plan until the program of 1966–70. The station will have a generating capacity of 440,000 kilowatts, consisting of four 110,000 units. A new town, Novoiliysk, replacing Ili, was under construction at the station site, which also necessitates the relaying of a section of the Turksib Railroad. Among the energy-oriented industries that may be fostered by the Kapchagay project is a nitrogen-fixation plant using hydrogen from the Mubarek natural-gas line, which was under construction to Alma-Ata via Frunze in the late 1960s.

The manufacturing industries of Alma-Ata itself long derived their electric power from a series of small hydroelectric stations built in the 1940s and 1950s along the Alma-Atinka, a mountain torrent south of the city. Most of the stations have a capacity of 2,500 kilowatts each, but the two nearest the city generate 15,000 kilowatts each, for a combined capacity of the entire Alma-Atinka series of about 45,000 kilowatts. A thermal power station, burning Karaganda steam coal, was inaugurated at Alma-Ata in 1962 to meet the growing industrial needs.

A multipurpose water project in southern Kazakhstan, west of Tashkent, is designed mainly for irrigation along the Syr-Dar'ya, but also contributes electric power to the Tashkent grid. This is the Chardara dam and reservoir, which was inaugurated in 1964 after six years of construction. The power station generates 100,000 kilowatts through four 25,000-kilowatt units. The storage reservoir, 35 miles long and 10 miles wide, is to provide irrigation water for a rice-growing district to be developed in the late 1960s and early 1970s along the left bank of the Syr-Dar'ya. The dam settlement of Syrdar'yinskiy, which had a population of 17,000 in 1968, was raised to the status of city in that year and renamed Chardara.

## Western Kazakhstan

In northwestern Kazakhstan, two industrial complexes may be distinguished: the petroleum-producing district of Emba and Gur'yev, extending southward into the Mangyshlak Peninsula since the development of newly explored deposits began there in the mid-1960s, and the Aktyubinsk chromium and chemical complex, based on nearby chromite deposits.

Although the Emba district, exploited since the first producing wells were drilled at Dossor in 1911 and Makat in 1915, never became a significant source of Soviet crude oil in terms of volume, it continued to operate despite high production costs because its crude oil yielded lubricating oils with low freezing points, especially useful under Soviet winter conditions. Emba crude oil was traditionally sent to plants specializing in the manufacture of lubricants, such as the old oil refinery at Konstantinovskiy, near Yaroslavl'. Production in the Emba district was maintained through active exploration and drilling of new wells to replace depleted wells, but total output never rose above 1.7 million tons, a high mark reached in 1961. After 1935, when a 550-mile-long pipeline was completed to the Orsk refinery, some of the Emba oil was also refined at Orsk.

The Gur'yev refinery, opened in 1945 with United States wartime aid, was designed to produce gasoline and diesel fuel and therefore used outside sources, including oil from Saratov on the Volga, Turkmenia, and even Baku. After 1958 the Gur'yev refinery also used some Emba crude oil in combination with Volga and Turkmen oils.

The Emba–Gur'yev district entered a boom with the discovery of the oil-bearing province of the Mangyshlak Peninsula in the late 1950s. A 400-mile-long railroad was completed in 1964 to the new coastal town of Shevchenko (called Aktau until July, 1964), which became the administrative headquarters of the peninsula (not to be confused with the older Fort Shevchenko, to the northwest).

Two fields presented immediate prospects for development. The Uzen' field, 100 miles southeast of Shevchenko, was the first to yield commercial crude oil, in the summer of 1965, after four years of exploration. The town of Novyy Uzen' (New Uzen'), with a population of 17,000, was inaugurated there in 1968. The Zhetybay field, halfway between Shevchenko and Uzen', where exploration began in 1959, had not begun producing by 1969. However, the Uzen' field alone yielded 5.5 million tons by 1968, or three times as much as the output of the old Emba field. Mangyshlak oil production was planned to increase to 7 million tons in 1969 and to 20 million in the early 1970s.

The Uzen' and Zhetybay fields are connected with Shevchenko by a railroad, highway and oil pipelines. Natural gas associated with crude-oil production supplies an ammonium phosphate factory and the heat and power plant at Shevchenko. This plant has operated a commercial desalting installation since 1963 to provide fresh water for the expanding economy of this desert region. An atomic reactor of 350,000 kilowatts, to be used both for electric power production and for desalting of Caspian water, was under construction at Shevchenko in the late 1960s. The city had a population of 28,000 in 1967 and was growing rapidly.

Because of the desert conditions of the Mangyshlak, housing for oil workers is to be concentrated in a few larger towns with adequate water supplies and other services rather than in scattered smaller settlements. The total manpower in the area was expected to increase from 3,000 in 1965, to between 35,000 and 40,000 by 1970, which would represent a total population of 200,000.

Pending the completion of long-distance pipelines, Mangyshlak crude oil was shipped by tank cars to the Gur'yev refinery and by shallow-draft tankers to the Volgograd refinery. Some amounts also moved to Orsk. The first long-distance pipeline for Mangyshlak oil was under construction in the late 1960s to the Kuybyshev refining complex, with a branch reaching the Gur'yev refinery in 1969. Other pipelines are being considered to Volgograd; to a newly planned refinery at Lisichansk, in the Donets Basin; and to proposed refineries at Chimkent, in southern Kazakhstan and at Chardzhou, in Turkmenia. Pipeline transmission of Mangyshlak oil presents special problems because of the high paraffin content (about 30 percent). Heating devices must be installed along pipelines to keep the crude oil from solidifying.

In addition to the Uzen' and Zhetybay fields, the Mangyshlak operation includes prospects at Tenge, southwest of Uzen', and Tasbulat, to the northwest. Another field is to be developed at Karamandybas, 50 miles south of Uzen'. Production was also being expanded outside the Mangyshlak Peninsula in the old Emba district. A new field opened in 1968 at Martyshi, just west of Gur'yev, and there were good prospects at Kenkiyak, 75 miles southwest of the rail junction of Oktyabr'sk.

To handle the increased flow of oil, the Gur'yev refinery was being expanded in the late 1960s, and an associated petrochemical plant was being built. Its first section, producing polyethylene, opened in 1966.

New applications for boron compounds in atomic reactors (as neutron absorbers) and in space exploration (as a coating material for solar batteries) have stimulated interest in the Soviet Union's principal borax deposit, worked since the late 1930s at Inderborskiy, on the Ural River, 80 miles north of Gur'yev. After the exhaustion of limited reserves of rich ore, a concentrator was built at Inderborskiy in the late 1950s to process leaner, disseminated ores. The construction of a railroad from Makat has been proposed to ease transportation, now dependent on trucking. The borax is processed at Alga, near Aktyubinsk.

The transport situation of the entire Gur'yev industrial district was being improved in the late 1960s. The area had been dependent on a single railroad leading northeast via Oktyabr'sk to Orsk, which was opened to operation in World War II. In 1967 a westward outlet was added with the completion of the Astrakhan'–Gur'yev railroad. In addition, work was nearing completion in the late 1960s on a 250-mile link between Kungrad, present railhead in the lower reaches of the Amu Dar'ya, and Beyneu, a station on the railroad to the Mangyshlak Peninsula. Completion of this missing section was to provide a long-planned direct rail connection between the western part of Central Asia and northwest Kazakhstan, to be extended ultimately to the Volga valley via the Inderborskiy borax mine and the railhead of Aleksandrov-Gay.

The chromium industry of the Aktyubinsk area is based on the Donskoye deposit, 50 miles east, where the mining town of Khromtau developed after 1943 (1959 population: 7,600). The deposit, mined in open-cut operations, supplies both high-grade ore for the production of ferrochromium and poorer ore for chemical purposes. The ore is shipped by rail via the junction of Oktyabr'sk (until 1967, Kandagach) to Aktyubinsk, where a ferroalloys plant has been in operation since 1943. In addition to its ferrochromium specialization, the plant has also been producing ferrotitanium since 1951. The city's chromium industry was further expanded with the construction of a plant (opened in 1957; enlarged in 1963) using lower-grade ores for the production of a wide range of chromium compounds. This, in turn, was to furnish the materials for a planned chrome-pigment factory. While the chromium ore of Khromtau moves to Aktyubinsk for processing, nickel–cobalt ores of the nearby Kimpersay deposit, where the mining town of Batamshinskiy (1959 population: 7,200) was founded in 1945, move north to a refinery at Orsk.

In addition to its chrome specialization, the chemical industry of

307

the Aktyubinsk area also includes an old plant built in the mid-1930s at Alga, 25 miles south of Aktyubinsk. Originally designed to use local phosphate rock for the production of superphosphate, the Alga plant was converted in 1942 to the processing of borax from the Inderborskiy mine when the discovery of the Karatau phosphate deposits offered a fertilizer source nearer to the potential consumers of Central Asia's cotton farms. Through World War II and into the early 1950s, Alga specialized in the production of boric acid and boron compounds, including additives for the fertilizer industry. It was only in 1952 that the need for superphosphate stimulated the production of this fertilizer at the Alga plant. At first long-haul apatite concentrate from the Kola Peninsula furnished the raw material in combination with Karatau phosphate, but as additional superphosphate capacity was completed in Central Asia, the Karatau phosphate was diverted increasingly to those plants. Since 1956 the Alga superphosphate plant has been using Kola apatite exclusively. A second plant, to produce double (concentrated) superphosphate, was under construction at Alga in the late 1960s. The source of the sulfuric acid at this fertilizer complex has been pyrite from the Urals

# 13

---

# CENTRAL ASIA

## Turkmen SSR

The Turkmen SSR, or Turkmenia, has been the main petroleum-producing republic of Soviet Central Asia, and a supplier of chemical raw materials (sulfur, iodine and bromine, and natural sodium sulfate), cotton, and karakul skins. Beginning in the mid-1960s, development plans were centered to a large extent on the opening up of newly discovered natural-gas deposits. In addition to being sent to central European Russia by pipeline, natural gas is expected to stimulate industrial development within Turkmenia by providing a fuel for new power stations and a raw material for a chemical industry.

Most of Turkmenia is covered by the Kara Kum Desert, which restricts settlement and irrigated farming to the valley of the Amu Dar'ya, on the eastern margins of the republic; and to the Murgab and Tedzhen oases and the foothills of the Kopet Dagh in the south. The petroleum industry is concentrated in the western part, on the coast of the Caspian Sea, around the cities of Krasnovodsk, Nebit-Dag, and Cheleken.

### PETROLEUM

Until 1949, oil production was concentrated in the Nebit-Dag field, 15 miles southwest of the rail town of the same name.

Crude oil output more than doubled in the years after World War II, rising from 629,000 tons in 1945 to 1.3 million tons in 1948. The oil was processed at the Krasnovodsk refinery, built with equipment evacuated during the war from the Black Sea port of Tuapse, in the Caucasus.

Beginning in 1948 the exploration and development of additional fields in western Turkmenia led to a rapid increase of crude oil production, from 1.3 million tons in 1948 to almost 13 million in the late 1960s. The first new development was the Kum-Dag field, 25 miles southeast of Nebit-Dag city, which in the mid-1950s accounted for about half the total Turkmen oil output, or about 1.8 million tons a year.

In 1950 new deposits were discovered in the Cheleken Peninsula, one of Turkmenia's earliest oil fields, which had not been producing for about 40 years. The new Cheleken deposits and offshore prospects were so promising that a production plan of 3.5 to 4 million tons was envisaged for these fields for 1970. A large part of the Cheleken output comes from offshore fields in the Zhdanov Bank, 11 miles west of Cheleken.

A major advance in oil production was the discovery in 1956 of the Leninskoye field at Koturdepe (Kotur-Tepe), halfway between Cheleken and Nebit-Dag. First put into production in 1959, Koturdepe soon became the principal oil-producing field of western Turkmenia. In the late 1960s it yielded 7.5 million tons of crude oil, or about 60 percent of the total output. Another new field, Barsa-Gel'mes, between the Koturdepe and Nebit-Dag deposits, was discovered in 1962 and was put into production in 1965. It is expected to rival Koturdepe as one of the leading Turkmen oil-producing areas in the 1970s.

Exploration for oil also extended southward along the Caspian Sea coast in the 1960s and resulted in the opening up of the Okarem field, 90 miles south of Nebit-Dag, in 1961, and of Kamyshldzha, 75 miles south of Nebit-Dag, in 1965.

To handle the increasing volume of crude oil, steps were taken to expand the Krasnovodsk refinery dating from World War II. It was a relatively small installation assembled in 1943 from equipment evacuated from the war-threatened refinery of Tuapse in the Caucasus. Expansion began in 1960. A straight-run distillation unit was opened in 1964 and a catalytic cracking unit, in 1967, for the production of high-octane gasoline. A catalytic reforming unit was under construction in the late 1960s. However, a large share of crude oil had to be shipped to other refineries, including Groznyy and Volgograd. Seaside oil terminals were operating in the Okarem field and at Aladzha, on the Cheleken Peninsula, for Koturdepe crude oil.

With Turkmen oil production scheduled to rise to 20 million tons or more in the 1970s, the need for a second refinery in the region became evident. Plans call for the construction of a pipeline eastward to the Chardzhou area on the Amu-Dar'ya, where a new refining and petrochemical center is to be built at Shagal, 35 miles northwest of Chardzhou. Work was to begin in 1969 on this complex, which would produce synthetic rubber, fibers, and plastics out of petroleum products. A new city of 120,000 is planned on the site of the present riverside mud village. The pipeline was also to be extended eastward to the oil refineries in the Fergana Valley.

NATURAL GAS

Until the mid-1960s, gas production was limited to casing-head gas from the west Turkmenian oil fields. For a long time only a small fraction (up to 20 percent) of the available field gas was collected. But in 1964 a gas pipeline was completed from Koturdepe, the main oil field, to Krasnovodsk, raising gas output fivefold, from a quarter billion cubic meters in the early 1960s to 1.25 billion cubic meters in 1967. A gas-collecting system centered on Nebit-Dag, and gathering field gas from the Barsa-Gel'mes oil deposit and from the Kyzylkum dry-gas deposit (discovered in 1951, just west of Kum-Dag) was also connected with Krasnovodsk in 1968.

These limited developments were overshadowed by the discovery of major gas deposits in the desert areas of eastern Turkmenia in the early 1960s, raising explored reserves to the level of the principal gas-producing districts of the Soviet Union. The first major gas development was in the Achak field, just southeast of the Khiva oasis, which was put in operation soon after its discovery in 1966. It was connected with the great transmission main completed in 1967 from Central Asia to Central European Russia and yielded 3.5 billion cubic meters in 1968. It was expected to produce about 6

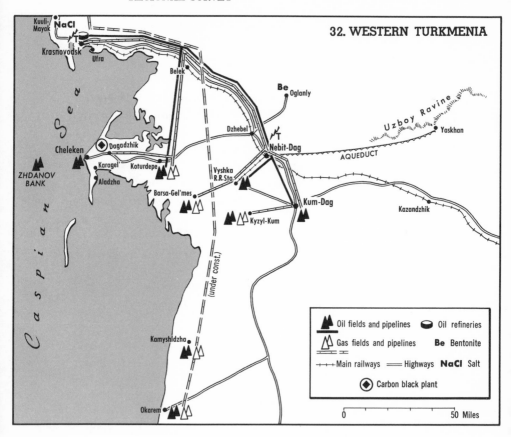

32. WESTERN TURKMENIA

Oil fields and pipelines
Gas fields and pipelines
Main railways ==== Highways
Carbon black plant
Oil refineries
Be Bentonite
NaCl Salt
0    50 Miles

billion cubic meters or half of Turkmenia's planned natural-gas output, by 1970. The gas-workers' settlement of Gaz-Achak was inaugurated near the field in December, 1967. Natural-gas liquids associated with the Achak deposit are being sent by pipeline to Pitnyak station, to the north, for shipment by rail to the petro-chemical complex of Fergana, pending completion of the petro-chemical center near Chardzhou in the 1970s.

Other major natural-gas prospects being prepared for production in the late 1960s were the Gugurtli field, on the left bank of the Amu-Dar'ya, 20 miles south of Dargan-Ata, and the Saman-Tepe field, on the right bank, 35 miles southeast of Chardzhou. Gugurtli, like Achak, was to feed gas into the Central Asia–Central Russia mains starting in 1969. Saman-Tepe is part of a gas field extending across the border into Uzbekistan that is unusually rich in hydrogen sulfide and is to be used for the recovery of elementary sulfur before transmission to gas-consuming areas.

Elsewhere in Turkmenia, natural gas was also discovered in the Mary oasis of the southeast. A 300-mile-long 22-inch pipeline, with a capacity of 2 billion cubic meters a year, was completed in 1969 from the Mayskoye field, just southeast of Mary, to Ashkhabad and Bezmein. The gas is to be used for household needs in the Turkmen capital and for power generation and cement production at Bezmein, an industrial town 15 miles northwest of Ashkhabad. The gas resources of the Mary oasis are also to be used as fuel for a 1.2-million-kilowatt power station under construction on the left bank of the Kara Kum Canal, just south of the city of Mary. The first 200,000-kilowatt generating units were to be installed in the early 1970s. Gas of the Mayskoye field and of the Bayram-Ali deposit, farther north, will also be the raw material for an acetylene-based plastics industry under construction at Mary. This plant, to produce vinyl acetate, polyvinyl acetate emulsion, acetaldehyde, and methanol, is also scheduled to go into operation in the early 1970s. Ultimately the gas resources of the Mary oasis may also be linked with the long-distance transmission mains to Central Russia.

One of the first desert gas deposits to be discovered in Turkmenia in the early 1960s was the Darvaza-Zeagli deposit in the central section of the Kara Kum. However, its remote location and unfavorable geological conditions, such as low reservoir pressure and water encroachment, have delayed development.

There are also plans for the long-distance transmission of natural gas from gas caps of the west Turkmen oil deposits, particularly Koturdepe, Okarem, and Kamyshldzha. Such a pipeline would be laid northward via the Kara-Bogaz-Gol sodium–sulfate complex and the gas-cap deposits of the Mangyshlak oil district to link up with the transmission mains from the east Turkmen–Uzbek district to Central European Russia.

For the time being, western Turkmenia's gas resources are being used locally. The Koturdepe field, in addition to serving Krasnovodsk, also feeds a carbon-black plant at Cheleken, opened to production in 1964. A second carbon-black plant is planned at Okarem.

ELECTRIC POWER

Electric power was relatively undeveloped until the construction of the Ashkhabad regional steam power station at the cement center of Bezmein and a heat and power station associated with the superphosphate fertilizer plant at Chardzhou. The two stations went into operation in 1958, and within a few years power output doubled, from 530 million kilowatt-hours in 1957 to 1 billion in 1962. The newly available gas reserves stimulated further development. In addition to the 1.2-million-kilowatt station under construction at Mary, which will triple Turkmenia's generating capacity, gas is also used as a fuel at a new 48,000-kilowatt power plant at Nebit-Dag. The plant is equipped with four 12,000-kilowatt gas turbines, of which the first went into operation in 1964 and the last in 1968. Another addition to the Turkmen power industry was the Krasnovodsk heat and power station No. 2, which was inaugurated in 1965. It reached a generating capacity of 170,-000 kilowatts in 1968.

Pending the construction of the Mary station, Turkmenia is expected to be dependent on the transmission of electric power from neighboring Uzbekistan. A 220-kilovolt line from the Uzbek grid reached Mary in 1966 via Bukhara and Chardzhou. Another 220-kilovolt line was under construction in the late 1960s from the Bezmein thermal power station via Ashkhabad and Tedzhen, which was reached in April, 1968. With the completion of the last link, between Tedzhen and Mary, the southern population and economic centers of Turkmenia will be linked to the unified Central Asian grid.

CHEMICAL INDUSTRIES

Turkmenia's chemical industry has been associated with by-products of the petroleum industry and with chemical mineral deposits. The oil fields have been a source of iodine and bromine, extracted from oil-well brines. An iodine–bromine plant, in operation in Cheleken since 1932, was reconstructed and modernized in 1963. A second iodine plant went into operation at Nebit-Dag in early 1969. Cheleken is also one of the Soviet Union's sources of ozocerite, a natural paraffin wax. North of Nebit-Dag, at Oglanly, is a large deposit of bentonite, a clay used in oil-well drilling muds, foundry sands, and as a bond in pelletizing iron ore concentrate. The Oglanly deposit, with reserves deemed sufficient for 200 years, has been mined since the 1930s.

The Kara-Bogaz-Gol, a vast salt lagoon off the Caspian Sea, is one of the world's largest deposits of natural sodium sulfate, a chemical used in the paper pulp, glass, and various chemical industries. However, because of its remoteness and primitive technology, the deposit has played a relatively limited role in the Soviet economy. Until the 1930s, the hydrous sodium sulfate, also known as mirabilite or glaubers salt, was simply collected along the shoreline of the lagoon where it washed ashore and dried in the sun. A lowering of the level of the Caspian Sea in the 1930s and 1940s virtually cut off the lagoon from the sea.

The resulting changes in hydrology and salt composition led to the use of the basin method of extracting the sodium sulfate. In this method, a basin is filled with brine in summer. In the autumn, after the water has evaporated, the sulfate precipitates, and is collected and bagged. As a result of the technological change in the industry, the center of activities moved from the old town of Kara-Bogaz-Gol, at the inlet from the Caspian Sea, 40 miles north to the Bekdash area, where the evaporating basins were situated.

A third technological advance was initiated in the 1960s when a sulfate dehydrating plant was being built to make the industry less dependent on weather conditions and to extract more of the other salts contained in the Kara-Bogaz-Gol brine. The production of bischofite, a hydrous magnesium chloride used as a defoliant on Central Asia's cotton farms, began in 1966. It was followed in 1968 by the experimental production of epsomite, the native Epsom salt, used in medicine and in the dyeing and finishing of leather and textiles. An electric power line was under construction in the late 1960s from Krasnovodsk to Bekdash to provide the power needed for artificial cooling of brines and dehydration of the native glaubers salt for the production of anhydrous sodium sulfate.

In eastern Turkmenia, a fertilizer industry is in the making, based in part on local sulfur and potash deposits. Exploitation of the native sulfur deposit at Gaurdak, linked by a railroad spur with

Mukry, began on a primitive scale after World War II, but was expanded and modernized in the 1960s with the construction of a large open-cut mine and concentrator. They went into operation in 1968–69. The Gaurdak mine supplies sulfur for the manufacture of sulfuric acid at the Chardzhou superphosphate plant, which also uses phosphate rock from the Karatau deposit in southern Kazakhstan. The fertilizer plant produced its first acid in 1960 and its first superphosphate the following year. It was converted in 1968 to the output of ammonium phosphate (400,000 tons a year).

The development of a potash deposit at Karlyuk, found in the early 1950s to have reserves of hundreds of millions of tons, was delayed though listed in the five-year plan of 1966–70. An unrelated mineral resource in the Gaurdak district is the Kugitang lead mine, in operation since the middle 1950s, which supplies lead concentrate to the smelter at Chimkent in southern Kazakhstan.

## TRANSPORTATION

An important factor for the Turkmen economy was the construction of the Kara Kum Canal, leading westward from the Amu Dar'ya near the Afghan border. Construction of the canal, planned already before World War II, began after the war but was soon shelved when attention was focused on the Turkmen Canal project, one of the Stalinist development projects of the early 1950s. This project, which would have tapped the water of the Amu Dar'ya farther downstream at Takhiatash in the Khiva oasis and would have crossed the desert from northeast to southwest, was judged unrealistic and was abandoned after Stalin's death in 1953.

Work was renewed on the more modest Kara Kum Canal. The first stage, to Murgab oasis, was completed in 1959; the second, to Tedzhen oasis, the following year, and the third, to Ashkhabad, in 1962, for an overall length of 500 miles. Plans call for extension of the canal westward to the area of Nebit-Dag through an aqueduct. The Bakharden area was reached in 1968. In addition to bringing irrigation water to new cotton fields, the canal also provided industrial water for new enterprises along the way. Although the canal is now said to carry 10,000 cubic feet of water per second near its headworks in the growing season, a steady year-round water supply will have to await completion of the great storage reservoirs on the headstreams of the Amu Dar'ya, such as the Nurek project on the Vakhsh River.

Economic development was also aided by the construction of the Chardzhou–Kungrad railroad in the early 1950s, linking the isolated Khiva oasis and the lower reaches of the Amu Dar'ya with the main centers of the republic. The importance of the Chardzhou–Kungrad railroad was greatly enhanced in the late 1960s with its extension northwestward to western Kazakhstan, providing a second rail connection between Central Asia and the manufacturing centers of European Russia.

## Uzbek SSR

The evacuation of manufacturing industries from European Russia to the Uzbek SSR in World War II clearly established this republic as the most industrialized region of Soviet Central Asia. However, the output of the resettled industries was largely for consumption within Central Asia, and the Uzbek contribution to the national economy continued to be primarily in the agricultural field—cotton, cottonseed oil, karakul skins, and fruits—and minerals such as copper, molybdenum, tungsten, and uranium.

The discovery and development of large natural-gas resources in the western part of Uzbekistan in the late 1950s brought about a major shift in the structure of the republic's economy. In addition to becoming a major supplier of gas for the industrial districts of European Russia, Uzbekistan began to develop new gas-based power stations of its own and to build a chemical industry using gas as a raw material. An expansion of the nonferrous metals industry made it one of the Soviet Union's major producers of copper, molybdenum, and tungsten metal.

Uzbekistan's population and economic activities are concentrated in five regions: the Fergana Valley, with diversified industry and cotton farms; the Tashkent–Almalyk–Angren heavy-industry complex; the expanding irrigated cotton lands of the Golodnaya (Hungry) Steppe on the left bank of the Syr Dar'ya, southwest of Tashkent; the Zeravshan Valley between Samarkand and Bukhara, with diversified industry and cotton; and the Khiva oasis and lower

317

reaches of the Amu Dar'ya, with a predominantly agricultural economy.

## FUELS

Exploration in the Bukhara–Khiva area, a promising gas-bearing province underlying the Kyzyl Kum Desert, on the right bank of the Amu Dar'ya, led to the discovery of vast resources of natural gas in the late 1950s. They included the deposits of Mubarek, discovered and explored in 1955–56 in an area 50 miles southeast of Bukhara; Gazli, discovered in 1956 in an area 60 miles northwest of Bukhara; Dzharkak, discovered in 1958 in an area 30 miles southeast of Bukhara; and Uchkyr, explored somewhat later between Gazli and the Amu Dar'ya. As of the beginning of 1965, explored reserves in the Bukhara region were estimated at 700 billion cubic meters, or one-fourth of the Soviet Union's total.

Dzharkak was the first deposit of the Bukhara region to be developed. A 28-inch pipeline from the Dzharkak field reached Bukhara in 1958, Samarkand the following year, and Tashkent in 1960. Subsequently the Dzharkak pipeline was extended to Chimkent in southern Kazakhstan, feeding newly constructed and converted power stations and industries along the way. The reserves of the Dzharkak deposit were limited and production never rose above 1 billion cubic meters a year. However, additional deposits of the Bukhara district also fed into the Dzharkak pipeline to make use of its full capacity of 4.5 billion cubic meters a year.

In contrast to the Dzharkak deposit, which was assigned to gas distribution within Central Asia, the Gazli deposit, accounting for two-thirds of the Uzbek reserves, was intended to feed large-diameter long-distance transmission mains to the Urals and Central European Russia. The first 40-inch pipeline extending more than 1,000 miles to the Urals around the west shore of the Aral Sea was built in 1961–63; a parallel line, also of 40-inch diameter, was completed in 1965. The two lines together can carry about 20 billion cubic meters of natural gas annually, or the fuel equivalent of 20 million tons of long-haul coal. The Gazli field, which began production in 1961, reached an annual output of 15 billion cubic meters in 1965 and 29 billion in 1968. Of the total 1968 output, 22 billion cubic meters moved out of Central Asia and 7 billion was consumed within Uzbekistan, Tadzhikistan, and southern Kazakhstan.

Gazli is also the point of departure for the great transmission mains to Central European Russia. The first, with a diameter of 40 inches, was inaugurated in 1967; the second, with a diameter of 48 inches, was under construction in the late 1960s. The two pipelines together have a capacity of 25 billion cubic meters a year. In addition to Gazli, they tap the gas fields of Uchkyr and Achak along the way. The Achak field, in northeast Turkmenia, began production in 1967. The Uchkyr field, west of Gazli, near the Amu-Dar'ya, was put in operation in 1968.

Since 1966, the Mubarek field feeds a second regional pipeline of 40-inch diameter laid parallel to the Dzharkak–Tashkent pipeline. Tashkent received Mubarek gas in 1968 at the rate of 2.4 billion cubic meters a year. In the late 1960s the gas transmission system originating in the Bukhara district was being extended beyond Chimkent by a 32-inch pipeline. It reached Dzhambul in 1968 and was expected to arrive in Frunze in late 1969 and in Alma-Ata in 1970.

The Bukhara gas pool was further supplemented in the late 1960s by the development of a gas deposit at Shibarghan in northern Afghanistan. Under an agreement with the Soviet Union, which helped explore and develop the Shibarghan site, Afghanistan was to supply 58 billion cubic meters of gas over an eighteen-year period (1967–85). A pipeline from Shibarghan was put into operation in the late 1960s, crossing the Amu-Dar'ya at Kelif, in the easternmost corner of Turkmenia, and feeding into the Mubarek pipeline to Tashkent. Afghan gas may also be used to reinforce Tadzhik gas deposits as a raw-material source for the gas-based chemical industry under development in Tadzhikistan at Kalinin-abad and Yavan. A 200-mile-long pipeline from the Kelif river crossing to Yavan was planned.

Mubarek is the center of gas fields containing an unusually high amount of hydrogen sulfide, and a plant for the recovery of elemental sulfur was under construction at Mubarek in the late 1960s. It will extract sulfur from the natural gas fields of Urta-Bulak (Uzbekistan) and Saman-Tepe (Turkmenia), to the southwest; the Uzbek fields of Pamuk and Kultak, south of Mubarek, and the Adamtash field, southeast of Mubarek.

Before the development of the great Bukhara gas province in the late 1950s, Uzbekistan's limited gas production was restricted

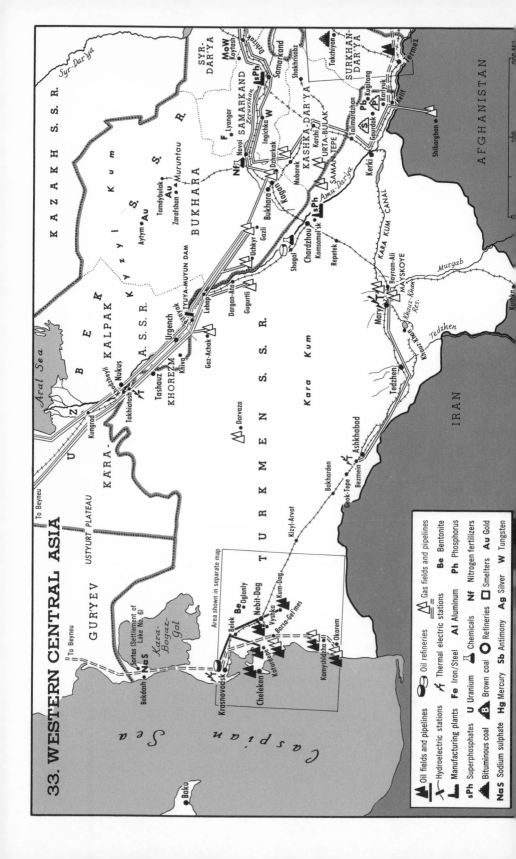

# 33. WESTERN CENTRAL ASIA

**KAZAKH S.S.R.**

**AFGHANISTAN**

**IRAN**

Aral Sea

Caspian Sea

Kara-Bogaz Gol

Kara Kum

Kara-Kalpak A.S.S.R.

Khorezm

Bukhara

Samarkand

Surkhan-Dar'ya

Kashka-Dar'ya

Syr-Dar'ya

Uzbek S.S.R.

Turkmen S.S.R.

Guryev

Ustyurt Plateau

Syr-Dar'ya

Zeravshan R.

Amu-Dar'ya

Murgab

Tedzhen

Kushka

Kara Kum Canal

Tyuya-Muyun Dam

Khauz-Khan Res.

## Legend

| Symbol | Meaning | Symbol | Meaning |
|---|---|---|---|
| Oil fields and pipelines | | Gas fields and pipelines | Be Bentonite |
| Hydroelectric stations | | Thermal electric stations | Ph Phosphorus |
| Manufacturing plants | | Fe Iron/Steel | Al Aluminum |
| sPh Superphosphates | | U Uranium | Nf Nitrogen fertilizers |
| Bituminous coal | | Chemicals | Au Gold |
| NaS Sodium sulphate | | B Brown coal | Ag Silver |
| | | O Refineries | Sb Antimony | Hg Mercury | W Tungsten |
| | | Oil refineries | | Smelters | |

Baku

Bekdash
NaS Sartas (Settlement of Lake No. 6)

To Beyneu

Krasnovodsk
Cheleken
Belek
Be Oglanly
Nebit-Dag
Vyshka
Barsa-Gel'mes
Kum-Dag
Koturdepe
Kamyshldzho
Okarem

Kizyl-Arvat
Bakharden
Geok-Tepe
Bezmein
Ashkhabad
Tedzhen
Bukharden

Mary
MAYSKOYE
Boyram-Ali
Komsomol'sk
Chardzhou
Repetek
Shagal
Sakar

Kerki
Kugitang
Karlyuk
Kelif
Termez
Takchiyan
Koytash
Dzhizak

Shiborghan

Gaurdak
S
Pb
Talimardzhan
Urta-Bulak
Karshi
Mubarek
Kagan
Bukhara
Nfti
Navoi
Ingichka W
Lyangar F
Shakhrisabz
Samarkand
sPh

Tamdybulak
Au
Zarafshan
Muruntau
Au
Aytym Au

Gazli
Uchkyr
Darvaza

Gaz-Achak
Gugurtli
Dargan-Ata
Lebap
Pitnyak

Urgench
Khiva
KHOREZM
Tashauz
Takhiatash
Biruni
Mangit
Chimbay
Nukus
Kungrad

To Beyneu

Area shown in separate map

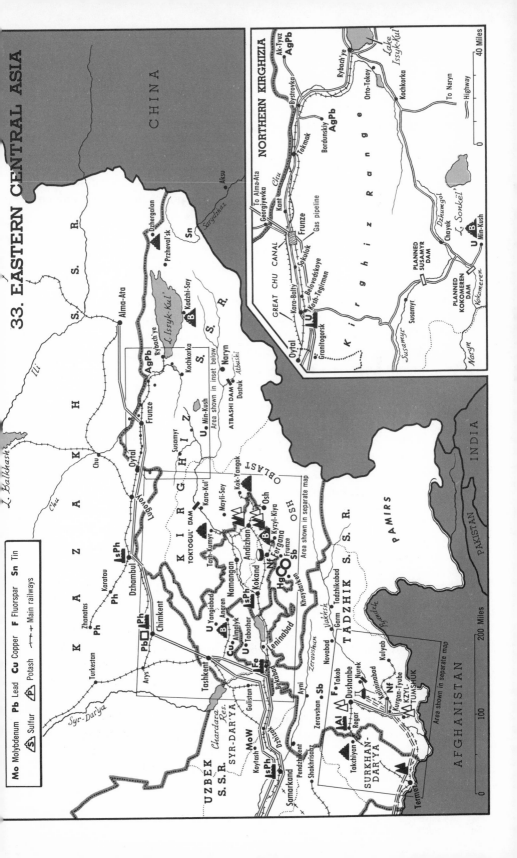

# 33. EASTERN CENTRAL ASIA

**Mo** Molybdenum  **Pb** Lead  **Cu** Copper  **F** Fluorspar  **Sn** Tin
**S** Sulfur  **P** Potash  **—+—** Main railways

## NORTHERN KIRGHIZIA

Ak-Tyuz **AgPb**
Rybach'ye
Bystrovka
Orto-Tokoy
Kochkorka
To Naryn
Highway
To Alma-Ata
Georgiyevka
Kant
Frunze
Gas pipeline
Bordunskiy **AgPb**
Tokmak
Dzhumgol
Chayek
L. Sonkel'
Min-Kush **U B**
GREAT CHU CANAL
Kara-Balty
Belovodskoye
Mosh-Tegirmen
Sokuluk
Oytal
Granitogorsk
Susamyr
Kokomeren
PLANNED SUSAMYR DAM
PLANNED KOKOMEREN DAM
K i r g h i z  R a n g e
Naryn
40 Miles

CHINA
C H I N A

S.  S.  R.

Sargidzhaz
Aksu

Dzhergalan
Przheval'sk
**Sn**
Kadzhi-Say
**B**
Alma-Ata
Rybach'ye
L. Issyk-Kul'
**AgPb**
Kochkorka
Naryn
ATBASHI DAM
Dostuk
Atbashi
Area shown in inset below
Frunze
Oytal
Chu
Susamyr
**U** Min-Kush
K I R G H I Z  S.  S.  R.
Kok-Yangak
O B L A S T
Kara-Say
Moyli-Say
**B**
Osh
OSH
Kara-Kul'
TOKTOGUL' DAM
Tash-Kumyr
Kyzyl-Kiya
Kok-Yangak
Andizhan
Fergana **Sb**
Frunze
Area shown in separate map

L. Balkhash
Ili
K  A  Z  A  K  H
Chu
Chu
Lugovoy
Oytal
Frunze

Zhanatas **Ph**
Karatau **Ph**
Dzhambul **SPh**
Chimkent
**Pb Ph**
Turkestan
Arys
Tashkent
**Cu**
Ilmolyk **B**
**U** Taboshar
Leninabad
**Fe**
Angren
**U** Yangiabad
Namangan
**SPh**
Kokand
**Hg Mo**
**N**
Khaydarken
Tadzhikabad
Garm
Tadzhikabad
Vakhsh
**TADZHIK  S.  S.  R.**
PAMIRS
INDIA
PAKISTAN
AFGHANISTAN

**UZBEK  S.  S.  R.**
Syr-Darya
Chardara Res.
SYR-DARYA
Koytash **MoW**
**SPh**
Samarkand
Pendzhikent
Shakhrisabz
Gulistan
Bekabad
Ayni
Zeravshan
Zeravshan **Sb**
Novabad
Takob **F**
Dushanbe
Regar
Takhiyaban
**Al**
SURKHAN-DARYA
Termez
Panj
Nurek
Kulyab
Kaninabad
Kurgan-Tyube
KZYL-TUMSHUK
**Nf**
Area shown in separate map

0    100    200 Miles
0    40 Miles

to the small oil and gas deposits of the Fergana Valley. A system of gas lines originating in the fields of Severnyy Sokh (northern Sokh), south of Kokand, and Khodzhiabad and Khartum, southeast of Andizhan, was built in 1958–60 to serve the industries of the southern part of the Fergana Valley, including Fergana, Kokand, and Andizhan. However, the valley's gas production of 500 million cubic meters a year was soon dwarfed by the spectacular developments in the western desert.

In oil production, too, the Fergana Valley has not developed into a major factor in the Soviet economy, although petroleum was first extracted in the area on a commercial scale as early as 1904, at Chimion, southwest of Fergana city. The old field became exhausted in the late 1930s, and after World War II the production of crude oil in the Fergana Valley shifted to newly developed deposits in the eastern section, near Andizhan, around Yuzhnyy Alamyshik, Khodzhiabad, and Palvantash.

Crude oil in the Fergana Valley was long processed by a small refinery built in 1908 to serve the old Chimion field. The refinery, situated at Alty-Aryk railroad station, gave rise to a small town known as Vannovskiy (renamed Khamza Khakimzade in 1963). Despite the limited crude-oil output in the Fergana Valley, a second larger refinery was opened in 1958 at Fergana city to process crudes from all Central Asian oil fields, including Turkmenia.

Two mineral deposits related to the Fergana Valley's petroleum resources are an open-cut mine producing ozokerite, a natural paraffin wax, and a small native sulfur mine, both at Shorsu, south of Kokand. The sulfur deposit became depleted, and the mine was closed in 1966.

Another small oil-producing district of Uzbekistan is in the Surkhan Dar'ya valley of the southwestern part of the republic. Production began in the area in the 1930s at Khaudag, followed in World War II by Kakaydy (Kokayty) and about 1950 by Lyal'mikar. Some of the Surkhan Dar'ya oil is relatively high in bitumen and suitable for use as road oil. The Lyal'mikar deposit also yields gas for local consumption.

The natural gas development of the Bukhara region has also been associated with some oil production. In 1966 this amounted to 350,000 tons, or 20 percent of Uzbekistan's total petroleum output, which ranged from 1.7 to 1.8 million tons in the 1960s.

Uzbekistan is the only Central Asian republic with a relatively economical coal-mining production, originating at the head of the Angren River valley east of Tashkent. The deposit of 2.8 billion tons of poorly transportable subbituminous coal was explored in the late 1930s, and the first commercial coal was produced in 1942. Mining was at first from small underground mines, but in 1948 the first open-cut mine was put into operation, and production increased rapidly thereafter, yielding more than 4 million tons a year since 1960 and exceeding the combined output of all the Fergana Valley mines. One-fourth of Angren coal is mined underground and three-fourths in open-cut mines.

Because Angren coal crumbles rapidly in transportation, it is used most effectively in local power generation. A large steam power station, Uzbekistan's largest at the time, went into operation at Angren in 1957 after four years of construction, and reached its designed capacity of 600,000 kilowatts in 1963. Surface mining was expanded in 1968 by construction of a tunnel diverting the Angren River from coal seams, and the quality of the coal was to be improved by beneficiation in a plant with a capacity of 4.5 million tons a year.

Further development of the Angren mining complex also hinges on the utilization of the kaolin overburden as a source of alumina for manufacturing aluminum. The Soviet Union has been experimenting for years with processes that convert clays into alumina and a pilot plant was under construction in the late 1960s at Akhangaran to experiment with the production of alumina from kaolin, yielding high-grade cement and, possibly, rare-metal components of the kaolin as by-products. If successful, this project would yield an alumina source far closer to the Regar aluminum plant, under construction in the Tadzhik SSR, than the Urals and Transcaucasian suppliers envisaged for the early period of aluminum production at Regar.

An attempt has been made to develop a deposit of higher-grade bituminous coal in an underground mine at the Shargun' deposit, in the upper valley of the Surkhan Dar'ya, 15 miles from the prospective Regar aluminum plant. The small coal-mining town of Takchiyan was built in the early 1950s and production from the mine began in 1958. It reached 160,000 tons in 1965, with some of the coal (37,000 tons) formed into briquettes for sale in the adjoining Tadzhik SSR. A production increase to 300,000 tons of coal, two-thirds in the form of briquettes, was planned for 1970.

## ELECTRIC POWER

Before the construction of Uzbekistan's first major steam power station, at Angren, hydroelectric stations accounted for more than half of the total installed generating capacity in the republic. The backbone of this system was a series of small hydroelectric stations built on the Chirchik River and Bozsu Canal, near Tashkent, beginning in the 1930s. By 1955 the combined installed capacity of the sixteen stations in the Chirchik–Bozsu system was 319,000 kilowatts. Another early hydroelectric station serving the industrialization effort in the late 1940s and early 1950s was the 126,000-kilowatt Farkhad station on the Syr Dar'ya at Bekabad (formerly spelled Begovat).

The construction of the 600,000-kilowatt Angren steam power station and of another coal-fed station at Fergana city, opened in 1956, inaugurated a new phase in Uzbek's electric power industry that was further promoted by the discovery of natural gas in the western desert. This phase involved the construction of large gas-fed power stations with generating capacities of millions of kilowatts. Larger boilers and turbine generators, increased plant size, and outdoor construction made possible by the warmer winters of Central Asia have resulted in lower capital and operating costs. The first gas-fueled station opened in 1961 at Navoi, a new town, whose chemical industry was also fostered by natural gas. By 1968, the Navoi power station had an installed capacity of 600,000 kilowatts, to be raised to 900,000 kilowatts in the early 1970s.

The gas pipelines from Bukhara fields also feed a major power station at Tashkent. The first unit of this installation, planned to reach 1.92 million kilowatts, went into operation in 1963. A capacity of 1,280,000 kilowatts (eight 160,000 units) was installed by mid-1968.

The largest gas-fed power complex in this region is under construction on the Syr Dar'ya near Bekabad. Its first section of two 300,000-kilowatt turbines is planned to go into operation in the early 1970s. A new town called Shirin was under construction at the station site. When completed, with a capacity of 4.4 million kilowatts, the power plant is expected to consume 6 billion cubic meters of gas annually.

The expansion of electric power generation after the late 1950s was associated with the linking up of previously isolated power grids. The Tashkent and Fergana systems were joined in 1959 via the Kayrakkum hydroelectric station, completed two years earlier on the Syr Dar'ya in the Tadzhik section of the Fergana Valley. In 1961 the Tashkent system was linked with Samarkand, and in the following years high-voltage transmission lines progressed westward toward Bukhara, Chardzhou, and into Turkmenia.

An effort was made to improve the power supply in areas not to be linked immediately with the unified grid, for example, the Khiva oasis and the Kara-Kalpak ASSR in the lower reaches of the Amu Dar'ya. At Takhiatash, on the site of the headworks of the abandoned Turkmen Canal project, a steam power station was opened in 1961, supplying electricity to the nearby towns of Khodzheyli and Nukus, and the more distant Khiva oasis centers of Tashauz and Urgench. Four units of 12,000 kilowatts each were installed between 1961 and 1964. Two additional generators of 100,000 kilowatts each were mounted in 1967 and 1969 to raise the station's capacity to about 250,000 kilowatts.

In keeping with the program of developing the hydroelectric potential of the Tien Shan mountain system, a number of projects are also envisaged for the outliers extending into the Uzbek SSR, in the basin of the upper Chirchik and its left head stream, the Chatkal. The first major station in this system, the Charvak plant with a planned capacity of 600,000 kilowatts (four units of 150,000 kilowatts) has been under construction since 1963 at the confluence of the Chatkal and Pskem rivers, which form the Chirchik. The Charvak dam and hydroelectric station are a multipurpose water-management project. Its huge reservoir, with a capacity of 2 billion cubic meters, is expected to regulate stream flow along the Chirchik River, prevent floods, and provide a more stable supply of water for irrigation. By increasing the flow of water in the normally dry winter season, the Charvak project is also expected to raise the generating capacity of the Chirchik–Bozsu system by 150,000 kilowatts. Completion of the Charvak station is planned for the early 1970s.

Long-range plans call for the construction of additional power stations with a combined capacity of 1.5 million kilowatts along the Pskem and Chatkal rivers. The upper Chatkal valley is now politically part of the Kirghiz SSR, though oriented toward the Tashkent area. It is possible that, for the purpose of Uzbek hydroelectric development, the upper reaches of the Chatkal may be ceded to Uzbekistan, as the valley of the Pskem River was ceded by Kazakhstan in 1956. The next project after the Charvak station is expected to be the 80,000-kilowatt Khodzhikent hydroelectric plant, just below the Charvak site.

## MINERAL INDUSTRIES

Mineral mining and processing industries have developed since World War II around the Almalyk–Akhangaran complex, situated southeast of Tashkent on the Uzbek slopes of the Kurama Mountains. The complex consists of the merging towns of Almalyk, a nonferrous-metals center with a population of 73,000 in 1967, and the cement-milling town of Akhangaran (1967 population: 22,000), which thus form an urbanized zone with a population of 100,000.

Development began in the late 1940s. The first mineral sites to go into operation were the lead–zinc mines of Kurgashinkan and Altyn-Topkan, on the Tadzhik slopes of the Kurama Mountains. The mining settlement of Altyn-Topkan, founded in 1951, reached a population of 6,500 by 1959. Though situated politically within the Tadzhik SSR, the lead–zinc mines shipped their ore for concentration to the Uzbek side by aerial ropeway. The lead–zinc mining center of Altyn-Topkan actually gave its name to the entire operation on both sides of the mountain although the city of Almalyk contained the major processing plants. Lead concentrates from the Almalyk concentrator were sent to the smelter at Chimkent in southern Kazakhstan, and the zinc concentrates to the Konstantinovka refinery in the Ukrainian Donets Basin. However, with the availability of more and cheaper electric power in the Tashkent area, an electrolytic zinc refinery was being added to the Almalyk complex in the late 1960s to eliminate the long haul of concentrates to the Ukraine.

While zinc–lead ore was being mined predominantly on the Tadzhik side of the mountains, a large deposit of copper–molybdenum ore was developed in the late 1950s at the Kalmakyr mine, on the Uzbek side, near Almalyk. A copper concentrator opened there in 1961, a smelter in 1963, and an electrolytic copper refinery in 1964. The cycle was to be completed in the late 1960s, with the installation of a rolling mill.

As part of further diversification of the Almalyk complex, a chemical fertilizer industry was added in the late 1960s. The production of sulfuric acid, utilizing smelter by-product gases, was inaugurated in late 1967 in preparation for the start of manufacture of concentrated ammonium phosphate fertilizer by 1970. The Almalyk product, manufactured from phosphoric acid (derived from Karatau phosphate and local sulfuric acid) in combination with Chirchik ammonia, will contain 46 percent available $P_2O_5$ and 11 percent nitrogen.

The Akhangaran cement mill, opened in 1961, more than doubled Uzbek cement output from 1.2 million tons in 1960 to 2.6 million tons in 1966. The town has been selected for the pilot plant that will experiment with the conversion of kaolin, from the overburden of the Angren coal mines, into alumina. The process yields 10 tons of cement as a by-product for every ton of alumina.

In addition to being produced in association with copper at Almalyk, molybdenum is also being mined together with tungsten in three mines developed during World War II in Samarkand Oblast and expanded in the 1950s. They are Koytash, in the Nura-Tau mountains; Lyangar, in the Ak-Tau mountains, north of the Zeravshan valley; and Ingichka, south of the valley. Tungsten concentrates from these mines, as well as molybdenum concentrates from Almalyk, are refined and manufactured into high-temperature alloys, wire, rods, sheets, and other end products at the Chirchik alloys plant, opened in 1956. By 1965 the Uzbek SSR was one of the Soviet Union's leading producers of tungsten and molybdenum.

Uzbekistan is also a major producer of fluorspar, the principal fluorine-bearing mineral, used as a flux in steel furnaces and for the production of hydrofluoric acid. The acid is used in the manufacture of synthetic cryolite, needed for aluminum electrolysis, as a catalyst in the production of high-octane gasoline, and in the processing of uranium. The fluorspar mill is situated at Toytepa (formerly spelled Toy-Tyube), halfway between Almalyk and Tashkent. One

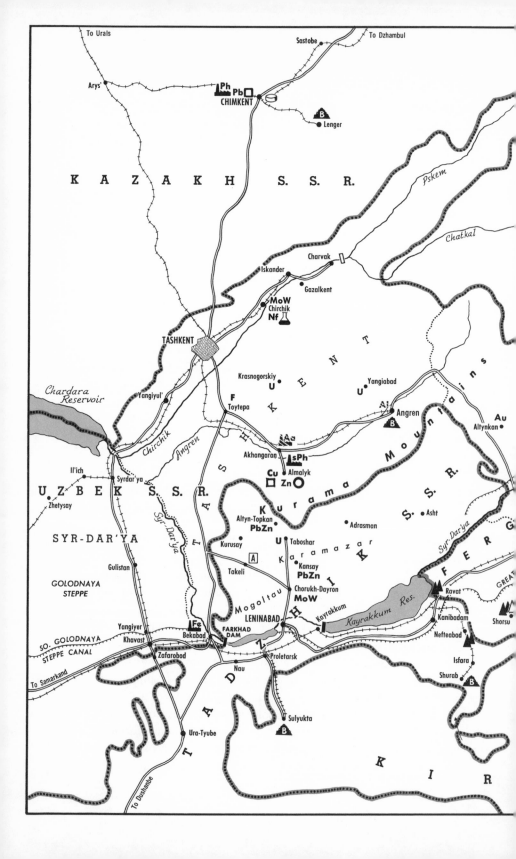

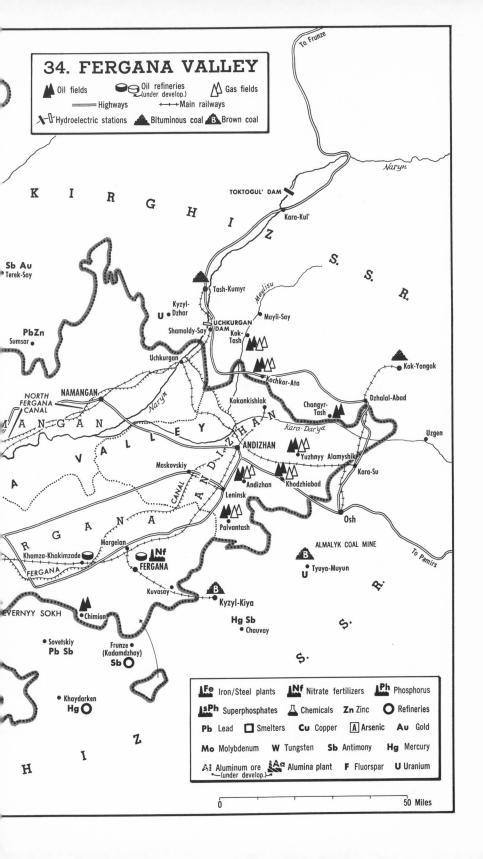

# 34. FERGANA VALLEY

| Oil fields | Oil refineries (under develop.) | Gas fields |
|---|---|---|
| Highways | Main railways | |
| Hydroelectric stations | Bituminous coal | Brown coal |

To Frunze

*Naryn*

K I R G H I Z    S. S. R.

TOKTOGUL' DAM

Kara-Kul'

**Sb Au**
Terek-Say

Tash-Kumyr

*Maylisu*

Kyzyl-Dzhar
**U**

Mayli-Say

UCHKURGAN DAM

Shamaldy-Say

Kok-Tash

**PbZn**
Sumsar

Uchkurgan

*Naryn*

Kok-Yangak

NORTH FERGANA CANAL

NAMANGAN

Kochkor-Ata

Kokankishlak

Changyr-Tash

Dzhalal-Abad

M A N G A N

*Kara-Darya*

Uzgen

A    V A L L E Y

ANDIZHAN

Yuzhnyy Alamyshik

Moskovskiy

Kara-Su

CANAL

ANDIZHAN

Andizhan

Khodzhiabad

R G A N A    A

Leninsk

Osh

Palvantash

A

Margelan

ALMALYK COAL MINE

Khamza-Khakimzade

**B**

**Nf**

FERGANA

**U** Tyuya-Muyun

FERGANA

To Pamirs

Kuvasay

**B**

EVERNYY SOKH

Chimion

Kyzyl-Kiya

**Hg Sb**

Chauvay

Sovetskiy
**Pb Sb**

Frunze (Kadamdzhay)
**Sb O**

R.

S.

Khaydarken
**Hg O**

S.

Z

H    I

| Fe Iron/Steel plants | Nf Nitrate fertilizers | Ph Phosphorus |
|---|---|---|
| sPh Superphosphates | Chemicals | Zn Zinc | O Refineries |
| Pb Lead | Smelters | Cu Copper | A Arsenic | Au Gold |
| Mo Molybdenum | W Tungsten | Sb Antimony | Hg Mercury |
| Al Aluminum ore (under develop.) | Ac Alumina plant | F Fluorspar | U Uranium |

0 _____ 50 Miles

of the mines supplying the mill, Naugarzan, opened in 1960, is situated on the Tadzhik side of the Kurama range and is reached by a 3-mile-long tunnel through the mountain.

To the extent that uranium-rich outliers of the Tien Shan system reach into Uzbek territory, the republic is one of the Soviet Union's producers of the nuclear fuel. Uranium mines are found in Uzbekistan on the southern slopes of two parallel mountain ranges, the Chatkal mountains, north of the Angren River, and the Kurama mountains, to the southeast. The principal uranium-mining and -concentrating center is Yangiabad, on the Chatkal slopes northwest of Angren. Founded in 1953, it reached a population of 9,500 by 1959. Under Yangiabad's jurisdiction is the uranium-mining town of Krasnogorskiy, 20 miles to the west, which was founded in 1955 and had a population of 7,800 in 1959. On the southern slopes of the Kurama mountains, facing the Fergana Valley, two smaller settlements have been associated with uranium mining. Uygursay, near the Syr Dar'ya, mined and concentrated uranium ore from 1947 to the mid-1950s when operations began at Charkesar, 15 miles northwest into the mountains. A rubber-goods factory was built in Uygursay in the late 1950s on the site of the former concentrator.

One of the Soviet Union's largest gold lode deposits was discovered in the Kyzyl Kum Desert in the late 1950s and was developed in subsequent years. The deposit is situated in Muruntau (41° 30′ N, 64° 15′ E), an outlier of the Tamdytau, a desert mountain range. A 180-mile-long railroad was built in the early 1960s from Navoi, the chemical center in the Zeravshan valley, northwestward into the desert gold field. There a huge open-cut mine was under construction in the late 1960s, and a miners' city, called Zarafshan (a variant form of the river name Zeravshan, meaning "gold-bearing") was being erected at a locality formerly called Sugraly. According to news reports, tall apartment buildings of nine and fourteen stories, presumably air-conditioned against the desert heat, are planned for the new town, and a 48-inch aqueduct was completed in 1969 from the Amu-Dar'ya, 130 miles away. The town of Zarafshan was officially inaugurated in January, 1967, and was expected to grow to a population of 40,000. Moscow reported the start of gold production at the concentrator in 1969.

A second major gold-lode deposit was under development in the late 1960s in the Fergana Valley, on the southern slopes of the Kurama Range, not far from the uranium mines of Charkesar. The lode deposit, situated in the Chadak area (40° 56′ N, 70° 45′ E), is to be worked both by open-pit (in the Guzaksay section) and underground (in the Pirmirab section) operations. A concentrator was under construction at the new town of Altynkan, which was officially inaugurated as a workers' settlement in late 1966.

Uzbekistan also has a small steel plant, the only one in the Central Asian republics. Built during World War II at Bekabad and put into operation in 1946 without having a local iron-ore supply, the plant uses mainly scrap and some long-haul pig iron. With an annual production of 400,000 tons of crude steel and 250,000 tons of rolled products, the small Bekabad plant meets only 15 to 20 percent of the steel needs of the four Central Asian republics and southern Kazakhstan. The rest must be shipped in from the Urals, Siberia, and the Ukraine.

### CHEMICAL INDUSTRIES

Until the discovery of the natural-gas resources, Uzbekistan's chemical industry consisted mainly of three fertilizer plants, one at Chirchik, producing nitrogenous fertilizer, and two small superphosphate plants at Kokand and Samarkand. The Chirchik plant, opened in 1940 and expanded in 1944, was the only Soviet installation in which hydrogen for ammonia synthesis was obtained from water by electrolysis. By 1955, it produced about 500,000 tons of ammonium nitrate and other nitrogen-based chemicals a year. Chirchik was converted to the use of hydrogen from natural gas in 1961 after the pipeline from the Dzharkak gas field had reached the Tashkent area, and the plant was expanded on the basis of the new gas source. The superphosphate plant at Kokand was opened in 1946, on the basis of a primitive fertilizer-mixing plant and additional equipment evacuated during the war from the Neva superphosphate plant in Leningrad and the Voskresensk plant near Moscow. The Samarkand plant, situated in the suburb named Superfosfatnyy, began operations in 1955. Both used phosphate rock from the Karatau deposit in southern Kazakhstan.

The opening of a new oil refinery at Fergana city in 1958 led four years later to the operation of an associated nitrogenous fertilizer plant, which obtains its hydrogen as a by-product of petroleum refining and from natural gas piped from the Fergana Valley fields. The Fergana plant added the manufacture of magnesium chlorate, a defoliant and drying agent, in 1965, and expanded its nitrogenous fertilizer capacity in early 1969 with the addition of an ammonium nitrate department.

A second fertilizer plant, opened in 1965 at Navoi (called Kermine until 1958), was related directly to the development of the natural-gas resources of the western desert. The Navoi chemical complex derives its hydrogen for ammonia synthesis from the natural gas brought by the Dzharkak pipelines. It also uses natural gas for the manufacture of acetylene, with cotton linters the basic raw material for cellulose acetate, and acrylonitrile, the raw material of the acrylic fiber called nitron. The nitron is to be manufactured at Navoi itself, which had a population of 27,000 in 1967 and continued to expand. The cellulose acetate is used for the manufacture of acetate rayon at an 800-ton mill at Namangan (dating from the late 1940s) and at a second mill that was completed at Fergana in the late 1960s.

Total fertilizer production in Uzbekistan rose from 634,000 tons in 1955 (including about 140,000 tons of phosphate fertilizer) to 2.1 million tons in 1965 (including 500,000 tons of phosphate). By the late 1960s, with the expansion of the Fergana and Navoi plants, the republic was to be self-sufficient in nitrogenous fertilizers for its important cotton crop. However, superphosphate needs were only partly covered by local production. In fact, the 1970 plan envisaged a cutback of superphosphate production to 300,000 tons (compared with 3.5 million tons of nitrogenous fertilizers).

IRRIGATION PROJECTS

In the agricultural field, the most spectacular development was the expansion of cotton growing in the Golodnaya (Hunger) Steppe. Opening up the area, on the left bank of the Syr Dar'ya, southwest of Tashkent, began in the 1920s with construction of the Kirov irrigation canal. In the mid-1950s a program of expansion to open additional parts of the area to settlement began. The South Golodnaya Steppe Canal, running westward from the Farkhad hydroelectric station near Bekabad, was inaugurated over a 50-mile-long section in 1960 and later extended to the Dzhizak area. The new town of Yangiyer (meaning "new land"), built as the headquarters of the reclamation project, has a population of about 15,000. The 75-mile-long Syrdar'ya–Dzhizak railroad, opened in 1962, provided a shortcut for rail traffic between Tashkent and Samarkand and, at the same time, provided an access route to interior sections of the Golodnaya Steppe yet to be reclaimed.

To reflect the development of the new area in political–administrative terms, a new oblast, Syrdar'ya, was established in 1963, combining the entire Golodnaya Steppe, previously divided between Kazakhstan and Uzbekistan, in a single political unit. The agricultural-processing center of Gulistan (known as Mirzachul until 1961) was made its capital.

Another Uzbek area envisaged for a major expansion of cotton production is the Karshi Steppe, on the right bank of the Amu Dar'ya. This development, involving construction of the great Talimardzhan reservoir, is dependent on completion of the Nurek hydroelectric station, which is planned to assure both a steady year-round water supply and electric power for pumping Amu Dar'ya water to the Karshi Steppe. In preparation for expansion of the Karshi area, a 90-mile-long railroad between Samarkand and Karshi was under construction in the late 1960s to provide a more direct link with the Tashkent area and the Fergana Valley.

## Kirghiz SSR

The Kirghiz SSR, or Kirghizia, has been the Soviet Union's principal producer of antimony and mercury metal, one of the nation's main sources of uranium ore and concentrates, and a major supplier of steam coal for Central Asia, particularly the Fergana Valley. Development plans in the late 1960s called for further expansion of the nonferrous metal industries, continued coal production at a level of about 4 million tons annually, and the gradual development of a major hydroelectric potential in the Tien Shan mountain system, which covers most of the territory of the republic.

A major part of its population and economic activities (agriculture and manufacturing) is concentrated in two lowland areas separated by the outliers of the Tien Shan. In the north is the Chu Valley, an irrigated area of diversified agriculture (grains, sugar beets, bast fibers), with a large Russian and Ukrainian population, and most of the republic's manufacturing. In the southwest are the Kirghiz fringes of the Fergana Valley, with cotton production and important Uzbek and Russian population elements. The republic's capital, Frunze (1967 population: 396,000), is the principal city of the Chu Valley. Kirghizia's second and third cities, Osh (1967 population: 119,000) and Dzhalal-Abad (1967 population: 42,000), are the regional centers of the Fergana Valley section. The Kirghiz, traditionally a herding people, of Turkic speech, are the principal ethnic element in the intermontane basins of the Tien Shan, of which the Issyk-Kul basin is the most important.

## ELECTRIC POWER

Some of these basins are expected to be partly flooded by the major hydroelectric developments envisaged for the republic. They are to be situated mainly along the Naryn River (a headstream of the Syr Dar'ya) and its tributary, the Kokomoren, with an estimated hydroelectric potential of 4 million kilowatts. The first power station in the Naryn series, the Uchkurgan hydroelectric plant, was completed in 1961–62 on the border of the Uzbek SSR, where the Naryn River issues from the mountains and enters the Fergana Valley. Originally planned for a capacity of 112,000 kilowatts when construction began in 1956, the station was soon redesigned for a capacity of 180,000 kilowatts (four 45,000 units). The town of Shamaldy-Say (1959 population: 4,500) arose at the station site. The Uchkurgan plant has been linked with the Fergana power system and has helped improve the power supply for both the Kirghiz margins and the central Uzbek section of the Fergana Valley.

The next project of the Naryn series, the Toktogul' station, has been under construction since 1963 at the new town of Kara-Kul', 40 miles northeast of the Uchkurgan station. The first 300,000-kilowatt generating unit of a planned capacity of 1.2 million kilowatts is scheduled to go into operation in 1971. The Toktogul' dam will create a lake in the Ketmen'-Tyube intermontane basin, a small farming and sheep-raising area, with a population of 30,000. The reservoir of 14 million acre-feet is expected to play a major role in regulating the flow of the Naryn River to maintain a year-round level needed for irrigation in the Fergana Valley and other cotton-growing areas downriver. The Toktogul' power station will be connected by a 500-kilovolt transmission line with Frunze and Dzhambul as part of a high-voltage grid linking the principal power-producing and consuming centers of Central Asia.

During the late 1960s, design work was going forward on the next station in the Naryn system, the Susamyr hydroelectric plant of 300,000 kilowatts, which would flood part of the Susamyr valley, an intermontane basin used as summer pasture. Next, in order of priority, is to be the design of the Kokomeren station (700,000 kilowatts), below the Susamyr dam, and the Kurpsay plant (500,-000 kilowatts), below the Toktogul' project.

A small project under construction in the late 1960s was the 40,000-kilowatt Atbashi station, on the Atbashi River (a left tributary of the upper Naryn River). The workers' settlement of Dostuk was inaugurated in 1968 at the project site, 25 miles southeast of the town of Naryn.

Until 1960, the principal power-generating complex of the Kirghiz SSR was a series of six small hydroelectric stations on the Chu irrigation canal in the Chu Valley, serving the manufacturing industry around Frunze. The last two stations in this series were opened in 1958, raising the combined generating capacity to about 20,000 kilowatts. In 1960, this system accounted for a little more than half of the republic's total power output of 870 million kilowatt-hours.

The power system of the Chu Valley was clearly inadequate to support industrial expansion and construction began on a heat and power plant in Frunze. The first 25,000 kilowatt-unit was inaugurated in 1961. The station reached a capacity of 200,000 kilowatts in 1963. Four 50,000-kilowatt units were added, one a year, from 1965 to 1968, raising the capacity to 400,000 kilowatts, and making the Frunze heat and power station the largest electricity producer of Kirghizia. An additional section with a capacity of 400,000 kilowatts is planned. In addition to the Chu Valley and the Issyk-Kul' basin, the Frunze station supplies power to the Naryn valley via a 110-kilovolt transmission line inaugurated in 1968. A 220-kilovolt transmission system connecting the Frunze power grid with

Alma-Ata and with Dzhambul was under construction in the late 1960s.

Until 1958, the Kirghiz SSR was Central Asia's largest producer of coal, supplying steam power stations in the Fergana Valley, other parts of Central Asia, and southern Kazakhstan. In that year, the Uzbek SSR took the lead in coal output with the rapidly expanding open-cut production at Angren.

Most of Kirghizia's coal mines are situated on the margins of the Fergana Valley and are served by rail spurs leading from the valley's railroad loop. Most of the coals are subbituminous, especially along the southern valley margins, changing to bituminous in the east. Predominantly underground mining adds to the cost of the relatively low-grade fuel and makes its use economical only at local power stations. Coal production doubled from 1.85 million tons in 1950 to 3.7 million tons in 1965, as new mines were opened in existing coal centers. Production has shifted slightly since 1957 to surface mines. About 22 percent of the 1965 output was produced by open-cut mines.

The two subbituminous coal centers on the southern margins of the Fergana Valley are Sulyukta (1967 population: 24,000) and Kyzyl-Kiya (1967 population: 36,000). Output at Sulyukta has been declining as expansion has been hampered by the low carrying capacity of the narrow-gauge rail spur that links the town to the Fergana Valley main line at Proletarsk. Kyzyl-Kiya, like the other Kirghiz coal towns situated on a wide-gauge spur, has been expanding. An underground mine, Dzhin-Dzhigan, with an annual capacity of 450,000 tons, was opened in 1964, increasing Kyzyl-Kiya output by almost 50 percent, and a 300,000-ton open-cut mine, Abshir, was added in 1967–68. On the outer margins of the Kyzyl-Kiya coal field, 30 miles eastward, a 180,000-ton open-cut mine went into operation in 1962 at Almalyk. This surface mine is situated in the area of the uranium-processing center of Tyuya-Muyun, 15 miles southwest of Osh.

Production in the two eastern coal centers of Kok-Yangak (1967 population: 18,000) and Tash-Kumyr (1967 population: 20,000), where coal is of bituminous grade, also expanded in the 1960s. At

Kok-Yangak, the 200,000-ton Sary-Bulak mine went into operation in 1960, raising the existing mining capacity at Kok-Yangak by about 30 percent, from 600,000 tons to 800,000 tons. At Tash-Kumyr, about half of the total production of 1 million tons originates in the Karasu open-cut, which began production in 1957. Less than 100,-000 tons of coal are produced at small isolated mines in the mountainous part of Kirghizia, including the 30,000-ton underground coal mine of Dzhergalan, east of Lake Issyk-Kul', which supplies the needs of the nearby town of Przheval'sk.

Oil and natural-gas production is of limited importance, with small reserves between the regional center of Dzhalal-Abad and the former uranium center of Mayli-Say along the eastern margins of the Fergana Valley. Oil was struck in the late 1930s at Changyrtash, 10 miles west of Dzhalal-Abad, but this site never yielded more than 25,000 tons of crude oil a year and was exhausted by the mid-1960s. In the early 1950s, additional deposits were explored farther west along the Mayli-Say River (or Mayli-Su), raising hopes for an upsurge in production. However, oil output in the new towns of Koktash and Kochkor-Ata dropped to about 300,000 tons in 1965 after having reached a peak of 490,000 tons in 1958.

Natural-gas reserves in the area are estimated at 7.3 billion cubic meters. A pipeline from the Mayli-Su field was laid to Dzhalal-Abad in 1964 and extended to Osh, the other regional center, the following year. Gas production was approaching 300 million cubic meters in 1968.

With natural-gas production within Kirghizia remaining negligible, the industries of the Chu Valley looked to the arrival of gas from the Bukhara fields as a source of electric power and an industrial raw material. A 32-inch pipeline under construction in the late 1960s reached Dzhambul in 1968 and was scheduled to arrive at Frunze in late 1969. Natural gas may furnish the raw material for a proposed nitrogenous fertilizer plant at Kosh-Tegirmen, a new uranium-processing town just south of Kara-Balty.

### MINERALS

Kirghizia is the Soviet Union's leading producer of antimony and mercury, which sometimes occur in conjunction with fluorspar. The principal deposits are found along the northern foothills of the Alay mountain range, which extends along the southern margins of the Fergana Valley. Antimony metal has been produced since the late 1930s by the Kadamdzhay smelter at the town of Frunze (1959 population: 4,776), which is situated 20 miles south of Fergana city and is not to be confused with the Kirghiz capital in the Chu Valley. Mercury metal has been produced since World War II by a smelter at Khaydarken (formerly spelled Khaydarkan), which had a population of 8,254 in 1959. Khaydarken added a concentrator for antimony and flourspar in 1968. A second mercury smelter and a large open-cut mine were under development at a cinnabar deposit in the Ulug-Too (or Ulug-Tau) hills, 15 miles northeast of Kyzyl- Kiya. Another mineral development on the southern margins of the Fergana Valley is centered at the mining town of Sovetskiy (1959 population: 2,142), 15 miles north of Khaydarken. At Sovetskiy, the Kan mine, opened in 1952, produces lead ore, and the Kamil-Say mine, opened in 1964, antimony in combination with lead.

On the northern margins of the Fergana Valley, on the south slopes of the Chatkal Range, lead is mined at Sumsar and antimony, in combination with gold, at Terek-Say. Both mines were developed in the early 1950s and a concentrator was under construction at Terek-Say in the late 1960s.

All the mines around the Fergana Valley are combined administratively in Kirghizia's Southern mining and metallurgical complex. The republic's so-called Kirghiz mining and metallurgical complex includes mineral and smelter operations in the northern part of Kirghizia around the Chu Valley. They include lead mines and concentrators at Ak-Tyuz and Bordunskiy, near the valley's eastern end, from where the concentrates are sent to the lead smelter at Chimkent in southern Kazakhstan, as well as uranium operations.

Kirghizia is one of the Soviet Union's leading sources of uranium. Soviet sources are not explicit on the location of mines and processing plants, but indirect evidence suggests the following distribution. A uranium-processing center is believed to operate on the site of an old mine of radioactive ores at Tyuya-Muyun, 15 miles southwest of Osh. Other early uranium-mining centers, both founded in 1947, were Mayli-Say (1967 population: 23,000), on the eastern margin of the Fergana Valley, and Kadzhi-Say (1967 population: 5,922), on the southern shore of Lake Issyk-Kul. Uranium reserves at these two centers became depleted in the early 1960s and electrical-equipment industries were introduced to provide employment and to make use of the available housing and plant facilities. One of the largest Soviet light-bulb factories opened at Mayli-Say in 1966, and an electronics plant producing transistors and other silicon products was placed in operation at Kadzhi-Say. A nearby brown-coal mine, the Tsentral'naya, yields 100,000 tons a year.

Uranium production now appears to be concentrated at the town of Min-Kush, founded in 1953 (1959 population: 10,907), in a tributary valley of the Kokomeren River in the Tien Shan. The ore is trucked for further processing to a mill at Kosh-Tegirmen (1959 population: 7,921), in the Chu Valley west of Frunze.

## Tadzhik SSR

Traditionally a supplier of cotton, dried fruits, and non-ferrous metal concentrates, the Tadzhik SSR, or Tadzhikistan, is developing into one of the Soviet Union's major producers of hydroelectric power. This newly developed resource, in turn, is attracting aluminum, chemicals, and other industries oriented toward cheap power availability.

Delimited on the basis of the settlement area of the Tadzhiks, a Muslim land-tilling people of Iranian language stock, the republic has a convoluted outline that extends from the Fergana Valley in the north to the Pamir highlands in the southeast. The principal economic and population areas are the Tadzhik (western) section of the Fergana Valley, focused on Leninabad, the republic's second largest city (1967 population: 100,000), and the valleys of southwestern Tadzhikistan, centered on the capital of the republic, Dushanbe (the former Stalinabad), with a 1967 population of 333,000. These two areas, which comprise almost all of Tadzhikistan's 2.3 million people, are separated by a series of transverse mountain ranges, the Turkestan, Zeravshan, and Gissar mountains, that form a significant climatic barrier and an obstacle to north–south transportation. The isolated Pamir highlands, with a sparse population of 85,000, mainly stockraising mountain tribesmen, play a minor role in the republic's economy.

Tadzhikistan's mountain streams flow in narrow gorges with occasional valley expansions that provide suitable sites for large power stations and their reservoirs. The large hydroelectric projects that are expected to shape the future economy are planned on the Vakhsh and Pyandzh (Panj) rivers, headstreams of the Amu Dar'ya. The total potential capacity of stations that could be built on these rivers and their tributaries has been estimated at 16 million kilowatts, or about half of the hydroelectric reserves of the republic. In addition to their generating capacity, the proposed projects will be a substantial aid to irrigation in the Amu Dar'ya basin by storing the increased summer runoff from melting mountain glaciers for use in the low-water period of autumn, winter, and spring. The deep gorge reservoirs are also expected to retain river sediments that normally clog irrigation systems farther downstream.

The first major hydroelectric station, under construction since 1961, is the Nurek project, 40 miles southeast of Dushanbe. The first of nine planned units, each generating 300,000 kilowatts, is scheduled to go into operation by 1971, with full capacity of 2.7 million kilowatts to be reached in the mid-1970s. A 1,000-foot-high dam of gravel and cobble fill on a concrete foundation has been designed to be resistant to local earthquakes. The reservoir, with a capacity of 8.8 million acre-feet will store water in the April–September period, accounting for 80 percent of the annual runoff, and discharge the stored water during the low-water stage in October–March. The regulation of the stream flow is expected to provide more water during winter for smaller hydroelectric stations farther downstream, eliminate extreme fluctuations in the level of the Amu Dar'ya, and improve the supply of irrigation water along the lower course of the river.

Construction of the Nurek station is to be followed in the 1970s by the 3.2-million-kilowatt Ragun (or Rogun) hydroelectric plant, 50 miles northeast of Nurek, just below the point where the Obi-Khingou and Surkhob rivers join to form the Vakhsh. Of eight potential hydroelectric power generating sites along the Pyandzh River, on the Soviet–Afghan border, priority is to be given to the Dashtidzhum project, with a capacity of 4.3 million kilowatts.

The principal industrial consumers of Nurek power will be an aluminum plant with a capacity of 200,000 tons, under construction at Regar, and an electrochemical complex based on salt and limestone deposits, which is being built at Yavan. The two installations are to be linked with the Nurek station by a 500-kilovolt transmission line, which is to be extended in the early 1970s to the Tashkent area via Samarkand.

The aluminum plant at Regar, a town of 15,000 before construction started in 1965, is situated at the western end of the Gissar valley, a broad depression that provided a convenient access route for a railroad to Dushanbe in the late 1920s. At least in the foreseeable future, the Regar aluminum plant will use long-haul alumina from the Urals and possibly from newly developed alumina sources in Transcaucasia, and ship most of its aluminum output to manufacturing centers in European Russia. Although a deposit of nephelite–syenite is known at Turpi, near Tadzhikabad, 150 miles northeast of Regar, it has not been sufficiently explored and is too remote to be a factor in short-range economic planning. There are plans to use the kaolin deposits of Angren, near Tashkent, as a source of alumina, but the technology of extracting alumina from kaolin still remains to be perfected before the Angren deposit will become of commercial significance.

The Yavan electrochemical complex, expected to give rise to an industrial town with a population of 100,000, will produce a wide range of chemicals based on local dolomite and salt deposits. The electrolysis of dolomite, containing a relatively high percentage of magnesium chloride, and of common salt (sodium chloride) would yield soda ash, magnesium metal, chlorine, and their derivatives. The start of production of the first unit, making calcium carbide, is planned for 1973.

The Yavan valley was an isolated dry steppe used for stockraising. In conjunction with the proposed industrial and irrigation development of the valley, provision had to be made for water and transportation. Water was obtained through a 5-mile-long tunnel completed in the spring of 1968 through the Karatau mountain range, which separates the Vakhsh from the Yavan valley, to the west. Water is diverted into the tunnel by the Baypazy diversion dam, 20 miles below the Nurek project.

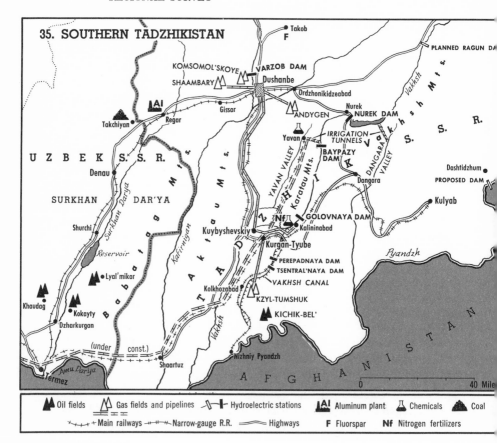

35. SOUTHERN TADZHIKISTAN

Takob F

PLANNED RAGUN DA

KOMSOMOL'SKOYE VARZOB DAM

SHAAMBARY Dushanbe

Ordzhonikidzeabad

Gissar

ANDYGEN

Nurek NUREK DAM

Takchiyan

Regar

IRRIGATION TUNNELS

Yavan

BAYPAZY DAM

UZBEK S. S. R.

Denau

Dashtidzhum

PROPOSED DAM

SURKHAN DAR'YA

Dangara

Kulyab

Shurchi

Kuybyshevskiy

GOLOVNAYA DAM

Kalininabad

Kurgan-Tyube

Reservoir

Pyandzh

Lyal'mikar

Kolkhozabad

PEREPADNAYA DAM

TSENTRAL'NAYA DAM

VAKHSH CANAL

KZYL-TUMSHUK

Khaudag

Kokayty

Dzharkurgan

KICHIK-BEL'

(under const.)

Shaartuz

Nizhniy Pyandzh

AFGHANISTAN

0    40 Mile

Termez

Oil fields   Gas fields and pipelines   Hydroelectric stations   Al Aluminum plant   Chemicals   Coal

Main railways   Narrow-gauge R.R.   Highways   F Fluorspar   Nf Nitrogen fertilizers

The provision of water to the Yavan valley was an essential preliminary not only for the planned irrigation of cotton, but also for the construction of a gas-fueled power station for the electrochemical complex. The first 60,000-kilowatt unit of the Yavan heat and power station was planned to go into operation in 1969 after completion of a pipeline from natural-gas fields near Dushanbe.

In planning a railroad to the valley, Soviet planners considered two alternatives: a relatively short extension from the nearby railhead at Ordzhonikidzeabad over difficult mountain terrain, or a considerably longer route from Termez that would pass over more level ground. Although the estimated cost of both routes was virtually the same, the second alternative was chosen, mainly because it would pass through the cotton-rich Vakhsh valley.

Despite its significance as the Soviet Union's leading producer of long-staple cotton, the Vakhsh valley has lacked a direct link with the national broad-gauge rail system. The valley has been served both by trucking services and by a narrow-gauge rail system. A narrow-gauge railroad was built in 1929–31 between Kurgan-Tyube, the main town of the valley (1967 population: 31,000), and Nizhniy Pyandzh, on the Pyandzh River frontier with Afghanistan. A northward extension to Dushanbe was completed in 1941, and an eastward extension, from Kurgan-Tyube to Kulyab, in 1957. The new broad-gauge railroad to Yavan, under construction in the late 1960s, runs from Termez eastward along the Amu Dar'ya, through Shaartuz and up the Vakhsh valley through Kurgan-Tyube to Yavan. It is expected gradually to eliminate the need for the present narrow-gauge system after completion about 1973.

The Yavan electrochemical complex, associated with the Nurek power plant, will not be the first power-oriented chemical installation in the Tadzhik SSR. A nitrogenous fertilizer plant went into operation in 1967 at Kalininabad, a town on the Vakhsh River, 10 miles east of Kurgan-Tyube. Kalininabad was founded in 1956 in conjunction with the start of construction on the Golovnaya (=head, headworks) hydroelectric station, at the head of the Vakhsh valley irrigation system. The 210,000-kilowatt station, which went into operation in 1962–63 with six 35,000-kilowatt units, provides power for Dushanbe and southern Tadzhikistan, including the Kalininabad chemical plant, which produces ammonia, urea, and other nitrogenous fertilizers, deriving hydrogen for ammonia synthesis from natural gas.

The first natural-gas deposit has been developed at Kzyl-Tumshuk, near Kolkhozabad (until 1957, Kaganovichabad), and a 70-mile-long pipeline was completed to Dushanbe in 1964. The Kzyl-Tumshuk gas field was reported to have limited reserves, estimated at 3.4 billion cubic meters, but larger reserves were discovered subsequently in the foothills of the Gissar range around Dushanbe.

The Komsomol'skoye gas field, on the northern outskirts of Dushanbe, went into operation in 1966. It was followed in 1968 by the Shaambary field, west of Dushanbe, where gas is associated with oil, and the Andygen gas field, southeast of Dushanbe. Gas transmission lines from Shaambary and Andygen to Dushanbe raised total output from 52 million cubic meters in 1965 to 350 million in 1968. If Tadzhik gas resources prove inadequate for the growing chemical industry, they are to be reinforced by natural gas from the Afghan field at Shibarghan via the proposed Kelif-Yavan transmission line.

Earlier electric power developments in Tadzhikistan were intended to serve mines and concentrating plants as well as manufacturing industries in the major urban centers. Two power grids took shape in the 1950s in the southern and northern parts of the republic.

Southern Tadzhikistan is supplied by a series of hydroelectric stations on the Varzob River, a mountain stream running south from the Gissar range past Dushanbe, and on the lower Vakhsh River. The 7,200-kilowatt Upper Varzob station was built in 1935–36; the 14,800-kilowatt Lower Varzob No. 2 station was completed in 1949–51, and the 3,500-kilowatt Lower Varzob No. 3 in 1952–54. Their total capacity is thus 25,500 kilowatts.

The lower Vakhsh system includes, in addition to the 210,000-kilowatt Golovnaya, two small stations on the Vakhsh irrigation canal—the Perepadnaya (30,000 kilowatts; completed in 1958) and the Tsentral'naya (18,000 kilowatts; completed in 1964).

To eliminate seasonal fluctuations in the power supply of the Varzob–Vakhsh system, entirely dependent on water power, a thermal power station was opened in Dushanbe in 1957. Originally based on long-haul steam coals from Angren and Shurab, the 218,000-kilowatt Dushanbe station was partly converted to gas when the pipeline from the Kzyl-Tumshuk field opened in 1964. The power plant had an original capacity of 12,000 kilowatts (two 6,000-kilowatt units) in 1957. A second stage of two 25,000-kilowatt units was added in 1962, followed by a third 6,000-kilowatt generator in 1963. A third stage of 50,000 kilowatts was inaugurated in 1964, and a fourth of 100,000 kilowatts in 1966. The total capacity of the Varzob–Dushanbe–Vakhsh system was thus raised to 500,000 kilowatts.

This power grid serves mineral centers north of Dushanbe. They include Takob, a fluorspar-mining town founded in 1950, which also processes tungsten–tin and lead–zinc ores. The tungsten ore comes from the Maykhura and Dzhilau mines on the southern slopes of the Zeravshan valley near Pendzhikent. Another mineral center is the town of Zeravshan, founded in 1952, where antimony associated with mercury is mined and concentrated in the Dzhizhikrut complex. An antimony smelter was under construction there in the late 1960s.

The principal electric power source in northern Tadzhikistan, which is integrated into the Fergana Valley–Tashkent power grid, is the 126,000-kilowatt hydroelectric station at Kayrakkum, on the Syr Dar'ya. Construction at Kayrakkum was begun in 1951; the first two 21,000-kilowatt generators went into operation in 1956 and the four others the following year. In addition to being linked with the Tashkent power system by a 220-kilovolt line and with the Fergana Valley at Kokand by a 110-kilovolt line, the new station improved the power supply of the mineral industries of northern Tadzhikistan and, through its 30-mile-long reservoir, helped regulate the flow of irrigation water for the cotton-growing district of the Golodnaya Steppe, downstream.

The mineral industries depending on the Kayrakkum station for electric power are situated to the north, in the Kurama mountain range, along the Tadzhik–Uzbek border, and in the southern outlying hills of Karamazar and Mogoltau. Since 1963, when the town of Kayrakkum, at the power station, was raised to the status of city, most of the mining settlements have been subordinated to it.

The tungsten center of Chorukh-Dayron, founded in 1945, has a concentrator for nearby mines at the eastern end of the Mogoltau. The principal ores are scheelite (calcium tungstate) and copper, with molybdenum, tantalum, and columbium as by-products. The lead–zinc center at Kansay, in the Karamazar hills, dates from the 1930s. It yields copper, gold, silver, and cadmium as by-products. The arsenic-mining center of Takeli, to the west, also dates from the 1930s. In the Kurama mountains are the lead–zinc mines of Altyn-Topkan (founded in 1951) and Kurusay (founded in 1953), which appear to be oriented toward the concentrators and smelters of Almalyk, on the northern (Uzbek) side of the mountain range. Finally this area contains the uranium mines and processing center of Taboshar.

Coal and petroleum are of negligible importance among the extractive industries of Tadzhikistan. Coal output at Shurab, where brown coal is mined underground, rose from 449,000 tons in 1950 to 800,000 to 900,000 tons a year in the late 1960s. The coal is shipped to adjoining areas of Uzbekistan, to Turkmenia, and by the roundabout rail route to southern Tadzhikistan, where it is burned at the Dushanbe thermal power station.

Crude-oil production at Nefteabad in northern Tadzhikistan has been a virtual trickle of 20,000 to 50,000 tons annually since the field was opened in the 1930s, and dropped to 16,000 tons in the early 1960s. The Nefteabad operation was surpassed in the mid-1960s by the newly discovered Kichik-Bel' field, in the Vakhsh valley near the Afghan border, which furnished a viscous product used as road oil. In 1965 the Kichik-Bel' field supplied 31,000 tons of crude oil, or two-thirds of the total Tadzhik output. Some of the production also came from the gas-oil deposit of Shaambary, west of Dushanbe. In the late 1960s, attention focused on a promising oil field in northern Tadzhikistan, at Ravat, north of Nefteabad.

# SELECTED BIBLIOGRAPHY

## General References

Ekonomicheskaya zhizn' SSSR. Moscow, Sovetskaya Entsiklopediya, 1st ed. in 1 vol. (1917–1959), 1961; 2d ed. in 2 vols. (1917–50 and 1951–65), 1967. A chronology of economic events in the USSR, such as openings of industrial plants, completions of railroads, canals, power lines, etc.

Kratkaya geograficheskaya entsiklopediya. 5 vols. Moscow, Sovetskaya Entsiklopediya, 1960–1966. An encyclopedia of place names and geographical terms.

RSFSR. Administrativno-territorial'noye deleniye. Moscow, Izvestiya, 1955, 1960, 1964, 1965, 1968. Administrative–territorial handbook of the RSFSR, published irregularly.

SSSR. Administrativno-territorial'noye deleniye soyuznykh respublik. Moscow, Izvestiya, 1954, 1958, 1960, 1962, 1963, 1965, 1967. Administrative–territorial handbook of the USSR, published irregularly.

XX s"yezd Kommunisticheskoy Partii Sovetskogo Soyuza. 2 vols. Moscow, Gospolitizdat, 1956. Proceedings of the 20th party congress, which approved the sixth five-year plan, 1956–60.

XXI s"yezd Kommunisticheskoy Partii Sovetskogo Soyuza. 2 vols. Moscow, Gospolitizdat, 1959. Proceedings of the 21st party congress, which approved the seven-year plan 1959–65.

XXIII s"yezd Kommunisticheskoy Partii Sovetskogo Soyuza. 2 vols. Moscow, Politizdat, 1966. Proceedings of the 23d congress, which approved the five-year plan 1966–70.

## Statistical Publications

Narodnoye khozyaystvo RSFSR v 1958 godu. Moscow, Gosstatizdat, 1959, and subsequent volumes (published by Statistika beginning in 1964). Statistical yearbook of the RSFSR, published annually from 1959 to 1968 (except 1967) with statistics of the preceding year.

Narodnoye khozyaystvo SSSR. Moscow, Gosstatizdat, 1956. The first postwar statistical handbook published in the USSR.

Narodnoye khozyaystvo SSSR v 1956 godu. Moscow, Gosstatizdat, 1957. The second postwar statistical handbook of the USSR.

Narodnoye khozyaystvo SSSR v 1958 godu. Moscow, Gosstatizdat, 1959, and subsequent volumes (published by Statistika beginning in 1964). Statistical yearbook of the USSR, published annually from 1959 to 1968 (except 1967) with statistics of the preceding year.

Promyshlennost' RSFSR. Moscow, Gosstatizdat, 1961. A handbook of industrial statistics for the RSFSR up to 1960.

Promyshlennost' SSSR. Moscow, Gosstatizdat, 1957. Handbook of industrial statistics for the USSR up to 1956.

Promyshlennost' SSSR. Moscow, Statistika, 1964. A handbook of industrial statistics for the USSR up to 1963.

RSFSR za 50 let. Moscow, Statistika, 1967. A statistical handbook of the RSFSR for the first fifty years of Soviet rule.

Strana Sovetov za 50 let. Moscow, Statistika, 1967. A statistical handbook for the USSR covering the first fifty years of Soviet rule.

Vneshnyaya torgovlya SSSR, 1918–1966. Moscow, Mezhdunarodnyye Otnosheniya, 1967. Foreign trade statistics of the USSR.

## Atlases

Atlas Mira. Moscow, Main Administration of Geodesy and Cartography, 1st ed., 1954; 2d ed., 1967. Large atlas of the world.

Atlas razvitiya khozyaystva i kul'tury SSSR. Moscow, Main Administration of Geodesy and Cartography, 1967. Economic and social atlas reviewing the first fifty years of Soviet rule.

Geograficheskiy atlas. Moscow, Main Administration of Geodesy and Cartography, 2d ed., 1959; 3d ed., 1967. A world atlas for middle-school teachers.

## Economic Geography of the USSR

Baranskiy, N. N. Ekonomicheskaya geografiya SSSR. 16th ed., revised. Moscow, Uchpedgiz, 1955. The standard Soviet textbook for the eighth grade of middle schools from the 1930s to the mid-1950s.

Breyterman, A. D. Ekonomicheskaya geografiya SSSR. Part 1: Geography of Heavy Industry. Leningrad University, 1st ed., 1958; 2d ed., 1965. A systematic college-level textbook covering fuels and power, metals, and chemicals

Cherdantsev, G. N., N. P. Nikitin, and B. A. Tutykhin, eds. Ekonomicheskaya geografiya SSSR. 3 vols. Moscow, Uchpedgiz, Vol. I: General survey, 1958; Vol. II: RSFSR, 1956; Vol. III: Other Soviet republics, 1957. A well-illustrated, regional economic geography of the USSR for use in teachers' colleges.

Ekonomicheskiye rayony SSSR. Moscow, Ekonomika, 1965. A regional economic geography of the USSR for use in schools of economics.

Lavrishchev, A. N. Ekonomicheskaya geografiya SSSR. Moscow, Ekonomika, 3d ed., 1967. A systematic economic geography of the USSR for use in schools of economics.

Lyalikov, N. I. Ekonomicheskaya geografiya SSSR. 4th ed. Moscow, Uchpedgiz, 1960. Standard textbook of economic geography of the USSR in the middle schools, replacing the Baranskiy text in the mid-1950s.

Nikitin, N. P., Ye. D. Prozorova, and B. A. Tutykhin, eds. Ekonomicheskaya geografiya SSSR. Moscow, Prosveshcheniye, 1966. A revised one-volume version of the Cherdantsev book.

Pokshishevskiy, V. V., ed. Geograficheskiye problemy razvitiya krupnykh ekonomicheskikh rayonov SSSR. Moscow, Mysl', 1964. A regional survey of geographic aspects of economic development of the USSR.

Saushkin, Yu. G., I. V. Nikol'skiy, and V. P. Korovitsyn, eds. Ekonomicheskaya geografiya Sovetskogo Soyuza. Part 1: General Survey. Moscow University, 1967. A college-level textbook on the economic geography of the USSR.

Shuvalov, Ye. L., A. M. Moshkin, and V. M. Zhuravlev. Ekonomicheskaya geografiya SSSR. Moscow, Prosveshcheniye, 1965. Standard textbook of economic geography of the USSR in the middle schools, replacing the Lyalikov text in the mid-1960s.

## Soviet Periodicals

Bakinskiy Rabochiy, Baku (daily)
Ekonomicheskaya Gazeta, Moscow (weekly)
Gazovaya Promyshlennost', Moscow (monthly)
Geografiya v Shkole, Moscow (six times a year)
Izvestiya, Moscow (daily)
Izvestiya Akademii Nauk SSSR, seriya geograficheskaya (six times a year)
Izvestiya Vsesoyuznogo Geograficheskogo Obshchestva, Leningrad (six times a year)
Kazakhstanskaya Pravda, Alma-Ata (daily)
Khimicheskaya Promyshlennost', Moscow (monthly)

Kommunist, Yerevan (daily)
Kommunist Tadzhikistana, Dushanbe (daily)
Komsomol'skaya Pravda, Moscow (daily)
Literaturnaya Gazeta, Moscow (weekly)
Neftyanoye Khozyaystvo, Moscow (monthly)
Planovoye Khozyaystvo, Moscow (monthly)
Pravda, Moscow (daily)
Pravda Ukrainy, Kiev (daily)
Pravda Vostoka, Tashkent (daily)
Problemy Osvoyeniya Pustyn', Ashkhabad (six times a year)
Razvedka i Okhrana Nedr, Moscow (monthly)
Sovetskaya Belorussiya, Minsk (daily)
Sovetskaya Estoniya, Tallinn (daily)
Sovetskaya Kirgiziya, Frunze (daily)
Sovetskaya Latviya, Riga (daily)
Sovetskaya Litva, Vilnius (daily)
Sovetskaya Moldaviya, Kishinev (daily)
Sovetskaya Rossiya, Moscow (daily)
Transportnoye Stroitel'stvo, Moscow (monthly)
Tsvetnyye Metally, Moscow (monthly)
Turkmenskaya Iskra, Ashkhabad (daily)
Vedomosti Verkhovnogo Soveta SSSR, Moscow (weekly)
Vestnik Leningradskogo Universiteta, seriya geologiya i geografiya, Leningrad (four times a year)
Vestnik Moskovskogo Universiteta, seriya geografiya, Moscow (six times a year)
Vestnik Statistiki, Moscow (monthly)
Voprosy Ekonomiki, Moscow (monthly)
Zarya Vostoka, Tbilisi (daily)

News notes of geographical interest gleaned from these periodicals are published regularly in *Soviet Geography*, the monthly translation journal of the American Geographical Society, New York.

## Minerals (general)

Antropov, P. Ya. Perspektivy osvoyeniya prirodnykh bogatstv SSSR, 1959–1965. Moscow, Gosplanizdat, 1959. A review of geological exploration plans during the seven-year plan 1959–65.
Bykhover, N. A. Ekonomika mineral'nogo syr'ya. Moscow, Nedra, 1967. The economics of the world's mineral industries, including the geology, production, and consumption of mineral fuels and ferrous and alloying metals.
Lyubimov, I. M. Poleznyye iskopayemyye SSSR. Moscow, Prosvesh-cheniye, 1966. A regional survey of the Soviet Union's mineral industries.

Shimkin, Demitri B. Minerals, a Key to Soviet Power. Cambridge, Harvard University Press, 1953. The basic English source on the Soviet Union's mineral industries up to 1950.

U.S. Bureau of Mines. Mineral Facts and Problems, 1965 (Bureau of Mines Bulletin 630), Washington, 1965. A useful reference work on production–consumption patterns and technological aspects of the world's extractive industries.

## Fuel Industries

### FUELS (general)

Bakulev, G. D. Toplivnaya promyshlennost' SSSR i ekonomicheskaya effektivnost' kapitalovlozheniy v yeye razvitiye. Moscow, Academy of Sciences USSR, 1961. A study of the comparative effectiveness of investment in the solid fuels and the oil and gas industries of the USSR.

Hodgkins, Jordan A. Soviet Power: Energy Resources, Production, and Potentials. Englewood Cliffs, N.J., Prentice-Hall, 1961. A review of the reserves and production of coal, oil shale, oil, and natural gas in the USSR, up to the mid-1950s.

Maslakov, D. I. Toplivnyy balans SSSR. Moscow, Gosplanizdat, 1960. Changes in the Soviet Union's national fuels budget from 1917 to 1958, and expected shifts during the seven-year plan 1959–65.

Mazover, Ya. A. Toplivno-energeticheskiye bazy vostoka SSSR. Moscow, Nauka, 1966. Prospects of development of the fuel industries of Western Siberia, Eastern Siberia, and Central Asia.

Mel'nikov, N. V., ed. Toplivno-energeticheskiye resursy. Moscow, Nauka, 1968. A comprehensive study of the geology and production of coal, oil, natural gas, peat, and oil shale in the USSR. A basic source on the Soviet mineral fuel industries.

Poleshchuk, N. G. Osnovnyye voprosy ekonomiki toplivno-energeticheskoy bazy SSSR. Moscow, Mysl', 1965. The economics of Soviet mineral fuel industries.

Razvitiye toplivnoy bazy rayonov SSSR. Edited by A. Ye. Probst. Moscow, Nauka, 1968. One of the most informative and up-to-date surveys of the fuel resources and production of the major regions of the USSR.

Riznik, A. Ya., and S. Ye. Litvak. Toplivno-energeticheskiy balans SSSR. Moscow, Statistika, 1965. The methodology of constructing a national fuels budget for the USSR.

Shimkin, Demitri B. The Soviet Mineral-Fuels Industries, 1928–1958: A Statistical Survey. Washington, U.S. Bureau of the Census, 1962. A review of output and productivity trends in the coal, peat, shale, oil, and gas industries of the USSR.

SELECTED BIBLIOGRAPHY

COAL

Andreyev, B. I., and D. V. Kravchenko. Kamennougol'nyye basseyny SSSR. Moscow, Uchpedgiz, 1958. A study of the geology and production of the coal basins of the USSR.
Ivanov, S. A., and M. D. Mezentsev. Ekonomika ugol'noy promyshlennosti. Moscow, Gosgortekhizdat, 1960. The economics of the Soviet coal-mining industry.
Ugol'naya promyshlennost' SSSR. Moscow, Ugletekhizdat, 1957. A statistical handbook on the Soviet coal-mining industry, covering the period 1940–1955.

PETROLEUM AND NATURAL GAS

Brenner, M. M. Ekonomika neftyanoy promyshlennosti SSSR. Moscow, Ekonomizdat, 1962. The economics of the Soviet Union's oil industry.
Bokserman, Yu. I., et al. Gazovyye resursy SSSR. Moscow, Gostoptekhizdat, 1959. A detailed survey of the geology and production of the natural-gas deposits of the USSR up to 1958, and plans for 1959–65.
Bokserman, Yu. I. Puti razvitiya novoy tekhniki v gazovoy promyshlennosti. Moscow, Nedra, 1964. Natural-gas production and pipeline construction in the USSR, up to 1963.
Chernykh, A. V. Neftyanaya i gazovaya promyshlennost' SSSR. Moscow, Vysshaya Shkola, 1964. The geography of the oil and gas industries of the USSR.
Dolgopolov, K. V., A. V. Sokolov, and Ye. F. Fedorova. Neft' i gazy SSSR. Moscow, Uchpedgiz, 1960. The geography of the oil and gas industries of the USSR.
Dunayev, F. F. Ekonomika i planirovaniye neftyanoy promyshlennosti USSR. Moscow, Gostoptekhizdat, 1957. The economics, technology, geographical distribution, and planning of the Soviet Union's oil industry.
Kortunov, A. K. Gazovaya promyshlennost' SSSR. Moscow, Nedra, 1967. A comprehensive survey of the Soviet natural-gas industry, including field development and pipeline construction up to 1967.
Lisichkin, S. M. Ocherki razvitiya neftedobyvayushchey promyshlennosti SSSR. Moscow, Academy of Sciences USSR, 1958. A history of the Soviet crude oil industry.
Malyshev, Yu. M., et al. Ekonomika neftyanoy i gazovoy promyshlennosti. Moscow, Nedra, 1966. The economics of the Soviet oil and gas industries.

Smyshlyayeva, L. M. Razvitiye gazovoy promyshlennosti i ekonomich-eskaya effektivnost' kapitalovlozheniy. Moscow, Academy of Sciences USSR, 1961. The Soviet natural gas industry from the point of view of comparative effectiveness of investment.

Umanskiy, L. M., and M. M. Umanskiy. Ekonomika neftyanoy i gazovoy promyshlennosti. Moscow, Nedra, 1965. The economics of the Soviet oil and gas industries.

Vasil'yev, V. G., ed. Geologiya nefti. Vol. 2, Book 1: Oil deposits of the USSR. Moscow, Nedra, 1968. A detailed geological description of the oil deposits of the USSR, with data on daily well produc-tivity and average annual production.

P.E A T

Torf v narodnom khozyaystve. Edited by A. M. Matveyev. Moscow, Nedra, 1968. A comprehensive, up-to-date account of the Soviet peat industry, including uses of peat for industrial fuel, briquettes, and soil improvement.

## Electric Power

Avakyan, A. B., and Ye. G. Romashkov. Proyekty blizkogo i dalekogo budushchego. Moscow, Geografizdat, 1961. A popular treatment of some of the great proposed water-management and river-diversion projects of the Soviet Union.

Chernukhin, A. A. Osnovnyye voprosy ekonomicheskoy effektivnosti kapitalovlozheniy v elektroenergetike SSSR. Moscow, Rosvuz-izdat, 1963. A study of the comparative effectiveness of thermal and hydroelectric power stations in the USSR.

Gidroenergeticheskiye resursy. Moscow, Nauka, 1967. A basic source on Soviet hydroelectric stations completed, under construction and planned.

Neporozhnyy, P. S., ed. Elektrifikatsiya SSSR, 1917–1967. Moscow, Energiya, 1967. A history of the Soviet electric power industry.

Novikov, I. T. Razvitiye energetiki i sozdaniye yedinoy energeticheskoy sistemy SSSR. Moscow, Ekonomizdat, 1962. The Soviet power industry and the construction of transmission lines in the seven-year plan 1959–65.

Oznobin, N. M. Elektroenergetika SSSR i yeye razmeshcheniye. Moscow, Ekonomizdat, 1961. A history of the Soviet electric power indus-try and its shifts in geographical distribution.

Steklov, V. Yu. Razvitiye elektroenergeticheskogo khozyaystva SSSR. 2d ed. Moscow, Energiya, 1964. A chronology of power-station completions.

Vilenskiy, M. A. Razvitiye elektrifikatsii SSSR. Moscow, Academy of Sciences USSR, 1958. A survey of the Soviet power industry.

Vilenskiy, M. A. Elektrifikatsiya SSSR i razmeshcheniye proizvoditel'nykh sil. Moscow, Sotsekgiz, 1963. Electric power as a factor in industrial location.

Zhimerin, D. G. Istoriya elektrifikatsii SSSR. Moscow, Sotsekgiz, 1962. A history of the electric power industry of the USSR.

## Metal Industries

### IRON AND STEEL

Bannyy, N. P., et al. Ekonomika chernoy metallurgii SSSR. Moscow, Metallurgizdat, 1960. The economics of the Soviet iron and steel industry.

Bardin, I. P. Zhelezorudnaya baza chernoy metallurgii SSSR. Moscow, Academy of Sciences USSR, 1957. The basic source on the geology and production potentials of iron ore deposits and mines of the USSR.

Bardin, I. P., and P. A. Shiryayev. Tret'ya metallurgicheskaya baza SSSR. Moscow, Znaniye, 1959. Plans for the development of the iron and steel industry east of the Urals.

Belan, R. V., and I. M. Denichenko. Perspektivy razvitiya chernoy metallurgii SSSR. Moscow, Ekonomizdat, 1962. Prospects of development of the Soviet iron and steel industry.

Braun, G. A., and M. A. Pokrovskiy. Razvitiye zhelezorudnoy promyshlennosti SSSR v 1959–1965 godakh. Moscow, Gosgortekhizdat, 1960. Prospects of development of the iron ore industry in the seven-year plan 1959–65.

Dolgopolov, K. V.; A. V. Sokolov and Ye. F. Fedorova. Zheleznyye rudy SSSR. Moscow, Uchpedgiz, 1963. The geography of the Soviet iron-mining industry.

Livshits, R. S. Razmeshcheniye chernoy metallurgii SSSR. Moscow, Academy of Sciences USSR, 1958. A basic study of the geographical distribution of the Soviet iron and steel industry.

Osmolovskiy, V. V. Ekonomika zhelezorudnoy promyshlennosti. Moscow, Nedra, 1967. The economics of the Soviet iron-mining industry.

### OTHER METALS AND NONMETALLICS

Belyayev, A. I. Metallurgiya legkikh metallov. 5th ed. Moscow, Metallurgizdat, 1962. Raw material sources and the metallurgy of aluminum, magnesium, beryllium, calcium, barium, and lithium in the USSR.

# SELECTED BIBLIOGRAPHY

Benuni, A. Kh. Razvitiye tsvetnoy metallurgii v 1959–1965 gg. Moscow, Metallurgizdat, 1960. Proposed development of the nonferrous metals industries of the USSR in the seven-year plan 1959–65.

Beregovskiy, V. I. Nikel' i yego znacheniye dlya narodnogo khozyaystva. Moscow, Metallurgiya, 1964. A review of the Soviet nickel industry.

Gratsershteyn, I. M. Razvitiye alyuminiyevoy promyshlennosti SSSR. Moscow, Metallurgizdat, 1959. A survey of the Soviet aluminum industry.

Gurvich, S. I., L. N. Kazarinov, and N. V. Khmara. Drevniye redko-metal'no-titanovyye rossypi, metody ikh poiskov i otsenki. Moscow, Nedra, 1964. Geological exploration of Soviet titanium placers associated with zircon, monazite, garnet, staurolite, and other heavy minerals.

Kazhdan, A. B. Osnovy razvedki mestorozhdeniy redkikh i radio-aktivnykh metallov. Moscow, Vysshaya Shkola, 1966. The geological exploration in the USSR for rare metals and radio-active ores.

Kislyakov, I. P. Metallurgiya redkikh metallov. Moscow, Metallurgizdat, 1957. Raw material sources and metallurgy of tungsten, molybdenum, columbium, tantalum, vanadium, titanium, zirconium, thorium, rare earths, uranium, beryllium, lithium, and minor metals.

Kitler, I. N., and Yu. A. Layner. Nefeliny—kompleksnoye syr'ye alyumi-niyevoy promyshlennosti. Moscow, Metallurgizdat, 1962. Soviet use of nephelite as a raw material for aluminum.

Pakhorukov, N. I. Alyuminiy i yego znacheniye dlya narodnogo khoz-yaystva SSSR. Moscow, Metallurgiya, 1964. A review of the Soviet aluminum industry.

Pervushin, S. A., et al. Ekonomika tsvetnoy metallurgii SSSR. 1st ed., Moscow, Metallurgizdat, 1960; 2d ed., Moscow, Metallurgiya, 1964. The economics of the Soviet nonferrous metals industries.

Popov, G. N., et al. Osobennosti razrabotki mestorozhdeniy radioak-tivnykh rud. Moscow, Atomizdat, 1964. The technology of uranium mining.

Rachkovskiy, S. Ya. Ekonomika gornorudnoy promyshlennosti SSSR. Moscow, Metallurgizdat, 1955. The economics of Soviet ore-mining industries.

Songina, O. A. Redkiye metally. 3d ed. Moscow, Metallurgiya, 1964. The resource base and metallurgy of rhenium, molybdenum, tungsten, vanadium, columbium, tantalum, zirconium, hafnium, ger-manium, uranium, gallium, indium, lithium, and other rare metals.

Sushkov, A. I., and I. A. Troitskiy. Metallurgiya alyuminiya. Moscow, Metallurgiya, 1965. A review of the raw-material base and metallurgy of the Soviet aluminum industry.

355

## Chemical Industries

Bobrovskiy, P. A. Khimiya v narodnom khozyaystve. Moscow, Ekonomizdat, 1962. A brief survey of the Soviet chemical industry.

Borodkin, I. A. Ekonomika i planirovaniye rezinovoy promyshlennosti. Moscow, Ekonomika, 1964. The economics and planning of the Soviet rubber-fabricating industry.

Bushuyev, V. M., and G. V. Uvarov. Sovetskaya khimicheskaya promyshlennost' v tekushchem semiletii. Moscow, Ekonomizdat, 1962. The Soviet chemical industry during the seven-year plan 1959–65.

Fedorenko, N. P. Ekonomika promyshlennosti sinteticheskikh materialov. Moscow, Ekonomizdat, 1961. The economics of the Soviet petrochemical, synthetic-rubber, man-made fibers, and plastics industries.

Fedorenko, N. P., and I. Ye. Krichevskiy. Khimicheskiye volokna v narodnom khozyaystve. Moscow, Ekonomizdat, 1963. The economics of the Soviet man-made fiber industry.

Kolobkov, M. N. Agronomicheskiye rudy vostochnykh rayonov RSFSR. Moscow, Nedra, 1968. Prospects of geological exploration of phosphates and potash in Siberia.

Kostandov, L. A., ed. 50 let—Sovetskaya khimicheskaya nauka i promyshlennost'. Moscow, Khimiya, 1967. A review of the Soviet chemical industry over the last fifty years.

Krentsel', B. A., and M. I. Rokhlin. Novaya khimiya i yeye syr'yevaya baza. Moscow, Academy of Sciences USSR, 1962. The raw material sources of the Soviet chemical industry.

Kryuchkov, A. P. Obshchaya tekhnologiya sinteticheskikh kauchukov. 3d ed. Moscow, Khimiya, 1965. The technology and raw material sources of Soviet synthetic-rubber production.

Lel'chuk, V. S. Sozdaniye khimicheskoy promyshlennosti SSSR. Moscow, Nauka, 1964. A history of the early period of development of the Soviet chemical industry.

Men'shikova, Z. I. Tekhniko-ekonomicheskiye pokazateli v kaliynoy promyshlennosti i perspektivy rosta proizvodstva i potrebleniya kaliynykh udobreniy na period do 1970 goda. Novosibirsk, 1965. A brief statistical review of the Soviet potash industry.

Nekrasov, N. N. Khimiya v narodnom khozyaystve. Moscow, Znaniye, 1958. A brief review of the Soviet chemical industry.

Nekrasov, N. N. Ekonomika khimicheskoy promyshlennosti. Moscow, Ekonomika, 1966. The economics of the Soviet chemical industry.

Strakhova, L. P. Khimiya i tekhnicheskiy progress. Moscow, Ekonomizdat, 1963. A review of technological advances in the Soviet chemical industry.

## Regional Publications

Regional monographs used in the preparation of this book are too numerous to be listed in the bibliography. Many of them yielded only one or two facts or dates or production figures. However, attention should be drawn to several regional series that were particularly useful:

1. The so-called Blue Series of regional economic geographies of the Soviet Union prepared under the general supervision of the Institute of Geography, Moscow, from 1955 to 1966.

Armyanskaya SSR. Moscow, Geografgiz, 1955.

Azerbaydzhanskaya SSR. Moscow, Geografgiz, 1957.

Belorusskaya SSR. Moscow, Geografizdat, 1957.

Dal'niy Vostok. Moscow, Mysl', 1966.

Dolgopolov, K. V. Tsentral'no-Chernozemnyy rayon. Moscow, Geografizdat, 1961.

Freykin, Z. G. Turkmenskaya SSR. Moscow, Geografizdat, 1957.

Gruzinskaya SSR. Moscow, Geografizdat, 1958.

Karel'skaya ASSR. Moscow, Geografizdat, 1956.

Kazakhskaya SSR. Moscow, Geografizdat, 1957.

Komar, I. V. Geografiya khozyaystva Urala. Moscow, Nauka, 1964.

Komar, I. V. Ural. Moscow, Academy of Sciences USSR, 1959.

Kutaf'yev, S. A., et al. RSFSR. Moscow, Geografizdat, 1959.

Litovskaya SSR. Moscow, Geografizdat, 1955.

Matveyev, G. P., et al. Volgo-Vyatskiy rayon. Moscow, Geografizdat, 1961.

Odud, A. L. Moldavskaya SSR. Moscow, Geografgiz, 1955.

Pomus, M. I. Zapadnaya Sibir'. Moscow, Geografizdat, 1956.

Povolzh'ye, Moscow, Geografizdat, 1957.

Rostovtsev, M. I., and V. Yu. Tarmisto. Estonskaya SSR. Moscow, Geografizdat, 1957.

Ryazantsev, S. N., and V. F. Pavlenko. Kirgizskaya SSR. Moscow, Geografizdat, 1960.

Severnyy Kavkaz. Moscow, Geografizdat, 1957.

Severo-Zapad RSFSR. Moscow, Mysl', 1964.

Shishkin, N. I. Komi ASSR. Moscow, Geografizdat, 1959.

Stepanov, P. N. Ural. Moscow, Geografizdat, 1957.

Tadzhikskaya SSR. Moscow, Geografizdat, 1956.

Tsentral'nyy Rayon. Moscow, Geografizdat, 1962.

Udovenko, V. G. Dal'niy Vostok. Moscow, Geografizdat, 1957.

Ukrainskaya SSR. Moscow, Geografizdat, Part I, 1957; Part II, 1958.

Uzbekskaya SSR. Moscow, Geografizdat, 1956.

Veys, E. E. and V. R. Turin. Latviyskaya SSR. Moscow, Geografizdat, 1957.
Vostochnaya Sibir'. Moscow, Geografizdat, 1963.

2. The series titled *Prirodnyye usloviya i yestestvennyye resursy SSSR,* published by the Institute of Geography, Moscow, beginning in 1963:
Kavkaz. Moscow, Nauka, 1966.
Ural i Priural'ye. Moscow, Nauka, 1968.
Sever Yevropeyskoy chasti SSSR. Moscow, Nauka, 1966.
Srednyaya Aziya. Moscow, Nauka, 1968.
Srednyaya polosa Yevropeyskoy chasti SSSR. Moscow, Nauka, 1967.
Srednyaya Sibir'. Moscow, Nauka, 1964.
Yakutiya. Moscow, Nauka, 1965.
Zapadnaya Sibir'. Moscow, Nauka, 1963.

3. The series titled *Sovetskiy Soyuz,* a popular geographic coverage of the Soviet Union in 22 volumes, whose publication began in 1966:
Armeniya. Moscow, Mysl', 1966.
Belorussiya. Moscow, Mysl', 1967.
Estoniya. Moscow, Mysl', 1967.
Gruziya. Moscow, Mysl', 1967.
Latviya. Moscow, Mysl', 1968.
Litva. Moscow, Mysl', 1967.
Tadzhikistan. Moscow, Mysl', 1968.
Uzbekistan. Moscow, Mysl', 1967.

4. The series titled *Razvitiye i razmeshcheniye proizvoditel'nykh sil SSSR,* published by the Council for the Study of Productive Forces, Gosplan USSR, beginning in 1967:
Razvitiye i razmeshcheniye proizvoditel'nykh sil Kazakhskoy SSR. Moscow, Nauka, 1967.
Severo-Zapadnyy ekonomicheskiy rayon. Moscow, Nauka, 1967.
Zapadno-Sibirskiy ekonomicheskiy rayon. Moscow, Nauka, 1967.

# INDEX

Kashpirovka, 24, 26, 134; map, 127
Katangli, 282; map, 275
Kaunas, 207, 208; maps, 22, 88, 204
Kavalerovo, 272; maps, 55, 270
Kayrakkum, 345; map, 328
Kaytakoski, 114
Kayyerkan, 256; map, 254
Kazakh SSR, 284-308; coal, 10, 11, 285-86, 292, 301; oil, 15, 304-6; electric power, 32, 286, 292-93, 300, 303; iron and steel, 36, 38, 39, 43, 286-87, 294-96; copper, 288-89, 297; map, 280; alumina industry, 294; lead-zinc, 297-99, 301; phosphate, 301-3; chrome, 307
Kazan', 82, 130; maps, 17, 23, 84, 127
Kazi-Magomed, 151; map, 153
Kazreti, 161
Kedainiai, 208; maps, 74, 204
Kegums, 209-10; map, 204
Keiv, see Keyv
Kelif, 319; map, 320
Kemerovo (city), 238; maps, 79, 236
Kemerovo Oblast, see Kuznetsk Basin
Kem' River, 112; map, 110
Kengir River, 288
Kenkiyak, 306; map, 290
Kentau, 301; maps, 54, 291
Kerch', 179-80; iron ore statistics, 36; maps, 41, 191
Kermine, see Navoi
Ketmen'-Tyube, 334
Keyv, 114; map, 110
Khabarovsk (city), 269; maps, 17, 270
Khabarovsk Kray, 269-70; maps, 270, 278
Khadyzhensk, 143; map, 144
Khaidarken, see Khaydarken

Khal'mer-Yu, 120; map, 111
Khamza Khakimzade, 322; map, 329
Khantayka River, 256; maps, 30, 254
Khapcheranga, 264; maps, 55, 249
Kharanor, 266; map, 249
Khariuzovo, 298
Khar'kov, 182-83; map, 191
Khartum, 322
Khaudag, 322; map, 342
Khaydarken, 338; maps, 54, 329
Kherson, 199; maps, 16, 191
Khevoskoski, 114
Khibiny Mountains, 115-16; map, 111
Khilly, 154; map, 153
Khingansk, 271; maps, 55, 270
Khodzhiabad, 322; map, 329
Khodzhikent, 326
Khol'bodzha, 263
Kholbon, 266; map, 249
Kholtoson, 262; map, 248
Khoronkhoy, 263; map, 249
Khovu-Aksy, 252; maps, 47, 248
Khrami River, 161; map, 152
Khrebtovaya, 260; map, 248
Khromtau, 307; maps, 40, 46, 223; 290
Khrushchev, see Svetlovodsk
Khrustal'nyy, 272; map, 270
Kichik-Bel', 346; map, 342
Kiev, 194, 195; maps, 22, 30, 88, 190
Kimovsk, 94; map, 96
Kimpersay, 228, 307
Kineshma, 105; map, 96
Kingisepp, 109; maps, 74, 110
Kireyevsk, 100; map, 96
Kirghiz SSR, 333-39; coal, 11, 336-37; oil and gas, 15, 337; electric power, 32, 334-36; minerals, 57, 337-39; map, 321
Kirishi, 108; maps, 16, 110
Kirov (city), 106; maps, 84, 111

372